A Genealogy of the Gentleman

EARLY MODERN FEMINISMS

Series Editor
Robin Runia, Xavier University of Louisiana

Editorial Advisory Board
Jennifer Airey, University of Tulsa; Paula Backscheider, Auburn University; Susan Carlile, California State University; Karen Gevirtz, Seton Hall University; Mona Narain, Texas Christian University; Carmen Nocentelli, University of New Mexico; Jodi Wyett, Xavier University

Showcasing distinctly feminist ideological commitments and/or methodological approaches, and tracing literary and cultural expressions of feminist thought, Early Modern Feminisms seeks to publish innovative readings of women's lives and work, as well as of gendered experience, from the years 1500–1800. In addition to highlighting examinations of women's literature and history, this series aims to provide scholars an opportunity to emphasize new approaches to the study of gender and sexuality with respect to material culture, science, and art, as well as politics and race. Thus, monographs and edited collections that are interdisciplinary and/or transnational in nature are particularly welcome.

Series Titles
Objects of Liberty: British Women Writers and Revolutionary Souvenirs, by Pamela Buck
Fictions of Pleasure: The Putain Memoirs of Prerevolutionary France, by Alistaire Tallent
The Visionary Queen: Justice, Reform, and the Labyrinth in Marguerite de Navarre, by Theresa Brock
Eliza Fenwick: Early Modern Feminist, by Lissa Paul
The Circuit of Apollo: Eighteenth-Century Women's Tributes to Women, edited by Laura L. Runge and Jessica Cook

A Genealogy of the Gentleman

WOMEN WRITERS AND MASCULINITY IN THE EIGHTEENTH CENTURY

MARY BETH HARRIS

NEWARK

978-1-64453-329-1 (cloth)
978-1-64453-328-4 (paper)
978-1-64453-330-7 (epub)

Cataloging-in-publication data is available from the Library of Congress.
LCCN 2023027111

A British Cataloging-in-Publication record for this
book is available from the British Library.
Copyright © 2024 by Mary Beth Harris
All rights reserved

No part of this book may be reproduced or utilized in any form or by any means, electronic or mechanical, or by any information storage and retrieval system, without written permission from the publisher. Please contact University of Delaware Press, 200A Morris Library, 181 S. College Ave., Newark, DE 19717. The only exception to this prohibition is "fair use" as defined by U.S. copyright law.

References to internet websites (URLs) were accurate at the time of writing. Neither the author nor University of Delaware Press is responsible for URLs that may have expired or changed since the manuscript was prepared.

∞ The paper used in this publication meets the requirements of the American National Standard for Information Sciences—Permanence of Paper for Printed Library Materials, ANSI Z39.48-1992.

udpress.udel.edu

Distributed worldwide by Rutgers University Press

*To the memory of Dr. Jim Harris, who was
all the best parts of the gentleman*

Contents

Acknowledgments   ix

Introduction   1

1. Gentleman Spectator as Desiring Author: *The Spectator* and Mary Davys's *Reform'd Coquet*   22

2. The Gentleman of Letters as Passionate Reader: Eliza Haywood's *Love in Excess* and David Hume's *Philosophy of Moral Sympathy*   53

3. Romancing the Gentleman Critic: Reading Criticism as Generic Courtship in Charlotte Lennox's *The Female Quixote* and Samuel Johnson's *The Rambler*   86

4. "Smartly Dealt With; Especially by the Ladies": The Women Writers of Samuel Richardson's *Sir Charles Grandison*   122

5. The Gentleman as Authorial Drag: Inverting Plots, Homosociality, and Moral Authorship in Elizabeth Inchbald's *A Simple Story* and Mary Robinson's *Walsingham*   153

Coda: But They Were All Written by Women   180

Notes   191
Bibliography   221
Index   233

Acknowledgments

My fascination and connection to the gentleman and the women who made him is at the intersection of my personal and professional influences, a winding road filled with the care, interest, and support of so many people. First, I would like to thank the fabulous Nush Powell, who plucked me from a Transatlantic Literature seminar and shaped me into the scholar I am today, who read and reread my work, my job documents, my anxious emails, and reminded me again and again that I could do this work, and that I could write a book. I wish to thank the incomparable and brilliant Rebekah Mitsein, whose meticulous intelligence and marvelous criticism made me feel like I could be occasionally shiny and brilliant too. The support and encouragement of my eighteenth-century cohort—Slaney Chadwick Ross, Jade Higa, Daniel Froid, Marie Balsley Taylor, Katie Sagal, Sarah Creel, and Jarred Weihe—have been invaluable. I also need to credit the wonderful support of my Purdue friends, Heather Wicks, Dana Roders, Nick Marino, Stacey Dearing, Lisa Curtin, Ryan Hubble, Mark Mengel, Leah Pennywark, Allison Layfield, and Nancy Farner, who have seen and supported me along this long road. Thank you to Molly Pim who was my first fellow reader on a long bookish journey.

I would like to especially thank Matt Townsley and Lauren Carpenter for their incredible copyediting services and support. I would like to thank Marilyn Francus for her invaluable guidance and feedback. Thank you to Susan Carlile and Kathy Lubey, whose work has so deeply inspired my own. Special thanks to Thomas Bonnell, for introducing me to the eighteenth century, as well as to Patricia Sayer, Linn Vacca, and my SMC family. I would like to thank the advisors and mentors who supported the inception of this project: Gerry Friedman, Emily Allen, Derek Pacheco, and Bradley Dilger. And I would also like to thank my wonderful colleagues at Bethany College, whose vibrancy make coming to work a joy even in the midst of struggles, especially my English colleagues Kristin Van Tassel and Marcus Hensel for their warm friendship, supportive mentorship, and exemplary teaching. Thank you to Adam Pryor, for your example as a scholar and mentor. Thank you also to Robyn Hensel and Rachael Pryor, who befriended me, fed me, made me part of your families, and gave me a place to belong. I must also thank Robin Runia, who encouraged me to submit to the Early Modern Feminisms series at the University of Delaware Press, and Julia

ACKNOWLEDGMENTS

Oestreich, whose generous attention has helped make the manuscript what it is.

Perhaps most importantly, I want to acknowledge that books take shape along with our lives in deeply personal ways. This book also owes a debt to my childhood home, which was made of both spaces and people; the book came from the cream-colored room where I watched my beautiful mother read books. Her frank, unselfconscious intelligence is a rare and wonderful gift. Much later, when I was drafting my chapter on *Sir Charles Grandison*, this book came from a sunroom where my father lived his last summer. I will always have a soft spot for Richardson's suntanned paragon because I discovered him while the best man I have ever known sat in the sun with me and let us all bask in his warmth. My parents gave me the gift of trust in myself, and our home gave me space to become a reader and a scholar in irreplaceable ways. This book is the outgrowth of all the vibrant, intelligent people in my family and my friend groups, especially the incredible women who have authored their own incredible stories, even if they haven't put them on paper; it is the product of the stories my grandmother Pat Minneman tells of her almost one hundred years on earth, of Joan Devitt's unending warmth, of the confidence of my aunts and uncles, the warmth of my cousins, and the love of my brothers and sisters-in-law and my niece, Lilly Harris.

A portion of chapter 2 was previously published as "Reforming Count D'elmont: Masculinity, Sympathy, and Reading in Eliza Haywood's *Love in Excess*," in *Tulsa Studies in Women's Literature* 38, no. 2 (Fall 2019): 285–311.

Introduction

Women do not write books about men.
—Virginia Woolf, *A Room of One's Own*

Rash young man!—why do you tear from my heart the affecting narrative, which I had hoped no cruel necessity would ever have forced me to review?
—Emma Courtney in *The Memoirs of Emma Courtney*

A Genealogy of the Gentleman: Women Writers and Masculinity in the Eighteenth Century poses a direct challenge to Virginia Woolf's claim that "women do not write books about men." Of course, women write and have almost always written books with men in them, but such books are neither principally about nor for men—or so the assumption has gone. Latent in Woolf's claim is a perception that has taken deep root in our critical bones, that women historically have been uninterested, incapable, or unable when it comes to writing books about masculinity or men. Women, struggling from their disadvantaged position within patriarchal systems, "do not write books about men" because they are too busy countering the "mass[es] of paper" that men have penned about women.[1] However, this is an assumption grounded more in the roots of criticism than in reality.

It is not even that the act of women's writing to or about men is in any way covert. The opening lines of Mary Hays's 1796 novel *The Memoirs of Emma Courtney* is a declaration to a young gentleman on the part of the titular heroine. From start to finish, *Emma Courtney* is structured as a series of letters between the heroine and Augustus Harley Jr., "the son of [Emma's] affection."[2] Emma is not revisiting her painful, passionate history for the education of her own daughter, who is deliberately and conveniently dead, but for her adopted son. *Emma Courtney* is thus a novel constructed with a male reader imagined as its in-text audience. Hays even references William Godwin's *Caleb Williams* (1794) as a source text for her novel, and she clearly imagines a mixed-gender audience.[3] Upon closer inspection, *Emma Courtney* is a novel deeply concerned with masculinity. Emma is surrounded by men: her rakish, neglectful father, her philosopher mentor, her volatile husband, and the sentimental yet secretive Augustus Harley Sr.

It is through Emma's eyes that these men are critiqued, judged to be desirable, and described as good, bad, or, more often than not, a combination of positive and negative characteristics. Masculinity is judged and taught by the central woman narrator of the novel, and it is treated as natural and appropriate that Emma's experience of and perspective on masculinity be used to instruct the future generation on masculinity.

It has been critics, both contemporary and historical, who have fallen into the comfortable pattern of dismissing the male characters written by women and of characterizing the works by women writers as exclusively feminocentric. Eighteenth-century critics, especially men, were quick to assert that novelists such as Hays were paradoxically both lesser than their male contemporaries and more threatening because they appealed only to women readers and dramatized women's passions. One reviewer claimed that he gave notice to Hays's novel only "to guard the female world against the mischievousness of [its] tendencies."[4] Thus, from a distance, the content and the reception of Hays's novel seem to suggest focusing on its female connections: female author, feminist themes, female protagonist, and female readers. And because of the critic's flagrant misogyny which feeds into the roots of the long-standing scholarly dismissal of women writers, feminist scholars have taken his dual assumptions to task. They have succeeded in repositioning women writers as the dynamic and influential contributors to literary culture that they clearly were and, in turn, have valiantly prioritized the female characters, readers, and authors of the eighteenth century and beyond.

However, an unintended consequence of this focus has been a recurrent dismissal of the male characters created by women writers as being unimportant, uninfluential, or even just poorly written. With the exceptions of Eleanor Wikborg's *The Lover as Father Figure in Eighteenth-Century Women's Fiction* (2002) and Megan Woodworth's *Eighteenth-Century Women Writers and the Gentleman's Liberation Movement: Independence, War, Masculinity, and the Novel, 1778–1818* (2011), there has been no sustained attention to the male characters or masculinities constructed by eighteenth-century women writers.[5] To be sure, individual studies have addressed individual male characters, and there has been interest in the queer and female masculinities presented by women. However, given the lack of sustained scholarly attention, our understanding of the ways in which women writers, with the notable exception of Jane Austen, have individually and collectively shaped cultural standards of masculinity has remained limited. Indeed, until very recently, most scholarship surrounding the topic has often expressed a sense of disappointment in the men written by eighteenth-century women.[6]

As my book shows, this blind spot has overlooked the vital legacy of eighteenth-century women writers in the construction of normative masculinity, specifically that of the gentleman. I have called this project a "genealogy" because the links between women's authorship and the gentleman were, and remain, vibrant in cultural ideals of masculinity. The gentleman is a defining ancestor of contemporary hegemonic masculinity, and if women have played a vital role in his construction, then their involvement challenges key aspects of how we continue to conceive masculinity and women's relationship to patriarchal history. Tracing the gentleman's genealogy matters because even if critics may find the gentleman boring, popular audiences have found him incredibly appealing in long-lasting, far-reaching ways. I need only mention my research to my friends or family members, and they immediately begin sighing over Mr. Darcy. By extension, if the gentleman is foundational to hegemonic masculinity, then his continued sexual and social appeal has played an important part in his maintenance. It has also played a role in reinforcing his patriarchal authority. As I argue throughout this book, men might have tried to write themselves into being the gentleman, but it was women writers who made the gentleman desirable, and it is this desirability that has continued to define this species of hegemonic masculinity even today.

The Gentleman's Entry into the World; or, the Origins of Hegemonic Masculinity

My fundamental argument is that the gentleman's masculinity is more persona than person, and that women writers capitalized on the inherently performative aspects of this masculinity to validate their own literary productions. However, to understand women writers' interventions into the gentleman, we first need to trace his emergence as the ideal man of the eighteenth century, his foundational position within the history of hegemonic masculinity, and the ways in which this masculinity was immediately tied to literary production. This trajectory is what allowed women writers to infiltrate and co-opt the gentleman, namely because his masculinity is a production of narrative. The key difference between his performance and other modes of gender performance is that he was constructed through the language of innateness, privacy, and contrast.

The gentleman emerged as the dominant standard of normative masculinity over the course of the eighteenth century, and the story of his emergence is one of the natural replacing the performative. According to eighteenth-century critics such as Thomas King, Erin Mackie, Shawn Lisa Maurer, Michèle Cohen, and G. J. Barker-Benfield, at the turn of the eighteenth century, the gentleman emerged as a cultural remedy for and rejection of the Restoration rake, and throughout the century, he gained cultural supremacy as the ideal of masculinity.[7] The contrast between the gentleman and the rake is entrenched in the history of gender and the history of subjectivity, both of which trace the marked shift from "a primarily performative toward a more essentialized notion of subjectivity."[8] Whereas the rake was performative, embodied, selfish, and verbal, the gentleman was natural, disembodied, selfless, and restrained.[9] Rakes were associated with ostentatious speech, dress, and sexuality; they were violent and rebellious and recognized no sovereignty but their own aristocratic selves, which were tainted with Frenchified Catholicism or atheism. The master of both foreplay and wordplay, the rake asserted his sexual, social mastery over others—women, boys, and other men—through his verbal and physical dexterity.[10] By contrast, the gentleman restrained his desires, sexual or otherwise, and was judged by the care and deference that he showed to women and people under his care.[11] The gentleman was the Christian hero, staunchly loyal to God, specifically the Church of England, as well as to country and family. His private subjectivity—a "properly disciplined inwardness"—was defined by his moral virtue, which took shape as heterosexual love, politeness, good taste, and sympathy.[12] Such subjectivity required him to move in the social world and provide useful regulation for society from the core security of an internalized, masculine self.

The story of the gentleman is the story of the foundation of *hegemonic masculinity* within the Western tradition. According to R. W. Connell, the gentleman is patient zero in the lineage of hegemonic masculinity, defined as "the configuration of gender practice which embodies the currently accepted answer to the problem of the legitimacy of patriarchy, which guarantees (or is taken to guarantee) the dominant position of men and the subordinate position of women."[13] It was through the eighteenth-century gentleman that this configuration first became solidified into a notion of man as the rational, ahistorical, and universal sex.[14] Before then, the gentleman was regularly considered to be the model of the "essential authentic self," which "above all . . . is a sexed self," a masculine self.[15] The rake's more fluid sexuality and courtly body align him with the ancien régime of identity described by Dror Wahrman and the one-sex model explored by Thomas Laqueur, both of which were gradually replaced with a so-called modern self that existed within a binary, two-sex system and inextricably internalized self and gender.[16] The gentleman became the masculine force at the center of the new system, and the poster boy of its gender structure.

Given all of his politeness, virtue, and hegemonic status, the gentleman surfaced as both the "masculine ideal" and the "dominant persona" of the literary world.[17] As numerous critics have argued, the gentleman was the ideal professional author: "masculine, genteel, disinterested."[18] He was also a "good reader"—that is, someone who was reliably rational and had "the ability to examine and separate ideas."[19] As a critic, the gentleman combined these skills to liaise between the public and authors. His literary authority was an extension of his masculinity, and it consequently relied on establishing and regulating relationships with women. As the ideal author, the gentleman validated his benevolent disinterest by speaking to and asserting his virtuous authority over the more passionate female reader. For their part, female readers were defined by their "unruly imagination . . . their general mental weakness . . . their susceptibility to the humoural disorders" and their overall inability to discern fact from fiction.[20] Thus, not only did the gentleman reader establish his rationality through a contrast with the female reader but also the underlying conception of gendered reading validated the need for the benevolent male author to guide female readers, as well as for the genteel critic to point them in his direction. As my project shows, in many ways the gentleman's connection to narrative was a pivotal means by which these gendered structures and patriarchal systems were and have been produced and maintained.

Part of the gentleman's allure was the way in which his literary authority dovetailed into a position of potential social mobility. Because the gentleman was a highly classed figure whose status depended not on his birth but on a combination of virtue, education, and breeding—things that could be cultivated—he created an avenue for a kind of narrow social mobility.[21] This characterization, coupled with his literary authority, meant that professional literary production could now operate as respectable social maneuvering. This new mobility was highly regulated by gender and evolving class markers, for "manly understanding was reserved for a privileged minority."[22] Even so, this minority was expanding, if slightly. As a new masculine ideal, the gentleman marked a new era, and he created an access point for privilege that could be entered through literary endeavors. Women, whose authorship had long been rebuked for violating rigid cultural standards, were clearly interested in casting their own work in this new light, as well as in co-opting some of this new social power for themselves.

Once More, with Performance

The scholarly story of the gentleman as the private subject is convincing but too easily goes unquestioned. Above all, it leaves out an important layer of the narrative: gender performance. I would like to recalibrate what critics have read as the gentleman's rejection of the rake's performativity and instead propose that the gentleman is not a rejection of performance but a new kind of performance, one that relies on contrast—not only with the rake but more importantly with women—to delineate its features. I agree with King, Karen Harvey, and Maurer, all of whom argue that the gentleman defined his masculinity through domestic, private relations and a *representation* of his subjectivity as internal and stable.[23] However, I argue that those features required a new kind of performance, not a rejection of performance. The gentleman portrayed inwardness, disinterest, benevolence, and virtue, and the role's performativity is what allowed women writers to enter the critical conversation about masculinity with such clarity and opportunity. Women writers wanted to get their hands on the various literary, professional, and social privileges attached to the gentleman, and what they realized through making him their character and casting him as the lead of their novels was that even the most normative masculinity is a narrative production.

Hence, women writers created the gentleman's masculinity as a narrative production, and recognizing it as such allows us to make sense of aspects of the gentleman's masculinity that critics have noted but left unquestioned. Critics have established, for instance, that what distinguished the eighteenth-century gentleman from his predecessors was a newly emphasized prioritization of his relationships with women; this emphasis included establishing the cultural value of heterosociality, along with the increasingly rigid definition of heterosexuality, all of which became entangled with the gentleman's literary status, itself also characterized through relationships with women.[24]

Why did relationships with women come to define the gentleman so intrinsically? My answer is because women wrote him that way. While Barker-Benfield, Harriet Guest, E. J. Clery, and other critics have noted the ways in which femininity and women were connected to the reform of masculinity throughout the eighteenth century, my book extends this connection a step further.[25] Scholars have long maintained that women could, hypothetically and even vaguely, influence the gentleman, but no one has yet theorized that women authored this influence themselves. Rather than registering women as peripheral or partial influencers within the history of masculinity, I argue that women were the chief agents of the shift in the character of the ideal man. Women novelists capitalized on the features initially meant to define the gentleman's masculinity through contrast—for example, between the benevolent gentleman author versus the vulnerable female reader—in order to expand the gentleman's dependence on women more broadly. They tapped into the ways gender is the product of narrative, and co-opted and rewrote the gentleman's masculinity as a narrative that gave them access to professional legitimacy and cultural influence. Given this dynamic, it is time to bring women into the conversation surrounding the creation of eighteenth-century masculinity. It is the logical and culturally necessary next step, especially for our understanding of the gentleman.

Exploring the ways in which women constructed the gentleman is also one of the best ways to make hegemonic masculinity visible as such. Hegemonic masculinity is challenging to study because "masculinity seems like an obvious thing, something we can and do take for granted. We know what it is when we see it: it is commonsensical, produced by testosterone or by nature."[26] This is what I call the "Jedi mind trick" of normative masculinity. It is never the gender you are looking for. There is far more language built around queer masculinity, female masculinity, and femininity because that language has been used critically and culturally to control, categorize, and make such masculinities and femininities visible, all while deliberately attempting to make normative masculinity invisible. But when we spotlight the ways women authors created the narrative of the gentleman through their novels, suddenly the performative aspects of normative masculinity become tangible. Women can perform the gentleman through their characters, and in many ways they do so more effectively than men because ideals are easier to imagine than to live up to.[27]

Even though studies of eighteenth-century masculinity have emerged as a vibrant field, its work has frequently sidestepped serious consideration of the men created by women writers.[28] Other than Jason Solinger's *Becoming the Gentleman: British Literature and the Invention of Modern Masculinity, 1600–1815* (2012), the field has not devoted serious attention to the normative masculinities constructed by women, and even Solinger's work positions women writers as responsive to a male-dominated standard and tradition.[29] Thus, despite commitments to theories of gender performance and histories of gender, we largely continue to present the construction of masculinity as an almost exclusively male production, even though we know better. We know that, as Jack Halberstam and Marjorie Garber point out, there is something especially threatening but also revealing about decoupling masculinity from the idea of innate male subjectivity or the material male body, because when we do, we "glimpse ... how masculinity is constructed as masculinity."[30] This possibility is why we need to bring women writers into conversations about normative masculinity. Their works make the constructions of masculinity visible as such, and, as authors, they played a vital role in narrating the contours of gender structures.

Resituating the Woman-Authored Gentleman

A Genealogy of the Gentleman challenges an underlying assumption that runs through scholarship on eighteenth-century women writers, namely that women were bad at writing men. This sentiment is clearly distilled in one of the earliest and only volumes ever devoted to men written by women, "Men by Women," the 1981 special edition of *Women's Writing*, in which Janet Todd declares, "Women writers [have an] inability to create great men in society."[31] Todd's word choice of "inability" feels especially jarring because it seems to reinscribe some of the binary limits between male and female authors that the recovery projects she led sought to interrogate. Underlying this implication is the assumption that, whereas Samuel Richardson could create a Clarissa or Daniel Defoe could create a Roxana, women writers could not create similarly "great men in society." This assumption not only positions masculinity as being beyond women's grasp, reified as something accessible to only men through nature and patriarchal hierarchy, but also positions men, as an audience open to influence, as beyond the woman author's reach. Consequently, as Todd states and as other scholars have echoed in the decades since, the men written by women, both in the eighteenth century and beyond, end up being read as unrealistic because they are effeminate or amount to fantasies who appeal only to a female readership.

However, when we utilize the historical discourse on masculinity to read works by women writers, we see that the assumption is false. Let's begin with a quick case study of perhaps the best-known eighteenth-century man written by a woman: David Simple. The titular gentleman of Sarah Fielding's *David Simple* (1744) is often read as being effeminate or even a woman in drag.[32] However, this characterization simply does not hold water with more contemporary studies of eighteenth-century masculinity. Such a perspective completely ignores the ways in which David's sentimental masculinity is entirely normative for his time. As Clery and Declan Kavanagh have argued, there are clear, important distinctions in eighteenth-century masculinity between the proper, normative feminizing of men and their slippage into effeminacy. Both point out how sentiment and softer feelings were part of masculinity in the mid-eighteenth century, when *David Simple* was written.[33] In the 1740s, men were supposed to be men of feeling, which was a popular, normative ideal of masculinity. David seems to be regarded as being effeminate almost entirely based on the fact that his author is a woman. Our labeling of David is more the product of our own policing of normative masculinity from a contemporary perspective than the reflection of eighteenth-century masculinity as it was.

By extension, David and other men written by women, especially the Mr. Glanvilles and Lord Orvilles of the literary landscape, have been categorized as fantasy figures. As Sarah S. G. Frantz and Katharina Rennhak argue, "When women construct and write about men in fictional worlds... they also construct their own realities, imagining alternative masculinities that are desirable from a woman's perspective."[34] Latent in the label of fantasy is often a quality of unreality, as if women are making men who exist exclusively in a feminocentric vacuum, which, though it may influence other women, seems removed from the world of "real" men and, coincidentally, "real" literary importance. The label also assumes that women's desires and what is desirable to women have no real-world impact on cultural ideals of masculinity. These assumptions are both counter to much of the more recent work on gender and readership in the eighteenth century. First, men were clearly a large part of women writers' readership, both actual and imagined.[35] The reality was that, although female literacy was on the rise, men continued to comprise the significant majority of the literate population, particularly early in the century. As consumers, men had nearly exclusive access to the sites of literary circulation: the bookshop and the coffeehouse. As a result, women writers had a clear material motivation to appeal to male readers. Second, the assumption that "fantasy" is somehow a dismissive label is problematic, for it wrongly assumes that gender ideals or fantasies are not hugely influential in the construction of norms. It also reflects a strange double standard for narratives of idealized gender: when we explore the men or women created by men, their hyperbolic gender standards are part of what we investigate as being powerful and critically important to our understanding of historical literature and culture. As cases in point, Clarissa and Pamela are entirely unrealistic idealizations of feminine virtue. Then why is this tendency toward hyperbole written up as a mark against the woman-authored gentleman? When we explore how women write men, the conversation suddenly reverts to the tethers of Wattian-style realism.

Fictions of the Gentleman: Courtship Novels and Male Essays

This book primarily focuses on courtship novels written by women, along with essays and periodicals written by men, in order to create dialectical pairings. I explain here why I have selected these genres and pairings for my first three chapters and how and why I depart from these pairings in later chapters. Broadly speaking, I have selected these genres because they occupy canonically important historical and critical places of prominence.

Within feminist criticism, women's novels have served as the formative source material for much of its recovery projects. In tandem, the essays of Joseph Addison and Richard Steele, David Hume, and Samuel Johnson are part of the oldest vision of the eighteenth-century canon within modern scholarship. Both women's novels and men's essays are now firmly entrenched in scholarly discourse. The courtship novel was the vital point for accessing the intersections of desire and influence over which women authors sought control. In parallel, I examine male-authored essays, philosophy, and periodicals, with the exception of Richardson's novel, to consider how male authors manifested the kinds of masculinity presented by women in their fiction. For my purposes, doing so affords a clear pathway for exploring the dynamics of the equally fictional performances of male literary and authorial characters across genres and authors.

It might seem odd to declare women's novels to be foundational or even canonical, but nearly fifty years out from the recovery projects of the 1980s, that is what they are. Although the novel as an idea or even a coherent thing is nebulous, the courtship novel does have some established generic and structural features. These novels are fictional prose tales of heterosexual relationships that typically end in the marriage of the central male and female characters.[36] They are foundational in the professional history of eighteenth-century women writers because it was gradually deemed acceptable for women to write as long as "their main subject would be love," and as long as such love was virtuous.[37] The courtship novel is also the genre in which the most attractive features of the gentleman were constructed and his long-lasting popularity was forged. I argue that this legacy is intertwined: the gradual value of the woman novelist, as women came to be regarded as moralists and thus as valuable writers, was due to the interventions and revisions that they made to the character of the gentleman in their courtship novels. As Patricia Meyer Spacks writes, "Art makes things happen in life, partly by altering perceptions,"[38] and that is precisely what women writers accomplished throughout the eighteenth century. By way of their novels, they slowly altered the contours of the gentleman in order to gain access to his literary authority. In doing so, they also altered long-standing perceptions of gender standards and of the value of women writers that persist to this day.

By no means do I think that courtship novels were the only vehicle that women writers used to cultivate and engage with masculinity. I do think, however, that courtship plots provided a distinct opportunity for women to manipulate and revise the form of the gentleman for their own ends. To support this claim, I draw on the work of critics such as Woodworth and Paul Kelleher and trace how the courtship plot became a tool in women writers' "radical quest for equality."[39] The courtship novel's plot was useful for eighteenth-century women writers because courtship was a phase of a young woman's life when the structures of power and desire shifted ever so marginally in women's favor. Although these structures were rigidly bound by norms—heterosexuality, intense standards of virtue, family pressure, and class—courtship was nevertheless a space in which particular young women were granted a certain amount of authority over their male suitors. As ideas of companionate marriage became popular, courtship readily became a space in which young women's desires and what they found attractive emerged as sources of power.[40] Men were not only expected to court women and present themselves as ideal candidates for marriage but were also required, at least in theory, to leave the ultimate decision about marriage up to the young women whom they courted. This norm explains why Mr. Spectator dedicates so much attention to young women's courtships and why he and other men were so threatened by the figure of the coquette, as I describe in chapter 1. It is also why Samuel Johnson presents *The Rambler* to his readers as if from a young lover to his lady in search of supplication and approval, as shown in chapter 3. I argue that, through courtship structures and narratives, women writers first capitalized on and then cultivated this norm in their courtship novels; they created the gentleman to be the ideal man in their tales and required that the gentleman's virtues and authority be based in women's desires.

A Genealogy of the Gentleman showcases that the key feature that women writers brought to the gentleman was desirability. Women wrote the gentleman into being attractive, and this constructed appeal is what male authors before and after have sought to live up to. The revision of the gentleman as desirable is why courtship novels were such an important vehicle for this masculinity. The plots of novels structure and are structured by desire;[41] this is what makes plots powerful and influential. The courtship plot is in itself one of desire: the desire of the male suitors and the desire of the heroines. However, because courtship was a period in which women had some say over the dynamics and were supposed to be supplicated to, if a gentleman wanted to be the ideal man, then he had to appeal to and be desired by women.

In turn, the stories of heterosexual love in courtship novels created unique spaces for defining male heterosexual desire.[42] In these spaces, the gentleman was positioned to prove his virtuous heterosexuality as the moral, noncoercive, but appealing choice. Authors presented him as a figure selected by the heroine instead of forced upon her. Consequently, women writers used this dynamic to make the gentleman suit their desires, both literary and sexual. The gentleman on paper, especially male-authored paper, was not initially attractive or desirable; however, when women placed him within the relational model of the courtship plot and used the setup to present him as desirable—as not only the virtuous but the attractive choice as well—they altered his chemistry. Women writers produced the gentleman's masculinity because "gender itself is a social relation obtained only through its materialization as practice."[43] They also marked this process to produce the gentleman materially through the structure of courtship as a narrative based on desire and power as chemical, a reaction to women's perspective, not the product of some innate, isolated, universal gender standard. By stressing the gentleman's dependence on women, women writers revised and cultivated him as a character who was desirable, attractive, and dependent on their authorship. Through their male characters, women writers not only constructed their own reality but also constructed *the* reality of masculinity.

The secondary genre I explore is the male-authored essay. In my first three chapters, I examine *The Spectator* (1711–1712), David Hume's mid- and late-century essays, and *The Rambler* (1750–1752). My approach to these texts was inspired, in part, by Catherine Gallagher's assessment of her own critical use of Hume's work: "I have chosen *A Treatise* not because it was an influential work in the eighteenth century, (it was not) but because literary critics are fond of quoting it to prove that eighteenth-century people believed that they naturally took on the emotional coloring of their human environment through the automatic operations of sympathy."[44] In fact, all three selected texts are often used in similar ways as shorthand for eighteenth-century norms and thoughts, which in some ways they may indeed be.[45] Much of this treatment, however, overlooks crucial genre conventions of periodicals and other essays. As Manushag Powell articulates, "The periodical . . . is a key element in the development of the *narrative* self."[46] The men who wrote the selected texts do not represent some sort of internal authentic selves in their essays but instead construct gentlemanly personas that lay claim to authenticity and internality. Theirs is a performance structured by narrative, and their texts are as fictional and performative as the novels that I present alongside them. Furthermore, as I show, these performances are increasingly dictated by the standards women authors set for the gentleman through their courtship plots and structures.

My exploration of male authors and texts repositions these essays as peers of, not authorities over, the novels that I discuss. Such male-authored texts do not somehow present eighteenth-century thought any more authentically than women-authored novels do. Solinger articulates a position widely echoed in scholarship on the gentleman in the eighteenth century: "A masculine ideal promoted across a spectrum of writing, the gentleman was the dominant persona of essayists, critics, and male conduct-book writers as well as the ideal husband imagined by the authors of heroine-centered domestic fiction."[47] In this characterization and in most other criticism, the female-authored gentleman is viewed as a response to a pre-established, male-authored gentleman. I challenge the ways in which male-authored essays' depictions of masculinity are treated as existing prior to or with more authority than the novels by women that I pair them with. In fact, I propose that the opposite is true—that the novels exerted influence over the essays. The essays constitute a site for exploring how men sought to reflect and perform the ideal of the gentleman, not for establishing masculine-embodied creation. As Gallagher points out, Hume is frequently referenced and used not because he was in fact popular but because we have made him so. My argument posits that the reason we have latched on to his performance of masculinity is because we have internalized the appeal and standards of the woman-authored gentleman, not because Hume is authentically a gentleman or textually all that desirable.

In my final chapters, I notably depart from my system of pairing in the first three chapters: Davys with Addison and Steele, Haywood with Hume, and Lennox with Johnson. In chapter 4, I flip the script and present a male novelist, Richardson, with female correspondents. I make this shift for a few important reasons. First, I want to showcase that although *Sir Charles Grandison* (1753) is a clear presentation of the eighteenth-century gentleman within a courtship plot, Richardson is not the father of the gentleman's genealogy, as he is so frequently presented, but instead an inheritor of the legacy of women writers. In chapter 5, I make a more dramatic shift by focusing solely on two women novelists: Elizabeth Inchbald and Mary Robinson. I make this shift before closing the book because my earlier chapters establish the reality of the described gender dialectic, which frees my final chapter to instead focus on how, by the late eighteenth century, women had such definitive ownership over the gentleman that they could interrogate the very plot structures that they had used to create him. Women not only crafted the gentleman through the courtship plot but also critiqued and revealed the ways in which his masculinity depended on plot and performance.

Chapter Summaries

As noted, *A Genealogy of the Gentleman* resists placing male and female writers in opposition but instead connects them dialectically in order to demonstrate how women drew upon and influenced the authorship of their now canonical male contemporaries. Chapters 1 through 3 pair female novelists and male essayists from the early through the mid-eighteenth century and explore how women writers took aspects of the gentleman designed to regulate women—his roles as didactic author, sympathetic reader, and moral critic—and created courtship plots that capitalized on his dependence on women to renegotiate the force of these powers. By revising rather than rejecting the gentleman's modes of authority, women writers transformed the gentleman into their own creature and constructed an influential masculinity that required women's approbation. In using this power to legitimize their authorship as being authoritative, moral, and culturally necessary, women writers slowly untethered the regulatory features from the gentleman as a private subject and co-opted his authority for themselves. By some contrast, chapters 4 and 5 transition from the mid- to the late century, specifically to women writers who confidently asserted their moral right to dictate and delineate proper masculine behavior and, in turn, revealed how a successful performance of gentlemanliness could have just as much impact as seemingly innate masculinity. By infiltrating classic structures of masculine power, these women writers established their own avenues to control morality and gender. However, they also became entrenched in and reinforced the patriarchal structures they criticized.

Chapter 1, "Gentleman Spectator as Desiring Author: *The Spectator* and Mary Davys's *Reform'd Coquet*," shows how performance is the foundation of the gentleman's identity. There is no wizard behind the curtain: the gentleman *is* the combination of author, persona, text, and performance. The gentleman's role as the didactic author depended on privatizing but not erasing his body and desires via textual performance, a distinction that could be realized by establishing a relationship with a desiring readership, especially female readers. I argue that Joseph Addison and Richard Steele's iconic periodical *The Spectator* (1711–1712) constructs the gentleman's role as professional author by performing neutrality, specifically a lack of selfish economic and sexual desires. However, interrogating the periodical's structure and style, with its eidolonic performances, subscription and circulation, and construction and critique of women readers, clarifies that the gentleman author's neutrality is a screen designed to code and hide his professional, economic, erotic, and narrative desires. In *The Reform'd Coquet* (1724), Mary Davys weaves this structure into the fabric of the courtship novel by constructing a gentleman lover-mentor, Alanthus, who performs the persona of the elderly bachelor Formator in order to reform the vivacious coquette Amoranda. Through masquerade, Davys reveals that Alanthus is just as fictional as Formator and that the gentleman's identity depends on reforming Amoranda's desires. However, the price that is paid for Davys's professional performance is her heroine's fortune. Amoranda must marry Alanthus if we are to fully understand the machinations of the gentleman's performance, and Davys is willing to bargain her character's fate for her own.

In chapter 2, "The Gentleman of Letters as Passionate Reader: Eliza Haywood's *Love in Excess* and David Hume's Philosophy of Moral Sympathy," we see that Haywood's 1719 novel and its central figure, Count D'elmont, anticipate the model of Hume's persona and philosophy, and that Haywood employs modes of gentlemanly sympathy founded on reading habits that Hume would later endorse. Although Haywood has long been established as a master of amatory passion, I argue that she is also a foundational authority on the connection between moral passion and codes of masculinity. Meanwhile, Hume has been read as a pivotal philosopher of moral sensibility, whereas his own authorial performance and the connection between his philosophy and his masculinity have largely been ignored. In response to both oversights, the chapter repositions Haywood as an author whose construction of masculinity anticipated the cult of sensibility and examines Hume as a character—and also a construction—in his own essays and writings. By presenting D'elmont as a reformed rake, Haywood moreover infuses the gentleman's role as sympathetic reader with a desirability that stems from the passion of moral sensibility and thus revises the force of seduction. As a result, her emphasis creates an exemplary standard of masculinity that male writers, including Hume, felt compelled to attempt to meet themselves, however unsuccessfully. In Hume's essays and treatises, he repeatedly attempts to present his body—both his actual body and his body of work—as desirable, and his failed bids to repackage his style in order to reach a wider audience and engage desiring female readers speak to the force of Haywood's idealized structure of masculinity, which depends on charging the moral passions with a covert erotic impulse. Ultimately, while Haywood exerted the influence, historically, Hume has reaped the reward because his imperfect gentlemanly performance still has the privilege of patriarchy.

By the mid-century, we see women writers questioning but also reinforcing the limits they constructed through the gentleman. Chapter 3, "Romancing the Gentleman Critic: Reading Criticism as Generic Courtship in Charlotte Lennox's *The Female Quixote* and Samuel Johnson's *The Rambler*," re-evaluates the relationship between Charlotte Lennox and Samuel Johnson through the lens of the gentleman's role as literary critic. For years, Lennox was read as a kind of protégé of the more established Johnson. However, my chapter argues that in the 1750s, Lennox and Johnson were colleagues, both on the cusp of their respective literary successes. Examining their correspondence from the 1750s, Johnson's *The Rambler* (1750–1752), and Lennox's *The Female Quixote* (1752) reveals a dynamic relationship that was negotiated through the gendered construct of criticism, within which both authors adopted and shed a variety of roles. In *The Rambler*, Johnson presents criticism as a heroic contest in which author and critic battle for literary greatness; this tension is presented with an air of romance. In *The Female Quixote*, Lennox recasts this model as Arabella's quixotic quest for narrative, which becomes a representation of female authorship. While Lennox revises the gentleman critic into a contingent ally of the woman writer through the comedy of Arabella and Glanville's courtship, she also criticizes the generic boundaries, frustrations, and hyperbolic expectations placed on women writers. The chapter concludes with a brief examination of Lennox's understudied piece of literary criticism, *Shakespear Illustrated* (1753–1754), a work that opens with Johnson adopting the role not of the gentleman critic but of Lennox herself: the woman author as critic. I argue that this performance highlights the performativity of both masculinity and criticism as well as represents the ways in which women writers created a space for their own critical voice, so much so that the man of letters adopted this voice himself.

Chapter 4, "'Smartly Dealt With; Especially by the Ladies': The Women Writers of Samuel Richardson's *Sir Charles Grandison*," re-evaluates the epistolary conventions of Samuel Richardson's *Sir Charles Grandison* (1753) in order to construct the gentleman as an object of revelatory desire by prioritizing a woman's authorial voice. I argue that it is far more accurate to read *Sir Charles Grandison* as having been coauthored by Richardson's numerous women correspondents than as the product of the single male author. As the chapter demonstrates in detail, the crucial struggle in constructing an ideal gentleman, especially one who is constantly virtuous instead of reformed, is establishing his very desirability. Richardson's third novel was meant to create the masculine counterpart to his epically virtuous heroines, a better hero than Tom Jones, Henry Fielding's lovable rogue. However, to create a desirable model of virtuous masculinity, Richardson relied heavily on his female correspondents, and this resource is woven into the epistolary structure of *Grandison*. Although Grandison's looks, fortune, sympathy, and character in theory speak for themselves, they are in fact spoken for and made desirable through the pens of women. The lively pens of Harriot Byron and the other women of the story comprise the channels of desire in the text and the desirability of Grandison's gentlemanly masculinity. In this way, the form of *Grandison* echoes its collaborative, women-authored composition. Yet, with this empowerment comes the uncomfortable recognition that these women are also the voices who are responsible for some of Sir Charles's most patriarchal views.

Chapter 5, "The Gentleman as Authorial Drag: Inverting Plots, Homosociality, and Moral Authorship in Elizabeth Inchbald's *A Simple Story* and Mary Robinson's *Walsingham*," posits that Inchbald's *A Simple Story* (1791) and Robinson's *Walsingham* (1797) not only firmly position the woman writer as the instructor for appropriate masculine behavior but also challenge late-century gender binaries, namely by revealing that the gentleman's power derives from structural relations that can be just as easily occupied by women. Both women writers interrogate the patriarchal architecture of homosocial triangles and argue that power emanates from that architecture's structural dynamics more than from biological determinism. On the one hand, through her provocative two-part novel, Inchbald reframes the heterosexual scenes between the coquettish Miss Milner and her lover-mentor Dorriforth/Lord Elmwood as scenes between a young gentleman, Rushbrook, and Elmwood. Inchbald does not disguise a woman in breeches, but instead uses plot to demonstrate how narrative structure makes and unmakes patriarchal power. In *Walsingham*, on the other hand, Sir Sidney's successful masquerade as a gentleman and her position as a disguised woman in homosocial relationships with other women invert male homosociality and transform Walsingham into an object of exchange between women. Sidney is by far a better gentleman than Walsingham. Taken together, both authors create characters and plots that successfully perform masculinity until they choose to reveal the woman writer behind the masculine curtain. In so doing, they reveal the constructed nature of binary gender and of the gentleman's masculinity and establish their own moral authority. However, while Inchbald and Robinson offer critiques that reveal the plotted reliance of the gentleman, they do not offer alternatives.

My forward-looking coda, "But They Were All Written by Women," gives a polite yet pointed nod to Jane Austen's gentlemen. After all, one cannot write about the gentleman without acknowledging Austen. However, rather than reading Austen as a departure or exception among women writers as authors of masculinity, as has often been the case, I resituate her as part of an ongoing legacy. In particular, I briefly explore Austen's first publication, *Sense and Sensibility* (1811), as her initial public foray into gentleman-making, one that seems to present two of her least impressive heroes: Edward Ferrars and Colonel Brandon. However, as the coda argues, the desirability of these heroes within the text draws upon their eighteenth-century predecessors, namely in the empowered and dominant role that the Dashwood sisters play in constructing the desirability of the heroes, who quite literally emerge from their reserved silences only through the narration, characterization, and revision of the women characters.

A Patriarchal Bargain

If we acknowledge the power and authority that women writers exerted over masculinity, then we also need to confront the complicated legacy this authority must have. If women shaped the gentleman, then they also played an active role in his patriarchal longevity. At times, I have wondered if this is actually what runs beneath declarations that the men women write are bad. If we believe male characters are not where women writers' literary efforts and investments lie, then we can excuse those writers as merely mimicking social norms or setting up a patriarchal surface against which to explore the limitations of female agency vis-à-vis their female characters. Recognizing that they had a literary and aesthetic investment in male characters must change the way we imagine their gender politics. The gentleman has been dismissed as women writers bowing to patriarchal standards, a necessary penance and way around "the censorship of critics."[48] What I propose here is that women did not yield to critics with their gentlemen but instead constructed the very contours of their critics and criticism itself, at least to a certain extent. After all, as George Haggerty points out, "No male character can avoid partaking in masculine privilege" in his relationships to female characters.[49] While we have acknowledged women's position or role within patriarchy, we are deeply uncomfortable with the ways women may have participated in that patriarchy.[50] The dual nature of the gentleman hero provides an ideal space for navigating the complex position held by women in a patriarchal society and the ways in which they have empowered themselves through and within it. At the same time, it also requires us to look squarely at the cost of their professional empowerment.

At his core, the gentleman is a fantasy of relief, not one of revolution. This is his fundamental structure and his problematic limit. This book's featured women authors' investment in the gentleman is a method of seeking access to a privileged system and structure, not an attempt to dismantle that system. As I explore in different ways throughout the book and most overtly at the end of chapter 4, the fantasy of the gentleman is that he is a version of patriarchy you can count on. He does not change the system; instead, he is a tool to intervene within it. He does not erase the rake's "threat of male sexual predation"; he merely steps in the rake's path to shield the heroine or the author or even women as a concept from the bombardments and vulnerabilities of patriarchal systems that he nevertheless does not erase.[51] The gentleman does not eliminate the heterosexual imperative of marriage as the ideal for women, and he does not grant women legal status to own their own property. He does, however, make the requisites of society more palatable by intertwining financial security with one kind of sexual attraction. Thus, despite the acknowledgment that female desire and sexuality are both important and possibly even virtuous, there are limits to this discourse. The gentleman is a fantasy that, if you follow the right plot, patriarchy will "yield a measure of authority," just enough to give some women breathing room.[52]

To return to Connell's definition of hegemonic masculinity, it is a masculinity that "embodies the currently accepted answer to the problem of the legitimacy of patriarchy, which guarantees (or is taken to guarantee) the dominant position of men and the subordinate position of women."[53] As an embodiment, the gentleman justifies this position through his kindness, generosity, and appreciation of women, but he continues to maintain a system that makes women vulnerable and thus dependent on patriarchy. In *Pride and Prejudice* (1813), Mr. Darcy does not protect Elizabeth from scandal by challenging the world's perspective on Lydia's elopement with Wickham or the standards that ruin her sisters by association. On the contrary, he protects her by legitimizing Lydia's relationship within a courtship plot and then marrying Elizabeth himself, thereby further shielding her from future scandal with his own patriarchal status.

Women writers wrote the gentleman as a bargain. However, this entailed not the uncritical reproduction of an oppressive system but a strategic cycle of intervention, endorsement, and critique, as well as an ongoing conversation with the strategies men were using to write themselves. This book traces the evolution of this complex negotiation, where the adoption of gentlemanly authority evolved from a means of seeking professional survival into a cultural category to be simultaneously challenged and validated. My goal is not to castigate these women writers—they were seeking footholds for professional status—but it is necessary to acknowledge the limits of what they imagined. Doing so enables us to interrogate our own continuing cultural attraction to the "gentleman" even as we may claim to find him boring, to recognize that the patriarchal bargain has meant that women creators are not recognized for their simultaneously remarkable and problematic contributions to literary tropes and production, and to expose the seemingly neutral and rational position the gentleman allegedly occupies as a performance.

My hope is that this book answers Susan Lanser's call to action to better interrogate the heteronormative plots of women's writing in the eighteenth century. By registering the gentleman as a performative masculinity and tracing how women actively constructed this type through their courtship plots, *A Genealogy of the Gentleman* provides "exposure of conventional practices *as* heteronormative, together with an interrogation of how that heteronormativity developed, functioned, and sustained itself."[54] One of the major ways that heteronormativity has continued to function so well is through the attractive packaging of the gentleman. Elizabeth Kowaleski-Wallace has articulated that, when we look at the legacies of women writers, we need to consider "the source of women's attraction to patriarchy."[55] One such source is the gentleman, and the added complexity is that the patriarchy was attractive because women penned those attractions themselves. This is both the power and the danger of women writers' influence: they succeeded where their male peers struggled; they made the gentleman attractive.

However, the limits are not theirs alone; they are also ours. Some critics might protest that they find the gentleman as presented in my book stuffy and boring—in a word, undesirable—because we, from our contemporary security, are too clever to fall prey to the lures of the eighteenth-century gentleman. Although we may indeed be too clever in some ways, I think that such a position is undercut by how clearly the legacy of the gentleman continues to exert influence over us today. As I repeat throughout my chapters, though women writers have defined the contours of the gentleman, male authors have reaped the rewards in terms of respect, canonicity, and critical attention. In unmistakable ways, this reality lingers at our critical doors. In a sense, these women authors did their job too well—so well that we stopped questioning the cultural importance of the gentleman without having accurately traced his origins. As an unspoken ideal or literary figure, the gentleman indeed continues to be incredibly popular, and many women still prefer, often unconsciously, to vote for men and want to see and support them in positions of power and leadership.[56] Even today it is often easier to imagine simply finding the right person, usually the right man, to place in a position of authority as a means to fix problems than it is to reimagine the systems of power responsible for these problems. For many of us, especially white, straight, cisgender women, doing so allows us to comfortably remain within our somewhat privileged positions.

We have also continued the pattern of not giving women credit for the production of the gentleman in its most widespread and popular forms. The gentleman still dominates women-authored novels. Perhaps this is why the romance novel industry remains the most popular in the publication world: it continues to sell the relief the gentleman provides. While features of the romance novel have evolved over time, its many fundamental generic aspects—courtship, female-centered desires, and the gentleman—remain stalwart aspects of its foundation. Similar to the woman-authored historical novels featuring gentleman, the romance novel also subsidizes more prestigious genres in publishing with its production and popularity while at once receiving no credit for serving as the backbone of a struggling industry.[57] Culturally, we are repeating the pattern of ignoring mass influence because it is woman authored and perceived as only being produced for women.

While there are complex and uneasy aspects of looking squarely at the woman-authored gentleman, there are also vital critical possibilities. It allows us a starting point to begin a wider exploration of how eighteenth-century women writers constructed masculinities in other venues and genres beyond the courtship novel, and to examine normative masculinity as a construction from its hegemonic inception, which, in turn, enables a clear critical vocabulary for articulating the performative modes and systems of this masculinity. Looking at the woman-authored gentleman allows us to take seriously that masculinity, even normatively, has always also been produced by women. Within eighteenth-century studies, this provides us with the opportunity for decentering canonical male authors by situating their works, their masculinities, and their male characters as dialectically integrated with those of women writers. The bastion of their masculine authenticity is now open for negotiation and critique in new ways. Beyond the eighteenth century, taking seriously how women writers have endorsed, committed to, and perpetuated tangible ideals of masculinity pushes us to interrogate our own political and cultural comfort zones. It opens possibilities of women's continued and adjusted influence, while challenging us to recognize how women have participated in our existing but potentially limited comfort zones. My hope is that *A Genealogy of the Gentleman* reminds us that the narratives of patriarchy are not impermeable and that masculinity, even at its most conservative, is a performance, and performances can be rewritten.

1

Gentleman Spectator as Desiring Author
The Spectator *and Mary Davys's* Reform'd Coquet

I ... do upon honour declare, I am pleased with what you have done; there is certainly a *secret pleasure in doing Justice*, though we often evade it, and a secret horror in doing ill, though we often comply with the temptation.
—Lord Lofty, *The Reform'd Coquet*

If I can any way contribute to the Diversion or Improvement of the Country in which I live, I shall leave it, when I am summoned out of it, *with the secret Satisfaction* of thinking that I have not lived in vain.
—Mr. Spectator, *The Spectator* no. 5

Mary Davys's *The Reform'd Coquet* (1724) follows the covert courtship of the coquettish Amoranda by her suitor in disguise, Alanthus. Alanthus disguises himself as an old man—Formator—in order to convert Amoranda from a coquette who loves flattery into a woman worthy of a man of sense. Along the way Formator/Alanthus and Amoranda foil kidnapping and seduction attempts by her other suitors, who use various forms of disguise and trickery to try to capture Amoranda and her fortune. The dynamic between Formator/Alanthus and Amoranda is the primary focus of this chapter; however, I would like to present Lord Lofty as a micro-example of the dynamic of performance and desire that Davys capitalizes on via her gentleman characters. All of Amoranda's would-be kidnapper-suitors end up dead, except for Lord Lofty. Lofty is the archetype of the aristocratic rake. He has previously tricked, seduced, and abandoned another young woman, Altemira. Through a bed-trick, Amoranda and Formator trap Lord Lofty into marrying Altemira, thereby fulfilling his contract with her: "When my Lord had looked sufficiently round and saw how matters went, he ... resolved to turn the Scale and show himself a Man of Honour at last." To make the best of his situation, Lofty proclaims that he will do the right thing: "I own my design was to wrong this innocent Lady, but I had an inward remorse, for what I was about, and I would not part with the present quiet and satisfaction that fills my breast to be Lord of the whole Creation" (*RC* 289). On the surface, Lofty's reform suggests that the rake is but a performance, obscuring the true, virtuous nature of the gentleman, which exists in the hearts of all men (of a certain status).

I propose a different significance for Lofty's declaration, which shapes the core courtship dynamics between Amoranda and Formator/Alanthus. Instead of reading this as a manifestation of true, innate masculinity as inherently virtuous, I argue that, at his core, the gentleman is a figure of performance and his secret pleasure of pleasing is the distinct product of his masculinity's links to authorship. After all, Mr. Spectator, the authorial persona of *The Spectator*, phrases his authorial satisfaction in words almost identical to Lofty's: he claims a secret satisfaction for his essays, based on their ability to instruct and delight his readers. Yet, Mr. Spectator's publication of this secret belies its very premise as a secret.

This play at secrecy reveals the layered performance of the gentleman. In *The Spectator*, we see the layered relationship between Mr. Spectator as eidolon and his authors, mainly Joseph Addison and Richard Steele. Meanwhile, in *The Reform'd Coquet*, Alanthus establishes his own gentlemanliness by disguising himself as Formator, the supposedly neutral, disinterested father figure, all the while taking increased satisfaction in Amoranda's reform and growing attraction to him as Alanthus. Like the secret pleasure of pleasing readers, the secret identity of these authors is not so secret. In both cases it is the performance (the eidolon or the disguise) that transfers gentlemanliness to its creator, rather than the innate gentlemanliness reverberating outward to the fictional identity. It is the fiction that makes the (gentle)man.

This chapter interrogates the idea of the gentleman as the emerging dominant form of masculinity in the eighteenth century and considers how this form of masculinity was dependent on a mutually constitutive relationship with women that took shape through literary authority (reading, writing, and criticism) and was defined by narrative structures (the periodical and the courtship novel). I will consider how *The Spectator* (1711–1712) built this relationship into its formation of the gentleman via its essay structure, aligning the gentleman with the periodical genre, not just the periodicalist. Thus, the periodical itself shaped the initial form of the eighteenth-century gentleman as he emerged as a man of birth and breeding into the cultural landscape of the eighteenth century. The periodical's popularity, overtly performative narrators (eidolons), and visible rhetorical situation make it ideally suited for my investigations.

The latter half of the chapter turns to Mary Davys's novel *The Reform'd Coquet; or, the Memoirs of Amoranda* and considers how Davys directly harnesses the essay structure and then transforms it into the core narrative of her courtship tale, dramatizing the rhetorical maneuvers of the periodical genre as the driving force of her novel. Formator/Alanthus is analogous to both the eidolon and its author, and his engagement with Amoranda mimics the form of *The Spectator* essays as they are presumed to be encountered by female readers. While Davys was an admirer of *The Spectator*, her hero is more than an homage to the gentleman spectator; her characterization is a vital step in the gentleman's transformation into the desirable lead of eighteenth-century courtship novels. Women writers, like Davys, contributed to the cultivation of this masculinity by making its formal aspects visible in their own narrative structure and style. Further, Davys is able to cultivate authorial power herself by revealing the machinations of the gentleman author's masculinity and detailing how the lessons to a female reader are necessary to the form of the gentleman, not because instruction is his ultimate goal but because his desires—that secret pleasure in pleasing—give shape to his masculinity. By revealing the contours of the gentleman author's pleasure and its reliance on a female audience, Davys demonstrates how a woman writer can deploy this structure for her own advantage. Her text embodies a pivotal moment when the gentleman became the lead of the courtship novel not just as a reflection of popular tastes but as a means through which women writers influenced that taste.

The Spectator; or the Gentleman as Authorial Performance

The Spectator's language and structure have long been associated with the links between authorship and hegemonic masculinity. The periodical emerged concomitantly with the figure of the modern gentleman around the turn of the eighteenth century. The genre and gender performance meshed similar goals: "to 'make [gentlemen] useful and acceptable to mankind.'"[1] Critics like Jason Solinger and Thomas King have explored how *The Spectator* specifically synthesized some of the most recognizable features of the gentleman: his usefulness, his combination of education and experience, his politeness, and his heterosociality.[2] Meanwhile, Manushag Powell, Erin Mackie, and Shawn Lisa Maurer have noted that the male authors of periodicals created ideals that defined this sphere as white, male, and heterosexual, and extended outward to regulate gender and literary standards.[3] In tandem, Kristina Straub and King have considered how the positions of subject and object were frequently defined through standards that positioned the masculine as the spectator and the feminine as the object of observation, which clearly draws on the spectatorial language of *The Spectator* and its predominantly male authors and their textual persona, the eidolon.[4] We see the threads of this woven into contemporary masculinity theory. As noted by R. W. Connell, hegemonic masculinity is routinely tied to a position of natural authority and invisibility, the authoritative observer of the world and its operations. These standards only reveal themselves in contrast to other genders.[5] Even dated theories like the Habermasian standard of gendered public and private spheres continue to linger in our narratives, critical discourse, and gendered ideals because of the resonance of texts like *The Spectator* and the ways that spectatorial language has been woven into our ideals of the masculine and, consequently, the normative. Therefore, linking *The Spectator* to eighteenth-century masculinity and the gentleman is a part of well-established territory.

However, the ways in which *The Spectator* defined and constructed masculinity have been somewhat misunderstood, or, perhaps more accurately, mislabeled. The narrative of masculinity and authorship in *The Spectator* has routinely fallen into the trap of assuming masculinity as innate and describing it as either invisible or disembodied. As Connell points out, "Mass culture generally assumes there is a fixed, true masculinity beneath the ebb and flow of daily life."[6] This idea of masculinity as being both part of the world but private and concealed, touching society and yet fundamentally untouchable at its core, echoes Mr. Spectator's claims: "I live in the World, rather as a Spectator of Mankind, than as one of the Species; by which means I have made my self a Speculative Statesman, Soldier, Merchant and Artizan, without ever meddling with any Practical Part in Life. I am very well versed in the Theory of an Husband, or a Father" (*Spectator* 1:4–5.1711). Thus, it may initially appear that Mr. Spectator personifies this untouchable masculinity. However, the perception that masculinity constructed as spectatorial equates to invisibility and disembodiment is an inaccurate picture of the gentleman as he emerges through the periodical, most specifically *The Spectator*.[7] Mr. Spectator deliberately constructs a body that is produced through authorship for himself, which allows for the construction of his masculinity to be generic, private, and theoretically neutral. In his first issues, Mr. Spectator articulates the typical markers of genteel masculinity. He is from an old gentry family, he has been properly educated, and he has seen the world (*Spectator* 1:1–2.1711). Yet, he also refuses to describe the cut of his coat or the shape of his nose; he refuses to present us with a physical body in the traditional sense. This combination fuels the vision of the gentleman as defined through his experiences and actions, while also maintaining a supposedly disembodied self.

However, these physical and familial features are not what ultimately construct his masculinity or what defines the core of the gentleman. Instead, they are the ways Addison and Steele construct their eidolon as a textual figure of authorship. Mr. Spectator declares, in his first issue, "When I consider how much I have seen, read, and heard, I begin to blame my own Taciturnity; and since I have neither the time nor Inclination to communicate the Fulness [sic] of my Heart in Speech, I am resolved to *Print my self out*, if possible, before I Die" (*Spectator* 1:5.1711, emphasis mine). He shall print himself out. That means the issues of *The Spectator* are him—they are his body, and that body is a textual one. Not only is it textual, it is also authored. He is doing the printing; he is both the content and the creator of himself, not disembodied, but authorially embodied. Thus, not only does Mr. Spectator have a body (and a voluminous one at 555 issues) but that body is also an active and ongoing production, not a stable, pre-existing entity.

The periodical constructed the gentleman's masculinity as private, not invisible, by linking form with gender. While the gentleman's body is existent, it is not public or visual in the same way women's bodies often were. Instead, as King argues, one of the central shifts in eighteenth-century masculinity was a move from public to private embodiment via the construction of a "properly disciplined inwardness," which stands in deliberate contrast with the performative public body of the restoration rake or, more and more frequently, the deviantly overt body of the fop or the molly.[8] The periodical participates in this restructuring. First, while the rake was noted for his speech (aligning him with the restoration theater), Mr. Spectator's heart is too full for speech, and he instead turns to print. Mr. Spectator can print himself out, allowing a textual body to circulate throughout England, while also maintaining a barrier between his imagined physical body and readers. This also creates a similar privacy guard between the eidolon—the created authorial persona—and the literal authors: Addison, Steele, and others. Instead of erasing the body, the periodical form and authorship allow for the gentleman's body to be both properly private and circulated through the social world, enacting his necessary social role as an authority on taste and a moral moderator.

Performed neutrality is the other key feature of the gentleman's masculinity in *The Spectator*, but this neutrality is now defined through heterosocial relationships. As Powell points out, Mr. Spectator's "power to remain an uninvolved spectator" is tied to the fact that he "is unmarried, childless, neutral, detached."[9] Mr. Spectator crystallizes for his readers how neutrality is the core of the gentleman because it is through his neutrality that the gentleman presents himself as lacking sexual or economic desires. In no. 4, Mr. Spectator professes this neutrality directly: "I have the high Satisfaction of beholding all Nature with an unprejudic'd Eye; and having nothing to do with Men's Passions or Interests, I can with the greater Sagacity consider their Talents, Manners, Failings, and Merits" (*Spectator* 1:19.1711). Mr. Spectator does not present himself as asexual—he dutifully acknowledges at least one serious, if failed, courtship—but he does not present himself as a desiring body.[10] He supposedly has no personal motives attached to profit or to women.

It is no coincidence that no. 4 is the issue where Mr. Spectator claims his vaunted neutrality and where he also directly addresses his prioritization and care for female readers: "The fair Sex . . . As these compose half the World, and are by the just Complaisance and Gallantry of our Nation the more powerful Part of our People, I shall dedicate a considerable Share of these my Speculations to their Service, and shall lead the Young through all the becoming Duties of Virginity, marriage, and Widowhood" (*Spectator* 1:21.1711). Whereas the rake is the sexual predator, who used and discarded women, the gentleman is their benevolent protector. Seeking women as readers was an emerging, if not quite new, aspect of the eighteenth-century gentleman. Contrast Mr. Spectator's attitude with the Earl of Shaftesbury. Whereas the Earl of Shaftesbury had advocated for learning, sociality, and politeness as markers of ideal masculinity, he and many other seventeenth-century thinkers were incredibly critical of women's influence on masculinity. Shaftesbury writes, "I have seen many a time a well-bred man, who had himself a real good taste give way . . . in favour chiefly of the tender sex" to false criticism and dismissal of manly literary labor.[11] But Mr. Spectator articulates in no. 57, "Women were formed to temper Mankind and sooth them into Tenderness and Compassion, not to set an Edge upon their Minds, and blow up in them those Passions which are too apt to rise of their own Accord" (*Spectator* 1:242.1711). Mr. Spectator links his neutrality with his relationship to female readers, and it is this combination that reveals the performative nature of his masculinity.

The Periodical Performing the Gentleman

Periodicals are voiced by eidolons, fictional figureheads who serve as the spokespersons for the essays, presenting a single unifying voice which is in fact written by multiple authors.[12] As Powell articulates, "Despite the eidolons' earnestness and conservatism about what an author ought to be—masculine, genteel, disinterested—there was a great deal of tension between the real identities of periodical authors and their eidolons." Mr. Spectator is the creation of Addison and Steele, along with others. This creates a shadowy but tangible distance between author and eidolon. The actual situations of many periodicalists and authors in general were far different in terms of their actual class status, education, and disinterest—sexual and economic—from their eidolons.[13] This distance between author and eidolon helps craft key aspects of hegemonic masculinity. As noted earlier, hegemonic masculinity is the rationalistic, innate, embodied gender of Western culture, and the gentleman is clearly a key, defining version of this category. However, what makes this "true masculinity" is not necessarily a definite or actual body. Instead it is linked to features that are categorized as innately masculine, like rationality, and while male bodies are clearly important sites for interpreting and coding masculinity, they are not necessarily (or even often) the origin of our conceptions of masculinity. In this way, the performative separation between eidolon and author, where the two were separate but sometimes not clearly delineated, became a defining aspect of modern, Western masculinity. Just as male bodies can be coded as representing a supposed authentic internal masculinity, the eidolon can be read as a vessel for the author's innate self. Hegemonic masculinity *performs* neutrality, naturalness, disinterest, rationality, and restraint in ways that mask its patriarchal power, its embodied desires (sexual or otherwise), and its deeply anxious self-interest.

The features of periodicals that "establish . . . whiteness, maleness, and middle-classness" as the defining features of authorship and the public sphere are constructed.[14] Mr. Spectator performs the role of gentleman author as a neutral spectator, and the distinction between his self and the actual authors' selves reflects the performative nature of the gentleman author. Mr. Spectator is a fictional characterization, performing the role of gentleman author on paper, and behind him are actual writers, primarily Addison and Steele. However, for readers there is a blurred sense of where one ends and the other begins. The gentleman author is both the textual performance and the context in which real authors produce that performance. Here is the complex nexus of the gentleman author's performative authenticity. Powell rightly points out that "the periodical, taken specifically, is a key element in the development of the *narrative* self, without which, contested as it is, our own society would be almost unrecognizable."[15] The gentleman is a figure of narrative who performs authentic subjectivity, who is constructed to create a sense of public and private self through narrative.

I argue that the ultimate goal of this textual self is to control and create desire, both sexual and economic, in ways that reaffirm the gentleman's masculinity. If we recognize the gentleman's neutrality as a performance and notably connect this to textuality, we can chart how it is actually language and narrative form that creates the gentleman. Despite the fact that readers know that the eidolon is not the author, there is no clear cultural dissonance around the authenticity of the gentleman author. This is because, by making the gentleman's masculinity a product of textual and narrative production, Addison and Steele recalibrate the relationship of authenticity to language. In an examination of Steele's "plain-style," Christina Lupton writes, Steele "loosens language's dependence on external references as a measure of truth while facilitating the claim that language might establish its sincerity through the internal relationship of argument to style."[16] According to this logic, Mr. Spectator's language, which is his body, rather than his true attachment to an external referent, is what makes him sincere. In fact, whereas the rake can separate his language and his sincerity—his body from his designs—Mr. Spectator's body is metonymically inseparable from his text. Both types of masculinities are performative, but whereas the rake is increasingly categorized as a deceptive body who disguises his intentions with words, the gentleman's words are tied to virtue and authenticity, which imply a body.

To be authentically a gentleman required a kind of adaptive performativity. Other authors and periodicalists clearly adopted this perspective, but Addison and Steele defined it in Mr. Spectator. There is a "shape-shifting quality" to the masculinity of the gentleman.[17] The gentleman shifts in and out of different spheres and performances. In perhaps the most frequently referenced essay in *The Spectator*, Mr. Spectator recounts, "There is no Place of general Resort, wherein I do not often make my Appearance" (*Spectator* 1:3.1711). He slips easily, almost invisibly, in and out of balls, the exchange, the coffee house, the theater, and the tea table, thus making himself a "Speculative Statesman, Soldier, Merchant and Artizan" (*Spectator* 1:4.1711). Mr. Spectator's experience is "speculative" rather than actual, but his ability to blend into different social arenas unnoticed, to belong to and own these spaces, marks his movements as those of the gentleman. Mr. Spectator defines this feature as the ability to move through the world, acclimating to the social circumstances with the kind of easy anonymity that indicates disguise but paradoxically maintains an authentic self. The gentleman, like the periodical, adapts to whatever situation he is in: that is what his knowledge of the world and good manners afford him.

This is all decidedly tied to the material circumstances of the periodical itself, a text that moved and circulated through space via subscriptions, social circulation, and conversation. This adaptable mobility allowed the gentleman to obscure his own desires: sexual, rhetorical, and commercial. As Powell and Mackie both explore, the periodical was entrenched in economic interest and market culture. Addison and Steele, and all periodicalists after them (male and female), wrote periodicals to sell them, to create profit. Thus, claims of gentlemanly disinterest ring false, but the need to perform this disinterest has created an undeniable legacy. The gentleman author must "*entice their audiences to read*, and thereby ensure both their own paychecks and the continued survival of the medium," and so "authors began to offer up more than advice: they offered up themselves, or rather, they offered up a version of 'the author' to be taken and mistaken for themselves."[18] Readers must be lured into reading periodicals because the "modes and attitudes" prescribed by periodicals "are instituted not through coercion but through persuasion."[19] His body, his supposedly private self, must be desirable and circulated if his product is to survive. This is why it is so vital that Mr. Spectator (and by extension Addison and Steele) both instruct and delight his readers.

The language of cajoling, pleasing, and winning takes on distinctive sexual overtones when we consider the dynamic between Mr. Spectator and his female readers. As with finances, Mr. Spectator claims not to have vested interest in his female readers beyond his altruistic benevolence. He is unmarried, and his one serious courtship does not go well. *Thankfully*, he still feels qualified to advise women about marriage. However, his description of ideal matrimony and courtship takes on the metaphorical dimensions of his relationship with his readers. Courtship is a process of close examination and critique: "Before Marriage we cannot be too inquisitive and discerning in the Faults of the Person beloved" (*Spectator* 3:516.1711). He is the embodiment of inquisitiveness, and continuously critiques and discovers the faults of those around him, theoretically out of benevolence and a kind of sociability. Mr. Spectator's recommendation of a long courtship equates to the desire for a long and continued readership. Unlike reading a novel or a play, reading a periodical takes on the dimensions of an ongoing relationship or a courtship. We could push this metaphorical courtship even further; the gentleman author's need to entice readers, to keep them interested and invested, speaks to flirtation and the cultivation of desire. The gentleman is perhaps not as distinct from the rake as he would like to define himself.

The gentleman cannot seduce women per se, but by interweaving his features with those of his authorship, he can gain a kind of erotic control over them. Namely, when he seeks to instruct and delight his female readers, he is explicitly teaching them to delight and desire him and his authorial instruction. As Maurer writes, in periodicals, "men's interest in and concern with women and with the norms of proper femininity served simultaneously to construct a masculine role of identity for the sentimental husband and father of the emerging middle classes."[20] In no. 92, Mr. Spectator claims, "I flatter myself that I see [women] daily improving by these my Speculations" (*Spectator* 1:393.1711). Mr. Spectator defines himself through his moral regulation of others; his character is formed through improving his female readers. After all, as a true gentleman, Mr. Spectator also sees it as his duty to protect the impressionable minds of women. Yet a distinctly competitive, self-interested thread runs throughout these periodicals. In no. 261, Mr. Spectator describes his failed courtship of a lady: he loses her to a dashing but seemingly shallow captain. He then spends a great deal of time describing the key features of a happy, companionate marriage. Mr. Spectator hopes to "keep [his women readers] from being charmed by those empty Coxcombs that have hitherto been admired among the Women, tho' laugh'd at among the Men" (*Spectator* 1:393.1711). When Mr. Spectator educates his women readers, he is teaching them to desire his version of masculinity over that of his competitors.

Similarly, his criticism of women proves self-interested. He critiques their fashion, both their love of dress and their vanity; he advises them to avoid being caught up in politics, as it is unfeminine and unbecoming of their sex. He advises them what to read (though more often he focuses on what not to read). These improvements or adornments of the fair sex are often directed at making them more attractive to men. In no. 73, Mr. Spectator writes: "I must return to the Moral of this Paper, and desire my fair Readers to give a proper Direction to their Passion for being admired: In order to which, they must endeavor to make themselves the Objects of a reasonable and lasting Admiration. This is not to be hoped for from Beauty, or Dress or Fashion, but from those inward Ornaments which are not to be defaced by Time or Sickness, and which appear most amiable to those who are most acquainted with them" (*Spectator* 1:315.1711). The ultimate goal of female cultivation is the admiration of men of sense. *The Spectator* creates a system where the veneration of women facilitates the regulation of women for the benefit of the gentleman. Women learn to seek and value his admiration above those of all other kinds of men, and to measure their own self-worth by his esteem. He creates a self-fulfilling loop wherein his own masculinity becomes the most desirable. Women must transform themselves into "Objects of reasonable and lasting Admiration," the standards of which are determined by him who is the "most acquainted with them," which validates his masculinity over the attractions of competitors.

This reciprocal relationship is constructed through literacy. Women are constructed as readers in *The Spectator*: even when they write, as they frequently do, it is to express their gratifications as readers. This is also true of Mr. Spectator's male readers, but the desiring appreciation of his female readers registers as especially important for his masculinity, because it establishes his sexual neutrality and textual desirability. The gentleman constructs women as desiring readers for several reasons. For one, it facilitates his position as a desirable author. For example, in no. 95, Mr. Spectator receives a grateful letter from Anabella, who opens her letter praising his kindness and benevolence: "As I hope there are but few that have so little Gratitude as not to acknowledge the Usefulness of your Pen, and to esteem it a Publick Benefit, so I am sensible, be that as it will, you must nevertheless find *the Secret and Incomparable Pleasure* in doing Good, and *be a great Sharer in the Entertainment you give*. I acknowledge our Sex much obliged, and I hope improved, by your Labours, and even your Intentions more particularly for our Service" (*Spectator* 1:404.1711, emphasis mine). What is most compelling about this letter is how it reveals the channels of desire that the gentleman author constructs through the periodical form and the depiction of female readers. This is a literary circuit. Anabella here, the model female reader, is literally parroting back Mr. Spectator's own presentation of his pleasures. She is a textual feedback loop that fuels his presentation of his authorship as attractive and desirable to women readers. Yes, Mr. Spectator objectifies women with his spectatorial gaze, but he also constitutes his own desirability as dependent on women.[21] The "*Secret and Incomparible Pleasure*" Mr. Spectator derives from his role as moral author is manifested through gratified female readers. This creates a reciprocal kind of pleasure, which is distinctly literary. Their correction constitutes his pleasure.

This authorial loop removes a layer of his supposed disinterest and links back to the actual material necessity of *The Spectator* being a desirable text; it must be desired for it to be produced at all. Without readers there would be no text, and without text there would be no gentleman author. However, by constructing a system where women readers act as respondents to Mr. Spectator, the periodical creates a system that reinforces the gentleman's hierarchical power. He is the author looking out on the world, and women are the subjects of his gaze and his critique—who are then the grateful, receptive respondents to his authorial production. But, as with pleasure, this structure does not accurately account for the reciprocity of these positions. Mr. Spectator only functions, and his identity only works, if there is an audience; as a genre, periodicals "often demand via their didactic appeals and intrusive narrators the active participation of the reader."[22] This extends outward along gendered lines. If Mr. Spectator is particularly interested in a female audience, then his identity is dependent on his interactions with them.

Mr. Spectator's compulsion to regulate women's reading reflects the gentleman's dependence on maintaining his position as a desirable author. To properly maintain his position of power and privilege, Mr. Spectator frequently mentions the need to monitor and adjust women's reading habits in order to help women cultivate proper kinds of femininity. They need him, he insists over and over again. In *Spectator* no. 37, he visits Leonora's library. Leonora is a lady-scholar of sorts, though her reading, like her library itself, is haphazard and scattered. Mr. Spectator reports, "As her Reading has lain very much among Romances, it has given her a very particular Turn of Thinking, and discovers it self even in her House, her Gardens and her Furniture." To aid Leonora, Mr. Spectator proposes to create a list of "such particular Books as may be proper for the Improvement of the Sex" (*Spectator* 1:158–159.1711). Advice on ladies' reading becomes one of the gentleman author's many forms of "self-commodification," except this one has erotic overtones.[23]

When Mr. Spectator claims he intends to "print himself out," we can now reinterpret Mr. Spectator and the gentleman's vaunted privacy, that authentic self, as a mechanism for creating and regulating desire. One of the functions of privacy—performed or otherwise—is to create desire in others, while delineating a restraint in oneself. As noted above, Mr. Spectator "was famous for *not* satisfying his readers' curiosity on the matter of himself."[24] If he leaves the readers unsatisfied on one level, he also leaves them desiring, and what they substitute for a traditionally physical body is his textual one. The denial of access to his "actual" body fuels a desire (both erotically economic and economically erotic) that is both satisfied and stoked by his textual body. His success relies on people, especially women, consuming his body through readership. Notably, Mr. Spectator continuously withholds his actual recommendations for their reading.[25] He covertly demands a kind of textual monogamy and monopoly. In a reversal of the rake who seeks to consume women, the gentleman seeks to be the desirable and consumable good, while still maintaining a patriarchal mastery over his readership by constructing them as perpetually dependent on him.

Any threat to this structure must be contained. One of the most frequent figures of Mr. Spectator's critique is the coquette.[26] As a gentleman, Mr. Spectator claims to criticize her because she falls into vice and away from the true beauty of her womanhood, thereby making herself vulnerable to the degeneracy of coxcombs and rakes. However, upon closer examination, it becomes clear that coquettes pose a challenge to Mr. Spectator's authorial control. For example, in *Spectator* no. 45, Mr. Spectator critiques a young coquette for disturbing his enjoyment of a performance of *Macbeth*. He writes, "She had...*formed a little Audience to her self*, and fixed the Attention of all about her. But as I had a mind to hear the Play, I got out of the Sphere of her Impertinence"; "This pretty Childishness of Behavior is one of the most refined Parts of Coquetry" (*Spectator* 1:194.1711, emphasis mine). She is a coquette because she dares to create an audience for herself, where her critiques of the play (she discusses Banquo in particular) become central. Mr. Spectator, as a purveyor of gentlemanly taste, critiques many plays in his essays. However, this young woman uses flirtation to invoke the same kind of authorial power as Mr. Spectator: she charms her audience for her own, and, to a lesser extent, their, pleasure.

The coquette is a "favorite satiric target of Joseph Addison and Richard Steele," because, as Juliette Merritt rightly points out, "she is an unsettling, even threatening figure" despite their obsessive attempts to "persuade us of the frivolous coquette's insignificance."[27] Coquettes seek and create their own audience, primarily composed of men, the way Mr. Spectator seeks to claim an audience for himself, and this is why they must be regulated and controlled. In delaying marriage and reveling in her own feminine display, the coquette sits "in open rebelling against the standard rules of courtship."[28] She also, and not unconnectedly, stands in opposition to standard rules of authorship, which "link . . . spectatorship to masculine privilege and superiority."[29] They are usurpers of authorship, and instead of occupying the comfortable space of a female reader, they seek to perform a brand of authorship for themselves. Furthermore, Mr. Spectator's removal from her sphere is reminiscent of yielding a field of battle, as if the coquette, because she seeks her own pleasure rather than responding to his as the gentleman author, is too powerful a rival for him to contend with. Even more dangerously, the coquette's use of desire reveals the similarity, rather than the contrast, between her authorship and that of Mr. Spectator. His forms are laid bare before him and potentially to the reader, and he leaves. This speaks to how fragile the controls of hegemonic masculinity are. They are powerful, but their mechanisms are perhaps rather easily subverted, hence the compulsion to label them as natural and therefore unquestionable.

Mary Davys: Dramatizing the Gentleman's Desires

Mary Davys and her work strike a discordant note in eighteenth-century criticism. On the one hand, she was deeply enmeshed in canonical circles of eighteenth-century literary culture. Her husband was a friend of Jonathan Swift's, and after his death Davys maintained an intermittent correspondence with Swift, repeatedly asking him for both literary and financial support. She admired *The Spectator* and also owned a coffee shop in Cambridge, seating her within established literary and masculine culture. She published her novels by subscription, a rising publication practice, and her list of subscribers was rather illustrious: Alexander Pope, John Gay, Martha Blount, Samuel Richardson, and at least two duchesses and other peers were among her subscribers for *The Reform'd Coquet*.[30] For these reasons, Davys has often anachronistically been read as a predecessor (often a less skillful one) of "the largely male-dominated developments of the realist novel."[31] In 1959, William McBurney semi-infamously described Davys as a forerunner of Henry Fielding and that therefore she had a "hearty, somewhat masculine temperament."[32] Davys was a woman who made her living by her pen and wrote popular novels that center on gender dynamics. Broadly speaking, Davys is often mentioned or footnoted in passing; she is included in general lists but quickly passed over for either more canonical or outrageous fare. Feminist criticism has struggled with what to make of Davys, and they find *The Reform'd Coquet* (1724) particularly troubling. The stumbling block for many readers is Amoranda's conservative reform from coquette to wife, and the (to use a technical term) creepy factor of the Formator/Alanthus manipulation of her character.[33]

The critical impulses to read Davys as either conservative or subversive have correct but incomplete instincts. First, the difficulty is that critics and scholars have attempted to locate Davys's protofeminist or conservative streaks in the fate of her heroine, Amoranda. However, if we consider the potential feminist aspects of Davys's novel as emerging from the structure and performative revelations of her text rather than in the destiny of her central female character, then new interventions appear within Davys's work—ones that allow us to put her at the forefront rather than banish her uneasily to the corners of our scholarship. Second, Davys was a popular author who used creative publication techniques (subscription) to define an independent authorial persona, and whose courtship structure of lover-mentor clearly took hold in the cultural imagination.[34] While Davys's rendition of this story is not the first, the semi-comedic marriage plot of *The Reform'd Coquet* is innovative, and does carry through to later authors like Fielding or even Jane Austen. The recognizability of the gentleman and our cultural attachment to him is almost unconscious and automatic, and it is because we are so familiar with plots like the one Davys creates here. In fact, I argue that the attachment of the gentleman to the courtship novel becomes the vital ingredient to his masculinity's power and long-standing appeal, and Davys is one of the earliest authors to manage this key integration clearly. If we can recognize the ways Davys deliberately crafted this structure to serve her own professional validation, then this structure pushes past what Eleanor Wikborg terms the "patriarchal lover": the "image of the powerful man . . . whose willingness to abstain from a measure of the sovereignty with which his maleness invested him would, at least in fantasy form, bring about a change in the power relations" between men and women.[35]

Reading the novel in conversation with *The Spectator* enables us to see that Davys does not just create an uneasy, pseudopatriarchal fantasy man; rather, she proactively draws on the constructed nature of the gentleman to suit her own innovations, and in doing so attaches the gentleman's masculinity to the courtship plot itself. The evidence for *The Spectator*'s influence on Davys's text is indirect but compelling. Besides being a reader of the popular periodical, Davys actually references *The Spectator* in the novel itself.[36] There are furthermore clear formal resonances between the structure of the periodical essay and the strategies Davys uses for framing the action of her narrative. Below I make a case for reading Formator/Alanthus as performance à la the eidolon, where Formator, the seemingly disinterested, benevolent bachelor, dispenses advice that creates desire for the gentleman—Alanthus—by transforming Amoranda from coquettish author into proper feminine reader. The performance of Formator, like that of Mr. Spectator (and unlike Formator/Alanthus's rivals), does not invalidate his power but rather facilitates it. However, Davys does not simply imitate *The Spectator*, nor does she buy wholesale into the gentlemanly model that the periodical offers. Her novel reveals the plotting of the gentleman author figure, deliberately incorporating letters and lectures that echo the style of *The Spectator*. In doing so, she reveals the machinations of the gentleman, and also takes advantage of the performative aspects of the gentleman author. If the gentleman author is a performance that validates the authorship of his creator, then a woman can deploy him as well as a man. Davys demonstrates an early and effective ventriloquism of masculinity itself.

Formator/Alanthus as Eidolon-Author

Formator's character, rather than just being an emblem of patriarchy, represents the eidolonic nature of the new mode of the gentleman. Davys focuses on him during the reform section of the novel because his masculinity is defined through its didacticism. At stake in *The Reform'd Coquet* is not Amoranda's femininity, or even her virtue, but Formator/Alanthus's masculinity. Tellingly, one of the most difficult struggles in writing about *The Reform'd Coquet* is how to reference Davys's hero: What name(s) should one use and when? Some critics refer to him by his assumed name, Formator, rather than by his "actual" name, Alanthus. Others refer to him by Alanthus throughout, and some opt for the Formator/Alanthus option. What I find so intriguing about this is how it sheds light on the constructed nature of the gentleman persona. In some ways, Formator, because his character is the most present to us, is more real than Alanthus is, or at least as real. More importantly, I argue, Alanthus is just as fictional as Formator; this is the crucial aspect of his masculinity within this text. Both are characters of manhood who operate under the constraints of constructed gender and wield a similar authorial power within the novel. This critical sense that Formator and Alanthus both are and are not the same person mimics the blurred lines readers created between eidolons and periodical authors. Mr. Spectator was not Addison or Steele, and yet his gentlemanly performance rubbed off on readers' perceptions of his authors as gentlemen. I argue that Formator is, fundamentally, Alanthus's eidolon who performs the disinterest of the gentleman author, covering the actual anxieties and desires of the engendered body of the gentleman himself. By reading Formator through the lens of the eidolon, we can see how Davys dramatizes the secret desires of the gentleman, connects his character to that new kind of performance, and demonstrates how his masculinity is dependent on creating a gendered author-reader dynamic, one that reforms Amoranda from a threatening coquette—a narrative rival—into a properly receptive and desiring female reader.

Formator bears all the markings of a gentleman author à la Mr. Spectator, which authorize his function in fundamentally the same way. He is a bachelor who enters Amoranda's life under the guise of reforming her coquettish behavior (as his name indicates, he will form her into a proper model of womanhood). Like Mr. Spectator, he is introduced in the form of a letter. Her Uncle Traffick, the source of her fortune and her absent guardian, writes a letter introducing Formator: "*Though he is an Old Man, he is neither impertinent, positive, or sour. You will, I hope, from my past Behavior towards you, believe you are very dear to me; and I have no better way of showing it for the future, than by putting you into such hands as* Formator's" (*RC* 267). His age provides a shield of neutrality for any presumptions of sexual ambition, as does his endorsement by her guardian. Amoranda is initially skeptical of Formator, but Formator protests in a very Spectatorish way: "Madam . . . you quite mistake me: I am not of that disagreeable Temper you have described; I would have both Young and Old act with that very innocent Freedom you speak of: but what I inveigh against, is an immoderate Love of Pleasure" (*RC* 268). Formator's moderation here is an echo of Mr. Spectator's, and Formator's qualification, his redefinition of pleasure, echoes Mr. Spectator's critiques of the fashionable world. Just as Mr. Spectator transforms his reticence into a valuable tool for his moral guidance, Formator recodes his age as something that provides him with perspective and appreciation for virtuous pleasure.

Formator delivers several lectures to Amoranda which follow the gendered pattern of Mr. Spectator's, inextricably linking her femininity with masculinity by critiquing female vanity and encouraging proper male attention. Formator begins by lecturing Amoranda on the failings of female vanity, often by first invoking nostalgia for a previous era: "When I was a young Fellow, we used to value a Lady for her Virtue, Modesty, and an innate Love of Honour ... those are unfashionable qualities, but they are still the chief Ornaments of your Sex, and ours never think a Woman complete without them" (RC 272). This echoes Mr. Spectator's proclamation: "Discretion and Modesty, which in all other Ages and Countries have been regarded as the greatest Ornaments of the Fair Sex, are considered as Ingredients of narrow Conversation" (Spectator 1:193–194.1711). Formator proceeds to critique coquetry: "Give me leave, Madam ... [to] tell you how great your misfortune has been," for despite her "Good-nature," her "want of Experience, together with a greedy Desire for Flattery" has led her astray (RC 272). He mimics Mr. Spectator's gentlemanly politeness, continuously asking leave before criticizing women. While this tactic does not seem particularly polite to us, Amoranda's reaction to it codifies it as politeness. She does not take offense, and instead feels charmed and eventually very pleased with Formator's lessons. In fact, she repeats with increasing frequency that she has "the greatest Inclination in the world to please" Formator because she "believe[s] him sincerely [her] Friend" (RC 271). Her response as a reader—which I will detail more fully later—validates his gentlemanliness as polite and useful, just as Mr. Spectator's female readers confirm his gentlemanly status. Finally, Formator links Amoranda's coquetry with problematic masculinities: her flirtation "has encouraged such a heap of Vermin about [her], as Providence would not suffer to live, were it not to give us a better taste for the brave, the just, the honorable and the honest Man" (RC 272). Formator reiterates the *Spectator*'s castigation of rakes and the veneration of gentleman.

However, this moral guidance is a mask for sexual and economic jealousy. Davys plays with her readers, deliberately revealing cracks in Formator's façade. It isn't just Amoranda's pleasure being reconfigured here; it is Formator/Alanthus's desire being justified through Amoranda's reform. When Amoranda tells Formator about Froth and Callid's plans to abduct her, "Formator's Cheeks glowed with Anger, and, in the highest Transport of Rage, cried out, How can such a Woman, such a lovely Woman as you are, subject yourself to such Company" (RC 268). Formator justifies this exuberance as the product of his duty to her uncle and his protection of her virtue. When he asks to disguise himself as her to thwart Froth and Callid's schemes, he declares, "Fear not, Madam ... this Arm can still do wonders in so good a Cause; a Vindication of *Amoranda*'s Honor fills my Veins with young Blood," which serves as a prejustification for how soundly he beats Froth and Callid despite his supposed agedness (RC 269). He claims that his cheeks became flushed and his arms became strong all for the sake of benevolent virtue, but Davys hints and then reveals that these are the effects of Alanthus's passion for Amoranda. There are hints of a lover's language throughout: "Every moment was lost to *Formator* that was not spent with *Amoranda*" (RC 275). As the intuitive spinster, Maria, points out close to the final reveal: "Formator's Intellects seem to be perfectly sound; and for his Outside, there is nothing old belonging to it but his Beard, and that, I confess, is a very queer one, as ever I saw in my life" (RC 313). By dropping hints, Davys is, I believe, testing the dexterity of her own readership, but also carefully indicating that the benevolence of the gentleman author is not as disinterested as it pretends.

As with *The Spectator*, there is an economic interest at work too. Amoranda is an heiress, and while Formator/Alanthus is wealthy and titled, there is a financial link between the power Alanthus gains by performing Formator and teaching Amoranda to desire his masculinity, which echoes the coded but very real mercantile desires of the periodical authors. The benevolence of the gentleman is revealed to be a layered, secret vehicle of self-interest.

Disguise and the Authentic Performance of the Gentleman

By reading Formator as an eidolon figure, we can unpack the complex and seemingly contradictory role of disguise within the novel. Davys makes a distinction between the performance of the gentleman and the performances of rakes, but she marks them *both* as performances. All of Amoranda's suitors attempt some sort of deception or performance, most especially Formator/Alanthus, who not only masquerades as the benevolent Formator but also, as Formator, masquerades as Amoranda in the scene with Callid and Froth. Yet, other characters are condemned for their use of disguise. For example, Beranthus disguises himself as a woman to gain access to Amoranda with the aid of Arentia. Amoranda confronts Arentia and Berintha/Beranthus and exclaims: "If... *Berintha* be a Man of Fortune and Honour, as you say he is, why has he used clandestine means to get into my Company? Do you think, Sir, *said she, turning to him,* I am so fond of my own Sex, that I can like nothing but what appears in Petticoats? Had you come like a Gentleman, as such I would have received you; but a disguised Lover is always conscious of some Demerit, and dares not trust to his right Form, till by a false appearance he tries the Lady" (RC 269). It is not the cross-dressing that is actually the issue within the broader novel. After all, Formator dresses as Amoranda in the scene with Froth and Callid.

Clearly it is not just the act or nature of the disguise that creates dishonesty or condemnation. In fact, Alanthus's justification for Formator sounds fundamentally the same as Beranthus's for Berintha: "I came to you, disguised like an old Man, for two reasons: First, I thought the sage Advice you stood in need of would sound more natural and be better received from an old mouth than a young one; next, I thought you would be more open and free, in declaring your real Sentiments of everything to me" (RC 316). Formator/Alanthus and Beranthus both disguise themselves as women for ostensibly the same purpose, to win Amoranda, but with different results: Formator/Alanthus wins Amoranda, and Beranthus is run through and killed by Alanthus. Amoranda's above speech seems to indicate that deception is the choice of cowards who are afraid to come as they are, and yet Formator is never censured for his disguise. Critics have extended Amoranda's judgment of Beranthus to include an indictment of Formator/Alanthus; however, I think such arguments miss the more nuanced nature of masculinity and performance in the novel. So what is the vital difference?

Undergirding the gentleman's performance is a current of desire, both the gentleman's and Amoranda's. It isn't that Formator/Alanthus's performance is more authentic, it is that his performance is more effective at creating readerly desire. If the gentleman's secret pleasure is in pleasing, then what validates his performance—what allows his pleasure to be secret—is the pleasing of others. What is actually revealed is that Formator is like the eidolon, who, for all of the differences between his character and his author, creates the association between his character and his authors in the minds of the readers through entertaining them. Alanthus's performance as Formator reflects gentlemanly value on him—rather than deception—because it creates desire in Amoranda. In contrast to the rake, the gentleman needs his lady to approve of him, and her desire must validate his virtues and translate erotic desire into a desire for guidance. Once he has introduced himself as Alanthus, the gentleman's continued disguise as Formator allows him a voyeuristic spectatorship of Amoranda's desires. Telling her guardian about the Beranthus event, "When she came to the part, where [Alanthus] was concerned, she blushed and sighed, saying, Oh *Formator*, had you seen the fine Man, how graceful, how charming, how handsome" (RC 302). When she receives a letter from Alanthus, we are told, "While *Amoranda* read this Letter, *Formator* watched her Eyes, in which he saw a pleasing Surprize [sic]" (RC 304). Later he has the pleasure of hearing her repeat his own lessons back to him, like Mr. Spectator's female readers, expressing gratitude: "I remember, *Formator, said she*, you told me some time ago, that a Woman's conduct vindicated by one single Man of sense was infinitely preferable to a thousand Elogiums, from as many Coxcombs ... [I] shall for the future, not only despise Flattery but abhor the mouth it comes from" (*RC* 302–303). All of this gratifies Alanthus's desire for Amoranda while coding it as Formator's neutral benevolence for her reform.

When an accidental house fire reveals his identity, he finally voices his own burning desires. He declares, "My adorable *Amoranda*, if I value myself for any Action of my Life, it is for carrying on so clean a Cheat so long a time" (*RC* 317). He asks her pardon for the "trial of your Love," for: "It was not possible for me to deny myself the exquisite pleasure I knew your kind Concern would give me" (*RC* 317). He prides himself on his masterful (and very gentlemanly) restraint: "I hope ... you remember, what a long time of Self-denial I have had, and that during *Formator's* Reign, I never dared so much as touch your Hand, though my Heart had ten thousand flutters and struggles to get to you" (*RC* 320). He has acted the gentleman, regulating her sexuality and using this control to demonstrate his own gentlemanly restraint. However, in revealing his restraint, Davys also reveals the deeply desiring and personal nature of the gentleman's character, which stands in stark contrast to claims of disinterest. It also reveals how the performance as Formator transfers gentlemanly behavior onto the author behind it. Alanthus uses his behavior while playing Formator—his lack of physical seduction or contact—to confer gentlemanliness upon himself after all is revealed. It is his successful performance of neutrality that makes him a gentleman, not actual neutrality.

The complex interplay of Formator/Alanthus's disguise and masculinity is one of the key ways Davys's novel reads back onto *The Spectator*: the gentleman's embodiedness. Through her construction of Formator/Alanthus, Davys provides us with a metaphor and language for understanding how the eidolon-author dynamic is not a denial of the gentleman's body but a disguise, which links the gentleman's physical body to text in new ways. As I have established, the gentleman's body is simultaneously private and textual. What creates the tension surrounding the gentleman's body is not whether he has one but whether it is desiring or not. The gentlemanly performance—the eidolon or Formator—requires a denial of selfish desire, specifically sexual or romantic desire (but also economic desire). The text of his body creates a desire in the reader (Amoranda), but it is supposedly nondesiring itself. However, there is another layer to the gentleman's desire: that of the actual author, or in this case Alanthus, which is personally, even selfishly, desiring. This is what Davys so powerfully illustrates by translating the eidolon-author into her central male character, and by translating the rhetorical situation of a periodical structure into the plot of her courtship novel.

Reforming the Coquette into a Proper Female Reader

When we read Formator/Alanthus through the lens of the performative author/gentleman we can illuminate the troubling aspect of Amoranda's reform as a necessary, if repressive, part of the formation of the gentleman's masculinity. As noted earlier, the coquette is a threatening figure for the gentleman because she wrests narrative control from him. Instead of conquering all those around him through his overtly sexualized body and language, like the rake, the gentleman is defined through an author-reader relationship with women. As the benevolent author, he takes shape through women's open and willing reception of his text/body. However, Davys's plot reveals that this seemingly mutual relationship is coercive. It lacks the direct seduction or forceful ravishment of a rake, and instead becomes about reforming—literally reshaping—women into receptive readers and removing them from positions of narrative authority.

Amoranda's reform is about transforming the feminine authorial and narrative power of the coquette into a proper female reader. Amoranda begins her tale "pleased with a Crowd of Admirers," that is, her own audience (*RC* 261). However, as the novel progresses she yields to Formator's authorial guidance. In the first two-thirds of the novel, whenever one of her suitors plots against her, Amoranda exerts narrative control over the telling of these adventures and over the suitors. When Froth and Callid plan to abduct her, she comes up with her own plot to thwart them: two of her footmen will dress up as her and her maid and cudgel the would-be abductors. She tells her plan to Formator, proclaiming, "What do you think, *Formator, said she*, will not my Contrivance do better than theirs?" (*RC* 269). She is a better schemer than the men she encounters. The connection between scheming and plotting and the narrative plot is deliberate in this novel. Amoranda crafts her own narrative, which defeats the masculine narratives of abduction. As an author figure, even when Froth and Callid are caught, she exerts her control to deny them narrative satisfaction. Callid starts, "But it is some Satisfaction to tell you how I would have used you had Fortune been so kind as to have put you in my power; know then, proud Beauty, I would—I know already (*said* Amoranda, *interrupting him*) as much of your designs, as you can tell me" (*RC* 274). She cuts off his speech, denying him any kind of sexual or linguistic satisfaction. When something of note happens, Amoranda usually recounts it. When Lofty is tricked into marriage (an Amoranda plot) and apologizes to Altemira, Amoranda steps in and accepts on Altemira's behalf: "My Lord...I dare answer for *Altemira's* pardon" (*RC* 289). Amoranda is a compelling author.

As Amoranda acquiesces to Formator's authority, she speaks and narrates less and less. Critics like Natasha Sajé see Amoranda's reform as a silencing, and in connection with *The Spectator* this train of thought seems accurate. As Powell has argued, many periodicals make women visible but not vocal or sensing.[37] Women are displayed, but not allowed the same subjectivity (sensate selves) as their male counterparts. After Alanthus reveals his true identity, his sister arrives to discover what has happened to him. At every juncture before this Amoranda has done the recounting, but here she yields the stage: "Lord *Alanthus* and Mr. *Traffick* are the fittest to give your Ladyship an account, which I leave them to do, while I beg leave to go and dress me" (*RC* 319). Amoranda, now fully invested in Formator/Alanthus's role as author of her behavior, leaves to dress, while the gentlemen tell the tale. Davys's reform of Amoranda displays this all the more vividly, because the heroine moves from vivacious coquette to virtuous wife-to-be, whose thoughts and will are realigned with patriarchal interests.

Amoranda's reform (or FORMATOR-ation) is marked by her evolution as a reader, which emphasizes and actualizes Formator/Alanthus's status as an author figure. Ten letters are exchanged throughout the novel, and eight of them are addressed to Amoranda. Most are authored by Alanthus and mimic the form of many of the Spectator's essays. One of the first letters she receives is an anonymous one from Alanthus: "*THIS Letter, Madam, does not come to tell you I love you, since that would only increase the surfeit you must have taken with so many Declarations of that kind already; but if I tell you I am in pain for your Conduct, and spend some Hours in pitying your present Condition, it will, I dare say, be entirely new to you; since (though many have the same opinion of your Behavior) none have Courage, or Honesty enough to tell you so*" (*RC* 265). Alanthus positions himself as solely interested in the good of Amoranda's character, and he declares that his criticism of her is courageous (i.e., masculine). It also echoes the supposed neutrality of Mr. Spectator, claiming that this is not about his love (i.e., his sexual desire for her) but his investment in her own self-interest. In terms of authorship, this letter throws a kind of gauntlet. Alanthus states that he will not be one of her admirers, that he will not tell her he loves her, and will instead critique her behavior from his position of masculine authority. When her maid, Jenny, suggests the author seems to mean well, Amoranda declares: "Mean well ... what good meaning can he have who persuades me to banish the Bees and live in the Hive by myself?" (*RC* 266). However, by the time Alanthus rescues her from Beranthus, Amoranda sees this letter in a very different light: "No, *Jenny, said she,* that Letter ... I now see with other Eyes and have reason to believe it came from a Friend" (*RC* 305).

She is now a proper reader, open to her gentleman's moral guidance, which is clearly linked to her newfound attraction to his physical body.

Once again the gentleman's body and his text are intertwined in their ability and mission to create receptive female desire. Amoranda compares the letter she receives from Alanthus after her rescue to the original; she recognizes the writing. She even uses the original letter to flirt with Alanthus; she teases him about the letter, "in which you tell me you don't love me" (*RC* 308). He then gives a justification that could be lifted from *The Spectator*: "I did not think Madam, you would have thought this Letter worth keeping so long, but you have put a very wrong Construction upon it; and I designed it as a very great Mark of my Esteem: I sent it to put you in mind of turning the right end of the Perspective to yourself, that you might with more ease behold your own danger" (*RC* 308–309). He begins from a point of modesty, and then explains why her reading is mistaken, further emphasizing her need for his guidance. Feminine behavior is linked to reading, and Alanthus reveals his eidolonic performance and corrects Amoranda's misreading, both of which he uses to establish his own gentlemanly virtue. Thus, Davys reveals the gentleman as a figure whose social role as morality monitor is tied to narrative production and control.

However, Davys subtly shifts this dynamic to reveal how reliant the gentleman's form is on narrative structure. She makes it clear that this narrative of silencing is not—as it is presented—about Amoranda's femininity or womanhood. At stake instead is the structure and style of the gentleman. Davys makes it clear that the regulation of female readers is inextricably linked with the construction of masculinity. By regulating her behavior and her reading, Formator/Alanthus influences Amoranda's access to and desire for her other (less savory) male suitors. Just as Mr. Spectator advocates that women read his body/text and avoid bad or more frivolous reading, so too does Formator limit Amoranda's access to other male texts and authors. Most notably he denies access to Lord Lofty, the rake figure. A witty and successful seducer, Lofty's rank and devious behavior links seduction and literacy—he uses a contract to seduce Altemira, and he reads Amoranda's mail without her permission—in ways that present him as a competing kind of male linguistic power and by extension a kind of authorship. This masculine contrast is a clear means of cultivating the metaphorical connection between Amoranda's readership and her taste in men, which is one of Formator's clearest goals: "*Formator* had by a daily application endeavored to form *Amoranda's* mind to his own liking; he tried to bring her a true taste of that Behavior which makes every Woman agreeable to every Man of Sense" (*RC* 291). By controlling and linking her reading and her access to men, he reforms her taste, which in fact forms her to his own ideal of womanhood. However, Alanthus's control through his persona Formator is not in fact a departure from the rake but a more covert version of his manipulations. Whereas Lofty attempts to manipulate Altemira and later Amoranda through covertly reading letters and stealing documents, Formator/Alanthus legitimizes a position of benevolent mentorship, which allows him to read and regulate Amoranda's letters and to watch her read and react to his own letters.

By designing Alanthus as Amoranda's love interest, Davys dramatizes the ways the gentleman author designs his texts to cultivate a yielding desire for himself. In his first anonymous letter criticizing her coquetry, he writes: *"Consider, Madam, how unhappy that Woman is, who finds herself daily hedged in with self-ended Flatterers, who make it their business to keep up a Vanity in you, which may one day prove your Ruin. Is it possible for any Fop to tell you more than you know already?"* (RC 265). This message is designed to deflate her coquetry, but also create a space for the Man of Sense. For, while a fop cannot tell her something she does not already know, the gentleman certainly can. Alanthus's goal, the reason he deploys the disguise of Formator, is to cultivate Amoranda's desire. He cannot abduct her as Froth, Callid, Beranthus, and, to a lesser extent, Lofty attempt to because the gentleman author, as a gendered identity, requires the yielding of his reader. His masculinity necessitates Amoranda declaring, "I own, *Formator*, the groundwork of this Reformation in me, came from those wholesome Lectures you have so often read to me; but the *finishing stroke is given by my own inclination*" (RC 303, emphasis mine). She must learn to be attracted to the Man of Sense. That is, theoretically, how the market of the gentleman author works.

On a structural level, Davys demonstrates how the gentleman can only manifest when he has cultivated female desire. *The Spectator* required the desire of its readers to continue to be; it would only be printed if there was a market for it, and, therefore, Mr. Spectator's textual body would only continue to be if readers desired it. In a similar way, Davys makes Alanthus contingent upon Amoranda's desire. He first appears as a literal text (his letter) and then as a figurative one (his eidolon Formator); however, he as an actual character and man is only revealed once Amoranda is well on her way to reform. He first "physically" appears during her harrowing encounter with Beranthus, and his continued presence—his visits and even the final reveal and marriage—depends on Amoranda's newfound attraction to the Man of Sense. Davys creates a plot that reveals the dependence of the gentleman on the complementary desire of female readers. His masculinity only truly comes into existence when Amoranda wants him.

Davys's plot is conservative: the gentleman author successfully reforms the vivacious coquette into a woman reader who allows his masculinity to take shape in a virtuous and desirable light. The plot of the gentleman, the construction of this masculinity, is inherently conservative. Davys does add a darker dimension that reveals how the construction of a desiring female readership comes at a stark price to women. Alanthus creates strategies of delayed gratification for Amoranda: he sends her letters but does not reveal his identity; he comes upon her being attacked by Beranthus and refuses to rescue her, only to return minutes later to save her at the moment of crisis; he visits her home but won't provide his full history, etc. Each of these encounters, like Mr. Spectator's reluctance to reveal his body or provide a library for his female readers, builds a kind of narrative anticipation, which becomes a trademark of the gentleman's character throughout the century.

In Davys's novel, this delayed structure takes on decidedly violent and manipulative proportions. The starkest example is when Alanthus comes upon Amoranda as she is about to be raped by Beranthus (who is still disguised as a woman): "Stranger, *said she*, for such you are to me, though not to Humanity, I hope; take a poor forsaken Wretch into your kind Protection and deliver her from the rude hands of a cruel Ravisher" (*RC* 299). His reply is cold and judgmental: "I presume, Madam, you are some self-willed, head-strong Lady, who, resolved to follow your own Inventions, have left the Care of a tender Father to ramble with you know not who." This is cruelly self-referential because the father figure he refers to is in fact himself. He then rides off, declaring, "Well Madam . . . I am sorry for you, but I am no Knight-Errant" (*RC* 299). He only returns and saves her from a gang rape after she cries out for Formator. After his true identity is revealed, Alanthus provides a particularly horrifying explanation for his behavior: "I put on an Air of Cruelty . . . and rode from you; I knew it would give you double terror, to see a prospect of relief, then find yourself abandoned; and I likewise knew, the greater your fear was then, the greater your care would be for the future. . . . I had yet a view in favour of myself, and had reason to believe the greater your deliverance was the greater value would you set upon your deliverer" (*RC* 317). His masculinity is linked to performance: he pretends cruelty he does not feel—justifying his performance as a necessary and virtuous act in *his* case. He deliberately instills fear in her to teach her a lesson about her own vulnerability, reinforcing the gentleman author's message that women are in desperate need of him. He also extends his reasoning to describe how making her wait for her rescue would exponentially increase her gratitude and desire for him.

Alanthus's control of the plot and the sequence of the narrative links this moment to authorship. He resents her attempts to "follow [her] own intentions" (*RC* 303). This manipulation is a dramatization of the gentleman author's cultivation of his appeal. Mr. Spectator withholds himself and, when it comes to creating a ladies library list, he withholds his assistance from his female readers, cultivating an increased sense of the need for his text, authorship, and guidance. Alanthus capitalizes on Amoranda's trauma to create a greater reward for himself through her increased desire for him and a greater need for his masculinity. She cries out for Formator and is rescued by Alanthus, demonstrating her desire for eidolon, author, and text all at once. But the sheer violence of this scene punctuates the coercive aspects of the gentleman's seemingly benign masculinity. It does not deploy the same kind of violence as a rakish ravisher, but thrives on a violent, passive aggression.

Davys's Co-opting the Gentleman's Authorship

Davys is certainly savvy in her dramatization of the gentleman's character, because she increases his dependence on her authorial terms. The greatest potential feminist power of *The Reform'd Coquet* is Davys's self-construction as an author. Critics have struggled so much with this text because feminocentric readings often seek to align the heroine with her author. However, Davys does not align her authorial persona with her heroine but with her hero and the larger plot structure. Critics have looked to Amoranda for signs of coercion or rebellion, but Amoranda's transformation is not presented as a negative outcome by the text. On this level, Davys spites our desires for such direct subversion. Instead, Davys uses the structure of this courtship/reform plot to chart a field for herself as an author, and the character who endows her with this authority is not Amoranda but Formator/Alanthus. Amoranda's ultimate submission to Alanthus/Formator is not just necessary for patriarchy but for Davys's authority. This is ultimately a powerful but complex and uneasy bargain that the woman writers examined throughout this book will make and negotiate again and again. The gentleman author's authority depended on his performance of moral instruction and cajoling pleasure. People voluntarily yielded to him, and Davys makes explicit the machinations of this yielding by dramatizing it through the lens of a courtship plot. However, she does not discard the yielding; rather, she utilizes the larger apparatus of her narrative structure in order to demonstrate that a woman author can pull these moral strings just as well as a male one. In her prefatory material she performs the same authorial disinterest and independence with a feminine twist. Davys takes advantage of the constructed and performative features of the gentleman. If the eidolon can be different from his author, but still lend the author his moral authority, then a woman author can adopt it as well as a man and validate her own ambitions. Yet, what is also made visible is that to access this authority, Davys is willing to play the gentleman's game, adopting and even endorsing his attractions while also dramatizing their manipulations.

If Alanthus's power comes from his ability to perform as Formator in order to direct Amoranda's reading, then it is important to note that there is another narrative voice who reveals itself to direct the readers of the novel: Davys herself. Davys continuously reminds her reader of her presence as the author through her narrator. Her intrusive, witty narrator is one of the features people connect to later male novelists like Henry Fielding. Her narrator interjects: "What an unhappy Creature is a beautiful young Girl left to her own Management, who is so fond of Adoration that Reason and Prudence are thrust out to make way for it; 'till she becomes a prey to every designing Rascal, and her own ridiculous Qualities are her greatest Enemies: Thus it might have fared with poor *Amoranda*, had not a lucky hit prevented it, which the Reader shall know by and by" (*RC* 264). This voice intrudes throughout the novel, reminding us that there is yet another author beyond the plots of Amoranda and Formator/Alanthus. Initially the narrator seems to empower Formator/Alanthus's role as author in the text—and to a certain extent, Davys does empower the gentleman's position within the text: his plot prevails. However, the narrator's intrusion also reminds the reader that Formator/Alanthus is Davys's construction. His plot is actually her plot, which she orders, despite not being a man herself, because the gentleman's power comes from his performance, not an actual private self. What is uneasy about this is that Amoranda's—the coquette's—authorial power is subjugated to reveal the contours of the gentleman's performance. The figure of the woman writer is not entrapped with her heroine, but instead intrudes to remind the reader that perhaps there is another power play in the works, that of the lived woman writer validating her craft. There is something terrible about Davys's bargain here; she opts to position herself within a structure that depends on subjugating women. Yet, her methods reveal the machinations of these power structures.

In her dedication and preface to *The Reform'd Coquet*, Davys commands the interdependence of masculinity and female readership in ways that mimic and then co-opt the prerogative of the gentleman author. As noted above, Davys published most of her novels by subscription, and therefore her prefaces are often dedications to "The Ladies of Great Britain" or "To the Beaus of Great Britain" rather than to a patron. In this way her actual authorial production is similar to periodical authors, like Addison and Steele. Mimicking the gentleman, the structure of Davys's dedication emphasizes how critiques of women's vanity paradoxically seem to lead to structures of masculinity. Davys begins her dedication "To the Ladies of Great Britain" by charting out a terrain of female readership, commenting on female vanity and pleasure: "At a time when the Town is so full of Masquerades, Operas, New Plays, Conjurors, Monsters, and feigned Devils; how can I, Ladies, expect you to throw away an hour upon the less agreeable Amusements my *Coquet* can give you?" (*RC* 252). Women's pleasures in theater and masquerades were often interwoven with criticism of female vanity. Davys also strikes a tone of polite didacticism: "If I have here touched a young Lady's Vanity and Levity, it was to show her how amiable she is without those Blots, which certainly stain the Mind, and stamp Deformity where the greatest Beauties would shine, were they banished" (*RC* 253). Davys is not describing Amoranda's faults in order to ridicule her but to instruct and to delight. She, like Addison and Steele, presents a portrait of female vanity to improve women everywhere.

However, like her spectatorial predecessor, Davys cannot present a lesson to the ladies without including its connections to masculinity. After focusing primarily on female and authorial vanities, Davys suddenly turns to the importance of distinguishing Men of Sense from flatterers: "One little word of Advice, Ladies, and I have done: When you grow weary of Flattery and begin to listen to matrimonial Addresses, choose a *Man with fine Sense*, as well as a fine Wig, and let him have some merit as well as much Embroidery: This will make Coxcombs give ground, and *Men of Sense* will equally admire your Conduct with your Beauty" (*RC* 253, emphasis mine). Davys's major criticism of female vanity was that it gets in the way of recognizing and appreciating Men of Sense. She also links the role of female readership with the gentleman. Remember, she offers her novel as a means to educate "the Ladies of Great Britain." Her book will help cure them of their vanity so they may recognize and then enjoy the better appreciation of Men of Sense instead of the vapid quantity of praise from coxcombs. What is especially exciting about this is that Davys was claiming for herself the same role as the gentleman; Addison and Steele have Mr. Spectator, and she has Alanthus/Formator. This changes the valence of Formator/Alanthus. It doesn't make him progressive or any less conservative, but it brings overt attention to the constructed nature of this figure and the masculinity he represents. That construction is made both dreadful and powerful. However, it also creates a space where a woman can manipulate the gentleman for her own ends. It also notably departs from masculine constructions of this dynamic in a key way: men should still be attractive to women. He should have "fine sense" *and* "a fine Wig," not instead of a fine wig. It is a subtle but important note that I argue women writers bring again and again to the construction of the gentleman that really makes him sing as a long, lasting vision of masculinity: he must be desirable. He always wanted to be, but it is women writers who make him so.

Davys co-opts the gentleman's prerogative to influence a cross-gendered readership; Davys claims the approval of male readers, just as *The Spectator* claimed the interest of its female readers. Davys was as concerned with addressing and categorizing her relationship to male readers as she was with female ones. Immediately following her dedication to the ladies, Davys's preface charts her relationship to male readers as a way to validate her authorship. However, Davys is careful to portray her relationship as creatively independent. She starts with the "worthy Gentlemen of Cambridge" whose "civil, generous, good-natured Behavior towards me, is the only thing I have now left worth boasting of" (*RC* 253, 254). She claims gentlemanly approval for her work: "When I had written a Sheet or two of this Novel, I communicated my Design to a couple of young Gentlemen, whom I knew to be Men of Taste, and both my Friends; they approved of what I had done, advised me to proceed, then print it by Subscription: into which Proposal many of the Gentlemen entered" (*RC* 254).

Davys herself performs the delicate dance of independence and modesty, which so many female authors learned to perform. She writes, "As this Book was written at Cambridge, I am a little apprehensive some may imagine the Gentlemen had a hand in it." Claiming a concern that such learned gentlemen will be thought guilty of writing her little novel she continues, "I do . . . assure the World, I am not acquainted with one member of that worthy and learned Society of Men, whose Pens are not employed in things infinitely above anything I can pretend to be the Author of: So that I only am accountable for every Fault of my Book; and if it has any Beauties, I claim the Merit for them too" (*RC* 254). Here, Davys claims an approving male readership but asserts her authorial independence. She flips and claims a key aspect of Mr. Spectator's authorial validation; just as he establishes his gentility through constructing fruitful relationships with his female readers, Davys creates a validating relationship between her and her male readers. She carefully balances indicating their interest and approval and marking authorship as distinctly and separately hers.

Davys plays a deliberately gendered game with her dedication and preface, which mimics the fluidity of Mr. Spectator's speech. Like the gentleman author, Davys adapts her own identity to move seamlessly within different circles. In her dedication to the ladies, Davys includes her own authorial brand of female vanity—"She who has assurance to write has certainly the vanity of expecting to be read" (*RC* 252–253)—but she justifies her authorial vanity as a motherly instinct: "All Authors see a Beauty in their own Compositions . . . as Mothers think their own Offspring amiable, how deficient soever Nature has been to them" (*RC* 252). On one level, Davys is clearly "capitalizing on [her] femaleness."[38] However, this combination of pseudo-self-deprecation and justification also strikes a similar tone to Mr. Spectator's revision of his quiet taciturnity to observational tool of authorship. Meanwhile, in her dedication, Davys constructs her authorship according to the rules of the gentleman. While she gestures to financial need, stating, "though I must own my Purse is (by a thousand Misfortunes) grown wholly useless to everybody, my Pen is at the service of the Public" (*RC* 253), that is not what has motivated her pen. Rather, Davys writes, "Idleness has so long been an Excuse for Writing, that I am almost ashamed to tell the World it was that, and that only, which produced the following Sheets." She even claims that her primary concern is for the "young unthinking Minds of some of my own Sex" (*RC* 253). Critics have read this gesture as indicating an actual and exclusive focus on female readers. Instead, Davys is mimicking the prerogative of the gentleman author. Davys claims the gentlemanly prerogatives of servicing the public, especially young women, and benevolent idleness for her novel. She utilizes the various aspects of male and female authorship that most serve her purposes. The sheer utility and dexterity of this gesture, perhaps as much as anything else, echoes the prerogative of the gentleman author who adapts and transforms to suit his purpose all the while claiming a kind of central authenticity.

Conclusion

Despite his normative and conservative power, the gentleman is by his nature a responsive performance of masculinity because he emerges as a figure of authorship and fiction. In *The Reform'd Coquet*, Davys reveals the desiring nature of the gentleman figure and how the coding of female readership is a gendered plot. She does not create his desire; she reveals it. The gentleman by definition requires a willing female audience. By making the gentleman author's desires visible and tying them to a courtship plot, Davys helps create a space where his desires are at the mercy of the woman writer. Female readers (as representatives for readers in general) must submit voluntarily to the gentleman's guidance. However, this dynamic transforms the gentleman into a contingent figure. For all of his supposed independence, he depends on pleasing women, and is shaped by and, later, for their pleasure. Despite his claims to disinterested disembodiment, the gentleman author repeatedly relies on metaphors of courtship and marriage to seduce his readers. This is what Davys capitalizes on; she takes the metaphor and makes it a plot, and in doing so, she tethers the gentleman to a new and emerging feature of his character: attractiveness to women. This feature above all else becomes the foothold of women writers into the construction of masculinity. If the ideal man must be a gentleman and he must be virtuously heterosexual, then for his masculinity to function women must want him. This wanting is both literal and literary. Male authors repeatedly seek to present themselves as attractive and desirable texts, and women writers again and again utilize this need to make the gentleman their creature.

However, in order to navigate this interplay, it was first necessary to reveal the ways the gentleman's masculinity was and continues to be performative, and that there are stakes to his construction for women. What emerges over the next several chapters is that these stakes are complex and mixed for women. On the one hand, women authors come to exert an increasingly confident and dexterous influence over masculinity. On the other, they create a masculine ideal that negotiates rather than undoes patriarchal systems for women's benefit. Most dangerously and importantly, they do it by making him attractive to women, thus entangling narratives of courtship, gender, and desire in a long-lasting system that from one angle benefits women as professional authors but through another endorses a masculinity that functions through its conservative position and power.

However, this complexity is precisely why revitalizing and rethinking our approach to authors like Davys and women authors more broadly is vital and necessary. Davys has sat on the sidelines not because her work was not influential or relevant but because we as a scholarly body did not know what to do with her. She did not fit within our more comfortable critical approaches or frameworks because her work is neither radically subversive nor moralistically stodgy. By situating her with the almost too easily canonical *The Spectator*, we can reimagine aspects of our critical discourse around women writers, genre, and masculinity. In *The Spectator* we can now see the ways masculinity was neither disembodied or natural but a complex performance based on genre, narrative, neutrality, and desire. Meanwhile, in Davys's work we see the complex dialogue between narrative impact and authorial control, between the protofeminist and the conservative, and finally between revealing gender performance and constructing that performance as desirable.

2

The Gentleman of Letters as Passionate Reader

Eliza Haywood's Love in Excess *and David Hume's Philosophy of Moral Sympathy*

In general we may remark, that the minds of men are mirrors to one another, not only because they reflect each others emotions, but also because those rays of passions, sentiment and opinions may be often reverberated.
—David Hume, *A Treatise of Human Nature*

Now will I appeal to any impartial Reader, even among the Men.
—Eliza Haywood, *The Female Spectator*

David Hume's comment on the "minds of men" operates on two levels. First, there is the universal construct of the minds of men, which implies both men and women but assumes men to be the de facto face of humanity. However, there is a second but no less culturally relevant or obvious assumption, both within and without the eighteenth century, that the construction of the minds of men is the reflection and province of other male minds, for they are the purest surfaces to reflect sentiment and opinions. As a result, critics have long considered the Enlightenment mind of male thinkers to be an ideal of eighteenth-century masculinity: seemingly rational, natural, and disembodied. These traits, as I have previously demonstrated, are the key features of the gentleman: an enlightened man whose mind appears to both create and then reflect itself through writing, culture, and gender. The wide-ranging reflective influence of the Enlightenment mind thus seems to create, naturalize, and reproduce itself in a sphere of masculine hegemony.

This chapter rethinks this perception by proposing a mirroring of minds not among men but between David Hume and Eliza Haywood. Critical discussions that have attempted to bring women writers into conversation with male Enlightenment thinkers typically position women as oppositional and responsive to their seemingly more dominant male counterparts.[1] I want to shift the focus of such criticism by considering the ways in which Haywood not only responded to but also shaped the discourse of masculinity and the gentleman reader through her male characters.[2] I argue that the "Fair Arbitress of Passion's" rays enlighten Hume's mind, specifically the contours of his masculinity, his status as gentleman, and the characteristics of that persona that require him to perform. As Haywood's epigraph indicates, the "impartial" character of the gentleman—his benevolent patriarchal light—is not as ingrained as he would have us believe. Instead, Hume's regulation of women's reading and, by extension, the gentleman's reading stems from anxiety about being desirable.

As a fictional construct, Hume's persona relies on the narrative structures of Haywood's fiction and, in turn, manifests the paradoxical anxieties of authority and responsive desire that define the gentleman reader. Reading reformed masculinity; it instilled proper sympathy into men and transformed them into gentlemen. The relationship between a gentleman's reading and his moral reform is both what Haywood dramatizes in *Love in Excess* and what Hume attempts to perform in his essays. For Haywood, reading is an antidote for rakishness, particularly in ways that participate in the cultural reform of male manners. Meanwhile, Hume uses the structures of this reform to rewrite the formerly stodgy, isolated man of letters as a social, attractive gentleman and, more specifically, to rewrite himself as a gentleman who inspires desire in his readers, especially women. Hume's metaphor of reflection is an especially apt starting point for this chapter because Haywood and, later, Hume use sympathy, passion, and imitation to define and revise the gentleman's authority as a moral reader. In this way, the gentleman, by reflecting the light of his text and his reading, creates a beam that others are meant to mirror. My chapter proposes that Hume imitates Haywood, for although he, as the man of letters, explicitly separates his gentlemanly reading from the reading of novels and decries the seductive effects on vulnerable female readers, he also attempts to co-opt their mechanisms of appeal and formal seductions for his own writings.

To be clear, in this chapter I do not argue for a direct line of influence from Haywood to Hume, nor do I claim that Hume read Haywood—though her popularity and longevity suggest that he may well have—and then directly transcribed her version of the gentleman onto his own literary performance. Instead, I argue that the modifications that Haywood brought to her gentleman character, D'elmont, reveal key aspects of the gentleman that became infused in Hume's own literary persona. At first glance, Hume's version of the gentleman seems obvious: the male author uses his gender and its accompanying characteristics to justify the regulation of women through literary and sexual channels. However, by positioning Haywood as a forerunner of Hume, it becomes clear that gentlemanly regulation stems from a more complex literary milieu. Through her amatory style and narrative of rakish reform, Haywood created a standard for the gentleman that depended on a potent, omnipresent desirability even more pronounced than the desire created by Joseph Addison and Richard Steele or, later, by Mary Davys. For the gentleman to be a gentleman, for his reading and sympathy to function and gain influence, women must desire him. His power thus depends on women. In that context, Hume sought to perform the impossible gender standard that Haywood set for masculinity, one demanding that men be powerful and influential as well as dependent on not only women's approval but also their sexual desire.

The Cult of Masculinity: The Gentleman Reader and the Reform of Male Manners

Part of the impetus behind this chapter is the fact that the writings of Haywood and Hume respectively occupy two key points on the trajectory of the cult of sensibility and its accompanying reform of male manners. Haywood's first novel, *Love in Excess* (1719), predates the cult of sensibility, typically associated with the era spanning the 1740s to the 1770s, and therefore serves as a precursor of its reform of men from rakes into gentlemen by cultivating sympathy and reading. Meanwhile, Hume is a constant touchstone in discussions about sensibility. Emerging from the tradition of the Earl of Shaftesbury, Francis Hutchinson, and the Scottish Enlightenment, prominent male thinkers such as Hume and Adam Smith "idealized sensibility in men and implemented their social affections among themselves."[3] Sensibility fit within not only their frameworks of sympathy but also the empiricist, social structure of morality.

A second impetus for this discussion is my hope that placing Haywood and Hume in dialogue reveals that while Haywood created a philosophy of masculinity in her novels, specifically via the gentlemen in her first foray, *Love in Excess*, Hume crafted a fictional identity for himself as a gentleman in his philosophical writings. Although critics often use Hume's philosophy to provide cultural or intellectual context for eighteenth-century ideals and principles, the textual, narrative, and structural aspects of the philosophical text have typically been ignored.[4] By contrast, Catherine Gallagher explains her focus on Hume's work as a reflection of eighteenth-century critical priorities, not cultural ones: "I have chosen *A Treatise* not because it was an influential work in the eighteenth century (it was not), but literary critics are fond of quoting it to prove that eighteenth-century people believed that they naturally took on the emotional coloring of their human environment through the automatic operations of sympathy."[5] Noting that Hume's philosophy of identity relies on fictional structures, critics have also examined his writing style but stopped short of reading Hume himself—that is, his persona in his philosophy and essays—as a fictional construction and examining how his style deliberately performs the character of the gentleman. Even though critics have thus linked Hume to the novel, to my knowledge only Rebecca Tierney-Hynes has connected his philosophy to the more "feminine" forms of fiction: romance, secret history, and amatory novels.

Meanwhile, the philosophical aspects of Haywood's work, especially in her novels, have gone unexamined until only recently.[6] Of particular value to my work here, Kathryn King has suggested that Haywood sought to be remembered as a poet and registered her own legacy within the contexts of sympathy and sensibility, while Paul Kelleher, April Alliston, and Stephen Ahern have all connected *Love in Excess* specifically to discourses of sympathy and sensibility.[7] However, if Haywood is only seldom referenced in conversations on sensibility, then she is almost entirely absent from discussions about its relationship to masculinity.[8] My chapter positions Haywood as an author who not only depicted moral sympathy but also deployed it to cultivate the gentleman, and thus anticipated Hume's persona and philosophy of the passions. The true complexity of exploring the relationship between their works is that neither author—indeed, no author—is entirely originary or reactionary. However, by placing both authors in dialogue, I hope to shift the valences that we usually ascribe to them.

Although the cult of sensibility is typically identified with the 1740s–1770s, in the early decades of the eighteenth century there was a progressive move away from the excesses of the Restoration and an ever-increasing embrace of ideals of sympathy, later epitomized by the sentimental novel and the philosophical works of Hume and Smith. This cultural evolution, as critics such as G. J. Barker-Benfield, Harriet Guest, John Mullan, and Betty Schellenberg have argued, was linked to shifting models of masculinity.[9] Barker-Benfield has labeled the shift as the "reform of male manners," in which an ever-increasing emphasis on sympathy and proper moral feeling was used to shift cultural ideals of masculinity.[10] The supposed ills of the Restoration were represented in the masculinity of the rake. Rakes were predatory, aristocratic consumers who indulged in luxury, violence, godlessness, and the debasement of women and who fundamentally lacked sympathy. To counter this version of masculinity, women, authors of both genders, and religious groups began advocating for a "new male ideal."[11] This new man is what we now identify as the gentleman, whose status and class were defined by his domesticity, his moral code of conduct, his taste and good manners, and his fine feelings—that is, his ability to monitor, understand, and care for those around him by interpreting and sympathizing with their feelings.[12]

Haywood anticipated several crucial touchstones of the reform of male manners. The cult of sensibility emphasized the reform of male manners because sympathy is empirical and experiential. Unlike other rationalistic moral philosophies, sympathy was regarded as an ability cultivated a posteriori. The cult of sensibility embraced the idea that with the right kind of cultivation and sociality, manners could be softened and morality could be instilled, which fit rather symbiotically with emerging ideas of the gentleman, according to which, being a gentleman was not an innate form of masculinity. Unlike the aristocrat, birth was only one feature of the gentleman, whose worth was defined by his experiences (i.e., education, cultivation, and travel) and his interactions with society (i.e., politeness, manners, and his ability to properly govern and influence others). Critics have remarked how Haywood's characters "are governed by an empiricist epistemology" and learn by way of passionate, embodied experience.[13] Haywood's narrative of the reformed rake moreover constructed a link between sympathy and masculinity. Sympathy not only distinguished the gentleman from the rake but also provided a potential antidote for rakishness; men could cultivate their moral feelings and reform from rakes into gentlemen. Thus, while the gentleman was more and more often set in opposition to the rake, as in Samuel Richardson's mid-century novel *Sir Charles Grandison* (1753), *Love in Excess* depicts the rakish seducer as being transformed "through suffering passion" into the domestic gentleman.[14] It is this transformation, as well as its very possibility, that locates Haywood's novel at the nexus of this cultural, philosophical evolution.

Published in 1719, Haywood's *Love in Excess* links the gentleman's sensibility, his sympathetic reading, and his relationships with women, all connections that would later be associated with the sentimental novel and philosophical writings of the mid-eighteenth century. Sympathy itself could also be cultivated through reading; after all, in bringing the experiences of others close to us in dramatic fashion, literature sparks sympathy by enabling us to relate others' experiences to our own.[15] This dynamic partly explains why the intersection between Hume's philosophy of sympathy and reading has been so popular among scholars of eighteenth-century culture.[16] Indeed, sympathizing with others was a way of reading the world. Hume explains, "Tis true, there is no human, and indeed no sensible creature, whose happiness or misery does not, in some measure, affect us, when brought near to us, and represented in lively colours" (*Treatise* 281). As Gallagher argues, "Hume's *Treatise* reveals why fictional characters were uniquely suitable objects of compassion. Because they were conjectural, suppositional identities *belonging* to no one, they could be universally appropriated."[17] Moreover, throughout his career, Hume repeatedly declared that literature was an ideal way of instilling sympathy.[18]

By extension, the masculinity of the gentleman was both a demonstration and an "effect of literacy."[19] Not only should the gentleman improve himself through reading, but he also had a particular moral duty "to *read* others and to modify and modulate" his behavior to suit whatever social context he was in.[20] The ability to read others and to act accordingly was associated with the reading of literature, considered to be "essential to the 'formation of taste.'"[21] By extension, taste was considered to be a regulating element for the passions. Hume writes, "I find, that [cultivating our taste] rather improves our sensibility for all the tender and agreeable passions" (*Essays* 93). The civilizing effect of reading thus became pivotal for reformers who sought to "improv[e] men through art" as a means of smoothing out their rougher aspects and encouraging their sensibility.[22] Because such masculine improvement naturally built on the gentleman's position as the ideal moral and didactic author (see chapter 1), the gentleman became *the* sympathetic reader.

This chapter demonstrates how writers such as Haywood developed sympathetic reading into a space for female influence over masculinity. In D'elmont, Haywood creates a "captivating performance of heterosocial politeness" for her own ends.[23] The reform of male manners by cultivating the gentleman's sympathetic reading, both literal and metaphorical, was tied directly to women's increased influence over masculinity. A new emphasis on heterosociality, especially for men, was vital to the cult of sensibility required for such reform.[24] In many ways, the reform of male manners was led by women, who gained new authority to "articulate ... their sense of real and potential victimization by men."[25] Furthermore, women were responsible for "polishing men,"[26] and "the mutual conversation of the sexes" was necessary for cultivating a gentleman's character.[27] The gentleman was paradoxically a dominant form of masculinity defined through a contingent relationship with women, who dictated the valence of value in the social circle, a realm given to conversation and social refinement. This configuration, especially in relation to the gentleman as reader, placed men who wished to be gentlemen in a dependent position, both morally and sexually. Because women's wishes, manners, and desires gave the gentleman shape, he had to be responsive to them before he could become influential.

Although critics have noted how the gentleman at least partly revised some of the class dynamics of masculine privilege associated with the rake, Haywood illustrates how this shift rewrote structures of masculine desire.[28] Part of reforming male manners involved rethinking and redefining class, specifically masculine class privilege.[29] Whereas the rake's aristocratic status authorized his pursuit of his selfish desires and his right to exert control and influence over the bodies of others around him, especially women's, the gentleman's desires had to function more reciprocally. It is this reciprocity that has made the gentleman appear passive or boring to critics; he lacks the sexual aggression and thrusting display of the rake while also struggling, if not failing, to perform the same sentimental, sexual vulnerability as the virtuous heroine. Because the gentleman has to sympathize with others and accrue status through his treatment of women, part of his desires, at least on some level, has to respond to women's desires, both moral and passionate. Although Haywood does not explode or erase male class privilege, she does revise masculine desire in order to create an access point for her own literary authority to exert influence over this gendered structure.

Eliza Haywood's Count D'elmont: A Character Study in the Literary Education and (Re)Form of the Gentleman as a Sympathetic Reader

In her first novel, *Love in Excess* (1719), Haywood constructs a model of masculinity in an exemplary male reader, the dashing Count D'elmont, for her own male readers to emulate. By intertwining D'elmont's excessively attractive masculinity with the cultivation of his moral sympathy through both literal and metaphorical reading, Haywood participates in and anticipates aspects of the reform of male manners and the cult of sensibility. Beyond that, she validates her right as a woman author to exert this influence. In the process, she challenges masculine critiques of novels and amatory fiction, thus anticipating Hume in another way, and presents a case that her novels are not only a valid but an ideal tool for educating her readers in moral sympathy and her male readers in particular in the ways of becoming desirable gentlemen. What Haywood adds to the gentleman is potent desirability steeped in her own generic conventions. As D'elmont transforms into a gentleman, he becomes more desirable, not less, and Haywood achieves this result by openly depicting feminine passion. D'elmont's desirability is thus crucial to the relationship that she constructs between appropriate masculinity, reading, and moral sympathy—a relationship that anticipates the rise of the cult of sensibility.

Love in Excess is one of the most studied texts in Haywood's oeuvre, and as with the larger critical conversation on Haywood, scholarship on *Love in Excess* has typically focused on feminocentric themes: female readership, female characters, genre and femininity, and expressions of female desire. Toni Bowers articulates this general position, arguing that "the central issue in *Love in Excess* is the problem of female sexual agency—the ability to recognize one's own desire and to express or act on it in an effective way."[30] Although such criticism has examined how portraits of female desire are potent and powerful in *Love in Excess*, the novel is largely about a man: Count D'elmont. As Kelleher and David Oakleaf have articulated, it is D'elmont's evolution from rakish seducer into domestic gentleman on "which a good deal of the novel turns."[31] He is the only character who appears in all three volumes of the novel, and his relationships with several (conveniently alliterative) groups of women shape the central action of each volume. The female characters absolutely present dynamic depictions of female desire and passion, but the narrative is also centrally concerned with D'elmont's moral and sexual development. Despite D'elmont's centrality, with the exception of Jennifer Airey's recent work, critics do not read *Love in Excess* as a novel fundamentally concerned with the proper construction of masculinity.[32] Ahern and Kelleher, however, acknowledge the centrality of D'elmont's reform to the sympathy structures of the novel.[33] Both read D'elmont's male typology and reform as part of a tipping point between Restoration and mid-century male ideals, but they tend to read him in parallel with Melliora, reading masculinity in balance with femininity in the novel's mission.[34] By contrast, I argue that masculinity is itself a key focus of the novel, and that this focus is what makes reading Haywood's first novel as an anticipatory note to the moral codes of the cult of sensibility so vital.

Haywood's Type? Rethinking Haywood's Male Characters and Readers

Haywood's male characters are almost universally typed as predatory vessels of patriarchy whose desires are "relatively straightforward... 'self-interested,' 'short-lived and end-directed,'"[35] "almost invisible," and "driven... by dumb lust or simple interest."[36] According to critics, the typical Haywoodian male is a predatory seducer who functions more as a plot device than as a distinct character. As such, he drives the narrative forward via his selfish, sexual potency, usually propelling the heroines toward seductions, unwed pregnancies, and broken hearts.[37] Meanwhile, male figures who depart from this model, including the overly modest Philidore of

Philidore and Placentia; or l'amour trop delicat (1727), are treated as exceptions who prove the rule.[38] Within this critical thrust, Haywood's male characters, especially in her earlier amatory fiction, are treated as a type. However, character type indicates a kind of static nature that, while popular in the eighteenth century, does not describe D'elmont.[39] D'elmont's desires may be self-interested, but they are not static. In part 1, D'elmont scoffs at the idea of love, but by the end of the novel he has learned to resist various temptations and become a "lovely" example "of conjugal affection." D'elmont's reform is all the more striking because the desires of the female characters, by contrast, remain relatively static.[40] Although their desires may nevertheless be significant and even vary from character to character, the unintended critical consequence of focusing exclusively on the text's female characters is that D'elmont's importance and the function of masculinity in Haywood's larger oeuvre have been overlooked.

Reading D'elmont as a model for male readers as well as masculinity in general challenges long-held beliefs that Haywood's readership was predominantly comprised of women. This perception is tied to nineteenth-century assumptions about "frothy minded" female readers and the purported femininity of genres such as amatory fiction and romance.[41] Despite its challenges to these problematic and gendered assumptions, contemporary criticism, from foundational recovery scholarship to much of the most recent work on Haywood, has consistently relied on the notion that Haywood's readers, both real and imagined, were primarily other women.[42] However, Laura Runge and William Warner both point out how this perspective on eighteenth-century women writers in general is inaccurate.[43] Furthermore, Jan Fergus argues that the primary audience for novels was young men and schoolboys, and within Haywood scholarship, K. King, Patrick Spedding, and Manushag Powell all consider men to be important, obvious members of Haywood's readership.[44]

Haywood herself was clearly aware of her multigender readership and addressed her male readers directly, as this chapter's second epigraph exemplifies. Moreover, in her dedication to *Lasselia; or the Self-Abandon'd* (1723), addressed to the Earl of Suffolk, a specific male reader, Haywood proclaims: "My Design in writing this little Novel (as well as those I have formerly publish'd) being only to remind the unthinking Part of the World, how dangerous it is to give way to Passion, will I hope, excuse the too great Warmth . . . for when the Expression being invigorated in some measure proportionate to the Subject,'twould be impossible for a Reader to be sensible how far it touches *him*, or how probable it is that *he* is falling into those Inadvertencies which the Examples, I relate wou'd caution *him* to avoid."[45] While masculine pronouns have often stood in for audiences of mixed gender, it seems clear that Haywood considers her text as potentially instructive and titillating for men as well as women. Haywood matter-of-factly declares that men are susceptible to the heat of her passionate scenes, and that such passion is morally instructive. In fact, for her, as opposed to modern scholars, the address to men comes across not as provocative or revolutionary but as a matter of course.

It has been critics, and not Haywood herself, who have relied on the ideal of a female reader, and despite how important the female reader is literally, symbolically, and politically, there are problems with assigning her to Haywood too exclusively. It is important to step back and recognize the *constructedness* rather than the *exclusiveness* of the figure of the female reader and to consider how actual readership departed from it in ways that open new critical possibilities. The emphasis on the female reader of the novel has instilled the long-standing image of "the novel as the desirable and vulnerable female body."[46] If we recognize that Haywood was aware of her male audience, or at least a mixed-gender audience, and consider how D'elmont acts as a model for this readership, the way Pamela, Melliora, and other heroines have been regarded as models of female readership, then the novel suddenly takes on a new association with a new desiring and desirable body: a male body. The desirability of D'elmont's body is one of the driving features of *Love in Excess*.[47] His desirability—that is, women's acting on their desires for him in defiance of social convention—as much as (if not more than) his personal male desires drives the action of the text. With this awareness, the constructedness of masculine reading, which like many aspects of dominant masculinity has become naturalized, invisible, and hegemonic, suddenly comes to the fore. Instead of an invisible body, Haywood presents us with the highly desirable and desiring body of D'elmont.

The Patterns of Love in Excess: *Teaching the Gentleman to Read through Sympathy*

In positioning D'elmont as the model for her readers, Haywood creates a narrative structure that reinforces and intertwines desirable masculinity, sympathetic reform, and reading. Moments of reading are followed by scenes of sympathy, followed by more advanced kinds of reading, followed by more properly deployed sympathy, all of which emphasize the connection between D'elmont's developing sympathy and evolving masculinity. Throughout the text, Haywood uses D'elmont's appeal to shape the reader's response to the novel. Because of his centrality, D'elmont's appeal becomes, in essence, the appeal of the novel as a whole. In this way, Haywood capitalizes on D'elmont's initial status as a rake, a figure whose performative allure is partly powered by his "status as an object of emulation."[48] To combat the dominance of the rake, the gentleman needed to become a figure that other men desired to emulate (and that women wanted). The fact that Haywood chooses to reform her rake rather than merely contrasting him with a gentleman demonstrates a keen savvy on her part. She takes advantage of the dangerous kinds of emulation that the rake inspires and sets up a structure that also reforms the desires of her readers. They begin by desiring the seductive rake but evolve into desiring the gentleman. This transformation fits directly into emerging models of moral sympathy, in which morality is not an innate faculty but the product of experience and, in Haywood's case, reading.

As the novel opens, D'elmont demonstrates all of the classic features of a rake. He is militaristic, magnetically attractive, wealthy, aristocratic, persuasive, and French, both in manner and lineage.[49] He consumes women to feed his "ambition ... the reigning passion of his soul" (*LE* 76). He pursues Amena for sexual conquest and marries the wealthy Alovisa to satisfy his social and financial ambitions.[50] D'elmont is so seductive that he makes a conquest of Alovisa (and seemingly every other woman) without any real effort or even knowledge of his seduction. From the outset, D'elmont appears to be the über-rake.

Although Haywood emphasizes the rake's nearly hyperbolic seductiveness, she also marks the rake's masculinity as frustrated and symptomatic of bad reading. The crucial feature that critics have almost universally overlooked is that D'elmont is not actually a successful rake. The rake proves his masculinity in displays: in battle, on the dueling field, and in the bedroom.[51] In the first breath of the novel, however, Haywood links D'elmont's rakish masculinity with foreclosure, namely with the ending of a war, "the conclusion of the peace taking away any further occasions of shewing [his] valour" (*LE* 37). D'elmont also never fights any duels. Most provocative is that, despite his overwhelming and ubiquitous allure, he does not consummate any of his seductions. In her later works, Haywood produces numerous other rakes who succeed in seducing, impregnating, and abandoning their ladies. However, D'elmont fails to achieve sexual gratification with the women he seeks. (D'elmont's marriage to Alovisa, though consummated, was for wealth, not sexual or romantic desire.) This does not mean there are no consequences for his seductions or that he is innocent, but by continually denying D'elmont sexual consummation, Haywood creates a situation that stresses distinct stakes for rakish masculinity. Amena's reputation is ruined regardless, but the impact on D'elmont's reputation depends on consummation, for rakish masculinity demands sexual gratification.

Instead of consummation, Haywood presents readers with a narrative pattern of anticipation and interruption. D'elmont lures Amena into a garden, but when "there was but a moment betwixt her and ruine [sic]," Amena's maid interrupts them, leaving D'elmont "half-blessed" (*LE* 58). The same pattern repeats twice in the second volume when D'elmont, despite being married to Alovisa, attempts to seduce Melliora. After sneaking into Melliora's bedchamber, "a loud knocking . . . put a stop to his beginning exstacy [sic]," and later D'elmont is again interrupted in a garden by Melantha (*LE* 118). Even when D'elmont believes that he has finally, illicitly bedded Melliora, he has in fact been tricked by Melantha into having sex with her. As Airey notes, the only time that D'elmont has sex outside of marriage is a rape scene, where he transforms from a "sexual predator to . . . sexual prey."[52] D'elmont is only able to gratify his sexual desire after he marries Melliora, which is allowed only after his lengthy reform.

Such frustration is not limited to D'elmont, for *Love in Excess* extinguishes all of its rakes by denying them satisfaction. The Baron D'espernay never successfully seduces Alovisa and is skewered by the Chevalier de Brillian at the close of volume 2. Meanwhile, the Marquess De Saguillier, who kidnaps Melliora, is reformed in part by D'elmont and reunited with his fiancée at the end of volume 3. In fact, the only character who gains clear sexual gratification outside of marriage is the coquettish Melantha. Throughout the novel, Haywood presents the path of the rake as an impotent, frustrated path of masculine sexuality.

Haywood also distinguishes D'elmont's potent appeal from his rakishness. Instead, Haywood emphasizes D'elmont's heterosocial appeal, which is significant because heterosociality was a crucial vehicle for cultivating sympathy and a defining feature of the gentleman's character. Within the context of the novel, the ideal man is passionately admired by both men and women, and Haywood writes of D'elmont, "The beauty of his person, the gaiety of his air, and the unequalled charms of his conversation, *made him the admiration of both sexes*" (*LE* 37, emphasis mine). His heterosocial popularity is founded not only on physical beauty and gaiety but also on "the unequalled charms of [D'elmont's] conversation." Heterosociality and charming conversation go hand in hand with the cult of sensibility and anticipate the philosophy of sympathy, and Haywood uses this crucial characteristic to indicate a unique potentiality in D'elmont. In a broad cultural context as well as in Haywood's other works, rakes were known for their charm and wit; however, in *Love in Excess*, the other two rakes lack this desirability.[53] Alovisa scorns the Baron as so different from D'elmont that he "seem'st not the same species of humanity, nor ought to stile [sic] himself a man" (*LE* 148). In contrast, D'elmont remains extremely desirable, both to men and to women, which indicates that his masculinity remains intact and that he does not become effeminate through his lack of consummation. Instead, he becomes more desirable as his failures begin to alter his morals. The shift signals that his masculinity can be reformed to suit more gentlemanly patterns and, in turn, enable male sexual satisfaction. In this way, Haywood uses heterosocial desirability to indicate D'elmont's gentlemanly potential instead of his rakish status.

Haywood also links the rake's impotence to dismal reading skills. There is a haphazardness to D'elmont's seduction of Amena that is spurred by a moment of misreading. After receiving an anonymous love letter (from Alovisa), D'elmont casually "[begins] to consider a mistress an agreeable, as well as fashionable amusement" (*LE* 40). He mistakenly attributes Alovisa's letter to Amena because he "fancie[s]" that he sees "something of that languishment in [Amena's] eyes, which the obliging mandate had described" (*LE* 42). When he discovers his mistake, he curses his "intolerable stupidity, when he consider[s] the passages of Alovisa's behaviour, her swooning at the ball, her constant glances, her frequent blushes when he talked to her" (*LE* 67). D'elmont misreads all of the physical and textual signs, and his inability to read Amena and Alovisa frustrates his own desires. Alovisa's jealousy disrupts his seduction of Amena, and his eventual marriage to Alovisa frustrates his later attempts to seduce Melliora.

It is precisely at the moment when D'elmont curses his misreading that Haywood introduces her first lesson in sympathetic reading: the inset tale of his brother, the Chevalier de Brillian. Through the Chevalier, Haywood anticipates several crucial mechanisms of moral sympathy and creates a symbolic moment of generic readership that contrasts and cultivates different kinds of masculinity. In doing so, she establishes the instructive potential of supposedly feminine genres for masculinity. Sympathy occurs when someone else's experiences and passions are brought close to us in such vivid ways that they become our own passions. Characters become an ideal vessel for achieving this effect because their experiences can easily be subsumed by our own imaginations. The Chevalier is an ideal sympathetic primer for D'elmont.[54] As brothers, D'elmont and the Chevalier share a "*great . . . resemblance in their persons*" as well as a "*sympathy of their souls*" (*LE* 68, emphasis mine). Moreover, the Chevalier is in love with Ansellina, Alovisa's sister, which parallels D'elmont's own immediate experience. Beyond these resemblances, the Chevalier functions as a literary, textual character that D'elmont relates to as a reader in ways that awaken and develop his sympathy, and the specific lesson that the chevalier teaches is the importance of sympathizing with and respecting women.

The Chevalier represents a different genre of masculinity than does his brother. Seeming more like a hero from Madeleine de Scudéry's works than anyone in Haywood's amatory fiction,[55] the Chevalier presents a love that is chaste, austere, and respectful, and the style, tone, and structure of his narrative mark both his tale and his masculinity as romantic instead of amatory or rakish. His distinct generic features and D'elmont's response to them mark the inset tale as a moment of sympathetic reading. The Chevalier's story is "accompanied with sighs, and a melancholly air immediately overspreading [his] face ... [which] raised an impatient desire in the Count [D'elmont] to know the reason of it" (*LE* 68). D'elmont's desire to hear his brother's tale is a desire for his narrative, the desire of a reader. As Patricia Meyer Spacks argues, fiction conveys its truths—political, social, or otherwise—by deploying plot to "engag[e] our desire."[56] D'elmont correctly reads his brother's body (so like his own), in contrast to his earlier misreading of Alovisa's. Describing his current separation from Ansellina, "the afflicted Chevalier could not conclude without letting fall some tears; which the Count perceiving ran to him, and tenderly embracing him, said all that could be expected from a most affectionate friend" (*LE* 75). D'elmont's response, sparked by sympathy, is that of a reader of sentimental fiction who sheds a tear at the sight of distressed virtue.

Haywood uses inset tales like the Chevalier's to emphasize the relationships amongst sympathy, reading, and masculinity. Critics have noted that Haywood frequently uses inset tales between women "to engage the female reader's sympathy and erotic pleasure."[57] The scene between the brothers shifts the didactic potential of Haywood's work from a female to a male reader and reveals that it is not only women's bodies that are texts.[58] Haywood contrasts the ways patriarchal structures give shape to the masculinity of the rake with how generic structures like romance, found in the inset tale, provide alternative lessons and masculinities. Romance "repeatedly inverts conventional value systems."[59] For instance, whereas D'elmont seeks "victory" over Amena to protect his "honours inclination," the Chevalier is "*the conquest*" of Ansellina (*LE* 46, 70, emphasis mine). What is at stake in these moments of homosocial narrative exchange is appropriate masculinity itself.

Haywood uses the Chevalier's narrative to prime D'elmont for his own first experience with love when he meets Melliora at the beginning of volume 2. D'elmont is called to the deathbed of his guardian and mentor, Monsieur Frankville, who entrusts D'elmont with the guardianship of his daughter, Melliora. Haywood writes, "The first sight of Melliora gave [D'elmont] a discomposure he had never felt before, he *sympathized in all her sorrows*, and was ready to joyn his tears with hers" (*LE* 86, emphasis mine). Although D'elmont's experience with women has not prepared him for the moment, his reading, by way of the Chevalier's story, has. The Chevalier's lesson on love, in which the man surrenders first, penetrates D'elmont's heart. Furthermore, D'elmont experiences the mutuality that his past relationships with women have lacked but that is emphasized in the Chevalier's story, which presents D'elmont and Melliora as a match, not as a predator and a victim: "Their admiration of each others perfections was mutual . . . and it was hard to say whose passion was the strongest" (*LE* 86). In mimicking the Chevalier's narrative more than his own experience with women, D'elmont's first real encounter with love emphasizes the instructive potential of reading.

D'elmont's new personal experience of passion immediately translates into further improvements in sympathetic reading. After bringing Melliora home to live with him and Alovisa, D'elmont is cast in a more sentimental mode of masculinity: "Real sighs flew from his breast uncalled" (*LE* 89). Haywood's emphasis on the reality of his sighs means that D'elmont is shifting away from the performative sighs of a rakish seducer and toward the genuine feeling of the gentleman. At this moment, D'elmont receives a letter from a convent-bound Amena: "Had this letter come a day sooner, 'tis probable it would have had little effect on the soul of D'elmont, but his sentiments of love were now wholly changed, what before he would but have laughed at, and perhaps dispised [*sic*], now filled him with remorse and serious anguish" (*LE* 92). When "by sad experience" D'elmont finds "what it [is] to love, and to dispair [*sic*]," he receives another letter from a convent-bound Amena, where she castigates D'elmont for seducing her (*LE* 90). Haywood chooses to manifest D'elmont's newfound sensitivity in a deliberate moment of sympathetic reading. His ability to properly feel, read, and respond to said reading has been made possible through the combination of his new personal experience with love and his practice as a sympathetic reader with the Chevalier. This reading of a woman's text is necessary for D'elmont's continued reform, for the rake's reform cannot be completed by another man but instead requires the influence of women.

Haywood uses Melliora to create a space for women to guide masculinity through the sentimental vehicle of polite heterosociality. The longest stretches of dialogue and conversation within the novel occur between Melliora and D'elmont, and though the subject is always their relationship, the stakes of their conversations center on D'elmont's masculinity. Melliora uses conversation and her own highly cultivated reading skills to reform D'elmont's rakish behavior, and she especially challenges him on specifically linguistic terrain. The rake does not speak the language of cultivated sympathy but one of seduction and conquest—a language that centralizes his masculinity and prioritizes his desires—and D'elmont argues with verbal (and sometimes physical) forcefulness. After sneaking into Melliora's bed, he responds to her protests by exclaiming, "What could'st thou think if I should leave thee? How justly would'st thou scorn my easie tameness; my dulness, unworthy of the name of lover, or even of man!" (*LE* 117). In response, as Bowers argues, "Melliora speaks what amounts to a different language" by referencing "her own desire" and "her position as dependent, resistant respondent."[60] While Bowers positions Melliora's language within a political framework of passive resistance, it also speaks to the shifting expectations of masculinity, which required gentlemen to consider and act in the best interests of those who were dependent on them, especially women. Melliora cries out during his intrusion: "O! hold . . . forbear, I do conjure you, even by the love you plead . . . unless you wish to see me dead, a victim to your cruel, fatal passion, I beg you to desist" (*LE* 117). Haywood thus uses Melliora's language of sympathy to counter the selfish discourse of the rake.

To become a gentleman, D'elmont must learn to speak the new language of heterosociality, a language grounded in sympathetic reading and women's influence. Melliora situates her authority on these matters in her ability to converse and to debate morality and passion based on her reading. In almost every scene in which D'elmont and Melliora debate, Melliora has been reading. When he confesses his love to her for the first time, she is reading by the lake. After his confession, Melliora's first real speech in the novel is set firmly within the context of polite conversation: an afternoon tea of both women and men. In response to Melantha's reading of amorous poetry, but also to D'elmont's earlier declarations, Melliora argues "against giving way to love, and the danger of all softning [sic] amusements," and "the force of her reason, the delicacy of her wit, and the penetration of her judgment" charm all of her listeners, including D'elmont (*LE* 107). Later, D'elmont catches Melliora reading Ovid and teases her for her hypocrisy, but she challenges his reading with her own: "Tis want of thinking justly" that leads lovers astray (*LE* 109). D'elmont then tries to play on her sympathy as a reader of him: "A thousand times you have *read* my rising wishes, sparkling in my eyes . . . by all the torments of my galled, bleeding heart, swear, that you shall hear me" (*LE* 111, emphasis mine). He appeals to Melliora here as a sympathetic reader but still prioritizes his happiness over her virtue. Although Melliora does not completely dispel D'elmont's passion and nearly gives into him numerous times, she also creates a conversational exchange that challenges his self-interested desires by confronting him with the consequences for her and the larger standards of morality. According to Schellenberg, a primary function of novels in the cult of sensibility was to circumscribe "socially threatening individualistic desire" within a heterosocial "community of consensus."[61] As a case in point, Melliora counters her individual desires and the selfish desire of the rake as a means to reform D'elmont into a gentleman: a man of community, consensus, and sympathy.

The final events of volume 2 remove the social and legal obstacles barring Melliora and D'elmont's love—Alovisa dies—but instead of rewarding the couple with marital bliss, Haywood delays their union. Melliora returns to the monastery plagued by guilt over Alovisa's death, and D'elmont sets out for Italy. At this point, Haywood marks a shift in her hero: "*Ambition*, once his darling passion, was now wholly extinguished in him . . . he no longer thought of making a figure in the world; but his *love* nothing could abate" (*LE* 163–164, emphasis mine). Gone is the rake's aristocratic pursuit of his own ambitions, and in its stead are the heterosocial desires of the gentleman. D'elmont's only hope is that Melliora promises to write to him, which shifts their whole relationship to one of male readership that agrees to abide by the dictates of female authorship.

The gentleman's ability to read others and to adjust his own behavior accordingly was a central feature of his masculinity. In volume 3, D'elmont demonstrates appropriate maturity in his gentlemanly reading by sympathizing with the lovestruck Ciamara and Violetta and doing what he can to mitigate their passions and discomforts. When he overhears Ciamara professing her passion for him, "No consideration was of force to make him neglect this opportunity of undeceiving her" (*LE* 177). Similarly, when Violetta trembles and stumbles over her words, D'elmont draws on "the experience he had of the too fatal influence of his dangerous attractions" and concludes "that his presence was the sole cause of her disorder" (*LE* 234). Gone is the "intolerable stupidity" that led him to misread Alovisa; D'elmont correctly interprets these women's passions, and rather than indulging in the "vanity . . . of being pleased that it was in his power to create pains," he seeks to ameliorate their feelings. He is not entirely effective, however; Ciamara throws herself at him, Violetta follows him through the country disguised as a boy, and both women die. But these drastic actions speak more to Haywood's investment in D'elmont's desirability, which is no less potent now that he is more virtuous, than to a failure of his sympathy. D'elmont's newfound sympathetic prowess has made him even more appealing to the fairer sex.

The lessons that D'elmont must embody include those of sexual restraint and virtue. Unlike the rake, the gentleman has sexual virtue and must protect it. The gentleman channels his sexual desires into marriage, thereby demonstrating through "chaste heterosexuality" his "exemplary self-control."[62] A continuing challenge of the gentleman as a literary figure is his being caught between the figures of the rake (his masculine opposite) and the virtuous heroine (his feminine counterpart). His virtue is not vulnerable to trauma in precisely the same way as a heroine's, and he cannot demonstrate his masculinity by performing the seductions of the rake. Haywood crafts a unique solution to this quandary: she inverts D'elmont's own rakish behavior by placing him in the same sorts of situations she normally reserved for her novels' heroines. Instead of attempting to seduce women and sneaking into bedrooms, D'elmont is himself "subjected to uninvited sexual advances."[63] When he visits Ciamara at her house, the Italian seductress hurls herself into D'elmont's lap, and "tho it was impossible for any soul to be capable of a greater, or more constant passion than [D'elmont] felt for Melliora," D'elmont is "still a *man*" and nearly succumbs to Ciamara's seductions (*LE* 225). Similar to the situations with Amena and Melliora, he is saved only by a timely interruption.

D'elmont learns a lesson from his close call with Ciamara and uses his newfound caution in a later scene with Melliora, one that presents the culmination of his reformation and shows that his masculinity now depends on and must respond to women's narrative power. While searching for Melliora, D'elmont and company happen to take shelter at the home of the Marquess De Saguillier, Melliora's kidnapper. That night, the Marquess's fiancée, Charlotta, helps Melliora to sneak into D'elmont's bedchamber, where darkness obscures her identity. As Airey notes, Haywood deliberately reverses D'elmont's previous bedroom invasions, when he snuck into Melliora's room to take advantage of her.[64] Although Melliora claims that she has only come to talk to him, her goal is clearly to test his virtue because she frames the conversation in sexual tones. Hoping that he is "more a chevalier than to prefer a little sleep, to the conversation of a lady," she clearly invokes the sexual innuendo of "conversation" (*LE* 249). These words, echoing Ciamara's insistence that he "know[s] how to act the *courtier*'s part," provoke D'elmont's anxiety (*LE* 171).[65] He worries that he has "met with a second Ciamara, and lest he should find the same trouble with this as he had done with the former, he resolved to put a stop to it at once, and with an accent as peevish as he could turn his voice to," he coldly dismisses Melliora. At this, Melliora again challenges his masculinity: "Is this the courtly, the accomplished Count D'elmont . . . who thus rudely repels a lady, when she comes to make him a present of her heart." D'elmont then continues his "peevish" defense by pompously declaring, "I can esteem the love of a woman, only when 'tis *granted*, and think it little worth acceptance, *proffered*" (*LE* 249). Although D'elmont does not recognize Melliora or realize that she is testing him, he does interpret the dangers of the scene in terms of his past experiences with Ciamara. As a result, he opts to protect his virtue rather than defend his former rakish reputation, which starkly contrasts his claims in volume 2 that leaving Melliora untouched would make him less of a man.

What is most striking about the scene is that D'elmont's strategy—affecting a false peevishness and excessive prudishness—is the same strategy that Melliora used on him during their first discourse on love. The conservative message of D'elmont's words seems to reassert "conventional representations of male agency and female passivity."[66] However, if we see the scene as depicting D'elmont's adoption of Melliora's polite lessons, then the dynamics of this conservative moment take on a different valence. D'elmont is ventriloquizing Melliora; he embraces her feminine influence and acts as a gentleman. Although the gentleman is indeed a conservative figure, Haywood complicates his conservative masculinity with repeated moments of sexual vulnerability. D'elmont almost lost his newfound masculine virtue with Ciamara, and his defensive response to Melliora in this later scene speaks to a position in which masculinity is sexually vulnerable. To protect his virtue from what he assumes is another predatory woman, D'elmont embraces Melliora's sympathetic heterosocial influence by mimicking her arguments and even adopting her narrative style. As with Melliora, D'elmont's prudishness is not a reflection of his actual desire but a defense. If volume 2 of *Love in Excess* demonstrates the usefulness of the Chevalier's lessons, then volume 3 proves that D'elmont has become a gentleman by putting Melliora's lessons into action. In this light, Haywood's plot delay facilitates the evolution of D'elmont's masculinity.

Beyond demonstrating D'elmont's virtue and validating Melliora's narrative tactics, the reunion also constructs D'elmont's desires as contingent upon female authorship. Volume 3 begins with D'elmont as a male reader of Melliora's letters, and this dynamic continues in the reunion scene. After she reveals her identity, D'elmont is initially transported by passion. Invoking the sympathies of her readers, both men and women, Haywood writes, "Those who have ever experienced any part of that transport, D'elmont now was in, will know . . . words were too poor to express what 'twas he felt." Even so, D'elmont ends their embrace to ask Melliora how she came to be in "the house of the young amorous Marquese D'Saguillier." She chides him to "cease" his "causeless fears,—where ever I am found . . . I can be only yours" (*LE* 250). D'elmont reacts with an abashed reflection on his own behavior: "These words first put the Count in mind of the indecency his transport had made him guilty of" (*LE* 251). D'elmont's reaction is one of virtuous shame; he feels guilty for being carried away by his passion for

Melliora. The exchange is a direct counter to earlier scenes of his frustration and aggressive, predatory bedroom invasions.[67]

Furthermore, his ability to step back, to engage her in conversation, and to feel guilt as a result creates space for Melliora to act as the authority within the scene. After his self-reflection, Melliora insists rather dictatorially that she will stay only if D'elmont gets into bed to keep from catching cold. She then tells him the story of her kidnapping by the Marquess, her virtuous resistance, her homosocial plotting with Charlotta, and so on. Thus, the pattern established by male homosocial inset tales becomes employed with Melliora acting as author and D'elmont sympathizing and being instructed. As a result, the female author's narrative incites intense sympathetic passion and desire. As Melliora finishes her story, "The greedy Count devoured [her words] as she spoke, and tho' kisses had made many a parenthesis in her discourse, yet he restrained himself as much as possible for the pleasure of hearing her; but perceiving she was come to a period, he gave a loose to all the furious transports of his ungoverned passion" (*LE* 258). The woman-authored narrative is a spark of passion for the sympathetic D'elmont. In this moment, he desires Melliora's narrative and her authorship as much as her person, if not more, and craves "the pleasure of hearing her" more than her kisses. In this way, all of the other lessons in sympathetic reading learned by D'elmont culminate in his most passionate, sympathetic response yet: a response to a woman author.

Haywood extends the importance of this moment outward to her own authorial control. After all, Melliora's tale is a microcosm of Haywood's own amatory style, and D'elmont's desire for Melliora's narrative reflects a readerly desire for Haywood. To remind readers of her authorial control, Haywood creates one more moment of narrative interruption. As the two lovers are interrupted when Charlotta knocks at the door, Haywood again deploys the mechanism of narrative delay to indicate her own power as the author to control and thwart D'elmont's desires as well as the desires of readers. While the passion of the lovers is mutual, Haywood makes the frustration D'elmont's: "A thousand joys *he* [would have] reaped, and had infallibly been possest [sic] of all" had they not been interrupted (*LE* 258, emphasis mine). Haywood makes her hero wait for consummation until the end of the narrative. By rejecting the rake's sexual consumption and embracing the feminine influence of polite conversation and the authority of female authorship, D'elmont is ultimately rewarded upon finally being united with Melliora. Haywood emphasizes this final satisfaction by closing her novel with a gesture to their "numerous and hopeful" issue. D'elmont has, at long last, consummated his desires (*LE* 266).

Haywood's Formal Seduction and the Desirable Gentleman Reader

In the character of D'elmont, Haywood charts a masculine reform from rake to gentleman and centralizes the roles that sympathy and reading play in this transformation. Deploying this narrative for her own authorial benefit, Haywood validates her right to influence masculinity and morality. She creates sympathetic readers, men and women alike, and uses the form and plot of her novel to seduce her readers into desiring the gentleman. Critics have often considered the gentleman an erotic bore; the Glanvilles, Orvilles, and Grandisons of the literary landscape are the correct and virtuous choices, but they lack the erotic thrills of the Lovelaces and Tom Joneses.[68] However, Haywood's form and style in *Love in Excess* infuse D'elmont's reform with an erotic pull. D'elmont's seductive appeal is not dimmed by his reform. In fact, he is more desirable as a gentleman than as a rake; women become more sexually aggressive with him, and men increasingly imitate him.

What enables Haywood to make reform appealing are two reciprocal formal elements: narrative delay and her passionate prose style. Haywood builds desire for D'elmont's reform by delaying his character's sexual gratification with his partner of choice; in parallel, Haywood makes her readers wait for satisfaction until the last paragraph of the novel as well. Through D'elmont's near seductions, Haywood continually seduces her readers but frustrates their narrative consummation. If, as Ros Ballaster argues, "the telling of a story of seduction is also a mode of seduction," then readers are being seduced into desiring the gentleman because it is only through him that they achieve narrative satisfaction.[69] Haywood employs what becomes the trademark, seductive style of her plot and prose to recalibrate her readers' desires from wanting the rake to wanting the gentleman.

Haywood's amatory style also increases the appeal of reform through a kind of narrative seduction. Functioning as what John Richetti calls an "erotic shorthand,"[70] the narrative creates, according to Kathleen Lubey, expert readers "adept in the grammar of eroticism that characterizes the heightened scenes in the novel."[71] These readers are then "drawn into or at least beckoned by the value system at work in the world of the text."[72] Haywood thus creates knowing readers who are enticed to grow with D'elmont. For example, at the height of his sympathetic powers, D'elmont correctly reads Violetta's countenance, and in this moment, Haywood deliberately invites the reader to join him. During their meeting, "[Violetta] trembled... but whether occasioned by any danger she perceived... or some other secret agitation she felt within, was then unknown to any but herself." What is striking about the passage is the seeming obfuscation Haywood's narrator exhibits in claiming that the lady's trembling manifests a "secret agitation" that only Violetta knows, when the secret is not a secret at all. D'elmont immediately recognizes the tell-tale signs of "the too fatal influence of his dangerous attractions," and so does the reader (*LE* 234). In this way, Haywood has trained her readers in the same sympathetic reading skills that D'elmont now possesses.

Haywood uses her amatory style to carve out a particular relationship between masculinity and readership. If D'elmont functions as an instructive model for other men, and if the rake is feared as a dangerous, reproducing contagion, then the gentleman is the cure who combats the disease of libertinage by reproducing other gentlemen and reforming rakes. In volume 3, D'elmont not only proves himself to be an effective reader but also becomes a didactic example of masculinity for both the Marquess and the younger Frankville, Melliora's brother. Both men are echoes of the earlier D'elmont. At first, in attempting to seduce Melliora, the Marquess abandons his obligations to Charlotta, while Frankville, specifically declaring that he is modeling himself after D'elmont, is "prompted" to travel by "hope of that renown" that D'elmont had "so gallantly acquired" during his military service (*LE* 187). As with D'elmont, "Love was little in [Frankville's] thoughts especially that sort which was to end in marriage" (*LE* 188). Later, however, D'elmont's model of reform initiates the desire for monogamy and domesticity in both men. After meeting Camilla, Frankville seeks sympathy from D'elmont by framing his own experience with love to reflect D'elmont's, particularly by declaring, "Language is too poor to paint her charms, how shall I make you sensible ... but by that which, you say, your self felt at the first sight of Melliora" (*LE* 191). In contrast to his own confidant, the Baron D'espernay, D'elmont helps Frankville rescue and marry Camilla, not seduce her. In cooperation with Melliora, D'elmont also reforms the Marquess into a happy husband by curing him of his desire for Melliora and reuniting him with Charlotta.

In fact, all three gentlemen embark on conjugal bliss together: "One happy hour confirmed the wishes of the three longing bridegrooms" (*LE* 266). Haywood's emphasis on the longing of the bridegrooms instead of the brides confirms that her novel is concerned with the reform of men, for where there were once three rakes, there are now three happy bridegrooms. In the last paragraph of the novel, Haywood tactfully indicates that it is not only D'elmont who will finally achieve the social and sexual satisfaction that he has pursued throughout the novel but every man who has learned to follow his model of proper sympathetic reading. Haywood presents marriage as the only acceptable option for the men in her novel. Every man who does not marry ends up dead (the Baron and Cittolini). The women have slightly more variety in their fates: Ciamara, Alovisa, and Violetta die; Melliora, Ansellina, Camilla, and Charlotta marry happily; Amena takes religious vows; and although Melantha marries, the coquette's bed-tricks and a hasty marriage do not fit neatly into the realm of domesticity. Haywood's lessons for her male readers are thus more rigid than those for her female readers.

By linking D'elmont's reading authority with her style, Haywood intertwines the project of masculine reform with her authorship and genre. She marks amatory fiction as a valid form of moral instruction and validates female authorship as a means of exerting proper and potent heterosocial influence over masculinity. According to Barker-Benfield, the reform of male manners was indeed fueled by "women's publication of their wishes and feelings on an unprecedented scale."[73] Critics have also noted the preponderance of women's expression of their desires in *Love in Excess*, which is a mode of publicizing their wishes.[74] Although feminine expressions of desire do not always succeed in *Love in Excess*, all of the women influence D'elmont's sympathetic development, and their desiring expressions help him to either transform into or prove to be a gentleman. By placing influence over masculinity firmly in feminine hands, the process makes female passion not only present within the novel but also powerful. Haywood justifies her right as a woman writer to instruct her readers, including male ones, on the ideal and proper shape of masculinity, thereby asserting for her writing the same kind of instruction that sentimental fiction would later claim.[75] Although the gentleman continued to be a conservative figure of patriarchal regulation, Haywood plays upon his sympathetic dependence on women to carve out space for her own literary authority.

A Reform of the Man of Letters: Hume's Attempted Desirability

Although the sheer popularity of Haywood's novel and her other writings seems to speak to the effectiveness of her narrative seduction, the desirability of her reformed gentleman carried forward into actual practices of masculinity.[76] I illustrate how the specific links that Haywood builds between the gentleman's desirability, reform, and reading integrate with the gentleman's authorial persona established in chapter 1. These intersections manifest in how later, mid-century male authors like Hume seek to present themselves to their readers. Whereas critics have identified Hume as a participant and contributor to the cult of sensibility, few other than Barker-Benfield and Jerome Christensen have directly connected his philosophical systems and writing style to masculinity.[77] At first glance, Hume seems to be the literary inheritor of the male-authored tradition of Addison and Steele; he even directly echoes their calls to bring philosophy out of the dark hollows of the university and into the light and sociability of the drawing room. However, if we also bring in the women-authored traditions of the gentleman, specifically Haywood's interventions on readership and reform, then Hume emerges as part of a wider gender dialectic, and we can illuminate heretofore overlooked aspects of his literary and gender performance. Too often critics have treated Hume's writing as a direct, pure reflection of a mind, self, or even a wider cultural consciousness, not as an authorial production or as literary text. Such criticism has rarely acknowledged that Hume's authorial persona is plagued by anxiety, especially about being found desirable. His persona, the style of his texts, and even his philosophy ultimately reflect the pressure to live up to the persona of the gentleman—not only Addison and Steele's version but the Haywood version as well.

The features that critics have used to mark Hume as a representative figure of the cult of sensibility—an advocate for heterosocial politeness and the links between moral sympathy and literary practice, especially reading—also mark Hume's investment in reforming himself as a gentleman and thus endow his work with moral authority and position him and his work as desirable fodder for readers, especially women, to consume.[78] I begin with a close reading of Hume's essay "Of the Study of History" (1741) as the most direct example of the entanglement of reading, gender, and desire with his own self-fashioning. After that, I move outward to explore how Hume seeks his own pathway of reform, which is an echo of Haywood's reform of the rake. However, Hume seeks to reform the stodgy man of letters into the ideal gentleman. He does so with reference to the playbook of Haywood's work: reading, sociability, sympathy, but also, crucially, desirability. Then, I consider how Hume's philosophy of the passions, despite reflecting Haywood's systems, attempts to reroute passion itself to serve his genteel reform: to literally systematize the passions in a way that feeds back into validating his work by cultivating modes of readership. Last, I circle back to consider what we gain by resituating Hume as constructing a narrative self enmeshed in a woman-authored legacy.

"Of the Study of History"; or a Covert Narrative Seduction

A recognizable, recurring feature of the gentleman author is his need to regulate women's reading. Throughout his work but pointedly in "Of History," Hume attempts to guide female readership as a means of demonstrating his gentlemanly restraint and refusal to play the rake but ends up relying on a seduction plot to create desire for his manhood in female readers. In the essay, Hume shifts between seduced and potential seducer. He opens with an anecdote about what is essentially his attempted narrative seduction of a young woman:

> I was once desired by a young beauty, for whom I had some passion, to send her some novels and romances for her amusement in the country; but was not so ungenerous as to take the advantage, which such a course of reading might have given me, being resolved not to make use of poison'd arms against her. I therefore sent her Plutarch's Lives, assuring her ... that there was not a word of truth in them from beginning to end. She perused them very attentively, 'till she came to the lives of Alexander and Caesar, whose names she had heard of by accident; and then returned me the book, with many reproaches for deceiving her. (*Essays* 388)

Similar to Haywood, Hume blends bodily and literary desirability. Being desirable is a central appeal of the gentleman, and Hume opens with a statement that emphasizes how the "young beauty" desires him independently of his passion for her. According to Spacks, because plots both represent and create desire, they illuminate "the history, politics, and manners of their age not only by embodying prevailing ideology but, often, by reshaping ideology closer to the heart's desire."[79] Hume plays with this concept of plotting, implying that he could seduce the young beauty with such forms of reading—that he could plot through their plots—but does not want to "take the advantage" that the plots of romances and novels might afford him. Despite clearly desiring the young woman, he seems to resist the rakish temptation to "make use of poison'd arms against her." Instead, Hume presents himself as the benevolent, seemingly disinterested gentleman, who would never take advantage of a young woman's weaknesses. In turn, he uses this moment to construct a narrative of his own gentlemanly virtue and ability to restrain his passions.

On the surface, Hume seems to present a countersystem to Haywood's. Whereas Haywood has created a gentleman whose reading is subject to feminine influence and who influences other male readers, Hume seeks to regulate female readers, which requires a kind of seduction—a gentlemanly kind. Hume dutifully opens "Of History" with a criticism of women's reading habits: "There is nothing which I would recommend more earnestly to my female readers than the study of history ... the best suited both to their sex, and education, much more instructive than their ordinary books of amusement, and more entertaining than those serious compositions" (*Essays* 388). At the same time, Hume clearly agrees with

Haywood that men's reading is vital to their character; after all, he recommends his particular brand of reading to the young woman to invoke her desire. Throughout his work, when Hume speaks of his own love of literature, he speaks of a love for poetry and the classics. Claiming that poetry can excite "all kinds of passions" and provides a kind of "satisfaction" in the reader that can be instructive,[80] Hume references Virgil, Homer, and other ancients, and often quotes Alexander Pope, whom he greatly admired. He also clearly enjoyed history, philosophy, and the periodicals of Addison and Steele. The gentleman likewise read many things, most of them written by other gentlemen, for the purposes of moral instruction and the cultivation of taste. However, the gentleman often claimed rather vocally, whether true or not, that "they didn't, above all, read romances," amatory fiction, or scandal writing of any kind.[81] These genres were seen as being not only unworthy of the gentleman's reading but also dangerous for female readers. "Of History" appears to capture this very canonical and misogynistic distinction.

However, a closer look at "Of History" showcases how such gentlemanly guidance is once again built on performance and that the confidence that Hume's authorial positioning strives for is founded upon anxieties of desirability. Hume's choice of reading is not as disinterested as it first appears; he recommends history, and in his lifetime, he was best known as a historian, not a philosopher. It was his six-volume work, *The History of England* (1754–1762), that gave Hume his financial independence.[82] Although Hume's histories were not published until more than a decade after "Of History," he had been conceptualizing the project for years. "Of History," first published in 1741, was revised and republished in editions of Hume's essays until 1760, after which it was removed.[83] Hume continued to publish an essay about tricking an attractive young woman into reading history as he himself became a renowned, popular historian. Writing himself into a genre that he perhaps thought would evoke desire, as he advises young women in general and the young beauty in particular to read history, he implicitly asks them to read him or, at the very least, authors with whom he aligned his authorial persona. By presenting a genre that became increasingly representative of his literary appeal as fiction, Hume attempts to co-opt or capture the seductive potential of the very genres that he critiques. The intended effect is similar to the one that Haywood creates for D'elmont: the ability to be seductive without continuing to be a seducer. However, Hume cannot achieve this effect; the young woman, a savvier reader than Hume has given her credit for, rejects his literary play and rebukes him for lying to her. Hume presents his readerly, mentoring failure in specifically gendered terms by offering a tale of a young woman and himself that, consciously or unconsciously, links his own work and position within a heterosexual, heterosocial dynamic.

Hume's self-characterization as a gentleman expresses this conflict of desires, a conflict that manifests in a Haywoodian structure of performed disinterest entangled with attempted seduction. Hume's criticism of more passionate or frivolous genres of reading reveals how the gentleman's role as moderator of reading is in fact an expression of his desire to be attractive, both textually and physically. Hume argues that "romances and novels" create "an appetite for falshood [sic]." His complaint is not only that these types of reading inflame women's more passionate sensibilities but that they also give women the wrong ideas about men. History offers an important departure from these genres because it provides women with "knowledge... *that* our sex, as well as theirs, are far from being such perfect creatures as they are apt to imagine, and, *That* Love is not the only passion, which governs the male-world, but is often overcome by avarice, ambition, vanity, and a thousand other passions" (*Essays* 388). The falsehood so objectionable in romances and novels is their portrayal of masculinity, which both gives women the wrong ideas about men and fails to represent the varying passions that affect men's decisions. Put differently, they present narratives that position women's desires as central instead of peripheral and subordinate.

Reforming the Man of Letters

The key intersection between the man of letters and the gentleman was literary. As noted, Hume's philosophy has become a popular site for critics of eighteenth-century culture to connect sympathy with reading, and Hume indeed explicitly links his identity as a philosopher with his love of reading. Through his language of the passions, he also implicitly connects it with his philosophy of sympathy. Hume opens "My Own Life" (1776) by writing, "[I] was seized very early with a passion for literature, which has been the ruling passion of my life, and the great source of my enjoyments" (*Essays* 1). By identifying literature as his ruling passion, he implicitly connects it to sympathy and morality. The passions direct moral feelings, and reading is the ruling, the most powerful passion that directs Hume's will and actions. A regulating element to temper the passions was taste, as Hume explains in "Of the Delicacy of Taste and Passion": "I find, that [cultivating our taste] rather improves our sensibility for all the tender and agreeable passions" (*Essays* 93). Therefore, his love of reading, instead of isolating the man of letters, transforms him into a man of passions who translates cultivated taste into moral sympathy—in a word, the gentleman.

However, authority without attraction is not enough, and the desire for desirability is precisely the tool that Haywood infuses into her own version of the gentleman. Hume's status as a gentleman, the pose that he strikes in "Of History," was not his by default. Positioned firmly within the cult of sensibility, Hume constructs his own careful reform of male manners more covertly than Haywood but no less deliberately. In "My Own Life" (1776), he seeks to align his own identity as a "man of letters" with that of the gentleman (*Essays* 3). Although the label may have a rather gentlemanly ring to modern ears, in the early decades of the eighteenth century "the historical separation between gentlemen and men of learning was . . . social and institutional."[84] The man of letters was considered to be the musty fellow of the university, full of specialized and esoteric knowledge but without any ability or interest in engaging a wider audience. Notably, based on his education, the man of letters was also categorically a figure of reading. Although he would become and often was a figure of authorship as well, at his core his identity was tied to his expert, if unsociable, readership. However, as being tied to literacy via his status as the ideal author and a sympathetic reader became a crucial feature of the gentleman, the features of the man of letters became newly valuable and appealing. Hume takes full advantage of the opportunity to present himself and his work as that of the gentleman, and his reading, as well as his writing, was part of that currency. His desire for a "union" between the learned world of scholarship and philosophy and the conversable world of politeness and social pleasure echoed Mr. Spectator's call to bring "Philosophy out of Closets and Libraries, Schools and Colleges, to dwell in Clubs and Assemblies, at Tea-Tables, and in Coffee-Houses."[85] Hume writes that the separation of these spheres is "one of the greatest Defects of the last Age, and must have had a bad influence on both Books and Company" (*Essays* 2). In this way, he positions his readerly identity as ideally suited, even necessary, for company and as the means by which he could be labeled a gentleman.

Similar to Haywood's reform of the rake, Hume's reform of the man of letters required a new embrace of heterosociality. For this reason, Hume rejected one of the primary masculine traditions that he is so often associated with, the traditions of the Earl of Shaftesbury and Alexander Pope. Although these earlier models embraced learning, taste, male camaraderie, and virtue, they also tolerated frequent vocalizations of a suspicion or an outright rejection of heterosociality and thus of women's influence.[86] In Hume, we see the result of the reform of male manners: for Hume, women must play a part in the cultivation of morality, and proper society must be heterosocial. Women are "the Sovereigns of the Empire of Conversation," he writes (*Essays* 2), whereas men reign over the learned sphere. Hume fancifully desires a "league" between these two states, or a "union"—in other words, what Schellenberg identifies as a mutually beneficial heterosocial sphere of cultivated, pleasurable understanding.[87] Within the proposed league, Hume presents women as vessels of delicate feeling and as the more necessary influence than men. In "Of Essay Writing" (1742), Hume "approaches [the ladies] with Reverence" and even goes so far as to say that "were not my Countrymen, the Learned, a stubborn independent Race of Mortals ... unaccustom'd to Subjection, I shou'd resign into [women's] fair Hands the sovereign Authority over the Republic of Letters" (*Essays* 369). The cultivation of moral sympathy required feminine influence that was directly linked to the shaping of masculinity, and I argue that Haywood played a decisive role in establishing this prerequisite. Whereas Christensen and Robert Jones see Hume as shifting, even constructing, the importance of women and heterosociality within this philosophical sphere, I argue that Hume in fact performs the structures created by Haywood. Even his posture of "Subjection," hypothetical though it may be, echoes the lesson that D'elmont learns from the Chevalier and the posture of the attractive, yielding gentleman.

If we read that part of what is at stake in Hume's writing is his own persona, then suddenly the proposed union takes on coded heterosexual as well as heterosocial implications. Again, we see performed neutrality as a shield of gendered desire. The union between these spheres is distinctly gendered for Hume, which by definition is necessary for heterosociality. Even so, the undercurrent of desire from "Of History" courses throughout this discourse. If he, as the man of letters, is to be seen and read as a gentleman, then he must be deemed appealing by the "Sovereigns" of the conversable world—that is, women. When he writes that "Learning has been as great a Loser by being shut up in Colleges and Cells ... this moping recluse Method of study," which has made philosophy as "chimerical in her conclusions as she was unintelligible in her Stile [sic] and Manner of Delivery," we can read it as reflecting his own authorial and masculine identity (*Essays* 3).[88] However, not only Hume but also his works were continually shelved and ignored because he does not capture the gentlemanly style of appealing and being found desirable by a heterosocial audience—for example, by an audience such as the young beauty. Furthermore, when he laments that conversation without recourse to "History, Poetry," "Politics," and "Philosophy" is unsuitable for rational creatures, we should read it as anxiety about his own place in this understanding of masculinity, not exclusively as a critique of women's discourse as a "Series of gossiping Stories and idle Remarks" (*Essays* 2). Thus, what initially appears to be rote misogynistic criticism of women's shallowness becomes an expression of Hume's own inability to live up to the standards set by Haywood and women writers.

Hume's attempt to recast himself as a desirable gentleman manifests in his ceaseless quest to recast his philosophical ideas in styles that are more appealing to a heterosocial audience. He cannot occupy his authority with taste and cultivation if he is neither attractive nor charming, and he was acutely aware of the interdependent relationship between positioning himself as a gentlemanly author and appealing to readers. In the advertisement for "Of Morals," the final book of *A Treatise of Human Nature*, Hume writes, "*I am hopeful it may be understood by ordinary readers, with as little attention as is usually given to any books of reasoning*" (*Treatise* advertisement). Hume explicitly links the goal for wide readership with his book on sympathy, and the focus of "Of Morals" was likewise the social system of sentiment. By politely hoping that a heterosocial audience of the conversable world will find his work instructive and agreeable, Hume claims a position as a gentleman author who seeks to instruct and delight his readers more for their own benefit than his own, even as he, similar to Addison and Steele, seeks to benefit himself as well. If the man of letters could fill the gentlemanly role of literary authority, then Hume himself could fulfill this ideal.

Unfortunately for the man himself, Hume's career was fundamentally a long, sustained, and mostly unsuccessful attempt to capture the kind of popular readership that Haywood's work enjoyed. Hume's reform of the man of letters and his gentlemanly posturing are at base expressions of anxiety, especially anxiety about desirability. In "My Own Life," Hume's autobiographical essay and a clear bid to cultivate his persona and legacy, he recalls, "Never literary attempt was more unfortunate than my Treatise of Human Nature. It fell *dead-born from the press*, without reaching such distinction, as even to excite a murmur among the zealots" (*Essays* 2).[89] Believing that the failure of his *Treatise* "had proceeded more from the manner than the matter" (*Essays* 3), Hume tried to adopt a more accessible style in his later works, including *An Enquiry Concerning Human Understanding* (1748) and *An Enquiry Concerning the Principles of Morals* (1751), as well as in his collected *Essays: Moral, Political, and Literary* (1741–1742).[90] Speaking of his *Enquiry Concerning the Principles of Morals*, Hume writes that the work, "in my own opinion (who ought not to judge on the subject), is of all my writings, historical, philosophical, or literary, incomparably the best," but nevertheless "came unnoticed and unobserved into the world" (*Essays* 4). For Hume, as with any author, formal appeal reflected on his character. Hume writes, "We choose our favorite author as we do our friend, from a conformity of humour and disposition. Mirth or passion, sentiment or reflection; whichever of these most predominates in our temper, it gives us a peculiar sympathy with the writer who resembles us" (*Essays* 281). The ideal sympathetic friend is the gentleman, the authoritative reader of sympathy, and if Hume's work lacked this appeal, then Hume himself was lacking as a gentleman. As with D'elmont, a character can exert gentlemanly influence only if one is desirable.

The Passions as Narrative Self

As shown in Haywood's *Love in Excess*, D'elmont does not reform into a gentleman simply because he falls in love with Melliora or because he sheds all selfish desires. On the contrary, he achieves his reform by learning to restrain his passions by way of proper heterosociality and an increased desire for proper moral sympathy via the cultivation of his reading. In Hume, we see a similar need for and emphasis on society's influence to redirect the passions and teach restraint. Even sympathy has a selfish streak, and Hume's philosophy of the passions struggles with these contradictory aspects of sentiment: "We naturally desire what is forbid, and often take a pleasure in performing actions, merely because they are unlawful. The notion of duty, when opposite to the passions, is not always able to overcome them; and when it fails of that effect is apt rather to encrease [sic] and irritate them" (*Treatise* 162). Morality becomes social because it is an external influence that prompts people to cultivate their passions in ways that allow them to overcome their potentially selfish impulses: "As we establish the *laws of nature*, in order to secure property in society, and prevent the opposition of self-interest; we establish the *rules of good-breeding*, in order to prevent the opposition of men's pride." Society gives structure to our sympathies and passions in ways that offset our self-interest for the greater good, for an effect that manifests in how we engage with society. The laws of good breeding, for instance, "render conversation agreeable and inoffensive" (*Treatise* 597). It is from this experience and polite interaction that Hume comes to believe that individuals can develop a *"strength of mind"* that allows them to prioritize "the calm passions above the violent"—in other words, to restrain their selfish desires and pleasure in the forbidden (*Treatise* 162).

Hume's gentlemanly persona reveals how the gentleman was the product of narrative: a literary construction clearly attached to the model of masculinity manufactured by authors such as Haywood and genres such as amatory fiction. Critics have discussed how Hume's "definition of personal identity turns on concepts of literary practice."[91] For Hume, there is no stable a priori self; instead, we create our sense of identity from the relationships that we establish between our ideas and impressions. Our perceptions "are link'd together by the relation of cause and effect.... Had we no memory, we never shou'd have any notion of causation, nor consequently of that chain of cause and effects, which constitute our self or person" (*Treatise* 261). The self thus becomes a narrative construct produced by reading our own experience.[92] Hume writes, "The identity, which we ascribe to the mind of man, is only a fictitious one" (*Treatise* 259). Not only identity in general but specifically the identity of the gentleman becomes a narrative construction.

The gentleman is a reader who enacts his gentlemanly moral prerogative by reading the world around him through the lens of moral sympathy, a right that he has cultivated through his own literal reading and the cultivation of his taste, which circles back to create his identity. From there, the cycle repeats again and again. If the gentleman is built upon his reading, then his identity is built upon character and plot. This dynamic presents the possibility that real-life gentlemen are formed by fictional gentlemen and blurs the lines between the two in ways that bring attention to the constructed, textual nature of the gentleman as a form of masculinity. More specifically, it directs attention to the influence of Haywood's model of masculinity and the gentleman's links to fiction by women. Genres that gentleman authors dismissed—amatory fiction and romance—create structures that become interwoven into the cultural practice and form of the gentleman.

Conclusion

To close, I would like to refer to my Haywood epigraph. Its broader context involves *The Female Spectator* (1744–1746), in which Haywood calls attention to the problems with men's barring women from "the most pleasant and profitable" of studies: philosophy. She criticizes, "O but, say they, Learning puts the Sexes too much on an Equality, it would destroy that implicit Obedience which it is necessary the Women should pay to our Commands:—If once they have the Capacity of arguing with us, where would be our Authority?"[93] Haywood then appeals to her impartial readers, male and female: "If this very Reason for keeping us in Subjection does not betray an Arrogance and Pride in themselves, yet less excusable than that which they seem so fearful of our assuming."[94] Unpacking this dimension of seemingly flat yet powerful, naturalized masculinity and its influence over women is what I have hoped to accomplish in this chapter. By pairing Haywood and Hume, I have charted how the gentleman reader's masculinity, linking sentiment and literary structures, became an important aspect of his cultural definition.

We often read *regulation* as the expression of cultural dominance and privilege, and those aspects are in Hume: men, specifically straight, white men of a higher class, are clearly privileged and given access to cultural control. This chapter is not an apology for their privilege, but I do think that it is important to examine the ways in which these oppressive mechanisms of regulation emerge from a complex system of influence that operates on more than the two levels of dominant versus subversive. If we shift focus and imagine regulation to be a need to rewrite women's desire, not merely for masculine pleasure but due to a performance anxiety that men feel over the definition and standards of masculinity, then we can demystify its cultural dominance and privilege and see how women played a role in its construction. This anxiety is the product of women's pens and of unrealistic gender standards for men that women such as Haywood crafted to create space for their own influence. To conform and perform to these standards, men such as Hume deployed their privilege to regulate women.

Last, this chapter highlights not only the power of the gentleman but also the dissonance in our critical memory of him as a figure. Hume, despite his lack of widespread popularity, has remained a canonical and representative figure of his time. Compared with Haywood's renown, Hume's lack of widespread popularity is startling. The difference, of course, speaks to a major aspect of feminist recovery projects that have adeptly pointed out how previously noncanonical female authors such as Haywood actually had as much, and, in her case, more popular impact and therefore influence than more canonical figures such as Hume. I find it intriguing that Hume was not popular with eighteenth-century readers; although the question of popularity is central to the masculinity of the gentleman, he, as the actual man, has become the representative of culture. By contrast, Haywood's fictional gentleman, whose impact and appeal was wider, has been ignored. We have, in essence, privileged the "real" man over the fictional one. Yet, as my chapter shows, the gentleman is a fictitious identity, one that is powerful and culturally important but no more achievable for men than Clarissa's feminine virtue is for women. Furthermore, just as men stood to gain power by controlling definitions of femininity, women stood to gain from influencing definitions of masculinity.

3

Romancing the Gentleman Critic

Reading Criticism as Generic Courtship in Charlotte Lennox's The Female Quixote and Samuel Johnson's The Rambler

> CRITICK ... 1. A man skilled in the art of judging of literature; a man able to distinguish the faults and beauties of writing.
> —Samuel Johnson, *A dictionary of the English language*

> Since you Sir have been so good to engage on my Side I think I may set these inhuman Criticks at defyance [sic].
> —Charlotte Lennox to Samuel Richardson, *Charlotte Lennox: Correspondence and Miscellaneous Documents*

The eighteenth-century critic, by definition, is a man, and frequently in the minds of scholars, the man—that is, *the critic*—is Samuel Johnson. Johnson defined the critic not only metaphorically but also literally in his *Dictionary*. Therein, with the support of passages from other male authors—Alexander Pope, John Dryden, and Jonathan Swift—the critic is defined both through and by the work of male authors. If the role of the critic is to judge literature and distinguish each work's beauties from its faults, then the features that qualify him for the role are his taste and his display of the signs of a classical education and experience in the world. Because the critic presents himself as the gentleman, not only he but also the categories of criticism—the beauties and faults—are gendered, whether overtly or covertly, in ways that exclude women from the role of the critic and from receiving the highest praise as such.

In this way, the gentleman critic seems to be the mortal enemy of the female author, a foe to be fought, as captured in the image presented in Charlotte Lennox's letter to Samuel Richardson quoted above. Lennox penned the letter while attempting to publish her second and most famous novel, *The Female Quixote* (1752), an endeavor in which Richardson and

Johnson were her correspondents and assistants. At first glance, it appears that the vulnerable yet defiant woman writer must rely on her male patrons, Richardson and Johnson, to defend her novel. However, as shown in their letters, all is not as it seems. Johnson, despite having defined the role, struggled in his performance as the gentleman critic, and in *The Rambler*, he overtly called attention to the performative aspects of the figure. Meanwhile, though Lennox turned to Richardson and Johnson to assist with her publication, she did not kowtow to them. Instead, as a savvy author, she pulled the prominent gentlemen to her side, transformed the gentleman critic from an opponent into her champion, and co-opted his power for her own authorial ambitions.

Previously, I explored how the features of the didactic author and the moral reader came to define the character of the gentleman. In this chapter, I want to shift the valence to show how the gentleman's literary authority as author, reader, and critic are all interconnected aspects of his cultural cachet. As the critic, the gentleman was once again deeply connected to women and femininity, which were often the subject and text of his critique, while women themselves were often his audience. This chapter evaluates the relationship between Lennox and Johnson through the lens of the gentleman's role as literary critic. For years, Lennox was read as a kind of protégée of the more established Johnson. However, this chapter argues that in the 1750s, Lennox and Johnson were colleagues, both on the cusp of achieving their own literary successes. When we examine Johnson's *The Rambler* (1750–1752), Lennox's *The Female Quixote* (1752), and their correspondence from the 1750s, a dynamic relationship emerges that is negotiated through the gendered construct of criticism, in which both authors adopt and shed a variety of roles. In *The Rambler*, Johnson presents criticism as a heroic contest in which author and critic battle for literary greatness. Though sometimes earnest or mock-heroic, the battle always has an air of romance. Johnson resists many of the periodical conventions of *The Spectator*, specifically ones that constructed women as desiring dependents and that defined the author as a gentleman via his neutrality. In *The Female Quixote*, Lennox recasts this model through the courtship plot. In the plot, the heroine's—Arabella's—quest for narrative comes to represent female authorship, which makes her both heroic and compelling, while the hero, Glanville, becomes the gentleman critic. The comedy of their courtship not only reveals the generic boundaries, frustrations, and hyperbolic expectations placed upon women writers but also revises the gentleman critic into a self-interested but contingent ally of the woman writer. This chapter concludes with a brief examination of Lennox's understudied piece of literary criticism, *Shakespear Illustrated* (1753–1754).

This text and its legacy, via Johnson, highlight the performativity of both masculinity and criticism as well as represent the ways in which women writers have created space for their own critical voices, so much so that the man of letters adopted the same structure for his criticism.

Recalibrating Lennox and Johnson's Relationship

We are firmly in a new age of Lennox-Johnson scholarship. Between Norbert Schürer's recent publication of a new cache of Lennox's correspondence and Susan Carlile's excellent biography of Lennox, we can now put the final pin into the old image of Johnson as Lennox's established mentor and Lennox as the dependent woman writer.[1] For decades, critics have rethought the cultural image of Johnson and his relationships to women writers.[2] Such revision has often been framed as separating Johnson as presented in James Boswell's formative biography, *Life of Johnson* (1791), from other accounts of him by women such as Hester Thrale and in his own writing and correspondence. Although Johnson was perhaps not a protofeminist, he was clearly an advocate and admirer of women, especially Lennox. As the recalibration of their relationship shows, in the 1750s, Johnson and Lennox were peers instead of mentor and mentee. Although Johnson was nearly twenty years older than Lennox, professionally they were at a similar turning point in their literary careers—namely, on the cusp of fame. In 1751, Johnson was "a minor celebrity with a big personality" who was working on his *Dictionary* and only beginning to publish his *Rambler* essays.[3] Meanwhile, Lennox's own "reputation was not insubstantial," for she had published two well-received works: *Poems on Several Occasions* (1747) and *The Life of Harriot Stuart* (1751).[4] Johnson and Lennox debated, corresponded, and developed a friendship that was intimate and professional. In fact, Lennox seems to have navigated her relationship with Johnson in a way that dodged some of his more overt codependences. Their mutual admiration and friendship in the 1750s clearly continued throughout their careers, albeit with some bumps along the way. As Johnson wrote to Boswell in 1784, "I dined yesterday at Mrs. Garrick's, with Mrs. Carter, Miss Hannah More, and Miss Fanny Burney. Three such women are not to be found: I know not where I could find a fourth, except Mrs. Lennox, who is superiour [sic] to them all."[5] Lennox was not only superior to other women; to Johnson, she was a friend, a colleague, and one of the finest authors of the century.

Johnson's professional respect for Lennox, as well as the tone of her correspondence both with him and other representatives of the male-dominated literary profession, captures how far the woman author had come by the 1750s.[6] Despite critical perceptions that women writers depended on the gatekeeping of "masculine approval,"[7] Lennox's correspondence does not portray a woman tiptoeing around male figures of authority. Instead, it reveals a savvy author seeking to achieve her own professional goals on her own terms while managing the men around her. Lennox used her male colleagues to form professional connections, as they did with each other and with her. In 1751, though already a published author, Lennox wanted to find a more advantageous placement for her second novel, *The Female Quixote*, and had her friend Johnson connect her to the famous author and publisher Samuel Richardson. Carlile recounts how even this initial introduction transpired on Lennox's own terms, for once Lennox and Johnson were at Richardson's door, she asked Johnson to leave. According to Johnson, Lennox stated, "'I am under great restraint in your presence; but if you leave me alone with Richardson, I'll give you a very good account of him.'"[8] She then leveraged her connections to Richardson and Johnson to convince prominent publisher Andrew Millar to publish her work.

Throughout the process, Lennox is shown to have taken an active role in cultivating her own professional identity and even to have refused some of the edits for *The Female Quixote* that Millar and his male readers suggested. One reader was especially adamant that Lennox remove the amatory tale of Miss Groves from the novel. In a letter dated November 22, 1751, Lennox wrote to Richardson, "The many alterations he insists upon being made . . . make it necessary to write a new Book if I woud [sic] please him."[9] Lennox pointedly refused to make the changes, and Richardson and Johnson both backed her against Millar and Millar's friend Lord Orrery. In this light, Lennox was the opposite of Jane Spencer's image of the woman writer who depended on male approval and was "careful to write in the way that men found acceptably feminine."[10] On the contrary, Lennox as author did as she saw fit, regardless of whether it contradicted the desires of critics. Later, she worried that the book would not be published until the next season, and, in need of funds, she pushed for an earlier publication despite Johnson's suggestion that "if you can stay until next year the prospect of [success] will be better."[11] But Lennox again had her way, and *The Female Quixote* was published in March 1752. It isn't that Lennox was a "man's woman" but that she was a professional and recognized as such by her male peers.[12]

As this chapter demonstrates more broadly, understanding Lennox and Johnson's relationship allows us to reconsider key aspects of both of their works, specifically *The Rambler* and *The Female Quixote*. Focusing briefly on the latter, when we register the ways in which Lennox operated as Johnson's colleague and peer, not as his protégée, it challenges some long-held critical nausea over the penultimate chapter and ultimate meaning of

The Female Quixote. Starting in the nineteenth century, and armed only with the evidence that Johnson was Johnson and that Lennox was a woman whom he knew, critics and scholars began theorizing that Johnson had written the chapter detailing Arabella's reform with the good Divine. However, we now have decisive evidence that Lennox wrote the chapter herself. On March 12, 1752, on the eve of the novel's publication, Lennox wrote to Johnson, "Permit me to intreat your acceptance of the inclosed Book, and of my sincere acknowledgment for your kindness during the Writing of it. if you do me the favour to read over the latter part of the second Voll. *which you have not seen* you'll find I have not cured my Heroine in the manner I proposd" (emphasis mine).[13] Johnson had not seen Arabella's cure.[14] Yet, for some critics the authorship has mattered less than the influence, and they have read the doctor of the cure to be "if not literally, at least metaphorically, Dr. Johnson."[15] However, if we embrace the reality that Lennox was Johnson's colleague, then this representation takes on new potential. Despite the Johnsonian elements in *The Female Quixote*, our understanding of them can shake off these restraints if we register them as the product of a dialectical relationship.

In this chapter, I explore the question of what happens when we read *The Female Quixote* not as deference but as dialogue. After all, a dialogue is what literally appears on the page. What does such a reading show us about the shifting power and authority of the woman writer if she felt free to engage, debate, and influence her male peers and especially gentlemen critics on the level of their shared profession? Furthermore, when we recognize Lennox as Johnson's friend and as an author whose skill and opinion he respected, in what ways does his own work reflect the shifting performance of the gentleman as author and critic, one who is overtly interrogated and influenced by his relationships with women and his own masculinity?

Gallant Criticism, the Gentleman Critic, and Samuel Johnson's Ambivalent Performance in *The Rambler*

The Rambler was published in 208 twice-weekly installments from March 20, 1750, to March 14, 1752, and identical to its author, the periodical paved the crossroads of numerous literary paths in the eighteenth century. It was read and reissued long into the nineteenth century, when it was possibly even more popular.[16] Similar to the works of the other male figures featured in this book—Joseph Addison, Richard Steele, and David Hume—*The Rambler* has become a favorite for eighteenth-century scholars seeking to provide cultural context for their arguments. In the wider critical vista, *The Rambler* has traditionally been read as part and parcel of how Johnson "dominated the literary scene through the middle years of the century, [and] offered, rigid prescriptions for novelistic propriety."[17] Nevertheless, as noted above, Johnson in the 1750s was not yet the towering moralist later described, and such readings tend to project the established vision of Johnson back onto his first periodical. Instead of establishing Johnson as the icon of the gentleman critic in the mid-eighteenth century, *The Rambler* reveals "contradictory impulses."[18] In his essays, Johnson struggled with performing masculinity. Instead of dictating to young women readers, criticizing "feminine" genres, and establishing his own gentlemanly credentials, Johnson emerges as a far more nebulous author who frequently reveals the constructed nature of masculine literary performance. By extension, his narrative-presentation reveals how successful the women-authored construction of the gentleman as a performance had been. In Johnson, we ultimately see the ways in which the efforts of women writers have loosened the gentleman's grip on the reins of influence—reins that Lennox confidently grabbed for herself.

Shifting in (and out) of Neutral: Johnson, Masculinity, and Criticism

Johnson has often been viewed as one of the big daddies of eighteenth-century criticism—a real "manly" author.[19] As I have demonstrated, the gentleman's masculinity became intertwined with his authorial power; he was the ideal author and reader, and when these powers combined, he readily became the ideal critic. This assumption of the role of the critic was clearly deeply gendered. As Laura Runge, Kathleen Lubey, and Martha Kvande have argued, the very act of discerning truth depended on gendered constructions of the mind, according to which men were rational while women were feeling.[20] As a consequence, the language of criticism itself reflected the gentleman's authority, or what Runge calls the "hegemonic function of criticism."[21] Just as overtly gendered language was used to declare literary value—good works and authors were spirited, vigorous, and manly—the language of universals reinforced the hegemony of the idea that "great" works and authors transcended the mundane and connected to the universal principles of reason and virtue. For example, in his *Essay on Criticism* (1711), Alexander Pope writes,

> But true expression, like the unchanging sun
> Clears and improves whate'er it shines upon;
> It gilds all objects but alters none.[22]

Such "true" expression—unchanging, improving, and shining—is the language of the ideal vision of the gentleman, writ large as the standard for literary value.

This tone of clear-eyed, masculine judgment has frequently, even infamously, been used to characterize Johnson's criticism, and it is easy to see why. Johnson makes the hallmark gesture of the gentleman on claiming a position of disinterested neutrality. In *Rambler* 18, he writes, "I, who have long studied the severest and most abstracted philosophy, have now, in the cool maturity of life arrived to such command over my passions, that I can hear the vociferations of either sex without catching any of the fire from those that utter them."[23] Johnson's emphases on his experience, discipline, and present but controlled passions are all classic markers of the gentleman and the critic, and it seems very on brand that the essay is the same that offers his perspective on marriage. In the inescapable critical go-to, *Rambler* 4, Johnson echoes recurrent anxieties about the "dangers of fictional models," especially ones "written chiefly to the young, the ignorant, and the idle."[24] Here is the ridicule of genres associated with the feminine-seeming romance, that "wild strain of imagination" with its crutch of the fantastic: "a hermit and a wood, a battle and a ship wreck." Such critiques are commonplace in the routine devaluation of supposedly feminine genres by the gentleman critic, a figure that Johnson helped to create with his own didactic persona (*Rambler* 3:20.1750).

The assumption that Johnson is playing Mr. Spectator's game overlooks the profound, frequent inconsistencies of *The Rambler*, and may be a projection of our own internalized expectations instead of Johnson's own expression. As Sarah Morrison points out, "Critics tend to bring women into a discussion of *Rambler* 4, *only* when they recall Johnson's concern for the impressionable reader of fiction" (emphasis mine).[25] Johnson is careful with his words; if he meant "women" explicitly in this essay, then the man writing the *Dictionary* would have said so. As established in chapters 1 and 2, there was certainly a clear precedent for such critiques. Instead, Johnson's approach to the role of the literary gentleman—author, reader, and critic—is at once more playful than, more anxious than, and, at times, even resistant to the traditional models presented by *The Spectator* or Hume.

Johnson overtly calls out the performative nature of the literary gentleman's role. In *Rambler* 1, he goes through some of the established periodical motions; his eidolon expresses his "desire for pleasing," establishes his investment in morality, and modestly professes that if his works are not beautiful, then they can be "pardoned for their brevity" (*Rambler* 3:4–7.1750). However, he is even less revealing than the taciturn Mr. Spectator.[26] He provides no biography, no credentials, no charming anecdotes, and no geography.

On the contrary, he directs attention to his act of entering the world and the performativity of it all: "Perhaps few authors have presented themselves before the public, without wishing that such ceremonial modes of entrance had been anciently established" (*Rambler* 3:4.1750). The figure of the Rambler also sounds remarkably similar to Johnson, who forgoes the periodical tradition of using "deliberately over-the-top rhetoric" to establish the constructed persona of the author's eidolon.[27] Although Johnson's rhetoric is over the top in and of itself, he seems to ask readers to assume that the Rambler is him in a more overt sense than typical eidolons. Even so, in a defiantly strange twist, Johnson does not completely collapse Mr. Rambler into his narrative self. For instance, in *Rambler* 18, he does not use his own marital experience to validate his perspective but rather relies on the gentlemanly conventions of experience and judgment. In not substituting a fictional eidolon's biography with Johnson's own, the text presents a noticeable gap and a play with the thinness of the veil. All of this disrupts the role of the eidolon, who is supposed to "point to the existence of *an* author" but not necessarily "meant to disclose the truth of *the* author."[28] By playing with this established form, Johnson calls attention to its performativity.

Johnson also overtly plays with the foundational feature of the gentleman's persona: his neutrality. To begin, he most definitely professes the required neutrality of a gentleman: the need to be "a kind of neutral being between the sexes" (*Rambler* 3:98.1750). Although such a declaration may seem rote, Kathleen Nulton Kemmerer shows how Johnson's proclaimed gender neutrality perhaps parodies Addison's "persistently calling that impartiality into question" in ways that "underscore . . . the difficulty of seeing the whole truth from one's own limited perspective, which is always inescapably gendered."[29] This is because Johnson even more frequently outs the literary currents of self-interest. Johnson once said to Boswell, "No man but a blockhead ever wrote, except for money."[30] But making this statement in private differs starkly from the alternative possibility of making it on the page. If "the authority of the eidolon comes from its *pose* of gentility, humour, or knowledge, not from intrinsic abilities associated with the anonymous author" (emphasis mine), then what matters is what is presented on the page.[31] On the page, Johnson frequently, though not always, refuses to play the part so easily. In *Rambler* 14, for example, he writes, "It is not difficult to conceive, however, that for many reasons a man writes much better than he lives" (*Rambler* 3:75.1750). Johnson also deliberately raises the reader's awareness of his posturing; in *Rambler* 93, he writes, "Criticks like all the rest of mankind, are frequently misled by interest" (*Rambler* 4:132.1751). This acknowledgment, what Helen Deutsch calls the "two-Johnson tradition," fits into the legacy of the gentleman author.[32]

Playing with another literary expectation, Johnson also rejected the posture of the gentleman by refusing to designate a "women's day" in *The Rambler*. In *Rambler* 34, he articulates that he has been "censured for not imitating the politeness of his predecessors, having hitherto neglected to take the ladies under his protection, and give them rules" (*Rambler* 3:129.1750). Throughout *The Spectator*, Addison and Steele criticize coquettes, bad women readers, lady gamblers, and so on. Here, Johnson calls out *The Spectator* and readers who seek to compare his *Rambler* to it, and his specific gesture to politeness is an unambiguous indictment of gentlemanliness. Speaking with women in a particular way, with a proper kind of condescension to their delicacy and interests was appropriate, and by not addressing them, Johnson, according to his readers, did not properly perform gentlemanliness. By calling out this departure, Johnson also directs attention to the apparatus for establishing literary, genteel masculinity.

Such resistance to gentlemanly periodicalizing marks an important shift in how Johnson perceived women readers and his own performance of masculinity. Johnson was acutely aware of the ways in which he did not fit the model of the gentleman. With his unruly body, physical tics, and middle-class upbringing, the "formal and moral transcendence of [Johnson's] literature resists but never quite detaches entirely from the famous deformities" of Johnson himself.[33] Although incredibly well read and versed in the classics and classical languages, Johnson lacked a university education. He also struggled financially for much of his career, and *The Rambler* itself was the product of financial necessity. Whereas previous authors may have dismissed this gap by performing neutrality and a disinterest they did not in fact possess, Johnson felt its weight. He knew from experience that this was performance, and the awareness of that dynamic and the anxiety that it produced manifest in his essays. Such a revelatory admission recognizes the distance between eidolon and author, if not also between authorship and life, but does not entirely preclude the transference of masculinity from authorial performance to the author himself. Although Johnson is still widely considered to be manly as an author and still an example of the transferable aspect of gendered performance, there is a recognition on his part that *this is a performance*.

The ever-present sense of his own performance shaped how Johnson related to women as readers. Some argue that Johnson's dismissal of gentlemanly, heterosocial benevolence signifies his misogyny or disinterest in women readers.[34] However, I am more inclined to agree with Kemmerer and Morrison that, instead of ignoring women readers, Johnson resists the gendered ideology claiming that some topics are beyond women's understanding.[35] Johnson was fairly liberal, if not radical, in his ideas about women's education and capacities, and he acknowledged the ways society was to blame for women's ignorance or superficiality.[36] Unlike *The Spectator*, which spends a great deal of time criticizing female types, Johnson presents human foibles that can appear in both men and women. He criticizes female card players in *Rambler* 15 but is equally critical of men's dissipation and wastefulness in *Rambler* 197. In *Rambler* 39–43, he defends women's rationality and acknowledges the "relationship of female rationality to male happiness."[37] There are nine essays in *The Rambler* addressing marriage and courtship; none are labeled as women's topics, and all include as many male correspondents as female ones.[38] Instead of distinguishing male from female topics and segregating his readership, Johnson presents his topics as being beneficial to all readers. This tendency becomes especially important for my rereading of Arabella's cure scene and her dialogue with the Doctor.

Johnson's different approach to women readers reflects cultural shifts about gender directly influenced by women's writing of masculinity. Although criticism was the gentleman's prerogative, he was no longer the exclusive moralizing voice. By the mid- and into the late century, "The beautiful and moral realm [had become] celebrated in gallant terms as the pseudo-literary field of women."[39] Women had gained a new kind of foothold in the terrain of the gentleman, particularly regarding the links between aesthetic and moral judgment. Whereas this moralizing function used to be more firmly planted in the gentleman's realm, such power began to shift owing to women's deployment of the performative features of the gentleman's masculinity for their own advantage.

There was room for other voices in the conversation, a reality that Johnson's essays recognize. For example, he emphasizes marriage as the likeliest source of human happiness, as well as of human misery, and often idealizes the domestic sphere and women's place therein. These markers are consistent with the courtship fiction written by women in the early eighteenth century, the difference being the moral and critical weight given to women. For instance, Johnson writes, "The men have, indeed, by their superiority of writing, been able to collect the evidence of many ages, and raise prejudices in their favour by the venerable testimonies of philosophers, historians, and poets" (*Rambler* 3:98.1750). In this way, authorship, as a masculine field, has empowered men and their representations of women. To me, Johnson's words seem to acknowledge how culture has become an accumulation of male narratives that have fed off each other and justified their own perspectives, in a kind of gendered echo chamber. To the ladies, by comparison, Johnson grants "the appeal of the passions" and a "more forcible operation than the reverence of antiquity," for even "if they have not so great a name on their side, they have stronger arguments"

(*Rambler* 3:98–99.1750). Johnson's dual awareness of the gendered production of literature, its critical value, and its authority, on the one hand, and the increased weight given to women, on the other, is a reflection of these cultural and critical shifts.

To a certain extent, these arguments have also obscured attention to what Johnson in fact writes. In *Rambler* 4, he does not identify women readers, as so many of his predecessors have, but uses the far more neutral language of "the young, the ignorant, and the idle." Nor does he call out women writers; instead, he is more concerned with the misleading nature of Henry Fielding's lovable rogues than with the wayward workings of women's pens. If we take Johnson's own interrogation of gentlemanly neutrality seriously, then it is entirely possible to read *Rambler* 4 as being addressed to a far more diversely gendered group. After all, if such neutrality and universality are a performance, then that performance or identification could be open to anybody. From there, the lines become more slippery. If Johnson plays at being a neutral being between two sexes while acknowledging the performative legacy of the position, then what is to stop others, namely women, from slipping into this role as well? The *Rambler* essays are not free of associations or context, but Johnson does not point us toward these contexts overtly. Instead, things hang, play, and resist simple categorization.

A Quixote Himself: Johnson and the Romance of Criticism

The second cloud hanging over Johnson's relationship to Lennox and *The Female Quixote* is the gendered criticism of romance. In discussions on *The Female Quixote*, Johnson's role is typically that of the anti-romance, masculine critic, which can largely be traced to an anecdote and to certain *Rambler* essays, particularly no. 4. As for the first, Boswell's *Life* relates Johnson's own fondness for romances and how, as a boy, "he was immoderately fond of reading romances of chivalry" and blamed "these extravagant fictions" for the "unsettled turn of mind which prevented his ever fixing in any profession."[40] This anecdote, reported in Johnson's biography and published far later, has been interpretively applied to *The Rambler* and led to generalizations such as, "In periodicals like *The Rambler*, Johnson spent a lot of time decrying romance as the . . . corruption of women."[41] It has thus become expedient to assume that Johnson reinforces romance as "the realm of excess and nonsense"—the realm of weak women readers and writers.[42]

However, as with his masculinity, Johnson's relationship to romance and romance's generic relationship to criticism are far more fluid. First, reading *Rambler* 4 as anti-romance is off the mark. The essay expresses much more anxiety about the emerging influence of what we term the "novel of formal realism" than about romance, and "contrary to the long historical tradition of romance criticism," Johnson denies romance the ability to exert dangerous influence.[43] This denial is entirely odd given romance's clear, profound influence on Johnson himself, both in anecdote and, more importantly, in how he imagined and structured literary criticism. For instance, in *Rambler* 2, only two publications earlier, Johnson claims that all readers are in some sense quixotes; similar to the "knight of La Mancha," "very few readers, amidst their mirth or pity, can deny that they have admitted visions of equally strange, or by means equally inadequate" (*Rambler* 3:9.1750). Throughout, Johnson likewise speaks about authorship and criticism in terms of gallantry. Imagining literary work as a kind of romance, the critic and the author are locked in a kind of knight-errant's struggle, and Johnson treats both figures with zest and satire. He also figures himself, both author and critic, as a kind of quixotic persona, one that is sometimes ridiculous, sometimes tragic, often heroic in intention, and, above all, performative.

Whenever Johnson positions criticism as being rational, even scientific, he does so by infusing the science with heroic romance imagery. Eithne Henson points out that even when Johnson, in *Rambler* 92, portrays criticism as being scientific, romance sneaks in: "Criticism reduces those regions of literature under the dominion of science, which have hitherto known only the anarchy of ignorance, the caprices of fancy, and the tyranny of prescription" (*Rambler* 3:144.1751). The images of overthrowing tyranny have strong ties to the knight-errant and his constant questing. In *Rambler* 3, Johnson follows that straightforward depiction of the author's morality with an "Allegory of Criticism," wherein the Goddess of Criticism—"the eldest daughter of Labour and of Truth"—gradually yields the immediate field to Time; in her absence her scepter is eventually tainted by Flattery and Malevolence, "and TIME passes his sentence at leisure, without any regard to their determinations" (*Rambler* 3:19.1750). She retreats "thenceforth to shed her influence from afar upon some select minds, fitted for its reception by learning and by virtue" (*Rambler* 3:16–18.1750). These select minds are described throughout *The Rambler* as being the "heroes of literature" (*Rambler* 3:17.1750).[44] The attainment of literary greatness is "garlands . . . gathered from summits equally difficult to climb with those that bear the civic or triumphal wreaths" (*Rambler* 3:117.1750). The allegory thus shows the proper duty "of the heroes in literature to enlarge the boundaries of knowledge by discovering and conquering new regions of the intellectual world" (*Rambler* 4:362.1751). In all of this figuring, Johnson transforms the polite, potentially mundane role of the moral critic and author into a heroic feat.

The gallant language of criticism is part of the legacy of women's influence over the gentleman and his literary function. During the eighteenth century, gallantry was both the language of criticism and courtship.[45] Mr. Spectator consistently addresses the ladies and declares them to be "the more powerful Part of our People" through "the just Complaisance and Gallantry of our Nation."[46] Such displays—deference to women and holding them up as vessels of virtue—are marks of the gentleman's politeness. As noted in chapters 1 and 2, this deference manifests in language that pays homage to women. Although I explore the gendered power dynamics of this configuration more fully in my reading of *The Female Quixote*, it bears highlighting that when Johnson positions the author and critic caught in a heroic struggle over virtue and truth, he draws on the language of gallantry. The true critic defends the Goddess of Criticism; the author and critic struggle for her favors. This arrangement is also the product of the woman author's pen; women novelists had so influenced the tone and structure of criticism that criticism had become linked to courtship. For decades, they had been positioning the gentleman within the courtship plot and increasingly positioning his literary authority via relationships with women, and by mid-century, the language had taken root in the structure of criticism.

Romance also lends itself to Johnson's more quixotic turns on criticism. At times, Johnson uses the same imagery of gallantry to satirize both the author and critic and thus imbues their "heroic" struggle with a quixotic tone. Such satirical potential was a recognizable function of romance as a genre, especially given the consistent, growing popularity of *Don Quixote* in the mid-eighteenth century.[47] In *Rambler* 176, the critic-author battle is "so powerfully ridiculous" that it takes on comedic overtones. Johnson continues, "Among the principal of comick calamities, may be reckoned the pain which an author, not yet hardened into insensibility, feels at the onset of a furious critick." A comedy of self-importance then ensues, in which the author, "full of the importance of his work, and anxious for the justification of every syllable, starts and kindles at the slightest attack," whereas the critic, "eager to establish his superiority, triumphing in every discovery of failure, and zealous to impress the cogency of his arguments, pursues him from line to line without cessation or remorse" (*Rambler* 5:164.1751). In these ways, the overly sensitive author and the zealous critic, caught tilting at each other's windmills, become figures of humor. It isn't that the struggle in authorship isn't virtuous to Johnson but that it descends into comedy when not pursued in its proper form.

My broader point is that Johnson uses romance, along with its influence on the language of criticism, as a multipurpose tool. I also argue that

Lennox similarly deploys romance but to far more pointed effect. Rather than reading Johnson or Lennox as pro-romance or anti-romance, I view them as participating in a dialogue on the structures of literature, gender, and criticism in which romance becomes an advantageous generic mode or symbol, one that readers and other authors recognize for its generic distinction. Furthermore, I want to showcase the ways in which romance is a flexible structure and made more so by the complex figure of the Quixote, who is not simply ridiculous, tragic, or celebratory but a multivalent, ever-shifting combination of the three.[48]

Johnson's romance-infused criticism uses three structures that Lennox interrogates and deploys in crucial ways. First, the satirical jabs at criticism, highlighted humorously by the language of gallantry, speak to the way criticism itself is somewhat arbitrary, at least compared with the more heroic act of authoring. Although Johnson is willing to laugh at both the author and the critic, he is often more critical of the critic. Within the paradigm of heroism, the author's "quiet and fame, and life and immortality are involved in the controversy," whereas the critic "hazards little": "The critick's purpose is to conquer, the author only hopes to escape" (*Rambler* 5:164–165.1752). The critic is by nature peripheral and his glory less than the author's because it requires less risk. Likewise, whereas Johnson protects hackneyed authors, he bashes bad critics.[49] In *Rambler* 158, he notes that good writing does not stem from critics, whose primary authority is based on "no other merit than that having read the works of great authors with attention" but who nevertheless expect "honour and reverence for precepts which they never could have invented" (*Rambler* 5:76.1751).[50] Although the error of critics initially seems trivial, Johnson points out that creating rules for literature based on convention instead of creation leads to generic stagnation.

Second, Johnson's own criticism was suspicious of conventional literary hierarchies, if not antagonistic toward them. On some level, Johnson demonstrated the proper masculine rigor of the critic—a good critic—by being the knight-errant taking on giants. Later, as explored in the coda, Johnson became even more pointed in his criticism of the literary giants of English literature: Milton, Dryden, Pope, and so on. Even in *The Rambler*, the narrator takes on the emerging literary canon. In *Rambler* 94, in one of his many critiques of Milton, Johnson writes, "Those who are determined to find in Milton an assemblage of all the excellencies which have ennobled all other poets, will perhaps be offended that I do not celebrate his versification in higher terms" (*Rambler* 4:142.1751). If Johnson's criticism of critics is their slavish devotion to the works of previous or established authors, it makes sense that he resisted the same in his own practice.[51] Johnson repeatedly points out—again, often in his criticism of Milton—that our assessment of language and its beauties changes.[52] It is the critic's task to sift through this change, to acknowledge the contextual nature of language and art, and to question the established rules of society and of literature if they do not serve the higher goals of authorship and virtue. In Johnson's text, such antiestablishment potential is deployed by a male writer who was an outsider but became part of the establishment. This structure is something that Lennox not only engaged with in her relationship to Johnson but simultaneously explored and exploded in *The Female Quixote*.

Third and last, Johnson's criticism leaves gaps between the value of criticism and gender. Despite a core association between masculinity and criticism in Johnson's *Rambler*—manly struggles of valor and all that—he does not write that men alone can engage in such struggles, and Lennox plays on his omission. Whereas criticism in general is merely implied to be masculine, failed criticism is made explicitly masculine. There are the shallow wits: "Men who have flattered themselves into this opinion of their own abilities ... and fruitlessly endeavouring to remedy their barrenness by incessant cultivation, or succour their feebleness by subsidiary strength" (*Rambler* 5:55.1751). Such men have access to all of the privileges afforded to men regarding education and supposed literary ability but have not cultivated their judgment or intellect into learning,[53] nor have they developed their conversation or politeness, which is the province of the gentleman and the influence of women.

Johnson's depictions of criticism and authorship do not escape gendered power structures either, for he uses romance language with strong ties to the language of gallantry. The critic should protect his readers, guard their virtue, and court their favor. Thus, when Johnson introduces his periodical and his authorship in *Rambler* 1, he compares his entrance as an author with that of an eager lover. Eager for praise, the author stepping onto the literary stage risks becoming one "who too soon professes himself a lover," which "raises obstacles to his own wishes"; by contrast, "those whom disappointments have taught experience, endeavour to conceal their passion till they believe their mistress wishes for the discovery" (*Rambler* 3:5–6.1750). This language positions the author, as well as the critic, as a masculine gallant or gentleman who lowers himself to beseech his reader, who is figured as feminine. It also creates a system that dictates the interdependence of the genders and the subordination of women. Johnson does not overcome this system in his language, and it is this aspect of his depiction of criticism that Lennox brings to the surface and reforms in her novel. What enabled this slippage was the way in which the gentleman was defined in context and in performance, neither of which was Johnson's invention. Women had made room for the unwieldy man of letters as long as he played the part. But when

Johnson rambled into the role, he also widened the gap, and Lennox capitalized on it. She took advantage of his anxiety about the connections between masculinity and literary authority to create a wider field encompassing an array of critics orbiting around a female author. She revealed the hegemonic systems that govern authorship while at once exploiting the cracks in them.

The Female Quixote: Criticism as Courtship

It seems entirely possible and even likely that *The Rambler* owes some of its style of criticism to *The Female Quixote*. Although Lennox's novel was published after the bulk of Johnson's periodical, Lennox and Johnson would have been preparing and working on their pieces with considerable overlap. As Carlile points out, "The themes of Johnson's *Rambler*, charity, good humour, and idleness, point to a lifelong preoccupation with life choices, a theme in *Harriot Stuart* as well."[54] Lennox finished *The Life of Harriot Stuart* in 1750 and published it in 1751, after which she would have written *The Female Quixote* before its release in early 1752. Upon its publication, Johnson famously crowned Lennox with a garland, thereby marking her, a woman writer, as a hero. In that same span of time, Johnson would have been writing and publishing *The Rambler* (1750–1752), in which he characterized authors as heroes deserving of laurels. It is also the era when he offered the knight of La Mancha as a model for readers, which connects reading and romance in the context of Lennox's first and second novels, both of which play upon romance conventions and themes. Although no letters conveniently state that Johnson's portrayal of the author as the reader's lover or his comic jab at the fashionable would-be critic were created in tandem with Lennox's portrayal of Glanville or Sir George, the similarity in theme is undeniable. Ideas do not exist in a vacuum, and it is unreasonable to assume that simply because Johnson's ideas appeared in print first that Lennox was merely responding to them so shortly afterward. Given their relationship, it is far more probable that their ideas emerged in dialogue between them, which is how I hope to present their ideas in what follows despite the necessity of acknowledging the chronology of their works.

The great question surrounding *The Female Quixote* has traditionally been whether Lennox's text criticizes romance or subversively embraces its feminocentric storytelling as speaking the "truth of female desire."[55] In going back and forth between these interpretations, critics have landed at every point along its spectrum.[56] However, we may alternatively ask how the gesture of including a distinct generic style—romance—illuminates gender and literary dynamics in the cultural relations between the author and the critic.[57] My central argument is that Lennox's novel dramatizes the gendered structures of eighteenth-century literary criticism and interrogates the language of gallantry as a critical mode associated with the gentleman critic.[58] Arabella and Glanville's courtship is fundamentally a prolonged debate of literary criticism, in which Arabella, the metaphorical female author, is critiqued by the gentleman critic, Glanville, as well as by various other characters. Within this structure, Lennox reworks the characterization of criticism from *The Rambler*. I argue that Lennox directs attention to the gendered implications of such gallant, heroic criticism by recasting the author, one of the "heroes of literature," as a would-be romance heroine, and thus emphasizes the ways in which criticism and its language of gallantry infuse the gendered relations between female authors and their gentleman critics with the power dynamic of courtship. Instead of reading *The Female Quixote* as situated at odds between the modern novel and the romance, I believe that Lennox uses the genres to depict the rigid expectations set for women writers, who, as the heroines of both, are expected to perform extreme, unrealistic forms of virtue and to gratefully accept the supposedly benevolent attentions of their male critics. Lennox then plays on the performative revelations, cracks in Johnson's gentlemanly persona, and constructs her own gentleman critic, all to reveal that some of the best critics are in fact women.

Lennox uses romance to establish that Arabella functions as a metaphorical figure for female authorship. Although critics have frequently read Arabella as a model for female readership, far less attention has been given to registering her as an author.[59] Arabella's "determination to create significance" is a fundamental desire of the quixote: to live out plot and seek narrative.[60] It is also the author's desire. Arabella not only seeks her own plot but also repeatedly exacts the authorial prerogative to rewrite the world to fit her own generic vision, one that plays upon Johnson's call to authors to create virtuous tales. Catherine Craft labels what I call "authorial prerogative" as a "refashioning of histories": "Arabella . . . not only refashions history, but also rewrites the stories of the women around her. She transforms Miss Groves into an unfortunate innocent lady . . . and turns a prostitute into a persecuted maiden, in defiance of the horrified Glanville."[61] In both episodes, Arabella creates fiction, and there is something decidedly *Rambler*-esque about her fictional impulses. Both of these episodes—Miss Groves's history in book 2 and the disguised mistress in book 9—have their own generic tone, namely one of amatory fiction. Miss Groves has been seduced by a rake, had two children out of wedlock, and is now in a secret marriage. Meanwhile, the officer's mistress is illicitly disguised in boy's clothes as she accompanies her lover in a public garden. Arabella rewrites both women as virtuous romance heroines, and, in doing so, she does not "so mingle good and bad qualities in their principal personages, that they are both equally conspicuous" (*Rambler* 3:23.1750). She may not represent life precisely as it is, but she commits to creating stories of intense virtue, which is, at least in theory, the duty of the mid-century author. Romance thus becomes the mode of Arabella's authorship and functions as a generic marker of authorial production.

If we accept Arabella as an author figure, then her commitment to romance brings important attention to the gendered dynamics of criticism and the role that masculinity plays in this dynamic. After all, Arabella's body is unambiguously aligned with and genders her authorship. In other parts of this book, I have resisted the alignment of the female author's body with her text; however, I believe that Lennox deliberately invites us to link Arabella's body with her desire for authorship, which is the desire to have a history of her own and to plot out her own life, all translated through the desire to be beloved. This desire was also common for critics, who would approach text in the language of gallantry or courtship. By aligning Arabella's body with her text and authorship, Lennox brings attention to the gendered dynamics of this phenomenon and uses it to revise the power dynamics between the woman author and the gentleman critic.

For Johnson, the author and the critic are combatants and mutual "heroes of literature." However, the structure changes when the author becomes a heroine instead of a hero. As Janet Todd points out, Arabella is limited because "activity in the world can only concern her relations with men—she cannot ride abroad like the Don or even tumble in inns like the quixotic Tom Jones."[62] A heroine, even a romance one, must in some sense take a passive role in her adventures in order to maintain the presentation of her unimpeachable virtue. The same is also true in terms of female authorship, the burdens and boundaries of which Lennox addresses through Arabella's quixotism. First, to escape charges of prostitution and justify the virtuous aspect of their economic needs, women authors were expected to demonstrate a disinterested, unimpeachable, yet vulnerable character.[63] However, this character is the same as the one performed earlier in the eighteenth century by the gentleman author. As Catherine Gallagher argues, the moral aspects of authorship were newly transferrable to women in the mid-century when a "new disinterestedness and high-mindedness was imputed to women as a sex."[64] Such "new disinterestedness" was the product of how women such as Mary Davys and Eliza Haywood co-opted and utilized the gentleman's persona in their fiction. Although such use yielded results, it also came with performative consequences. The extreme demands of romance's standards of female virtue thus also highlight the hyperbolic commands of eighteenth-century femininity, especially for women writers.

Mr. Glanville: A Gentleman Critic

Linking the language of gallantry with criticism to Arabella as a female author figure urges new interest in the often overlooked Mr. Glanville. Despite being the novel's leading man, Glanville has routinely been passed over for *The Female Quixote*'s more colorful characters: Arabella, Charlotte, Sir George, and even the Countess and the Doctor, both of whom appear abruptly and only briefly at the novel's end. By contrast, Glanville has been read either as the bland vehicle of patriarchy—as Mr. Blandville—or damned with faint praise.[65] He is better than "those suitors whom tyrannical fathers or guardians impose on romance heroines,"[66] and "his non-interference and his continuing concern prov[e] him more acceptable than others."[67] However, combining Arabella as an author figure with the courtship-infused discourse of criticism repositions Glanville as *the* gentleman critic of the novel, whose relationship to Arabella becomes a metaphor for the relationship between the woman writer and the gentleman critic.

Glanville is without a doubt a gentleman. He is polite, avoids gossip, and spends a great deal of the novel attempting to protect Arabella from ridicule. He has also read as a gentleman; he can discourse on "*Grecian* History" with Arabella for hours, and he has also read Richardson and Johnson, specifically *The Rambler*.[68] He enters the novel "having just returned from his Travels," which has completed his experience of the world (*FQ* 27). Bar Arabella, he is the most dexterous conversationalist because he takes "a great deal of Pains to turn the Discourse upon Subjects, on which" Arabella "could expatiate, without any Mixture of that Absurdity" (*FQ* 153). Despite her romantically principled resistance to her father's choice, even Arabella has "too much Discernment not to see Mr. *Glanville* had a great deal of Merit; his Person was perfectly handsome; he possessed a great Share of Understanding, an easy Temper, and a Vivacity which charmed every one" (*FQ* 30). In short, Glanville checks all of the boxes.

Lennox clearly links her gentleman lead to Johnson's mode of criticism, and it shifts our perspective on Glanville's desire for Arabella's reform. He approaches her and his courtship with a desire to mediate between her and the wider world, which marks him not only as a reader but a critic. His desire is not simply a conservative gesture of the benevolent gentleman seeking the best for the female reader but a revelation of the gentleman critic's lack of neutrality, his self-interest, and his compulsive need for self-justification. Johnson reveals the performative nature of the gentleman critic's neutrality by openly and repeatedly declaring that critics are also motivated by self-interest. He writes, "There are prejudices which authors, not otherwise weak or corrupt, have indulged without scruple; and perhaps some of them are so complicated with our natural affections, that they cannot easily be disentangled [sic] from the heart" (*Rambler* 4:132.1751). Lennox's courtship narrative makes this feature of the gentleman critic explicit. In the role, Glanville has a vested interest in reforming Arabella's literary ambitions to his liking; he will receive only part of her fortune if she refuses to marry him, but acquire it all if she agrees. He wants her to abandon her romances so that she will not demand such great sacrifices of him and therefore yield to her father's injunction to marry him. Put differently, he wants to rewrite her into a less stylistically extreme version of the courtship plot. Moreover, similar to the Johnsonian critic, Glanville's emotions are not presented as nefarious, but they are indeed entangled and absolutely self-interested.

This self-interest is linked to the critic's and the gentleman's need for self-justification. Johnson writes in *The Rambler* that critics, unlike authors, need to justify their existence, which explains why they so desperately seek to intervene in manuscripts. In *Rambler* 23, Johnson describes how differently critics behave with a published novel versus a manuscript. Whereas a published book "is considered as permanent and unalterable; and the reader ... accommodates his mind to the author's design ... often contented without pleasure, and pleased without perfection," if the text remains a manuscript, then the critic "considers himself obliged to show, by some proof of his abilities, that he is not consulted to no purpose, and, therefore, watches every opening for objection" (*Rambler* 3:127.1750). Just as a critic approaches a manuscript, Glanville approaches Arabella assuming that she needs his intervention in order to protect her from the public: "Her Character was so ridiculous, that he could propose nothing to himself but eternal Shame and Disquiet, in the Possession of a Woman, for whom he must always blush, and be in Pain" (*FQ* 117). Glanville's criticism is marked by self-interest, as well as self-justification, for he needs Arabella to reform or else possessing her, despite her other merits, would reflect poorly on him. However, Lennox also reveals the dependent position of the gentleman critic, as Glanville serves no textual or narrative purpose without Arabella. He, just as with the critics in *The Rambler*, is markedly secondary. He produces no plot or action but only comments and reacts to the plots of others, usually Arabella's. In seeking to reform her, Glanville justifies his narrative presence. As Lennox interweaves the gentleman's dependence on women with the critic's dependence on authors, criticism becomes a courtship wherein the gentleman critic has no choice but to depend on the woman writer for production.

Through *The Female Quixote*'s courtship structure, Lennox interrogates the superficiality of gallantry as a rhetoric for criticism. In particular, she reflects the ways in which this discourse is limiting for women writers and constricts their work within the cultural conversation. As a romance heroine, Arabella is inured to the language of gallantry. When Sir George takes the opportunity of "saying a hundred gallant Things to her . . . she received [them] with great Indifference; the most extravagant Compliments being what she expected from all Men." Arabella accepts flattery as her due, and "provided [Glanville] did not directly presume to tell her they loved her, no Sort of Flattery or Adulation could displease her" (*FQ* 119). In a real way, Arabella's quixotism is a quixotism of gallant criticism. By way of her heroine, Lennox takes the flattering language of courtship and criticism at its word and, in turn, takes advantage of Johnson's humorous play with the language of gallantry. Lennox takes the language to comedic extremes, but the joke is less on Arabella than the gentleman, because the woman writer is merely taking the gentleman critic at his word. His flattery is expected because it is conventional.

Lennox reveals the coded power structure of this critical framework. Whereas for Johnson criticism takes on the form of combat—between author and critic—for Lennox the conflict is packaged as courtship. Although the contest accommodates the role of heroine and her would-be lovers, Lennox continues to capture the combative undertone of this gendered relationship. When male authors and critics establish their gentlemanly credentials through their gallant treatment of women, they present themselves as subservient: Hume presents himself as a supplicant to the rulers of the polite sphere and Mr. Spectator as the benevolent caretaker of his women readers. However, coded within this structure is male-dominated power. Just as with courtship, the gentleman's slavishness is a "temporary subordination" that he uses to achieve his own ends and empower his own status. Though the male lover courts his lady with gallant words and subservience to her wishes, such displays disappear once they marry. Likewise, the gentleman author, reader, and critic can "defend his generous attention to women as the actions of a benevolent patriarch."[69] On some level, the obsequiousness of the gentleman's politeness is a veil for the power dynamics of gender relations because it is also the language of courtship. This was also, metaphorically, a dominant structure of literary agency. The critic courts the author by praising and seeking their approval, but the author's power can be transitory, which is exactly what lurks beneath the surface of Arabella's deferred courtship narrative.

In the tension between what Arabella wants and what men want from her, there is a struggle for whose vision will win the day, a struggle that reflects the conflict between the woman writer and the gentleman critic. An awareness of this configuration is built into Arabella's desire for romance itself. After her father declares his desire that she marry Glanville, Arabella is taken aback: "Tho' she always intended to marry some time or other, as all the Heroines had done, yet she thought such an Event ought to be brought about with an infinite deal of Trouble" (*FQ* 27). Deferral is the prerequisite for narrative. While Glanville, similar to Mr. Spectator, laments how coquettes think "it a mortal Injury done to their Charms, if the Men about them have Eyes or Ears for any Object but their faces," his desire to possess Arabella is frustrated by her refusal to hear such talk or to receive such compliments as anything but her due (*FQ* 148). If she, as an author, is worthy of love and consideration, then it is due to her virtue and beauty, not the critic's intervention. By accepting but also resisting the gallantry of the critic, Arabella also resists this gendered power structure.

Lennox also uses her heroine to disrupt the critical and gendered power structure of gallantry. By denying Glanville the language of courtship, Arabella pushes him into a discourse that highlights her diverse abilities as an author figure. Glanville is forced to talk to Arabella about a much wider variety of topics than the typically feminine ones of love, courtship, and domesticity. The pair has the most extended dialogues in the novel, with the possible exception of Arabella and the Doctor's conversation at the end. Their first extended exchange, occurring after Arabella has stopped attempting to banish Glanville for offending her, addresses the obligations created by love. Arabella wins the debate, because Glanville agrees to abide by her rules and stop speaking to her about love until she gives him permission. From then on, they speak of Greek history, the nature of beauty, and the proper use of raillery;[70] Arabella's advice on the proper use of raillery, which could be lifted from *The Rambler* or *The Spectator*, is given an entire chapter. Here, when the gentleman critic quits insisting that the woman writer respond to his gallantry, he finds that she can discourse on all the vital topics that her male peers can but that she often does it better. In Glanville's eyes, Arabella shifts from being superior to other women to being superior to everybody. Early in the novel, Glanville repeatedly praises her in comparison to other women; however, as the text progresses, Arabella is increasingly compared with traditionally masculine figures.[71] Sir Charles proclaims that she "speak[s] like an Orator" and that "if she had been a Man, she would have made a great Figure of Parliament" (*FQ* 269, 311). These compliments "give great Joy to *Glanville*" because others see the same merit in Arabella that he sees (*FQ* 311). Lennox thus charts a path whereby the woman writer, once freed from the constraints of the criticism of gallantry, can be heard and valued on the same grounds as her male peers and applauded by the gentleman critic for it.

Although the courtship structure reveals the gendered tension within criticism, Lennox also deploys her gentleman critic to serve her own authorial ends. Glanville's role as critic evolves and is ultimately less top-down than it might first appear. Despite being entangled in his own self-interest, he ends up highlighting Arabella's superiority to other authors and critic figures in the novel. Lennox parrots Johnson through her gentleman critic to interrogate male literary privilege and shift the balance of power to the woman writer and critic. If the courtship dynamic echoes Johnson's humor, then Glanville's criticism of male literary figures in the novel plays upon Johnson's suspicions of literary hierarchies, as well as his performance anxiety, and ultimately exploits the widening gap between the critic and masculinity.

Arabella's first rival is Sir George, the "deceitful upper-class gentleman of leisure" and the character that critics have most frequently identified with authorship in Lennox's novel given his attempt to woo Arabella by constructing his own romance history.[72] But what prompts Sir George's history is Glanville's criticism of his character. Adopting decidedly Johnsonian tones, Glanville—in one of his longest speeches of the novel—sharply criticizes Sir George as a "Critic at the *Bedford* Coffee-house." Sir George is a "Demy-wit," and he and his other fashionable brethren "sit in Judgment upon the Productions of a *Young*, a *Richardson*, or a *Johnson*. Rail with premeditated Malice at the *Rambler*; and, for the want of Faults, turn even its inimitable Beauties into Ridicule: The Language, because it reaches to Perfection, may be called stiff, laboured, and pedantic; the Criticisms, when they let in more Light than your weak Judgment can bear, superficial and ostentatious Glitter . . . then give shrewd Hints, that some Persons, though they do not publish their Performances, may have more Merit, than those that do" (*FQ* 253). Seeming to echo *The Rambler*, Glanville renders Sir George as the image of the "swarm of reasoners . . . who, instead of endeavoring by books and meditation to form their own opinions, content themselves with the secondary knowledge, which a convenient bench in a coffee-house can supply" (*Rambler* 4:281.1751).[73] Glanville's criticism of Sir George's coffee-house critiques especially echo *Rambler* 2, in which Johnson writes, "Censure is willingly indulged, because it always implies some superiority . . . a train of sentiments generally received enables him to shine without labour, and to conquer without a contest" (*Rambler* 3:9.1750). Sir George, "shin[ing] without labour," mimics the genres and writings of others and criticizes established authors while producing nothing of merit himself.

By presenting Sir George as an author figure and subjecting him to Glanville's criticism, Arabella's authorial merit becomes clearer by contrast. In *Rambler* 93, Johnson writes, "For the duty of criticism is neither to depreciate, nor dignify by partial representations, but to hold out the light of reason, whatever it may discover; and to promulgate the determinations of truth, whatever she shall dictate" (*Rambler* 4:134.1751). The critic's job is to reveal the merit of an author or text to readers, which is precisely what Glanville does. Glanville recognizes that Sir George is not only a hack but a dangerous one, whereas Arabella is an author who commits fully to virtue. Arabella's own virtue shines forth in scenes such as the one with Sir George. She is not taken in by his story; she believes that it is true, but she sees his lack of virtue, which highlights her own virtue and understanding. As Johnson writes in *Rambler* 4, "Virtue is the highest proof of understanding, and the only solid basis of greatness; and that vice is the natural consequence of narrow thoughts" (*Rambler* 3:25.1750). Motivated by greed, Sir George is an author of narrow thoughts and thus an inferior author to Arabella, whose "Charms of Mind and Person" make her Follies seem "inconsiderable and weak" (*FQ* 117). In this way, Arabella collapses the divide between Johnson's author and his writing. In *Rambler* 168, Johnson writes, "Those who profess the most zealous adherence to truth are forced to admit that [truth] owes part of her charms to her ornaments, and loses much of her power over the soul, when she appears disgraced by a dress uncouth or ill-adjusted" (*Rambler* 5:126.172). Arabella's authorship is like this truth; her beauty and ornaments afford a power over the souls of others but only if she is virtuous.

Lennox also uses Glanville to amplify the performative aspects of the gentleman critic. In his long-winded critique of Sir George, Glanville immediately sounds like Johnson, especially in the length of his sentences and his emphasis on light and virtue. However, rather than viewing the moment as a bow to the gentleman critic, I understand it as Lennox's playing with his performativity, as her callout to *The Rambler* in the voice of its narrator demonstrates. Lennox can parrot Johnson, both suddenly and deliberately, and thereby highlight the superiority of her heroine-author over the would-be male hack. Her deliberate explosion of Johnsonian language in Glanville's critique is only the first of many times when Lennox demonstrates her ability to play the part of Johnson for her own gains.

In her characterization of Mr. Selvin, Lennox also calls out the hierarchy of learning that has lent credibility to the gentleman critic. Once again, Glanville's voice indicates how we should judge the would-be scholar-critic. When Glanville calls attention to Mr. Selvin's "Custom to mark in his Pocket-Book all the Scraps of History he heard introduced into

Conversation, and retail them again in other Company," Mr. Selvin becomes a comedic send-up of the gentleman's claim to literary authority based on education, specifically classical knowledge, and the effect fully illuminates the superficiality of the gendered implications of knowledge (*FQ* 273).[74] Mr. Selvin "*affected* to be thought deep-read in History, and never failed to take all Opportunities of displaying his Knowledge of Antiquity, which was indeed but *very superficial*" (*FQ* 264, emphasis mine). In satirizing Mr. Selvin, Lennox challenges one of the great bastions of the gentleman's critical authority: his classical education. Although the gentleman's experiential knowledge was meant to distinguish him from the pedant, a crucial feature of his critical voice was his classical education.[75] By revealing how superficial and silly Mr. Selvin is, Lennox calls out these markers of masculine literary privilege. In fact, she equates the grand masculine domain of the classics with the supposedly feminine field of gossip and superficial coffeehouse echoes. Mr. Selvin does not fundamentally differ from the blabby beau Mr. Tinsel, for both comment primarily on the sexual escapades of women. Mr. Tinsel tells the "Histories" of some scandalous ladies at the ball, while Mr. Selvin recounts the "history" of Princess Julia, who, "Tho' the Daughter of an Emperor, she was, pardon the Expression, the most abandon'd Prostitute in *Rome*" (*FQ* 274, 273). Lennox reveals that what the classical version of history reinforces is exactly the social purpose of gossip: patriarchal control over women's bodies. Here again is a gendered echo of Johnson's own suspicions of literary hierarchies and establishments. Perhaps Lennox also nods to Johnson's own ability to demonstrate such learning without the proper pedigree.

The criticism of Mr. Selvin again reveals the superiority of Arabella's literary force. Instead of studying deeply, Mr. Selvin has memorized a few "Anecdotes by Heart"; he seeks "Attention" rather than actual knowledge (*FQ* 264). He resembles one of Johnson's coffeehouse critics, one of the "Echoes" who "adopt the criticisms and remarks" from learned individuals (*Rambler* 4:281.1751). Glanville notes that Mr. Selvin has written down Arabella's romance versions of historical figures such as Julia and Cleopatra, and he does "not doubt [Mr. Selvin] would make a Figure with the curious Circumstances *Arabella* had furnish'd him with" (*FQ* 273). The woman author thus reveals the superficiality of the pendant's supposedly masculine knowledge.

After critiquing the representatives of traditionally masculine literary privilege, Glanville serves his most valuable critical function: validating women's voices and knowledge. Although he admires the Doctor, the most frequent recipients of Glanville's critical approval are women, particularly Arabella and the Countess, both of whom precede and potentially exceed the Doctor in Glanville's estimation. His praise of Arabella only grows throughout the novel. Likewise, when the Countess enters the scene, Glanville's approval of her and desire for her assistance create a scenario in which a woman can be just as effective and insightful a critic as a man. Lennox's description of the Countess is especially pointed: "This Lady, who among her own Sex had no Superior in Wit, Elegance, and Ease, was inferior to very few of the other in Sense, Learning, and Judgment" (FQ 322). The Countess has wit and elegance, as well as sense, learning, and judgment, all of which Runge identifies as the exclusively masculine realms of the critic. Seemingly deliberately, the parallel descriptions of the Countess's features enable Lennox to create a female character defined by her possession of critical faculties. In Glanville's estimation as gentleman critic, women frequently outperform the men in criticism; Lennox thus uses her own gentleman to make room for women to have valuable critical voices.

Although Mr. Glanville validates Arabella, her literary sway is not determined by his influence. The woman writer does not need the gentleman critic the way he needs her. For instance, she finds Sir George at fault for lacking virtue in his own romance history; regarding genre, he does not live up to her more expert criticism, experience, or standards. Similarly, while Glanville fears society's reception of Arabella, especially as represented by the superficial Selvins and Tinsels, Arabella's literary force is undeniable, as clarified when she attends her first ball. After hearing of her unusual dress in the style of Princess Julia, society is ready to pounce on Arabella: "It is not to be doubted but much Mirth was treasur'd up for her Appearance . . . when the Sight of the devoted fair One repell'd . . . the designed Ridicule of the whole Assembly." However, everyone is "aw'd to Respect by the irresistible Charm in the Person of *Arabella*, which commanded Reverence and Love from all who beheld her" (FQ 272). Literally dressed in her own generic authorship, Arabella sways the public with her literal and metaphorical textual beauty. Glanville's critical fear that society will ridicule Arabella is largely unfounded. Instead, Glanville functions, like a good critic should, as a guide not for the author but for the reader. We take nods from him about these subpar male literary figures and increasingly see the social world, not Arabella, as the joke of the novel.

Reform as Critical Dialogue

Perpetually looming over any analysis of *The Female Quixote* is Arabella's reform because it feels as if the male characters get their way. Arabella, the wayward female Quixote, is reformed at the intervention of the Doctor and to the benefit of Glanville. However, in recontextualizing Lennox's relationship with Johnson and by tracking how Lennox uses the gentleman critic to interrogate and restructure some of this masculine authority, I want to rethink the novel's ending not as the deus ex machina of masculinity but as a dialogue that culminates in both acknowledging the authority of women writers and feminine genres, while also addressing the limits placed on them and their writing.

Arabella is not the first character to undergo a reform; Glanville reforms first. In his reform, Lennox positions the woman writer as an incredibly influential figure, one who, rather than yielding to her male critic, makes him first adapt and defer to her. Glanville indeed ends up yielding to Arabella's romance codes. As Laurie Langbauer and Eve Tavor Bannet acknowledge, Arabella is a compelling force who blurs the lines between quixotism and reality through the sheer force of her presence. She is incredibly beautiful, virtuous, and wealthy, all of which create "the need to please her ... [and] force polite and desiring men to do her wishes, even against their better judgment."[76] Arabella's delusion is supposedly that all men, or at least a significant majority of them, will fall in love with her, and that their love will dictate their actions. However, "Arabella ... is very much a romance heroine."[77] Most of the men who meet her desire her, both for her incredible beauty and wealth, and several of them perform complicated maneuvers to attempt to win her favor. Among them, Mr. Hervey unsuccessfully attempts to send letters to her through Lucy in book 1, while Sir George fabricates his own romance history for all of book 6 and both creates and executes the complicated Princess of Gaul ruse in book 11. In the same book, Glanville spies Sir George and a veiled lady whom he believes to be Arabella emerging from a secluded cottage. Glanville reacts with all the righteous jealousy of a romance hero: "Transported with Rage at this Sight, he snatch'd up his Sword, flew down the Stairs into the Garden, and came running like a Madman up the Walk in which the Lovers were" (*FQ* 357). As displayed by his jealous duel with Sir George, Glanville has embraced the rules and interpretive structures of romances. The gentleman critic has not reshaped the woman writer to his taste but adapted to hers. Similar to the crowd awed by Arabella at the ball, the gentleman critic is ultimately swayed by her force, which can be viewed as one of the benefits of paying attention to the supposedly innocuous gentlemen.

In part, Glanville's critical authority validates supposedly feminine genres of reading and authorship. Rather than uniformly declaring romance to be a dangerous and superficial genre, Glanville's critical perspective validates or decries romance based on authorship, and his endorsement falls along surprisingly gendered lines. Whereas Sir George's romance is ridiculed as manipulative, Glanville continually remarks on the inherent virtue of Arabella's motives and therefore her narrative, despite his personal frustrations with her plots. Likewise, whereas Sir George uses romance reading in a bid to manipulate Arabella, Glanville presents the Countess as a critical authority and potential paragon, partly because of her romance reading. The Countess knows "the Language of Romance" and can return Arabella's "Compliment in a Strain as heroick as hers" (*FQ* 325). In this way, the Countess brings knowledge and insight to her interactions with Arabella that Glanville himself lacks. Her romance knowledge is valuable, whereas Sir George's is superficial. What emerges is a pattern of the gentleman critic's valuing romance when deployed by women and criticizing its use by nefarious men. On the one hand, the pattern reinforces the categorization of romance as a feminine genre. On the other, it marks women's increasing critical and moral authority in the literary landscape. In Glanville, we have a crucial representation of the gentleman critic's prioritizing the authority of women and an acknowledgment that what is flawed is not the genre but its usage.

If we read Glanville as reforming and revising his stance on genre and authorship first, then we can reconsider the final debate between the Doctor and Arabella in a more nuanced light. The Doctor is not the text's sole voice of authority despite having long been read as the representative of Johnson and male control, a critical perspective that frequently overlooks the structure of the dialogue between Arabella and the Divine. The Doctor, far from always being in control of himself or the discussion, makes several missteps throughout the dialogue and is often "completely embarrass'd" (*FQ* 370). The tone of the dialogue deliberately departs from the structure of gallantry as the Doctor gets carried away by "Vehemence . . . [and finds] himself entangled" several times throughout the debate (*FQ* 374). He explains that he is "accustom'd to speak to Scholars [with] Scholastick Ruggedness" and worries that "in the Heat of Argument" he will depart from the "Respect to which [Arabella has] so great a Right, and give Offence to a Person I am really afraid to displease" (*FQ* 371). The Doctor speaks to Arabella not as a vulnerable, subordinate female reader but as a critical counterpart capable of withstanding a more combative style. Permitting him to proceed, she asserts that she is "content . . . to obtain Truth upon harder terms" (*FQ* 372). The response marks the Doctor, like Johnson and Lennox, as an outsider who is hostile to traditional genteel structures and who is not a gentleman but gains his authority nonetheless.

The power dynamics in the dialogue do not exclusively or even primarily privilege the Doctor. Instead, Arabella gives as good as she gets and is repeatedly positioned as being the more compelling, collected, and capable participant in the discussion. Declaring her superiority, the Doctor states outright, "Madam . . . whoever is admitted to your Conversation, will be convinc'd that you enjoy all that Intellectual Excellence can confer" (*FQ* 370). Rather than being browbeaten and led by the proverbial wrist, Arabella sets the terms of the debate and of the Doctor's proofs and tasks him with proving that romances are "Fictions," "that they are absurd," and "that they are Criminal" (*FQ* 374). In many ways, the impulse to read the exchange as masculine manipulation comes from a misunderstanding of Johnson and Lennox's relationship and from assumptions that a woman writer would not have felt capable or socially able to take on the giant Johnson. As noted above, such thinking does not accurately capture Lennox and Johnson's dynamic.

By contrast, I read the final dialogue as representing their relationship as one of dialectical equals. After all, the timing of the writing of *The Female Quixote* and *The Rambler* allows for such discussions to be part of the authors' real-life literary and philosophical exchanges. To be clear, I do not read the discussion as being between Arabella as Lennox and the Doctor as Johnson but as a dialectical representation of two literary figures philosophically playing with and debating values and critical ideas. Although the Doctor indeed sounds like Johnson: "Arabella and the good doctor reason much alike."[78] Arabella has also espoused Johnsonian ideas throughout the novel—in one instance, by declaring to Mr. Tinsel that vice ought only be shown "to make its Deformity appear more hideous"[79]—ideas that the Doctor has not given to her (*FQ* 277). She engages with him on this terrain, ground on which she has already been validated by Glanville as a compelling authority. In this light, the debate is not Johnson's defeat of Lennox but a representation of how literary criticism can be voiced and engaged with by multiple people. This is Lennox's ultimate message. She has used her gentleman to position two nongentlemen, namely an unwieldy, aggressive man and a confident woman writer, as the novel's ultimate authorities on literary criticism.

Critics are right about one thing: the ending of *The Female Quixote* feels unsatisfying. When Arabella, now reformed of her quixotism, marries Glanville, it deliberately underscores the limitations placed on women writers by gendered expectations of genre and the limited opportunities that the gentleman makes viable for them. Women writers had gained much in professional status and legitimacy by the mid-eighteenth century but were often bound by generic expectations nonetheless. As Katherine Rogers points out, "Women were expected to write romances."[80] Critics are frequently disappointed with Arabella's reform because they see more protofeminist potential in romance than in the domestic novel. As Catherine Craft argues, "The language of romance is women's language, a tongue that men cannot understand."[81] However, Lennox does not ask us to choose between genres; Arabella's romance and her courtship novel would theoretically end the same way, with Arabella's marrying Glanville. Lennox is not interested in an exclusive "women's language." On the contrary, she validates the power of genre through Arabella's influence over Glanville and her ultimate superiority to all of the other male author figures in the text. Even so, I do not think that "romance tells the truth of female desire," or at least not the whole truth.[82] Romance contains female desire within heterosexual love stories, which, despite delaying marriage, do not avoid it. Love and relationships with men remain very much at the center of heroines' lives. True, they have histories and adventures to share, and they build bonds with other women, but it all serves the larger narrative trajectory that bounds through captivity, battle, and hermitage to marriage. Glanville is Arabella's inevitability, but he is not one imposed on her by men; instead, he is the product of a woman-authored investment in the gentleman. By rethinking Glanville's role as the gentleman in the novel, we see how he is validating for the woman author, but he also remains a constraint. The gentleman's window of opportunity is still structured within courtship narratives, which were developed and defined by women writers.

If Arabella's quixotism is a desire for authorship, then it also represents the narrow professional borders available to women authors who end up bound by rigid gender and generic prescriptions. At several junctures, Arabella's own desires conflict with her romance plots. Other than acknowledging that she "Does not hate" Glanville, she cannot express her desires any better than a realist heroine in domestic fiction. As David Marshall[83] points out, Arabella's "subservience to the authority and prescription of romantic forms almost kills her" (*FQ* 122). This tendency extends outward to Lennox's arguments about authorship, which reveal the continued cost that women authors pay for their investment in the gentleman. Although Arabella's dedication to romance endorses feminine forms, it also indicts the limited possibilities of genre for a woman writer. In the Doctor's final point, he begins, "Love, Madam, is, you know, the Business, the sole Business of Ladies in Romances"; however, when Lennox informs us that "*Arabella's* Blushes now hinder'd him from proceeding as he had intended," it is the final straw that makes Arabella's "Heart yield... to the Force of Truth" (*FQ* 381). The exchange feels gendered in problematic ways until we consider that perhaps the Doctor is speaking not to female sexual desire but to authorial desire. This recognition is why the ending is unsatisfying: Arabella follows her authorial ambitions while we continue to feel the limitations of her literary potential. The woman who can discourse on so many things is restricted by generic expectations, and these expectations, despite serving the metaphorical validation of female authorship and restructuring the gentleman critic's authority, still feel deliberately confining. Lennox uses specific genres to create an argument about who is allowed to speak, and in what ways, about how literary agency is deeply gendered.

What we must reckon with are the ways women have played a part in crafting these gendered terms. While investing in the gentleman persona and the courtship tale provides avenues for narrative, validation, and critical intervention, they also lock women into generic conventions and their prescribed performances. The performative structure of these constraints is echoed in Arabella's own words: "Turning to Mr. *Glanville*, whom she beheld with a Look of mingled Tenderness and Modesty, To give you myself, said she with all my remaining Imperfections, is making you but a poor Present in return for the Obligations your generous Affection for a Partner for Life by a Man of your Sense and Honour, I will endeavour to make myself as worthy as I am able to such a favourable Distinction" (*FQ* 383). Although Arabella's obsequiousness feels like a violation of her authorial power, she merely echoes the refrain of the eighteenth-century preface, a refrain common to authors of all genders. What colors the scene is how Lennox reveals the ways in which the refrain is inflected by an author's identity. Whereas Johnson, Addison and Steele, and Hume all make claims to such authorial trepidation, Arabella's claim becomes the common plea of the female author: a plea of modesty, unworthiness, nothingness, and dependence. It is a pose that, albeit potentially sincere, is what Gallagher identifies as a professional tool used by women writers.[84] As so many authors do, Arabella is speaking to her critics, and by recognizing it as a clichéd performance, we can recognize that Lennox is calling out the larger cultural structure, not abdicating to it. Nevertheless, Arabella remains locked within the structure and turns to Glanville to help her, a gentleman who has been constructed to support but not to release female ambition from these critical structures.

"For You Are a Bird of Prey"

Lennox stepped out from the above-described courtship structure and fittingly followed *The Female Quixote* with one of the first major works of literary criticism in the eighteenth century, *Shakespear Illustrated* (1753–1754). Thus, as an author, she immediately moved from dramatizing the gendered structures of literary criticism for women and constructing a gentleman critic for her own purposes to stepping into the gentleman critic's role herself. Lennox's work of literary criticism also provides a benchmark for tracking how she, as a woman writer, shaped the contours of male-dominated criticism. Reading it leads us back to Johnson but with a new awareness that illuminates how, as Johnson settled into the figure of the gentleman critic, much of the pose came from his relationship with Lennox. It also requires our critical community to acknowledge that part of the reason why women authors remain locked into courtship novels and gentlemanly structures is because we, as critics, have continuously reinforced them.

Published a year after *The Female Quixote*, *Shakespear Illustrated* was advertised as containing "Critical Remarks . . . By the author of the Female Quixote."[85] In this work, Lennox combines "neoclassical precepts with the authority of female domesticity in her unseasonable criticism of Shakespeare," as well as traces and summarizes the source materials for Shakespeare's plays, many of which are romances.[86] The work has been characterized as one that ruffled feathers and was summarily dismissed.[87] In finding fault with the rising forefather of the masculine literary canon, Lennox left "a legacy of irritated responses" in her wake, including those from formidable figures such as David Garrick.

However, the results of her painstaking work locating, translating, and analyzing Shakespeare's source materials are accurate and were used repeatedly throughout the century.[88] For reference, her closest predecessor was Gerard Langbaine's *Account of English Dramatic Poets* (1691), and "while Langbaine's inventory [of Shakespeare] is seventeen pages long, Lennox offered three volumes of summaries, translations, and commentary."[89] In time, *Shakespear Illustrated* became popular and respected enough to warrant a reprinting in the 1790s, one that referred to Lennox's "critical sagacity" and how "the Public was pleased to see so much merit in the performance," which was "received with very general favour, and was honoured by such marks of attention, as not to acknowledge would argue rather arrogance than modesty."[90] Carlile's own detailed analysis of the work supports these claims: "*Shakespear Illustrated* certainly was not neglected at the time that it was published; in fact, in numerous venues, Lennox was seen as a scholar giving evidence to audiences and readers who doubted uncritical Shakespeare worship."[91] Carlile expertly traces the influence and positive reception of Lennox's criticism of the Bard, including by citing positive reviews in *The Monthly Review* and *The Gentleman's Magazine*, in which critics such as Joseph Warton and Thomas Barker praised her work as "very judicious, and truly critical."[92] Her *Shakespear* was regularly cited by such publications as being the authority on Shakespeare's reference material, and Lennox clearly influenced later Shakespeare scholars such as Richard Farmer, whose *An Essay on the Learning of Shakespeare* (1767) refers to the "ingenious Mrs. Lennox's" commentary.[93] Despite the disapproval of figures such as Garrick and criticism that she was not as deferential to Shakespeare as she should have been, Lennox's critical work was treated seriously, and it did not damage her literary standing in any substantial way or stop her from publishing extensively and successfully throughout the rest of her life. If anything, the work seems to have enhanced her reputation.

Again, our perceptions of Lennox as a critic have been inaccurately filtered through a dated perception of her relationship with Johnson and the literary establishment, namely a perception that she was not a part of it. For example, Jonathan Brody Kramnick has argued that *Shakespear Illustrated* came into being to assist Johnson's own Shakespearean endeavors.[94] However, this understanding is largely unsubstantiated, and I am more inclined to agree with Carlile that "the degree to which [Johnson and Lennox] disagree about Shakespeare's inventiveness ... makes this possibility unlikely."[95] One of the performances obscuring this interpretation is Johnson's authorship of the preface to *Shakespear Illustrated*, in which he masquerades as Lennox in the dedication to Lord Orrery. In the role, Johnson proclaims that Shakespeare's "works may be considered as a Map of Life, a faithful Miniature of human Transactions, and he that has read *Shakespear* with Attention, will perhaps find little new in the crouded world."[96] By contrast, she writes about *Measure for Measure*, "I think, wherever Shakespeare has invented, he is greatly below the Novelist; since the Incidents he has added, are neither necessary nor probable" (*SI* 1:24). Lennox is notably more critical of the Bard in her remarks.

In these moments, Lennox and Johnson play at each other's voices but not in ways that involve Johnson's apologizing for Lennox's prickliness. On the contrary, it is a far more equal exchange. In *The Female Quixote*, Lennox repeatedly invokes Johnson through multiple characters; sometimes Glanville takes on his sentiments and even his voice, as do the quixotic Arabella and finally the Doctor. The imitations can be read, however, not as mockery but as an inside joke or homage between friends used to explore criticism and voice. Regarding the more deferential, feminine pose of the preface to *Shakespear Illustrated*, they seem to be direct echoes of Johnson's performance in the preface to *The Female Quixote*, wherein he had also masqueraded as Lennox. Lennox plays Johnson in the novel, and Johnson plays her in the preface. Such play speaks to a mutual sense of performance as being not only filtered through cultural ideas of gender but also self-aware that the literary world is one of posturing. Johnson plays at being a gentleman in his work but was not in fact a gentleman; Lennox plays at voicing Johnson, whom she was obviously not; and Johnson plays at being a submissive female author that Lennox was decidedly not. There is something poetic in Johnson, the emerging critic, assuming the role of the vulnerable woman writer as Lennox, the woman writer, steps into the role of the gentleman critic. Moreover, both of them built important literary careers and reputations on these performances.

To be clear, the evidence suggests that Johnson's criticism, including his own edition of *Shakespeare*, was influenced by Lennox's, not the other way around. Johnson most definitely admired Lennox's critical work. In a letter written in either April or May 1753, Johnson expressed his unequivocal delight in Lennox's criticism: "I should be sorry to lose Criticism in her bloom. Your remarks are I think all very judicious, clearly expressed, and *incontrovertibly certain*. When Shakespeare is demolished your wings will be full summed and I will fly you at Milton; for you are a bird of Prey, but the Bird of Jupiter."[97] If anything, as Runge argues, Johnson's preface was a sign of his esteem for Lennox, not of a paternalistic need to intervene.[98]

Johnson not only wrote this privately but also used Lennox's work, especially *Shakespear Illustrated*, as references in his *Dictionary of the English Language* (1755). In the *Dictionary*, "Lennox is among the few women cited as an authority," and she is quoted twenty times.[99] *The Female Quixote* is referenced ten times—see the definitions of "Talent" and "Visionary"—as is *Shakespear Illustrated*, with the entries for "Unnecessary" and "Wonderful." Notably, *Shakespear Illustrated* is the only reference for the word "Starry." Johnson's comment about flying Lennox—now transformed into Criticism itself—at Milton also reflects his enthusiasm. Johnson was sharply critical of Milton throughout his career and expressed some of these sentiments in *The Rambler* but was even more direct in his *Lives of the Poets* (1779–1781). Therein, Johnson writes, "Surely no man could have fancied that he read *Lycidas* with pleasure had he not known its author."[100] Similar to Lennox, Johnson does not fear taking on an author whom many consider to be untouchably canonical. What echoes Lennox most directly is Johnson's repeated insistence that Milton cannot capture reality. Although Johnson does admire *Paradise Lost*, "The reader finds no transaction in which he can be engaged, beholds no condition in which he can by any effort of imagination place himself."[101] There is a lack of reality, of believability, in the characters' motives, which is precisely Lennox's criticism of *Measure for Measure* and many of Shakespeare's other works in *Shakespear Illustrated*.

Lennox repeatedly stresses the value of originality, even in adaptations, an idea that Johnson seconds throughout his critical works. Speaking again of Milton, Johnson writes, "The highest praise of genius is original invention"; and of Milton adapting Homer; "But of all the borrowers from Homer Milton is perhaps the least indebted."[102] Lennox's whole project analogously traces how Shakespeare borrowed ineffectively from his source materials. He "has altered and added a good deal" to *Measure for Measure*, for instance, "yet has not mended" (*SI* 1:25). In a sense, Lennox is only holding Shakespeare to the standards that she herself was held to. Henry Fielding, praising Lennox's quixotic tale in *The Covent Garden Journal* on March 24, 1752, compared *The Female Quixote* to *Don Quixote* and argued that Lennox's novel "comes nearer to Perfection than the loose unconnected Adventures of *Don Quixote*": "Upon the whole, I do very earnestly recommend it, as a most extraordinary and most excellent Performance."[103] Thus, when Lennox holds Shakespeare to account, Lennox is, like the good critic (i.e., the gentleman critic), holding him to a consistent standard. She has, for all intents and purposes, taken on the role of the gentleman critic, a role that she has helped to fashion and refashioned as her own.

Johnson's *Shakespeare* owes a debt to Lennox that has long gone unacknowledged. It is not a coincidence that "during these years [the early to mid-1750s] Samuel Johnson was also expanding his writing repertoire and had discussed the idea of doing an edition of Shakespeare."[104] I agree with Carlile that "Johnson began his own career in comprehensive Shakespeare criticism by impersonating Lennox" and in his 1756 proposal for the edition set himself up to fundamentally repeat Lennox's project.[105] He promises not to lavish "praises ... without reason ... on the dead."[106] He also claims that "Shakespeare with his excellencies has likewise faults, and faults sufficient to obscure and overwhelm any other merit."[107] After making note of Shakespeare's sources and annotating the plays, Johnson, again like Lennox, promises that at "the end of most plays, I have added short strictures, containing general censure of faults, or praise of excellence."[108] Johnson, now the established Johnson, sets forth his major critical voice, and it is a direct performance of the voice that Lennox created for her critical work, which came from the legacy of *The Female Quixote*. In this case, the male critic literally parrots the woman writer, her critical voice, and her fictional-turned-literal prerogative, which has emerged not from a top-down or bottom-up intervention but from a responsive relationship between gender performance, fiction, and criticism, all swirling through the structures of eighteenth-century masculinity, the gentleman, and the professional status of the woman writer.

The goal of this book is to highlight these connections because they have been overlooked and invisible for too long. This is not because they are not tangible and traceable but because they have been systematically subordinated or outright erased through a biased critical retrospective. Johnson's *Shakespeare* "was soon looked upon as the definitive critique of Shakespeare," and even into the twentieth century, it "was being praised as exceptional."[109] This development emerged despite the fact that his work was not as thorough or as critically well received as Lennox's. Moreover, his edition does not contain the detailed annotations, connections to source material, or even the pointed criticism of faults that his proposal promised: "Reviewers saw this lack in Johnson's *Shakespeare*. They criticized Johnson for sweeping statements in his preface that did not include careful study."[110] Despite being his biggest cheerleader, Boswell had to acknowledge that "his researches were not so ample, and his investigations so acute as they might have been."[111] Even so, Johnson's less critically rigorous work became the dominant one as Johnson became JOHNSON.

Johnson's becoming Johnson owes a debt to Lennox, especially the play with performance and masculinity that she cultivated and that Johnson participated in. We do not remember this, however, because as in Johnson's *Shakespeare*, Lennox goes unnamed in the references. Despite their long and continued friendship, Johnson does not mention Lennox by name even once in his 1756 proposal or his actual *Shakespeare*. Instead, he "alludes to Lennox several times without naming her."[112] Although she is footnoted in the *Yale Edition* of Johnson's works, he himself does not recognize her by name. He does, however, name a host of male Shakespeare editors: Alexander Pope, Lewis Theobold, Thomas Hanmer, and William Warburton. As Carlile writes, "Leaving out Lennox is an oversight that is hard to reconcile. Johnson clearly valued Lennox's mind, but he did not see fit to refer to her scholarship."[113] I do not have evidence to speculate on why Johnson omitted Lennox, especially given his regular, effusive praise of her before, during, and after this period in personal and public writings. However, I do know that we, as a scholarly community, have largely reproduced this silence. We have fallen into the pattern that hegemonic masculinity wishes to establish: that it is an eternal, naturally produced constant. My hope is that by tracing the far more complex legacy of Lennox and Johnson, we can continue this vital challenge to our established assumptions about the relationships between women writers and their male contemporaries. In his preface to *Shakespeare*, Johnson writes, "Yet it must be at least confessed, that as we owe every thing to [Shakespeare], he owes something to us; that, if much of his praise is paid by perception and judgment, much is likewise given by custom and veneration."[114] I would like us to apply the same consideration to Lennox in our assessment of Johnson—he owes much to her—but also to the gentleman and the critic as wider cultural ideals. We must also confront the ease with which we fall into the very performance of the gentleman crafted by women, a performance that is lulling in its familiarity and convenient in its expediency. It is a legacy of women writers, and when we unknowingly reproduce it, we both ignore its production and mitigate its hegemonic legacy.

4

"Smartly Dealt With; Especially by the Ladies"
The Women Writers of Samuel Richardson's Sir Charles Grandison

> Could I have proceeded with Harriet and *your* good man (your's he is—he owes the existence he has to you), I should have been better
> —Samuel Richardson to Lady Dorothy Bradshaigh, *The Cambridge Edition of the Correspondence of Samuel Richardson*

According to some, *Sir Charles Grandison* (1753) is the book Samuel Richardson didn't want to write.[1] So maybe *he* didn't, or at least he didn't do it alone. My epigraph comes from Richardson's correspondence with Lady Dorothy Bradshaigh. Bradshaigh was Richardson's most prolific correspondent; she began writing to Richardson in 1748 under the pseudonym Belfour while he was publishing *Clarissa* (1748). By the time he was writing *Grandison*, she had revealed her identity, and, as remarked above, Richardson declared Sir Charles more her creation than his. Critics have taken Richardson's flattery of his correspondents, especially the numerous women of his circle, with a grain of salt, often reading it as self-indulgent lip service or condescension on Richardson's part. However, I would like to shift this paradigm and take Richardson's words seriously. I argue that women, including Bradshaigh, Lady Elizabeth Echlin, Hester Mulso, Catherine Talbot, Elizabeth Carter, Susanna Highmore, Sarah Wescomb, and more, played a direct and active role in Richardson's construction of Sir Charles. In fact, I contend that it is far more accurate to read these women as coauthors of *Grandison* than it is to continue to place them as color commentary surrounding Richardson's oeuvre.

Sir Charles Grandison is usually read as "the stepbrother of Richardson's other novels."[2] General disdain aside, there is some truth to such comments; the writing and publishing of *Sir Charles Grandison* took a much different shape from Richardson's first two novels. Whereas Richardson had carefully plotted out *Pamela* (1740) and *Clarissa* (1748), *Grandison* was created as he went, with significantly more input from his various correspondents, especially his women correspondents. Richardson had always been anxious about readers' responses to his novels, and he was often frustrated by their unwillingness to read and want as he wished. Therefore, he devoted revisions, prefatory material, indexes, and letters to attempt to correct his readers, but what distinguishes *Grandison* is the ways readers, especially women, played such an active role in its composition. Bradshaigh, her sister Echlin, Mulso, Talbot, Carter, Highmore, Wescomb, Francis Grainger, and more, not only responded to and critiqued *Grandison* as they had all done with *Clarissa*, they helped define and create the text and its titular gentleman through their correspondence with Richardson from 1749 through his death in 1761. As Richardson wrote in a 1754 letter to Bradshaigh, "I really like to be smartly dealt with; especially by ladies."[3] This chapter takes Richardson at his word, and examines the vital role that these women played in Richardson's novel about the ideal man. In fact, I argue that Richardson not only incorporated and relied on these women's correspondence in shaping his novel, but the figure of the gentleman, especially by mid-century, necessitated women's input. *Grandison* is the product of the cultural and gender trajectory I have been tracing throughout this book, and Richardson's compulsive, even anxious codependence on women shaped both the form and the networks of desire structuring his book and the figure of its central gentleman. Rather than reading *Grandison* as a diminution of male genius, I read it as a vital sign of the ways authorship, masculinity, and women writers had become inextricably intertwined.

As this chapter demonstrates in detail, the crucial struggle in constructing an ideal gentleman—especially one who is constantly virtuous, rather than reformed—is his very desirability. Richardson's third novel was meant to create the masculine counterpart to his epically virtuous heroines and to one-up Henry Fielding's lovable rogue, Tom Jones. However, to create a desirable model of virtuous masculinity, Richardson himself relied heavily not on male-authored constructions but on his own female correspondents, and this resource is woven into the epistolary structure of *Grandison*. While Grandison's looks, fortune, sympathy, and character in theory speak for themselves, they are actually spoken for and made desirable by the pens of women, especially within the initial, most compelling phases of the text. It is the lively pen of Harriet Byron that composes the channels of desire in the text and the desirability of Grandison's gentlemanly masculinity.

Richardson's Stepson

Despite the highly canonical status of Richardson, his gentleman, Sir Charles, is almost universally considered uninteresting. This is because the transition from the mid- to late-century gentleman is not, on the surface, critically exciting. This is the era of the boring gentleman. Gone are the reformed rake narratives of the early century as well as the morally nebulous play with disguise and transformation; instead we have the gentleman from birth[4]—the gentleman who starts as and remains a gentleman, a constant pulse of masculine virtue, beating the drum of heterosocial politeness and domesticity throughout. This gentleman "has birth, the kind of cosmopolitan, polite education that goes with wealth and birth, and the personality to convey his breeding and engage his companions."[5] Richardson's gentleman has received much less attention than *Pamela* or *Clarissa*. One has only to glance at the critical discussion of *Sir Charles Grandison* to register the general scholarly disinterest in this mode of masculinity. The sheer amount of critical disdain for Richardson's gentleman is so palpable as to feel almost like a critical requirement. Elaine McGirr summarizes this feeling when she writes, "The general tone of modern scholarship on *Sir Charles Grandison* is apologetic or amused,"[6] and much of it, as Emily Friedman points out, seems to focus on "debating the precise nature of *Grandison's* boringness."[7] As Jocelyn Harris writes, "Richardson created a blank where a character ought to be."[8] Critics who take on *Sir Charles Grandison* more than occasionally do so with an air of begrudging necessity. The consensus is that male virtue is boring, unaffecting, and unappealing. To a certain degree, this is understandable. After all, unlike the patriarchal regulation of female virtue, male virtue feels optional, or at the very least negotiable. These paragons of male virginity and social perfection seem like the most unnecessarily smooth pathway for character.

When Sir Charles is acknowledged and when his masculinity is addressed, he is frequently labeled as a *new, feminine,* and *fantasy* man.[9] The "newness" of his masculinity, that is, the masculinity of the gentleman, is a feature this book recontextualizes. It isn't that the mid- to late-century gentleman is brand new, emerging from nowhere; instead, as detailed in my first three chapters, he is the evolution of masculinity, which has largely been shaped by women writers. However, the second two markers—feminine and fantasy—are not so much incorrect as tonally misleading. Both have been used repeatedly to dismiss the masculinities produced by women writers as somehow unrealistic, catching critical discussions and investigations of masculinity in the pesky net of Wattian realism. As discussed throughout this book, the gentleman, especially when written by women, gets labeled as feminine for his heterosocial politeness and dependence on women characters. To label these features as feminine is not inaccurate, but the tone of this label misses the ways that the gentleman's masculinity was built on these characteristics and that their potential femininity is not a counter to the highly normative nature of this masculinity.[10] These feminine aspects are not novelties; they are an expectation.

Furthermore, I want to rethink the label of Sir Charles's masculinity as a fantasy. The story goes that Sir Charles functioned as a kind of patriarchal reward for good girls. Women who confined themselves to the rules of society and excelled within them were treated to a handsome, supposedly benevolent prize. Sir Charles as an archetype of this structure then spawned several similar models of men: Lord Orville in Frances Burney's *Evelina* (1778) is a frequent example, but you could also read many of Jane Austen's heroes this way. Critics have debated the conservative and subversive potentials of these trajectories, but that is the fundamental structure most seem to agree exists.[11] However, what I call into question is the connotation we assign to the label of "fantasy." We so frequently use this label to dismiss the work and productions of women, as if gendered fantasies are not an incredibly real, incredibly powerful, and frequently dangerous force. No, I don't argue that Sir Charles is a hyperrealistic figure—whatever strange magic that alludes to—but I interrogate how the structure of his fantasy is actual and incredibly potent.

Grandison is a text scholars seem to turn to because it is instructive rather than delightful. One of the most frequent uses for *Grandison* is tracing various legacies. As noted above, it has been read as producing "heirs," frequently in the work of women writers, a kind of canonical filial production.[12] I think this is partly because of the above labels, which serve as pointed, if perhaps unconscious, critical dismissals. I argue Sir Charles's supposed "boringness" actually serves a vibrant, literary function and has an important and still powerful appeal within modern constructions of normative masculinity. In my examination of Richardson, I reposition *Sir Charles Grandison* as the legacy not of the pinnacle of male-centered canonicity but as the product of a network of novel writing that is highly dependent on women readers and writers. In my estimation, Richardson is not just responding to the male tradition of Joseph Addison's *Christian Hero* (1714), Henry Fielding's *Tom Jones* (1749), or his own prior male models, but to a woman-authored tradition of creating desirable gentlemen, which directly manifests in his obsessive and direct engagement with his women correspondents.[13] This fundamentally shifts the legacy of *Grandison* from one where the male author produces female inspiration and imitation to one where the male author works in a coterie of female-driven expression and desire, which then leads to lasting literary influence.

A Good Man Is Hard to Write

Richardson's correspondence has become an integral part of his authorial legacy. Richardson himself thought to publish his correspondence, but an edition would not come into being until Anna Laetitia Barbauld's *The Correspondence of Samuel Richardson* in 1804, which for decades cast the author as a gossipy, middle-class printer.[14] The recent and forthcoming Cambridge editions of his correspondences have added invaluable new letters and context for Richardson scholars. Women dominate large swaths of Richardson's correspondence. Richardson wrote to and with an array of women. There were the aristocratic sisters, Bradshaigh and Echlin; the literati of Mulso, Talbot, Highmore, and Carter; and Wescomb and Grainger, the daughters of wealthy merchant families. Finally, there were numerous and continued fan letters written by or presented as written by young women.

Critical perception of Richardson's relationships with his women correspondents varies from polite nods to overt condescension. Much of the condescension comes from older scholarship, but scholarship that is still deeply central for Richardson studies. For example, biographers T. C. Duncan Eaves and Ben D. Kimpel describe Richardson's relationship with Sarah Wescomb—the daughter of a wealthy merchant family—with a bemused condescension: "[Richardson] was evidently genuinely fond of the girl, and she as evidently deserved it, in spite of or because of her utter lack of intellectual pretensions, even to correct spelling. Their correspondence is almost barren of substance and is as repetitious and trivial as possible."[15] These women are often characterized as well meaning but inadequate: "Under-educated, inexperienced."[16] Yet, as John Dussinger rightly points out, Eaves and Kimpel's dismissal of Wescomb—and similar dismissals of other women—is deeply problematic. That is, "Given the considerable emotional investment in writing more than thirty thousand words to [Wescomb] over a period of fourteen years," Richardson's own middle-class education, and the variety of eighteenth-century spelling, Eaves and Kimpel's dismissal of Wescomb is a bit ridiculous.[17]

This censure ratchets up when it comes to *Grandison*, with the criticism of these women increasing along with acknowledgment of their contributions. Jocelyn Harris both acknowledges and laments the input of Richardson's correspondents on *Grandison*. In fact, she blames what she sees as the stylistic failings of *Grandison* on Richardson's overreliance on feedback from his readers. Bradshaigh and Echlin both wrote alternative endings to *Clarissa*, seeking to mitigate or undo the tragic ending. Harris argues that these alternative endings were a denial of *Clarissa* by two "shrewd but unsophisticated readers" who were "unwilling to confront pain, complexity and death as Richardson (or Euripides or Shakespeare) had done.... Such wretched misreading was far from being creative, and it brought Richardson down from the imaginative daring of *Clarissa* to the prevailing self-consciousness of *Grandison*."[18] Harris problematically reiterates the image of Richardson as genius and these women readers as bringing him down to some lower, pop-culture level, away from the heights of other (male) geniuses like Euripides and Shakespeare.

When recent critics incorporate these women into their analyses of Richardson, they usually avoid condescension, but they often make these women peripheral: convenient background quotes to situate a larger thematic argument about Richardson. This chapter shifts that; it takes seriously Richardson's call to Bradshaigh in 1751: "You blame me for not thinking of publishing in my life-time. You deny me assistance" (*CC* 5:194). Rather than seeing the input of these women readers and letter writers as a "sad tale of response and counter-response," I would like to explore the revelatory potential of resituating Richardson—the most canonical, moralistic male novelist of the century—as part of an authorial network, largely made up of women.[19] I fall much more in line with Peter Sabor's assessment that, rather than being "stung ... to the quick" by the responses and interventions of these women, Richardson instead "welcomed them.... Richardson, after all, never thought of the texts of his novels as stable entities."[20] These women played a vital and necessary role in his authorship, which was not about stable entities but ongoing productions. Richardson exchanged thousands of letters with these women. The current Cambridge edition of his correspondence with Bradshaigh and Echlin alone is three full volumes, spanning the last thirteen years of his life and hundreds of exchanges. He also clearly adopted feedback from them, using their input to guide his multiple revisions. Mulso's criticism of *Clarissa* with regards to Clarissa's obsessive obedience to her tyrannical family pushed Richardson to revise Clarissa's foreboding over her father's curse.[21] Bradshaigh's marginalia-filled copy of *Clarissa* sits proudly in the Princeton Library, kept as a valuable piece of archival material. Sabor notes that Richardson "made substantial use of Lady Bradshaigh's commentary, adopting many of her proposed revisions in the fourth edition of *Sir Charles Grandison*."[22] He similarly adopted and sought corrections from Highmore, Mulso, Talbot, Carter, Echlin, Wescomb, and others.

Finally, Richardson himself frequently declared that their reading and judgment mattered to him. During the composition of *Grandison*, he wrote to Mulso stating, "You are one of my best girls, and best judges."[23] Sabor notes, "Contending with Lady Bradshaigh about his novels was among his favorite activities."[24] To Wescomb he declared, "What charming advantages, what high delights, my dear, good, and condescending Miss Wescomb, flow from the familiar correspondences of friendly and undesigning hearts!" (*CC* 3:6). Rather than taking this merely as polite condescension, though that thread is there (especially in his insistence at adopting a fatherly role with them, even with older, married women like Bradshaigh and Echlin), I argue that it represents the state of gentlemanly masculinity and authorship at the mid-century.

Richardson needed these women, and this relationship is especially vital to *Grandison*. This falls in line with Betty Schellenberg's examination of mid-eighteenth-century coteries. Like Sabor, Schellenberg is one of the main critical voices that takes the contributions of correspondents and readers to Richardson's work seriously. Schellenberg writes, "At this junction in the process of" writing *Grandison*, "the reading circle is invited into the text, well beyond mere stylistic correction or moral pointing, to its very heart: the nature of the protagonist as the 'truly good man.'"[25] She specifically notes that the timeline of *Grandison* was at the height of what she reads as Richardson's main literary coterie, which spanned 1749–1755, with one primary circle including Thomas Edwards, Highmore, and Mulso.[26] Through "its practice of social authorship" and "mutual . . . improvement" by the exchange of literary texts, this group meets Schellenberg's definition of a coterie.[27] However, Schellenberg also recognizes the influence of Richardson's other correspondents: Talbot's focused involvement in the drafting and editing process,[28] Bradshaigh's extensive correspondence, and the letters of Wescomb, Carter, and other women.[29] However, I would like to recognize these women as distinctly part of the coterie and, as a wider network, as coauthors with Richardson. Through this authorship, rather than Sir Charles regulating women, it was women who regulated Sir Charles.

Historically, it makes sense that with "*Sir Charles Grandison*, Richardson allowed his readers to take a still more active part."[30] In a 1751 letter to his French translator, Jean Baptiste de Freval, Richardson wrote, "I am teased by a dozen ladies of note and of virtue, to give them a good man, as they say I have been partial to their sex, and unkind to my own" (*CC* 10:41–42). This teasing covers for the very serious contributions and work these women were already doing and would continue to do. Richardson sought to be a man of letters, and as discussed in chapter 2, by the mid-century there was concerted pressure for the man of letters to also be a gentleman.

Richardson's persona as a gentleman author was predicated on his ability to instruct and delight a desiring readership, especially among women. He was, fundamentally, a more successful version of David Hume; his works were widely beloved, and women and men alike consumed Richardson's work. However, like his less successful peer, Richardson felt pressured to be found desirable as an author. These feelings were perhaps fueled and exacerbated by his own awareness of his middle-class status as a printer and not a born gentleman.

A Ladies' Gentleman: *Sir Charles Grandison* as Representation of Correspondence

Women writers dominated *Sir Charles Grandison* from production to page. Richardson dramatized his own correspondence and used directly and thematically the input of these women. The epistolary structure reflects this letter-writing community. Most overtly, Harriet Byron as the central narrator in a novel about a male paragon embodies this structure, whereby the masculinity of the gentleman only takes shape and gains appeal through women's pens. Most notably, Harriet, like the women in Richardson's circle, is a lively, detailed, and voracious correspondent—a prolific writer. This might strike readers as unusual, given Sir Charles's status as the titular character. After all, Pamela is the almost sole narrator of her novel, and Clarissa is certainly a dominant and prolific voice in hers. In *Grandison*, Harriet is the central authorial figure of the text, serving in that capacity as the dominant narrative voice, editor, transcriber, and commentator. Out of the 319 total letters in the novel, Harriet writes 178. In contrast, Sir Charles, who doesn't even appear for about 137 pages, only writes sixty-five, forty of which are copied by Dr. Bartlett to recount his initial Italian adventures, meaning only twenty-five letters are written by Sir Charles during the main action of the text. Notably, 240—over three-quarters—are written by women. Women narrate the gentleman, and Harriet is the figurehead of this female endeavor. As Richardson himself wrote, "It is more in the power of young ladies than they seem to imagine, to make fine men" (*Letters* 164). Schellenberg points out, "The phrasing here suggests first the women ... have a unique creative or formative power over men."[31] They absolutely did.

Harriet Byron is the compilation of Richardson's women correspondents, literal and fictional. Richardson himself declared Harriet a hybrid of his fictional women writers: "His new heroine Harriet Byron he designed to 'keep the middle course' between Pamela and Clarissa, and Clarissa and Miss Howe."[32] Harriet is without a doubt the most central narrator of

Sir Charles Grandison. She also reflects the styles and characteristics of Richardson's correspondents. Like many of them, Harriet is well read, unmarried, and genteel. Likewise, she is not aristocratic, though her immediate acclimation to a higher station as Lady Grandison reflects the experience and status of Echlin and Bradshaigh. Her frankness and willingness to debate and critique, especially in the early volumes, reflects the style and tone of much of Richardson's correspondence with these women; Mulso and Bradshaigh were quite famous for their debates with Richardson. Meanwhile, Carter once playfully wrote to Richardson, "Do not be frightened, my good Mr. Richardson, I am set down with no vixen dispositions, but you shall have a letter as gentle and quiet as a heart can wish" (*CC* 10:80). This sounds remarkably like the playful tone Harriet takes with her Uncle Selby. Harriet repeatedly teases and is teased by her uncle about women's characters and vanity, especially her own. She writes, "But after all, may not, methinks I hear my correcting Uncle" jokingly chide her for a variety of flaws.[33]

Via the reform of male manners and other shifts, masculinity in the 1750s must be measured by women. *Grandison* is a novel about masculinity, which is told and defined through the voices of women. The ladies requested a good man from Richardson, who is deemed good by his worthiness of a heroine. Talbot wrote to Richardson in March of 1750, encouraging him to oblige all his women writers: "They much wish also, that he may have Leisure, Spirits and Inclinations to comply with the repeated Requests of his Agreeable Incognita [Bradshaigh], and shew the World such a Man as would neither have been unworthy of a Clarissa, nor unagreeable to a Miss Howe" (*CC* 10:8). This makes Harriet's construction, as a halfway point between these fictional women, yet another inspiration of Richardson's correspondence.

Harriet Byron is immediately positioned as the critic of masculinity, who "describes and details not only a masculine model of eighteenth-century virtue" but also critiques bad masculinities.[34] Much of the anticipation for Sir Charles is established by cataloging less desirable forms of masculinity. The first letter of the text is written by one of Harriet's suitors, Mr. Greville, and her very first act of authorship is a critique of his. After reading this letter, Harriet declares to Lucy, "The hyaena, my dear, was a *male* devourer. The men in malice, and to extenuate their own guilt, made the creature a *female*" (*SCG* 1:24). Greville is part of an initial trio of unsuitable suitors: Greville, Mr. Fenwick, and Mr. Orme. Greville is the entitled rake, the first of the text's libertines. Harriet objects to Mr. Greville's "immoralities" because "a man of free principles, shewn by practices as free, can hardly make a tender husband, were a woman able to get over considerations that she ought *not* to get over" (*SCG* 1:24). They know of at least three women he has seduced, besides the most recent unfortunate woman from Wales he brought with him into the country and then abandoned. Mr. Fenwick "*avows* not free principles," but he just keeps his indiscretions secret, and is therefore equally objectionable (*SCG* 1:26). Meanwhile, Orme is a sickly, sentimental send-up of Richardson's previous good-man attempt, Hickman, virtuous and full of sighs but not desirable.

Upon arriving in town, more specimens of masculinity present themselves for Harriet's keen assessment. Mr. Fowler is not "disagreeable in his *person*. But he seems to want the *mind* I would have man bless'd with" (*SCG* 1:32). The condescending and pedantic scholar, Mr. Waldon, who "despis[es] everyone who has not had the benefit of an University education," and the inoffensive Mr. Singleton, who is good at managing his estate but laughs to cover a lack of understanding, are both found wanting (*SCG* 1:42). Harriet's criticism of masculinity extends beyond men. Miss Barnvelt is ridiculed by Harriet for being "a lady of masculine features, and whose mind bely'd not those features" (*SCG* 1:43). Finally, there is Sir Hargrave, who reveals the depths of rakish arrogance. Harriet writes: "I viewed [Sir Hargrave] steadily several times; and my eye once falling under his, as I was looking at him, I dare say, he at the moment pity'd the poor fond heart, which he supposed was in tumults about him; when, at the very time I was considering, whether, if I were obliged to have the one or the other, as a punishment for some great fault I had committed, my choice should fall on Mr. Singleton, or on him" (*SCG* 1:46). Harriet is presented as the authority on modern masculinity's foibles, and clearly these men are measured by whether they are worthy of someone as exceptional as Harriet. She certainly measures them with this lens. Worthy and agreeable, the gentleman must be; in other words, virtue must go with attractions. So, when he does finally appear, he not only rescues Harriet from the villainous Sir Hargrave, preventing a second *Clarissa* tragedy, he also becomes the hero "amidst an epic cast of inadequate men."[35] What establishes Sir Charles as the hero, as the ideal, is Harriet's voice and her critical eye for masculinity.

Harriet's descriptions and critiques of men and Sir Charles are often lifted directly from the descriptions and critiques of Richardson's correspondents. Bradshaigh's critique of Alexander Pope sounds remarkably like Harriet's disdain for the pendant Waldon and the mean-spirited nature of Sir Hargrave's humor, which "such a one as rather shewed ridicule than mirth" (*SCG* 1:47). Bradshaigh writes, "I have not so good an opinion of Mr. Pope since I read his Dunciad. A little spiteful wasp! . . . what pity—so much wit should be blown over in so dirty a mean-spirited manner!" (*CC* 5:149). Some of the common and pleasant features of Sir Charles also emerge from direct descriptions of men by women. In the summer of 1750, Mulso praised her own brothers as being exemplars. We do not have her letter, but Richardson quoted her words back after meeting her younger brother, reprinting her praise and echoing her sentiment that, "It is indeed, 'a pleasing discovery to me, to find a set of young gentlemen who have spent their lives in London, yet remain untainted with modish vice, uncorrupted by the mean selfish maxims of the world; and who, at the hazard of being laughed at by *men of spirit and fashion*, dare avow and act up to the principles of religion and virtue!'" (*Letters* 3:163–164). Richardson applies this standard when he describes to Mulso how her youngest brother "stood particularly well with every body at North-End. . . . In the praises of every one of these, which all . . . overflowed with after their departer, the agreeableness of manners, the modesty of behavior, the complacency of temper, of this young gentleman, together with the intelligence apparent in his countenance, were taken great notice of" (*Letters* 3:164–165). Sir Charles is frequently remarked as having lived in the world while being untouched by its vices. His dedication to Christian principles is repeated almost ad nauseum. The pleasure and effect he has on company to his ability to leave his impression behind and be talked of, even while he is in Italy settling a possible obligation and divided love, are clearly transplants of Mulso's own assessments of good masculinity in her brothers.

Similarly, Sir Charles's devotion to family and domesticity is the influence of Bradshaigh. Speaking of her brother-in-law Edward Stanley, the Earl of Derby, in 1750, she wrote, "Indeed, all who know, must value and love him, for a better Man lives not. He would be a Friend to the *Public*, if he *could*: But to his own Family he is *inestimable*. May God long continue the Blessing to them!" (*CC* 5:146). In the sixth volume of the novel (originally published in 1753), Sir Charles declares to Harriet, "My chief glory will be, to behave commendably in the *private* life. I wish not to be a *public* man; and it must be a very particular call, for the Service of my King and Country united, that shall draw me out into public notice. Make me, madam, soon, the happy *husband* I hope to be" (*SCG* 3:99). The ideal gentleman prioritizes the domestic over the public, as a rule. On the one hand, these are common kinds of descriptions of exemplary gentlemen. Yet, given that Richardson was anxious that such a man would be found unbelievable, he was likely reassured by Mulso's and Bradshaigh's own descriptions of their real brothers and applied this to his descriptions of Sir Charles right down to the praise coming from admiring sisters, first Charlotte Grandison and Lady L and then later the "adopted" sister of Harriet Byron (*SCG* 2:301). Furthermore, the specific praise of the man who could do great things for the public but elects to perform his grace in private is pointed. Richardson practically lifts Bradshaigh's language and plants it into Sir Charles's mouth to be copied by Harriet's pen. Overall, there are clear points of contact between *Grandison* and Richardson's women correspondents. These qualities are the reflection of what women writers voiced as valuable in men.

It was not just literal descriptions of men that Richardson lifted from his women writers into the persona of Harriet Byron and her characterization of Sir Charles. Richardson expressed a great deal of anxiety about women's desires for men. He was deeply skeptical that you could make a good man appealing, and he struggled with and resented that the gentleman was so dependent on women for his desirability. He wrote to Mulso, "A fine task have I set myself! to draw a man that is to be above the common foibles of life; and yet to make a lover of him! to write, in short, to the taste of girls from fourteen to twenty-four years of age" (*Letters* 3:172–173). This is the Hickman problem or the Lovelace legacy. Richardson was flabbergasted by his women readers' reactions to his previous versions of the good man and the bad man. Hickman the incredibly dull, virtuous man of *Clarissa* was widely dissatisfying to readers. Meanwhile, Lovelace, even after the rape of Clarissa and Richardson's own revised editions that sought to emphasize his villainy, was widely appealing to readers, especially the ladies. As Bradshaigh, writing under her pseudonym Belfour declared, "I cannot help being fond of Lovelace" (*CC* 5:5). This disparity between what Richardson wanted from his women readers and his inability to control or dictate their desires clearly frustrated him. When asking for Highmore's help creating the good man, he declared, "But no Hickman! How can we hope that ladies will not think a good man a tame man?" (*Letters* 2:236). Yet, he knew he needed women: women to help him, to guide him, to revise this man, and to want this man. Women's desires were now inextricably woven into the gentleman, and there was no getting around that.

One of the ways Richardson drew upon this previous criticism and tried to circumvent it was by presenting remakes of Hickman and Lovelace early in *Grandison* and then quickly setting them aside: Orme and Sir Hargrave. Orme is indeed, as Bradshaigh describes Hickman, "*starch'd ... creeping ... whining*" (*CC* 5:176). This caricature seems designed to signal to his women readers that Sir Charles shall not be another Hickman. The more challenging obstacle is the appeal of rakes, which also plays a definite role in Sir Charles's character; but, before dealing with the ideal gentleman's rakish threads, I want to quickly note how Harriet's narration of Sir Hargrave subverts the appeal of the rake. Harriet's description of Hargrave was not entirely unappealing to Richardson's women correspondents. Richardson had been sending drafts of *Grandison* to Wescomb as early as 1751, and

Wescomb told Richardson how attractive she thought Hargrave was: "I really liked his Person, Air, & Life considered! (for I see in him) something so very smart and clever" (*CC* 3:147).

Now, Dussinger argues, "In contrast to her acute insights regarding the character and plot of *Clarissa*, Wescomb was usually off the mark when commenting on the various drafts of *Grandison*."[36] In his reading of this as a failure on Wescomb's part, I would argue that it is Dussinger who, despite his usual insights, is off the mark, because Wescomb's attraction to Hargrave is, in some ways, designed by the text, designed by his marked similarity to Lovelace: aristocratic, handsome, verbal, and manipulative. What Dussinger misses is the importance of the mechanism that reshapes Wescomb's reading: Harriet. Wescomb continues, "[Harriet Byron] has searchd & tried [Sir Hargrave] and he is come out to be a very sad Man! . . . has she not unmasked him & does there not already appear the strongest & worst Passions in him how sorry I am that I should ever have entertained a favourable thought" (*CC* 3:147). It seems as if Harriet served Richardson's purpose here; she swayed the desires of Richardson's female reader. This weight, given to Harriet, is the weight Richardson gave to his women correspondents, and we see it on effective display.

More powerful than undoing the appeal of the rake was the necessity of making the gentleman attractive. Literary references provided a narrow window for women to explain the necessity of making Sir Charles sexually attractive. The most overt example comes directly from Bradshaigh, which is unsurprising given her statuses: Bradshaigh was both Richardson's social superior and, unlike many of the other women included here, married and middle-aged. Bradshaigh was the formative advocate for the good man being a "Rake in his Address" and appearance. She did not invent the "good man," as Gerard Barker points out, but she did provide the specific imagery, description, and language that Richardson used to infuse his good man with desirability.[37] In the great tradition of gentleman writers, Richardson blamed women's preference for Lovelace over Hickman on the oft-stereotyped idea that women prefer rakes because they love flattery. He wrote to Mulso in September 1751, "The result of the matter is this, with very many young women:—they will admire a good man; but they will marry a bad one.—Are not rakes pretty fellows?" (*Letters* 3:180). Yet, in a November 1750 letter, Bradshaigh loudly and repeatedly declared, "I still say, Sir, you are too severe in persisting, that young Ladies prefer Rakes, *because they are Rakes* . . . excuse me, if I pretend to know my Sex, in this Particular, better than you" (*CC* 5:149). She continued another letter, writing that she is "very sure many would prefer a good man with an equal appearance; which proves they would not chuse a rake, because he is a rake, and which is all I contend for" (*CC* 5:167).

Richardson felt an insistent need to make his good men physically unattractive, or at least physically and fashionably unremarkable. This emerges in his initial resistance to Bradshaigh's suggestion. Writing in 1751, Richardson scoffed: "Will you be pleased, Madam, to give me particulars of the taking dress of a rake? Will you be pleased to describe the address with which the ladies in general shall be taken?—the rake is, must be, generally, in dress a coxcomb; in address, a man of great assurance; thinking highly of himself, meanly of the sex; he must be past blushing, and laugh at those who are not. He must flatter, lie, laugh, sing, caper, be a monkey, and not a man. And can a good man put on these appearances?" (CC 5:169). But Bradshaigh pushed back. First she argued, "Is a *bad Person*, a *bad Address*, necessary to complete a *good Man*?"; "why must a good man have a tame appearance? It sounds so like a thing that will fetch and carry. I am sure every good man is not a Hickman or an Orme" (CC 5:177, 180).[38] She bites back, "You write my *Words* without taking my *Meaning*" and then cleverly uses his own words against him:

> The *Dress* and *Address* of *such a Man (without his Vice)* is what I would recommend to the *sober Men*, who are too often *formal*, and disagreeable in their Manner, for want of a *liberal Education* . . . but would a *good Man* be the worse for carrying the *Outside* of such a Rake as I mean? And you know I mean no *bad Men*, tho' you will not own it. Would it hurt a Man's *Morals*, to have the *Appearance* of even Lovelace, as Miss How describes him at Colonel Ambrose's Ball? Let me see—I'll give you her Words: "So little of the *Fop!* yet so *elegant* and rich in his Dress! His Person so *specious*! His Air so *intrepid*! So much *Meaning* and *Penetration* in his *Face*! So much *Gaiety*! Yet so little of the *Monkey*! Tho' a travelled Gentleman, yet *no Affectation*! No mere *Toupet-man*! But all *manly*! And his *Courage* and *Wit*, the one so *known*, the other so *dreaded*!" Now, Sir, I suppose this was designed to be thought an *amiable Appearance*. Do not *you* think it was?-You answer, *Yes*.—Well then, To, *this Body* let us join a *great* and *good Soul*. And pray, Sir, what Fault have you to find with the *Union*? . . . Ask either Miss Howe, or Miss Byron. I durst venture to put the Question to a *Clarissa*. (CC 5:176)

The tension between Richardson and Bradshaigh was one of desire, and Bradshaigh closes with an appeal to women's desires: "Ask either Miss Howe, or Miss Byron," even the angelic "*Clarissa*."

Bradshaigh cleverly found a way to use fictional women to advocate for a rather scintillating request. As Juliet McMaster points out, the term "person," "like so many other terms in Richardson, comes to have a particularly sexual meaning."[39] Bradshaigh's emphatic insistence that a good man also have a good person is sexual. It is about the good man having a desirable body. The good man must be physically and socially attractive because women need to desire him, and that desire must be sexual. The marriage plot leads to the marriage bed, and if the gentleman is to outpace the rake and win over the ladies, part of what he must capture is their sexual desire and not just their polite, social accolades. If virtuous women characters are models for virtuous women readers, they must also model virtuous desire. Nobody wants to sleep with Hickman, and many people want to sleep with Lovelace. If Sir Charles Grandison is to even the scale he must be physically attractive; he must have the attractive shell of the rake at the very least. He must not creep; he must entertain. He must not be a coxcomb, but he must dress well. He must absolutely be handsome.

Bradshaigh carried her point; by the time he appeared in print in 1753, Sir Charles appeared as she designed him, and Richardson signaled her contribution directly. Helen Thompson argues that "Richardson rejects Lady Bradshaigh's" suggestion as problematic "sugar-coating," but the evidence of her influence is directly present on the page. When he emerged in print, Sir Charles was a "Rake in his address, and a Saint in his heart" (SCG 3.92). Richardson even puts this description in the mouth of Charlotte Grandison, who many, including her own sister, thought was either a characterization of or actually written by Bradshaigh.[40] The physical description Bradshaigh highlights also appears in the novel. There is a direct comparison between Sir Charles and Sir Hargrave that details exactly the distinctions of dress, education, and character that Bradshaigh suggested: contrasting the rake with the gentleman and finding the rake wanting on all counts. Both are handsome and genteel. They both have complexions that are "naturally too fine for a man," but whereas Sir Hargrave is "a little of the palest," Sir Charles has a suntan, or as Harriet describes, "his face is overspread by a manly sunniness," "as if he were above being regardful of it" (SCG 1:45, 1:181). They both have fine teeth, but while Sir Charles is not vain, Sir Hargrave "forgets not to pay his respects to himself at every glass" while he is in company (SCG 1:45). They both dress well, but while Sir Charles dresses to abide by social conventions, Sir Hargrave is overly fashionable. While Sir Hargrave has "remarkably bold eyes; rather approaching to what we call googling," Sir Charles's "eye shews, if possible, more of sparkling intelligence than that of his sister" (SCG 1:45, 1:181). (This, given Charlotte's similarity to Bradshaigh, could be another compliment to Bradshaigh and her contributions to Sir Charles's character.) Their physical attributes are put side by side, and though they are rather similar, their characters are distinct, with Sir Charles positioned to emphasize his gentility, intelligence, and modesty, while Sir Hargrave's same features mark him as a rakish, vain man of fashion.

Similarly, their travel and education distinguish the use a gentleman puts such experiences versus the rake: "Sir Charles Grandison, my dear, has travelled we may say, to some purpose" (SCG 1:182). He is what Lady Bradshaigh describes as "a Man who has *seen the World*, and has had Opportunities of *improving* himself" (CC 1:177). Meanwhile, "Sir Hargrave, it seems, has travelled: But he must have carried abroad with him a great number of follies, and a great deal of affectation, if he has left any of them behind him" (SCG 1:45). It is not the dress, the looks, or even the education that defines the gentleman, but the use or regard he has for them. Here are all the distinctions Bradshaigh suggested, laid out directly and overtly in the long-awaited introduction of Sir Charles's charms. Richardson cannot help claiming, via Harriet, that Sir Charles "has such an easy, yet manly politeness, as well in his dress, as in his address (no singularity appearing in either) that were he *not* a fine figure of a man, but were even plain and hard-featured, he would be thought (what is far more eligible in a man, than mere beauty) very agreeable" (SCG 1:181). Yet, he is still not only made a handsome man, but *the most* handsome man of the novel, who "break[s] half a score of hearts" when he marries (SCG 1:182).

In this characterization, Richardson prioritizes his women correspondents' suggestions over his male ones. Richardson had a range of male correspondents as well, several of them downright celebrities: figures like Samuel Johnson, Colley Cibber, and David Garrick. Yet his women correspondents were the ones he relied on most directly for his shaping of the gentleman and who, I argue, participated most actively in the production of *Grandison*. While several men wanted Sir Charles to be virtuous but not saintly, there is a specific instance in the definition of male charm and male virtue where Richardson emphatically sided with the ladies: Sir Charles is a virgin.[41] During their debate about rakes in appearance, Richardson described Cibber's input, which detailed that a man may have some sexual exploits but still be considered a good man. Bradshaigh was scandalized by this suggestion: "Appearance is *all* I want, not meaning it *any* Part of his *Character*. Nor will my Words, if duly considered I think, admit of your Construction, 'That to draw a good Man, he must be a *moderate Rake*; must qualify himself for the *Ladies Favour* by taking *any Liberties* that are *criminal*.'—Give me Patience!—*Scurrilous!*" (CC 5:176). Yet again, *this* is the emphasis given to Sir Charles. Harriet declares, "I have met with persons, who call those men *good*, that yet allow themselves in liberties which no good man can take. But I dare say, that Miss Grandison means by *good*, when she calls her brother, with so much pride, *a good man*, what I, and what you, my Lucy, would understand by the word," that is, a virgin (SCG 1:183). It isn't enough to be a Mr. Fenwick (perhaps a direct callback to Cibber's suggestion) and just keep your vices secret, to "*avow* . . . not free principles" (*SCG* 1:26); one must put their manhood where their mouth is. Further parroting Bradshaigh, Harriet later declares, "A fine reflexion upon the age; as if there could not be *one* good man in it! And as if a good man could not be a man of vivacity and spirit!" (*SCG* 3:138). Richardson parted from his own original conception here and embraced the view of the women correspondents, which he echoes and enacts through the voices of women in the novel, and he prioritized women's voices over men's to construct his gentleman. The novel embodies this structure as well, focusing on two women confirming that the good man is sexually virtuous and still desirable to them and admired by all the men, especially the rakes, of the novel.

Circles of Women: Circulation, Pleasure, and Ownership

Schellenberg and Tita Chico have examined the role of community in *Grandison* and in Richardson's own circle.[42] They have talked about Sir Charles's influence as the central power of the text, shaping community in his own image. However, I would like to consider how the widening circle of women writers in *Grandison* reflects Richardson's own networks of women writers and readers. Richardson did not communicate unilaterally with each of these women; rather, he circulated their ideas amongst each other, sometimes sending them actual letters, sometimes quoting them to each other, and other times alluding to their general ideas. We see this throughout the composition of Grandison, from his declarations about the fair sex teasing him for a good man as a general allusion to more specific instances. In December 1750, he wrote to Bradshaigh, "I am at present engaged with a most amiable young lady of little more than twenty, Miss Mulso, on the subject of paternal authority and filial obedience, grounded on Clarissa's duty to her persecuting parents and on her dread of her gloomy father's curse. Miss Mulso is a charming writer" (*CC* 5:153). He also alludes to the importance of Talbot's insights as the "British Minerva" to Mulso, and likewise praises Carter for her and, by extension his, admiration of Talbot. These women frequently expressed admiration for each other. Bradshaigh, in response to Richardson's praise of Mulso, wrote, "I should be greatly delighted to see the correspondence between you and the young lady you mention. Some time or other, I hope to be favoured with it" (*Letters* 5:156). Mulso praised Bradshaigh's criticism of Sir Charles's divided love.[43] Meanwhile, Carter praised Talbot directly for her influence over the final novel: "Every body, I am sure, will be struck with the advantageous differences of the language, though but few can observe it with the peculiar pleasure that I do."[44]

Correspondingly, Harriet's letters are never truly private; they are always meant to be read by a community, first by her family at Selby house, but eventually they circulate through the Grandisons and their widening circle of influence. As George Haggerty points out, "Harriet's letters become the public property of her family once they are written."[45] This circulation is a meme; it spreads throughout the text, inspiring other women to take up their pens. Harriet and her network of women are the actual power structure of the novel, circulating Sir Charles as *their text*. It is the network that exerts influence, not the gentleman's radiance.

The benefits of women's writing circulating amongst and through other women are presented in the novel as advantageous for both the women and for the reputation of the gentleman. Harriet's authorship creates a community of women writers. As noted above, Harriet is the dominant narrator of the text. However, the next largest source of authorship is other women. Harriet inspires Charlotte to take up her pen, who then pushes Lucy Selby into writing, even functioning as a critic of Lucy's work. Finally, even Emily Jervois, Sir Charles's lovesick ward, takes up the pen. She writes to Harriet of her would-be-suitor, "Here every-body is fond of Sir Edward Beauchamp. He is indeed a very agreeable man. Next to my guardian, I think him the most agreeable of men" (*SCG* 3:443). On the surface, it looks as if Sir Charles is firmly planted as the sun, with other men orbiting around him. However, in her critiques of masculinity, Emily is actually echoing Harriet.

Sir Charles only takes shape through Harriet's pen, and now Emily has taken up her own to give Beauchamp some shape, using Harriet's epistolary model as her guide. The mark of her emerging maturity is not her fading infatuation with her guardian but her ability to mimic Harriet as a critic of proper masculinity. Similarly, once Lucy starts writing, she dismisses the advances of Greville (seeking Lucy as a backup and access point for Harriet) and moves on to her own suitable suitor, one of Sir Charles's anonymous groomsmen. The unmarried ladies have found their own blank gentleman to assess and fill in. Even Clementina takes up her pen for the first time in the final volumes, asking for intercession with her parents and the liberty or at least the time to make up her own mind about marriage and, more pointedly, her suitor, Count Belvedere—once again, a man similarly lacking in defining features. It speaks to Harriet's ownership of the title Grandison, both as Lady Grandison and as the narrative voice of *Grandison*, that her former rival has now adopted her authorial tactics. This textual community reflects the structure of Richardson's actual community. Women's writing circulates and gains influence, and its subject is consistently critiques of courtship and masculinity.

This circulation also reverberates outward from the text in several ways. First, the ending of the novel functions as both an acknowledgment of and invitation to Richardson's women correspondents and readers in general. The ending is remarkably open-ended. Other than Lucy, many of the young women of the novel remain unmarried and in the midst of possible courtships. Most notable and frustrating for eighteenth-century readers of *Grandison* are the unknown fates of Clementina and Emily. While his women writers frequently asked Richardson to "finish" the novel, this ending is perhaps another nod to their influence. There was a great deal of disagreement among these women about how Clementina's story should end. Mulso "and a few of her Favourites" were "most romantically averse" to Clementina marrying the Count, who is seen as beneath the angelic Italian" (*Letters* 2:348). Meanwhile, Bradshaigh wrote, "What ever Miss Mulso, or any body may think of it, I am absolutely for Clementina being the wife of the Count of Bellvedere" (*CC* 2:359). The very openness of the ending is perhaps a sign of Richardson's desire to please these women. He could not please them all, so he left the ending open.

The openness invites further authorship from these women. Richardson encouraged both his correspondents and his general readers to fill in the ending themselves. He wrote to Bradshaigh in 1754:

> An ingenious Gentleman has written a Letter in answer to what I told You I had been writing in Defence of my Concluding Part. He has made a Proposal, in order to induce me to write another Volume: It is this: That every one of my Correspondents, at his or her own Choice, assume one of the surviving Characters of the Story, and write in it. . . . I shall pick and choose, alter, connect, and accommodate, till I have completed from them, the requested Volume. Will your Ladiship, who would make a most Charming Lady G. contribute to the Temptation?—I think myself absolutely worn out. I am in Earnest. (*CC* 6:450)

This could be read as posturing, but the very nature of the posturing speaks to my argument. Richardson felt obligated to perform deference to these women writers, for the sake of his fictional gentleman and his own authorial reputation.

However, there is ample evidence that Richardson was serious in his offer. He asked Mulso and another young woman (unidentified) to provide short prefaces for the novel, and declared himself "greatly in earnest" (*Letters* 3:195). He asked that these women continue the novel, if they wanted a continuation so badly. He requested that they each write a letter from the voice of one of the characters. In August 1754, Richardson wrote Mulso about this, and the roles he would cast each of these ladies in.

He asked her, "Sweet reasoned!—How I love your reasoning pen!—Give me a letter of your Clementina to your other favourite Harriet (you know her inmost soul)" (*Letters* 3:209); meanwhile, Bradshaigh

> has written one in the character of Charlotte. Your Miss Highmore is inclined to write me one in the character of Harriet. Perhaps, through you, the *meek-eyed Goddess of Wisdom*, our British Minerva, will honour the character of Mrs. Shirley in another; and who knows but, on seeing yours, she will add another in that of Sir Charles, making him shine in some new acts of beneficence? You will flatter yourself, you say, that my pen is at work. It is not;—nor, in my conception, ever can be, but by such inspiration. To me, my imagination seems extinguished. (*Letters* 3:210)

Ultimately, Bradshaigh was the only one to oblige him, writing a sample letter from Charlotte, which Richardson declared made Charlotte even more of a vixen.[46] He wrote back to Mulso after her refusal to write a letter that he "was [again] very much in earnest" (*Letters* 3:215). There seems no reason to assume this invitation was disingenuous, other than our deep-rooted assumption of singular, male authorial genius.[47] Yet this version of masculinized authorship ignores the ways the gentleman author was dependent on women for his status, as detailed in chapters 1–3. Furthermore, we have seen the evidence of these women in the text itself; we have just as much, nay, more reason to take Richardson at his word here. After all, many of these women were accomplished authors in manuscript or print, and if nothing else, their massive amount of labor and letter writing to Richardson about his novels, especially *Grandison*, is definitely a valued and literal kind of authorship.

"The British Minerva" here is Talbot, and Richardson's suggestion that she write as Sir Charles is especially provocative but also not that surprising. After all, Sir Charles had already been written by and through these women. Richardson writes that Talbot "will add another in that of Sir Charles, making him shine in some new acts of beneficence." In the same letter to Mulso where he chastises her for not writing a letter for him, Richardson continues, "I should not have dared to hope for Miss C. in Sir Charles' character; but that I wanted to make him rise in it, were I to have proceeded. Particularly I wanted a better hymn for him than he had before given us" (*Letters* 3:216). On the one hand, he expresses a sense that Talbot would not write such a letter, but, at the same time, he articulates that her writing as Sir Charles could only improve him. She would use her own authorial talents, poetry, and religious reflections to improve the male paragon. She would write him a better hymn than Richardson. Thus, not only does Richardson acknowledge throughout his correspondence that

Sir Charles is more these women's creation than his, but he also articulates that they could improve him; in fact, that they are entitled to improve him. The gentleman is only elevated by women's pens. He is their vehicle.

Even the preface and appendixes Richardson published speak to his public and private engagement with women writers. His appendixes are directed toward letters signed by women. The first asks for a continuation of the story to settle Clementina's fate, to which Richardson replies, "Do you think, Madam, I have not been very complaisant with my Readers, to leave them the decision of this important article" (*CC* 3:496). This letter, though presented as from a lady, was actually from a man, writing incognito. Yet this narrative disguise speaks to the ways the wider readership registered that women were an audience with influence, over both Richardson and his gentleman novel. This is a kind of inversion from Bradshaigh's own initial camouflage as Belfour, which allows for the possibility that when one was writing about a rake and young woman, writing as a man may have held more sway, while when it came to the gentleman—to *Grandison*—there was an impulse to present one's concerns through a woman. His second letter of the appendix strengthens this possibility; treating criticism over Sir Charles's offered compromise with Clementina's family over the religion of their children also empowers women readers as the authoritative force. Richardson writes, "I had a very nice and difficult task to manage, to convince nice and delicate Ladies, who, it might be imagined, would sit in judgment upon the conduct of a man in a Lovecase" (*CC* 3:472). He specifically cites women's authority to judge men, to judge them in love. Richardson was deliberate about his appendixes; they were a way to guide his readers. Here, Richardson uses this structure to perform his own gentlemanly persona and defend his authorial choices, but this structure also presents women's voices and women's writing as valid and contextually important for understanding *Grandison*.

These women certainly felt the power of their influence. For these women writers, power and pleasure created a sense of ownership over *Grandison*. As Harris writes, "*Grandison* was immediately popular," especially with these women correspondents.[48] Carter wrote to Richardson in September 1753, "And yet, who loves Sir Charles Grandison more than I do? Who is more interested for him than I, and who consequently has a better right to be informed of the state of his affairs?" (*CC* 10:143). Here, Carter encapsulates the coupling of pleasure and ownership these women felt for *Grandison*. These women prided themselves on their authority over *Grandison*; Bradshaigh wrote, "I heard it was said, by a Lady who pretended to know *something*, that sir Charles was to be drown'd, at which I laugh'd and look'd wise" (*CC* 6:374). This possessiveness speaks to both the character and the text itself. After receiving a manuscript from Richardson in October of 1753, Carter declared, "If it was known Sir Charles was in the Town I apprehend there would be so much scratching and clawing that it would be impossible to keep him in my possession" (*CC* 10:148). Why shouldn't Carter, Bradshaigh, and the rest feel this pride of ownership? Sir Charles and *Grandison* are, in a Lockean sense, their possessions via their feedback and their labor. These women were authors, readers, and critics of *Grandison*, expending a tremendous amount of labor for Richardson and doing all the things demarcated as the gentleman's in chapters 1–3 in order to construct a gentleman of their own. Bradshaigh wrote in March 1754, "I believe I have wrote you a hundred pages at least, within these four months but I hope I can prevail with myself, not to write another of four months to come" (*CC* 6:428). But this sense of possession and ownership also came with a deep sense of pleasure. We see this in Carter's effusive pleasure, and in Bradshaigh's letters: "Thank you Sir! now I *adore* you, he has said *every thing* I wanted him to say, and even, (tho' I own my self vain while I write it) the *very words* I wish'd him to say" (*CC* 5:328). Ownership and pleasure are comingled throughout these women's letters. Sir Charles is delightful because he belongs to them; he is quite literally everything they wished and wrote him to be.

The Challenge of Polite Desire

A key facet of Harriet's role as the narrator and as a critic of masculinity is to create anticipation and desire for Sir Charles. As discussed throughout, the gentleman's character had to create desire specifically in women—as characters and as readers. Richardson wrote to Highmore emphasizing that his women correspondents were "extremely earnest with me to give them a *good* man. Can you help me to such a one as is demanded of me. He must be wonderfully polite" (*Letters* 2:236). This wonderful politeness takes on a kind of code for desirability in the text. So, what or who invests politeness with this wonder, this appeal? Harriet. It is what she models in her own desire and encourages—emphatically—in her readers: Sir Charles is "an irresistible man" (*SCG* 6:240). Yet this desire comes from Harriet, not from Sir Charles himself. Sir Charles's character is the product of Harriet's authorship. She literally carves out a space for him in the text by making us feel his absence amidst a sea of lesser men, building our anticipation for the title character to appear, but she also literally writes the letters that define his character, highlights his appeal, insists on his desirability, and constructs his desire to her liking. Harriet uses the structure of the novel, her narrative voice, and suspense to insist that the reader feel as she does. When she declares, "this man is every-thing," she is fundamentally speaking of her own authorial creation and power (*SCG* 4:346).

What constructs this desire is the very blankness, or more accurately, the malleability of Sir Charles's character. Harris argues that Sir Charles is a "blank," and she continues that this creates a kind of readerly frustration: "Readers keen to 'carve' found nothing there to work with."[49] Harris's sense that this blankness creates a narrative impulse, the keenness to "carve," is precisely what I see in Sir Charles. However, I disagree with her conclusion; I think this blankness enabled a very potent kind of creation, where women got to carve out the gentleman to their liking, using their own coded desires and ambitions to do so. It not only leaves room for women, it requires women to fill in the narrative work. Sir Charles's blankness, his lack of interiority, "institutes the need for Harriet's observation—and interpretation—of him."[50] Sir Charles does not drive the authorship; he cannot. Harriet does. She produces the narrative around him, and he, like a good gentleman, does not interfere. He does not challenge her in writing. Her primary role is not, as critics have argued, merely "to display through narration the virtue of Sir Charles."[51] She creates his virtue. Her authorial voice structures his character, form, and desires. She then gets space to repeat and insist that readers also find him attractive, and his blankness leaves little authority besides hers to interfere with this interpretation. If Lovelace's voice and his seductive power defied the larger moral authority of the text, then in *Grandison* there is no such competition. There is only Harriet, and a chorus of like-minded women, telling us over and over again how delightful, how irresistible Sir Charles Grandison is. When she declares "What a man is this, Lucy!" no one naysays her and a chorus of women are there to yea her (*SCG* 2:62).

This delight seems to transfer outward to *Grandison*'s other women authors. Bradshaigh described a young fan, "She is quite outrageous to see Sir Charles" (*CC* 5:263). Bradshaigh herself was pleased with the delayed gratification of *Grandison* and its hero: "And so Sir Charles is the man! I make him one of my very best courtesies, and say all the handsome things that ought to be said, upon being introduced to an acquaintance so agreeable. I shall be impatient to know more of him" (*CC* 5:190). His merits are the construction of women, and whether we in a contemporary sense are swayed by these women or not, it is important to note that women are the ones who speak for, even over, the gentleman to determine his desirability. This delight is not one created by Sir Charles himself, but it is the delight of construction, of authorial creation. Harriet and Bradshaigh's delight is a mode of self-congratulatory pleasure and the power their construction allows them to feel.

Sir Charles's very entrance into the novel is the by-product of women's narrative desire. Richardson's correspondents and his wider readers had pleaded for Clarissa Harlowe's life. My personal favorite is Bradshaigh's plea, which is more threat than sympathetic appeal. Still writing as Belfour, she wrote: "If you disappoint me, attend my curse:—May the hatred of all the young, beautiful, and virtuous, for ever be your portion! And may your eyes never behold any thing but age and deformity! May you meet with applause only from envious old maids, surly bachelors, and tyrannical parents! may you be doomed to the company of such! and, after death, may their ugly souls haunt you! Now make Lovelace and Clarissa unhappy if you dare!" (*CC* 5:5).

But Richardson did make Lovelace and Clarissa unhappy, at least based on these kinds of outcries and expectations. *Grandison* creates a kind of déjà vu, but with a fan-service reimagining. In volume one of *Grandison*, once again a young, exceptional woman is kidnapped and threatened with violence by a handsome rake. However, instead of facing down thousands of pages of tense threats of ruin, ruin fulfilled, death, and then grief, Sir Charles Grandison emerges from out of nowhere and intervenes. If the novel did not bear his name—if, like its predecessors, it was named *Harriet Byron* and not *Sir Charles Grandison*—one would never have seen him coming. This narrative abruptness is a kind of fan fiction made manifest. (I do not use the label fan fiction to in any way diminish these women's influence, but rather to recognize the ways readership and authorial creation can manifest together through fandom.) Clarissa Harlow and Anna Howe shall not be violated by Lovelace or reduced to Hickman; they shall instead escape both fates for a man created by women for them.

It is as if, in her moment of distress, Harriet uses the only weapon at hand, her pen, to manifest a weapon against Sir Hargrave. She cannot physically overpower Sir Hargrave, but Sir Grandison can beat him soundly (*SCG* 1:140). True, our first mention of Sir Charles is not actually from Harriet; her cousin, Mr. Reeves, first meets and writes about him after Harriet's mysterious disappearance. However, from the first, the intervention of Sir Charles is a response to Harriet's narrative voice. Reeves recounts that Sir Charles says he heard Harriet cry out for help: "'Help!' Again cried she, but with a voice as if her mouth was half stopt." Sir Hargrave claims this is his fugitive wife, but Sir Charles believes the muffled voice crying "O no, no, no!" (*SCG* 1:139). The bar is low, as Bonnie Latimer points out, but on the most basic level, Sir Charles first appears as a man who believes a woman, even one (gasp!) dressed for a masquerade, over another man.[52] After this, it is Harriet who makes the stakes of this clear to the reader. It is she who supplies the desperate circumstances of her kidnapping: a condensed and less elegant version of Lovelace's tortures of Clarissa, where Hargrave takes pleasure in her suffering, women refuse to aid her and abet her kidnapping, and a group of male cohorts participates in the scheme. Sir Hargrave mocks Harriet, "By my soul, this will be a pretty story to tell when all your fears are over, my Byron!" (*SCG* 1:163). This narrative taunt is structurally what Harriet answers with Sir Charles. It is a "pretty story," but one where Hargrave loses his teeth, good looks, and health, and can lay no claim on Harriet Byron. A gentleman structured by women emerges from her pen to protect her own narrative impulses. Harriet describes Sir Charles randomly emerging on a darkened road. She does not lose control of her narrative to a Sir Hargrave; he is not her narrative counterpart, the Lovelace to her Clarissa. Nor does she truly have to share the page with Sir Charles.

Here we see the first key feature of the gentleman's desirability: he gets in the way and provides relief. Sir Charles's delay "combines with the reader's anticipation of the appearance of the title character in a deliberate effect of desire heightened by delay."[53] However, structurally, the desire created by his arrival is one of relief. We often discuss desire in terms of tension. However, the erotic offerings of the mid-century gentleman's politeness work on the other side of the desire coin: relief. After all, what is all the tension building toward if not an eventual release, which provides relief? The gentleman's politeness offers relief: relief from the threat of sexual violence, relief from the invalidation of women's opinions, relief as breathing room to speak, and relief from the pressure to deny feeling desire at all. In this way, the gentleman is built for the woman writer's pleasure. The polite gentleman gets in the way of predatory masculinity. Heroines, women writers, and women in general live with constant threats of male violence: physical, verbal, textual, sexual, and more. The gentleman's appeal is that he provides a barrier; he, quite simply, gets in the way.[54] Sir Charles happens to appear on the road to thwart Hargrave. Men behaving badly in patriarchal structures do not give women room to breathe, room to speak, or room to act, and the gentleman simply steps in the way. He also provides a potential retaliation. Harriet cannot smash Sir Hargrave's teeth in, but Sir Charles can politely end up with his hilt in the path of Sir Hargrave's precious pearly whites. Harriet authors all of this.

What helps facilitate the gentleman's relief is his adaptability, a characteristic more frequently attributed to the rake. Bradshaigh wanted Sir Charles to not only be a rake in his appearance but also in his address. Critics have remarked on Sir Charles's rakish or "protean aspects" of his character: his ability to adapt and his manipulative qualities.[55] Sir Charles "is an accomplished manipulator."[56] He has the annoying patriarchal quality of marrying off everyone around him and of muting the more rambunctious characters. As McMaster notes, "A modern reader cannot but feel that Sir Charles' haste in pushing Charlotte into marriage with a man she despises is a betrayal, although it is clearly not meant to appear so."[57] With Harriet, Sir Charles even owns this aspect of his character. In volume 6, he tricks Harriet into signing an agreement for an early wedding date, and when he is caught, declares, "My dearest creature, said he, I *am* a designer" (SCG 3:108).

However, this seemingly rakish component of Sir Charles's character—his designing qualities—is not the exclusive property of the rake, as detailed in chapter 2. These features actually reinforce both the performative aspects of the gentleman's masculinity and their debt to women. Critics have positioned Sir Charles as the heir to a rakish inheritance, both literal and literary.[58] He is the literal son of a rake, Sir Thomas Grandison, who ignored his virtuous wife in favor of town life and spending, was tyrannical over his daughters, and, after his wife's death, installed his mistress as his housekeeper. Sir Charles is the heir of a Lovelace, "handsome, amorous, and martial."[59]

Yet, manipulation, adaptability, and a sex drive are not the exclusive property of the rake. Philip Carter and Bonnie Latimer have both noted the protean aspects of genteel masculinity.[60] Latimer cites Sir Charles's performance as a waiter at his wedding in volume 6 as a key example of this. At Mr. Selby's joking insistence, Sir Charles, "with an air of gaiety that infinitely became him, took a napkin from the butler; and, [put] it under his arm" (SCG 3:232). After acting as the most perfect of all waiters, Mr. Selby declares, "Adad! . . . looking at him with pleasure—You may *be* any-thing, *do* any-thing; you cannot conceal the Gentleman. Ads-heart, you must always be the first man in company—Pardon me, my lords" (SCG 3:233). Latimer argues, "His impersonations show him off as the paradigmatic gentleman."[61] The shades of this, especially with regards to the ladies, are highlighted explicitly by Harriet in an earlier scene. Sir Charles, as is his gentlemanly wont, has inserted himself into a family squabble between his friend Mr. Beauchamp and his stepmother Lady Beauchamp. The lady is surprised by Sir Charles's free, rather flirtatious behavior: "'I have heard much of you, Sir Charles Grandison: But I am quite mistaken in you: I expected to see a grave formal young man, his prim mouth set in plaits: But you are joker; and a free man; a *very* free man, I do assure you.' 'I would be *thought* decently free, madam; but not *impertinent*. I see with pleasure a returning smile. O that ladies knew how much smiles become their features'" (SCG 2:274). The grossness of Sir Charles telling Lady Beauchamp she is prettier when she smiles should not be passed over, but within the structures of the novel this virtuous rakishness takes on a seductive quality. Lady Beauchamp asks, "Was you ever, Sir Charles Grandison, denied by any woman to whom you sued for favor?" To which he replies, "I think, madam, I hardly ever was: But it was because I never sued for a favour, that it was not for a lady's honour to grant" (SCG 2:277). This is seduction within the boundaries of virtue.

Sir Charles represents desire and desirability deployed for the social good, which Harriet calls out for its overt performativity:

> See him so delicate in his behavior and address to Miss Mansfield, and carry in your thoughts his gaiety and adroit management to Lady Beauchamp, as in this letter, and you will hardly think him the same man.... He but accommodates himself to the person he has to deal with:—He can be a man of gay wit, when he pleases to *descend*, as indeed his sister Charlotte has often found, as she has given occasion for the exercise of that talent in him;—and, that virtue, for its own sake, is his choice; since had he been a free-liver, he would have been a dangerous man. (SCG 2:272)

While set up to value and perform domesticity and private virtue, Sir Charles's appeal and gentlemanly qualities are marked as overtly performative. As Latimer rightly calls out, "Richardson's split characterization of his last hero as saintly on the inside and smooth on the outside reveals an understanding of moral masculinity as performative and consciously strategizing."[62] It isn't so much that Richardson hybridizes the qualities of the good man and the rake, as Thompson, McGirr, and Harris have suggested, but rather that this adaptability is an integral part of the performativity of the gentleman's masculinity.[63]

However, despite its manipulative potential, the gentleman's performativity combines with his relief structure to create space for the expression of female desire. Because the gentleman is a kind of mutable space for women, he is a safe space for them to express their sexual and literary desires. The gentleman is presented as providing a socially acceptable tablet for voicing female sexual desire. When Harriet's love is discovered before it is officially returned, she has an out: Sir Charles is *so perfect*. Harriet writes, "Dr. Bartlett guesses, that I am far from being indifferent to Sir Charles Grandison: He must be assured, that my own heart must be absolutely void of *benevolence*, if I did not more and more esteem Sir Charles" (SCG 2:62). Harriet's love, the expression of her desire for this handsome man, is justified because "it is inspired by Sir Charles' merit."[64] As McMaster puts it, "To fall in love with Sir Charles . . . is almost a virtue in itself, since it shows a proper and rational admiration for virtue."[65] The gentleman may not be a contemporary magnet for feminist scholars, but the possibility that heroines could create a gentleman, express their desire for him, and encourage other women to desire him too, is powerful. It is a relief from the constant constraints of modesty. It is a loophole in the social structure that insists that young women (and women in general) never express desire without parental approval, or without the man expressing himself first. After all, if the man is a Sir Charles Grandison, how could the young woman help herself? She only desires as society would have her.

When bosoms heave for the gentleman's politeness, it is because he leaves women room to breathe, literally and textually. In part, this is because they have been frantically combating the most overt manifestations of patriarchy: direct threats of gendered violence. However, it is also because the gentleman is defined by his politeness, which takes the form of a kind of patient blankness. He can be a space for women to speak. The heroine-author can express her distress, write and shape her narrative, and project features and attributes onto the gentleman of her own choosing. The woman writer can create a sense of ownership over the gentleman; he requires her to have room to write and to plot, and then politely contours himself to her wants and desires. He also desires her writing. Sir Charles, like so many Richardson men, falls in love with Harriet through her writing. When he is convincing her of his attachment, he tells her, "Let me tell you madam, that you had not been *Miss Byron*, FOURTEEN days after I was favoured with the sight of those Letters, had I been at liberty to offer you my heart, and could I have prevailed on you to accept it" (*SCG* 3:130). Women's writing is desirable to the gentleman. He allows them to express their desires, reflects them, and validates their writing as narrative ambition.

This desire structure metaphorically represents the professional desires of the woman writer. The woman writer, like the heroine, has to navigate a range of social constraints about if she should write, what she should write, how, for whom, and in what context. As noted in chapter 3, even as women writers were professionally recognized, they often had much narrower social constraints placed on their work. The gentleman, as the symbol of the literary establishment, presents a fantasy. As Sir Charles frequently declares to Harriet in the last volumes of the novel, "The heart of the man before you, madam (to me) in sincerity and frankness, emulates your own" (*SCG* 3:53). He depends on them; he is theirs, and therefore can work for them. The desire for the gentleman, expressed by the heroine authors, echoes and validates a professional desire for literary legitimacy, something these women writers, through the vehicle of Richardson, successfully achieve. They do it; they make the gentleman their character, and their writing is received as legitimate and worthy.

The Gentleman's Legacy: Rethinking a Powerful and Problematic "Fantasy"

I would like to close this chapter by revisiting *Grandison* and the midcentury gentleman's relationship to fantasy. Frances Burney was an admirer of *Grandison*, which was truly very popular. In her journals, Burney recounts an exchange she had with Mr. S., an admirer of her oldest sister:

> Mr. S.: . . . Now Sir Charles Grandison is all perfection, & consequently, the last Character we find in real Life. In truth there's no such thing.
> F.: Indeed! Do you really think a Sir Charles *never* existed?
> Mr. S.: Certainly not. He's too perfect for human Nature.
> F.: It quite hurts me to hear any body declare a really & thoroughly good man never Lived. It is so *much* to the disgrace of mankind.[66]

This exchange speaks to the issues I want to close this chapter with: on the one hand, we have a dismissal of the ideal gentleman as unreal, as stuff for women. On the other hand, we have a woman who would go on to be an influential writer, and who would use Sir Charles as a model for her own ideal gentleman, Lord Orville, just a few years later. The question is, what influence did Burney see in the gentleman, and what are the inherent problems with this continued labeling of the gentleman as a silly fantasy?

Richardson and *Grandison*'s legacy is one of women. As this book has hoped to show, it sprang from the pens of women. Sir Charles's hybrid quality is the legacy of the gentleman as created by women. Sir Charles's adaptability and charm, as the waiter at his wedding, the matrimonial pusher, and the wooer of Lady Beauchamp, are much like Alanthus's from *The Reform'd Coquet*, using a variety of tactics to accomplish his goals and cultivate desire. As Barker notes, this chain of influence is entirely probable because "a 'Mr. Richardson' (along with 'Alexander Pope Esq' and 'Mr. Gay') is included among the novel's subscribers."[67] Sir Charles's ability to seduce and attract without actual seduction is the legacy of Count D'elmont and Eliza Haywood's amatory tradition. Meanwhile, his complex and often problematic blending of admiring and criticizing women's behavior is an echo of Glanville's character in Charlotte Lennox's *The Female Quixote*, which Richardson read while writing *Grandison*. Therefore, the numerous women who called for and who cultivated this aspect of Sir Charles's character can and should be read as part of a woman-authored tradition, and, as the gentleman author, Richardson had to heed this legacy.

Grandison's own critical legacy has been one created by women. One of the features of *Grandison* that seems to irk contemporary scholars to no end is the fact that so many wonderful women writers loved this book. Frances Burney, Jane Austen, and George Eliot all expressed delight with *Grandison*, and critics, who find *Grandison* so boring, cannot fathom how these dynamic women writers loved this supposedly dull, conservative gentleman.[68] Here is where the dismissive connotation of "fantasy" seems to worm its way into our discourse. We don't really like that these women liked this book, so we label it in such a way as to dismiss it as both useful and harmless, which is deeply problematic. This is when we get statements like Barker's that "Sir Charles's idealized, shadowy character offered women novelists, who, like Fanny [Frances] Burney and Frances Sheridan, were ill at ease in the world of male psychology, a means to create a hero perfectly equipped to complement their genteel heroines."[69] As if women writers borrowed Sir Charles as an easy, but ultimately unrealistic, template because "real" men were too much of a psychological mystery. This is clearly reductive and, if this book has been persuasive at all, demonstrably untrue. Women had long been writing men and had specifically created and structured the gentleman. Sir Charles is not a male innovation that women gratefully adopted; he is, from his literary roots through his composition, the product of women's constructions of masculinity.

The argument that comes the closest to what I would like to explore here is Eleanor Wikborg's about figures like Sir Charles and Lord Orville, the good gentleman of women's writing. Wikborg explores the dynamics of lover–father figures in women's writing, of which Sir Charles is a core example. She articulates that in the complex appeal of these figures for their heroines "lies the hope that he [the paternalistic lover] will reciprocate the gesture, that he in turn will yield a measure of authority to [the heroine] and, by so doing, author(ize) her."[70] In a sense, part of this appeal is the ideal of a patriarchy, but one you can count on, one that yields its power to make room for you. This is where the idea of "fantasy" becomes both dismissive and dangerous. There is a critical impulse to present this as unrealistic, as impossible, and as somewhat ridiculous. However, this is a dangerous reaction because it ignores the ways this "fantasy" is in fact very real as a working model of masculinity and how women played an active role in its appeal and actuality. It allows us to step back when women actively participate in this brand of patriarchy, but it also ignores the real influence that women had over the construction of masculinity.

Sir Charles, as a symbol of this masculinity, provides space for women's desires and women's authorship, but this does not mean he is free of patriarchal ties and controls. The truth is the gentleman is not just presented or attractive to women because he is the patriarchy you *can count on*, but because he is the patriarchy you can *make*. Whereas it is tempting to lay

Sir Charles's more misogynistic qualities at Richardson's feet, it is vital to recognize how even these features emerge from the pens of women writers. Remember, Sir Charles's rakish tone with Lady Beauchamp can be traced back to Bradshaigh. So too can one of the—to use a technical term—icky conversations about gendered intelligence in volume 6. In this conversation, Sir Charles engages a collective of women: Charlotte, Mrs. Shirley, Lucy, a variety of other young women, and Harriet. He and Charlotte are debating whether men are actually more intelligent than women: "Why has nature made a difference in the beauty, proportion, and symmetry, in the *persons* of the two Sexes? Why gave it delicacy, softness, grace, to that of the woman ... strength, firmness, to men?" (SCG 6:247). The ultimate conclusion is that because it is natural that the sexes be complementary. Men are in fact superior in a traditionally intellectual sense. This galls; "the presumption of male superiority in *Grandison* is overt and direct,"[71] and moments like these highlight the "the masculinist, anti-egalitarian nature of its hero's benevolence."[72] *Grandison* is not a novel espousing progressive gender equality.

What is left out of this image is the fact that this conversation springs from Richardson's correspondence with women. While Mulso and others argued for a more egalitarian vision, other women such as Bradshaigh openly declared in 1751 that "I should be ashamed of having more learning than my husband" (CC 5:156). It is Richardson who, while not as progressive as Mulso, argues that, "If a woman has genius, let it take its course, as well as in men; provided she neglect not any thing that is more peculiarly her province" (CC 5:158). In this scene, Sir Charles may perhaps be voicing the attitudes of a woman, just not in the ways we would prefer. We would rather he voiced Mulso's views, but that doesn't mean this dialogue and its masculinist views should be laid entirely at Richardson's door. It isn't as straightforward as a patriarchal male author taking women's perspectives up to a point where he reasserts his male prerogative. Bradshaigh's correspondence and its similarity to the dialogue of Sir Charles force us to recognize that the gentleman's character is much more intermingled than that. When Sir Charles becomes a mouthpiece for these patriarchal views, he also still acts as a woman-authored creature. He has, to return to Bradshaigh's aforementioned quote, "said *every thing* I wanted him to say, and even ... the *very words* I wish'd him to say" (CC 5:328).

5

The Gentleman as Authorial Drag

Inverting Plots, Homosociality, and Moral Authorship in Elizabeth Inchbald's A Simple Story *and Mary Robinson's* Walsingham

---

> No; by woman alone can man be rendered amiable.
> —Lady Aubrey in *Walsingham*

Lady Aubrey's above declaration comes at a moment of gendered, pedagogical standoff with Mr. Hanbury, her son's tutor. Arguing with Lady Aubrey about how she is educating her son, Sidney, but ignoring her nephew, Walsingham, Mr. Hanbury claims that men should be modeled after the ancients—that is, by the company of other men. Lady Aubrey insists that only under the guidance of women do men become appealing. Their standoff shapes the action of the novel. When Mr. Hanbury is dismissed, he takes Walsingham with him to educate him in his way, whereas Lady Aubrey proceeds with educating Sidney. In the end, Lady Aubrey wins the standoff; Sidney is by far the most attractive, amiable, and appealing gentleman of the novel, whereas Walsingham is a frantic, misogynistic, Rousseauian mess. Even after Sidney is revealed to be a young woman raised as a gentleman to maintain control over her father's estate, I contend that Lady Aubrey's declaration holds up. Although a woman, Sidney is also the ideal gentleman of the novel. It is this combination of insistence and self-confidence that gives shape to this final chapter, in which I likewise insist that only by women are gentlemen made amiable.

Late-eighteenth-century women writers designed their gentlemen to demonstrate how gender categories could be used to their advantage as writers and to challenge late-century gender binaries in the process. This literary mode of drag presents characters as gentlemen who are later revealed to be literally or structurally women. Elizabeth Inchbald's *A Simple Story* (1791) and Mary Robinson's *Walsingham; or, The Pupil of Nature* (1797), for example, reveal that the best gentleman is both absolutely a gentleman and most definitely a woman. Through an examination of Inchbald's male characters and her novel's two-part structure, I demonstrate that she marks the coquette, given the figure's passionate wit, as the most appropriate role model for masculinity. Although critics typically read Matilda as the inheritor of her vivacious mother's legacy, I argue this reading is a binary narrative trap that the novel asks readers to resist. Instead, Rushbrook, the handsome young gentleman, is actually the reincarnation of Miss Milner's vivacity. Meanwhile, Robinson's *Walsingham* is structured around a literal drag reveal, and I read Robinson's tale as the bolder, more established version of Inchbald's gentlemanly play. For both narratives, I examine how this confident performance of the gentleman is deployed to reveal how power structures built upon binary, innate gender—specifically male homosociality—can be interrogated through such self-assured infiltration. In the end, both women writers showcase their established authority over the gentleman and all of his literary terrain.

This chapter follows Lady Aubrey's lead by focusing exclusively on the men made amiable by women authors. It thus marks the culmination of my book's larger argument: if we take seriously that the gentleman's masculinity is performed and constructed and that the construction is largely the product of women's writing, then at a particular juncture we no longer need literal men to validate the import of their performance. This is not to say that one could not pair either Robinson or Inchbald with other male writers or peers and gauge the influence of their gentlemanly plots, but that is beyond the scope of my project at this point, and I believe that those connections have been well established in my other chapters. Instead, I want to direct attention to the seemingly paradoxical but delightful play of the gentleman and his plots as forms of drag in the late century. I have emphasized the gentleman's deliberate entanglement with the courtship plots of novels written by women. Here I argue that because such a connection was so firmly established, Inchbald and Robinson are able to play upon that structural link and to create their own plots and novels that utilize and critique these earlier narrative structures. As I noted in the introduction to the book, scrutinizing the men imagined by women writers provides the kind of critical foothold that Jack Halberstam and Marjorie Garber articulate for female masculinities because it allows us to "glimpse . . . how masculinity is constructed as masculinity."[1] Inchbald's and Robinson's authorial drag, along with the way in which they utilize the intertwined relationship between the gentleman's masculinity and courtship plots, affords a glimpse into how they use the more rigid binary gender structures of the late century to their advantage while also presenting sharp critiques of these categories.

The Late Eighteenth Century: Binary Gender and Gentlemanly Homosociality

Inchbald's and Robinson's novels represent the highly structured nature of gender in the late century and reveal those structures to be constructed on a foundation of narrative performance. Keenly aware of the power of performance in their own professional lives, both moved within similar intellectual circles, including ones with William Godwin and Mary Wollstonecraft, though Inchbald publicly quarreled with the couple after their marriage. While Robinson has often been presented as the more scandalous of the two, both she and Inchbald were very much aware of and in control of their public images. According to Ben Robertson, Inchbald's good reputation was largely due to her careful self-fashioning; she maintained a "personal . . . unsullied" reputation while also managing "the professional persona that she projected as an actor and writer."[2] Inchbald helped to widely circulate an anecdote about how, as a young actress, she had to thwart the advances of Thomas Harris; to protect her virtue and stop him from kissing her, she supposedly yanked his wig off and then fled the room.[3] Meanwhile, Robinson, following her very public albeit short-lived affair with the Prince of Wales, managed to reinvent herself as a well-respected poet and editor, and in her memoir *Perdita* (1801), she and her daughter rewrote the events of her life to recast her as a sentimental heroine and celebrated author. The same awareness of performance is on full display in their two best-known novels, *A Simple Story* and *Walsingham*, both of which perform gentlemanly plots and conventions. On the one hand, *Walsingham*'s frame narrative involves a gentleman, Walsingham, instructing a female reader, Rosanna, while narrating his life in the hope that she will learn from his sorrows and sympathize with the pain of his rivalry with his cousin, Sir Sidney Aubrey, and his supposed love for Isabella Hanbury. On the other, *A Simple Story* presents two masterful plays of generically defined courtship plots—the reform of the coquette and a sentimental novel—each with the guiding figure of a gentleman mentor.

Both *Walsingham* and *A Simple Story* display the surety of women writers' authority over the masculinity of the gentleman in the latter decades of the eighteenth century, even if such a claim may initially seem counterintuitive. After all, the late century was the era of rigid binary gender models, and by the time that Inchbald and Robinson wrote their novels in the 1790s, most scholars agree that gender identity had undergone what Dror Wahrman calls the "gender-play-to-gender-panic" transition.[4] The gentleman became, in a fuller sense than before, the protector and guardian of these gender boundaries; it was his role to regulate this system to make it seem appealing. This more rigid aspect of gender also translated into a more restrained form of masculinity for the gentleman. As George Haggerty, Candace Ward, and Megan Woodworth all explore, the man of sentiment's overt displays of feeling were now viewed with suspicion, whereas the ideal gentleman was marked "through being in control of his desires and passions."[5] He still had to have desires and feelings—had to feel sympathy properly—but he also had to restrain them. In tandem, as critics like Eve Tavor Bannet, Harriet Guest, and Karen O'Brien point out, women's roles as moral arbitresses and civilizing agents allowed them to play a powerful part in constructing these gender categories, and such complementarity gave them a pointed kind of moral and literary influence.[6] Crucially, this structure made the gentleman more dependent on women. As Woodworth aptly explains, "While women must please men, men must make themselves worthy of being pleased—they must be sufficiently manly and must prove themselves worthy of their positions of power and authority."[7] While binary gender made the gentleman more rigid and more powerful, it also made him more dependent on women, and his power required him to be pleasing according to the moral standards of women.

Although late-century women writers had become established as moral arbitresses, most scholarship, with the exception of Woodworth's, sees this influence as being largely, if not exclusively, directed through women as characters or readers.[8] However, in the later decades of the eighteenth century, women writers frequently spoke directly to male readers, whether literal or metaphorical, and used first-person male narrators. For example, Frances Burney begins *Evelina* (1778) with an exchange of letters between Lady Howard and Mr. Villars, Evelina's adoptive father. However, once Evelina leaves the nest, the bulk of the novel is presented through her voice as she writes to Mr. Villars. Although she is admittedly a young woman seeking advice and guidance from a male father figure, the novel also prioritizes her feminine perspective in presenting her world experience to a male reader. By the time of Mary Hays's *The Memoirs of Emma Courtney* (1796), the novel, as discussed in my introduction, opens with an inversion of *Evelina*'s structure. Instead of seeking advice from a male guardian figure, Hays's heroine presents her life story retrospectively as advice to the inexperienced Augustus Hartley, her adopted son.[9] Charlotte Smith also placed a male perspective at the center of her epistolary novel *Desmond* (1792), and Maria Edgeworth even created a series of first-person male narrators. Her first novel, *Castle Rackrent* (1800), presents the unreliable comedy of Thady Quirk's character, and *Ennui* (1809) and *Harrington* (1817) likewise use first-person male narrators with their own distinct voices. In *Ennui*, Edgeworth literally unmakes and then reforms Glenthorn into a gentleman, and something about the puppetlike quality of his narrative voice gestures toward Edgeworth as the gentleman's puppet master.[10] Of course, looming at the turn of the nineteenth century is Jane Austen, the Übermensch of gentlemen (as my coda will address more directly). That handful of samples represents a larger trend in the late eighteenth century, one that carries over into the early nineteenth, in which women writers took an increasingly direct voice in their depictions of the gentleman.

Instead of binding women to exclusively female audiences, the late-eighteenth-century climate seemed to mark a turning point in the confidence and authority of women writers to control, narrate, and dictate the proper behavior of the gentleman. This is not a brand-new phenomenon but the concentrated legacy of women writers throughout the eighteenth century. Whereas the gentleman used to speak and dictate to women, women writers now had their own authority to speak and dictate to men. Therefore, Robinson's *Walsingham* and Inchbald's *A Simple Story* are not exceptions when it comes to late-century women writers but part of a far broader pattern.

What Inchbald's *A Simple Story* and Robinson's *Walsingham* both present in a particularly direct and narratively unsettling fashion is the authorial drag of the gentleman, which allows them to infiltrate, critique, and upset binary gender and its patriarchal power mechanism: male homosociality. I use drag as a structural and theoretical metaphor because, unlike transgender identity, drag resists a commitment to internal subjectivity. Drag is the performance of gender and can be not only hyperbolic or even comedic in its exaggeration but also powerful and often serious in its implications.[11] I am obviously drawing on Judith Butler's theorization that "'imitation' is at the heart of the *heterosexual* project and its gender binarisms, that drag is not a secondary imitation that presupposes a priori and original gender, but that hegemonic heterosexuality is itself a constant and repeated effort to imitate its own idealizations."[12] But this is indeed the revelation of Inchbald's and Robinson's play with the gentleman: the lack of a priori gender identity, specifically one disposed to hegemonic masculinity. The gentleman is always drag and always an idealization imitating itself.[13] It is the ideal of normative masculinity that confers power.

Both Inchbald and Robinson reveal and deploy the drag of the gentleman to rethink narrative structures, which create a kind of gender simultaneity. Despite its dated terminology, Madeleine Kahn's theory of transvestism provides a useful framework: "Transvestism temporarily suspends the rules of logical consistency. The transvestite is a woman *and* he is a man." This is a figure of paradox: "[They assert] that something both is and is not true at the same time."[14] This is how I theorize the drag of the gentleman: in both novels, it relies on a kind of passing. Sidney passes for a cisgender man for most of the text, and Rushbrook is one, which is revealed to be grounded in performance. Sidney ultimately reveals himself to be a woman, and Rushbrook becomes the recasting of Miss Milner's narrative and character.[15] However, in both cases, the drag persona, the gentleman, is not made illegitimate or inauthentic. They both *are* the gentleman and *are* women within the arc of their texts.

Inchbald and Robinson reveal that masculine privilege is permeable because it is the performance that confers privilege, not biology. From there, they also play on and invert male homosocial structures to reveal the performative bones of masculinity and its systems.[16] Sidney and Rushbrook are both convincing in their portrayals of the familiar, stylized type of the gentleman, and their passing is powerful because it causes the world and narrative to react in normative ways. Or, put differently, the world's reaction, not a trick of dress or lighting, constructs their passing. Sidney *is* the gentleman because the world treats him as one. This point is where Eve Kosofsky Sedgwick's foundational theory of male homosociality comes into play: patriarchy runs on triangulations of male homosocial desire, in which men consolidate "control over the means of production and reproduction of goods, persons, and meanings" through their bonds with other men.[17] To this familiar structure I bring Todd Reeser's point that such bonds protect male dominance, for the triangle "keeps men from serving as objects of exchange," even though "these kinds of triangles do not always function in a neat or stable way."[18] My readings of both novels play with Reeser's provocative questions: "What happens if women control the configuration of the triangle and co-opt it for feminist ends?" and "Can a transsexual, a cross-dressed man or woman, or someone of indeterminate sex, hold a position in the triangle?"[19] Inchbald and Robinson answer that if Dorriforth, Walsingham, and their larger narratives treat Rushbrook and Sidney as men and create these triangulations through rivalry or inheritance, then even if Rushbrook's and Sidney's gentlemanliness is revealed to be drag, their masculinity can still be authentic. Instead, masculinity is revealed to be systemic, structural, constructable, and social, and as such, it and patriarchy are also permeable. Such play allows Inchbald and Robinson to infiltrate patriarchal homosocial structures, interrogate them, and ultimately revise them.

Plot in Drag: The Homosocial Plots of Elizabeth Inchbald's *A Simple Story*

Inchbald's two-part novel has proven to be a rich, critically challenging text. Part 1 traces what appears to be the plot of a standard domestic novel, the tale of a reformed coquette, between Dorriforth, a Catholic priest, and his beautiful ward, Miss Milner. After Dorriforth is released from his vows to become Lord Elmwood, Miss Milner's illicit desire is made legitimate; she learns the error of her coquettish ways, and after misunderstandings and near misses, the lovers are eventually united in holy matrimony. In the turn of the page between part 1 and part 2, seventeen years have passed, and "the beloved Miss Milner" is "no longer beautiful—no longer beloved—no longer . . . virtuous."[20] Lord and Lady Elmwood were happy, but after Lord Elmwood traveled to the West Indies and was noncommunicative for three years, Lady Elmwood had an affair with her rakish suitor. At the time of part 2, she is dying in banishment with her and Elmwood's daughter, Matilda. She bequeaths Matilda to her father, and part 2 traces his initial rigidity but ultimate reconciliation with Matilda.

The leap in time between parts 1 and 2 of *A Simple Story* is a decidedly provocative feature that has divided critics' interpretation of the novel right down the line. Setting the tone for much of the current scholarly engagement with the text, Terry Castle's dynamic reading of the temporal shift views the novel as unapologetically feminist and subversive: "The pattern of rebellion is linked to the struggle for power between men and women."[21] Despite interpreting part 2 of the novel as being less transgressive than in Castle's view, many critics have maintained the gendered opposition within the text. Most base their readings on whether or not Matilda is the second coming of her mother and, in turn, whether or not they read Matilda as another form of feminine rebellion or, more often, a "kind of atonement . . . for the boldness" of part 1 and Miss Milner.[22]

However, pairing Miss Milner with Matilda places parameters around how we understand the structural possibilities of the text, parameters that are grounded in overly rigid assumptions about gender categories. A closer look reveals that Inchbald has dressed her plot in drag and thus hidden the subversive energy and pleasure of the coquette in the passionate young gentleman. Because the witty, sentimental Rushbrook is the true reincarnation of Miss Milner, the narrative power of the vivacious coquette is not banished or even reformed but instead dressed up as the gentleman. Inchbald reveals how plots create and construct desire and gender in ways that recoup the narrative power of the coquette in the gentleman. Inchbald uses this gender reversal to interrogate late-eighteenth-century truisms about innate gender difference, with a keen awareness of the role that plot plays in defining these standards through structures of power and desire. One of the pivotal structures that Inchbald reinterprets is male homosociality. After all, if Rushbrook is indeed the new Miss Milner, then the channels of desire and power between him and Dorriforth shift from a straightforward exchange of Matilda as a woman and thus property into a revelation about the ways in which patriarchal power creates narrative. This dynamic allows us to revise the courtship plot and the figure of the supposedly reformed coquette, for if Rushbrook is the second Miss Milner, then the coquette is not reformed into the sentimental heroine but reincarnated as the young gentleman. Ultimately, by constructing her most refined gentleman, Rushbrook, to have so much in common with a vivacious coquette, Inchbald creates a model of masculinity that questions and resists the binaries that it plays with.

The text itself presents the pairing of Miss Milner and Matilda as a narrative trap, one that we are asked to resist. Initially, the characters who present us with this reading, Dorriforth/Elmwood and Miss Woodly—Miss Milner's and later Matilda's virtuous companion—consistently misread Miss Milner in part 1. Miss Woodly and Dorriforth both misinterpret Miss Milner's forbidden passion for Dorriforth as a passion for the rakish Lord Frederick. These misreadings from two of the supposedly most rational and virtuous characters—the two most immune to the fashionable world—act as a warning. In fact, the text explicitly asks us to question the resemblance between Miss Milner and her daughter. As Matilda examines her father's portrait, Inchbald writes: "In the features of her father, she [Matilda] was proud to discern the exact moulds in which her own appeared to have been modeled; yet, Matilda's person, shape, and complection [sic] were so extremely like her mother's that at the first glance she appeared to have a still greater resemblance of her . . . but her mind and manners were all Lord Elmwood's" (SS 220). The text not only aligns Matilda with her father more than with her mother but also positions a physical resemblance to her mother in a cursory "first glance" that fails to identify the more important aspects of her character. Inchbald challenges our desire for a homosocial return of Miss Milner, and we desire her character and perceive her narrative absence to be a vacuum. In seeking to fill this void, we mistakenly look for embodied resemblance—that is, gendered resemblance—and in approaching the text in this way, critics have inadvertently repeated the same binary gender structures that they often seek to critique.

Critics do have correct instincts about the "important patterns of duplication" between the two parts of *A Simple Story*.[23] They are also correct to suspect the subversive energies of masquerade in the text. As Catherine Craft-Fairchild argues, "Masquerade [is] the creation of an image or spectacle for the benefit of a spectator,"[24] one that represents a "distance or proximity between the representation and the self beneath."[25] In the novel, we see both of these forms of masquerade. Matilda is a masquerade of supposed proximity that leads the spectator astray from the far more interrogative masquerade of Rushbrook. Although Rushbrook is the most ignored character of the novel, it is his childhood banishment that first reveals Elmwood's tyrannical streak and foreshadows the banishment of both Miss Milner and Matilda. Rushbrook's mother, Elmwood's sister, married without her brother's consent, and when she dies, Elmwood maintains the son but refuses to see him. However, few critics discuss Rushbrook as a character beyond noting that he falls in love with Matilda in part 2. In this light, Rushbrook and his courtship of Matilda are considered to be "almost an afterthought."[26]

Rushbrook is the character that most resembles Miss Milner in part 2, given the overt similarities in their physicality, demeanor, treatment by other characters, and the structure of their plots. They have the same strengths and foibles. Miss Milner is all "sprightly vivacity ... natural gaiety" and "beautiful beyond description" (SS 13, 50). Likewise, Rushbrook is an "extremely handsome young man" and "a perfect man of fashion." Similar to Miss Milner, he also has "an elegance and persuasion in his manner almost irresistible," as well as a "youthful, warm, generous, grateful but unthinking mind" (SS 230, 241). Beyond temperament and attractiveness, both Rushbrook and Miss Milner tend to engage in performative behaviors, and both bend the truth or even lie to protect the secrets of their hearts. Miss Milner lies about loving Lord Frederick in order to protect Dorriforth from dueling with him, and she also plays the haughty mistress in order to test Dorriforth's love. Similarly, Rushbrook conceals and obfuscates with Elmwood in order to protect Miss Woodly and Matilda. Elmwood turns up unexpectedly when Rushbrook and Miss Woodly are talking about Matilda, and Rushbrook, "with the most natural and happy laugh that was ever affected," covers for them both, thereby protecting Miss Woodly, Matilda, and himself from Elmwood's wrath (SS 234). Owing to such behaviors, other characters view them as frivolous and fickle. Despite their foibles, however, both characters are saved from division with Lord Elmwood by deus ex machina interventions. Within their respective parts, neither of them is punished for their performances. Instead, their performances serve to create narrative.

Rushbrook is the reimagined Miss Milner, and he is *the* gentleman of the text. Critics who engage with Rushbrook mistakenly read the fact that he is less domineering and rigid than Elmwood to mean that he is "juvenile, helpless, and ultimately, if implicitly, impotent."[27] However, doing so, as other chapters have established, misunderstands the key features of the masculinity of the gentleman. Genteel masculinity is not fundamentally interested in macho tyranny, and Rushbrook's features are decidedly aligned with those of the gentleman. Rushbrook's ability to charm, please, and feel sympathy is properly rather than aberrantly masculine. In fact, he is a very accomplished gentleman: "He had made an unusual progress in his studies, had completed the tour of Italy and Germany" (SS 230). If anything, Rushbrook is the ideal gentleman of the text when compared with Dorriforth/Elmwood and his tyrannical rigidity. Rushbrook is not effeminate—he is properly feminized as the gentleman should be but not effeminate—and Miss Milner is likewise not a masculine woman. If both Rushbook and Miss Milner are properly masculine and feminine and yet so similar, then their similarity interrogates the ways in which character was understood to reflect innate gender. Pairing the gentleman with the coquette thus presents a challenge to late-eighteenth-century binary gender.

Circular Triangles of Reading: Re-forming the Reformed Coquette Plot

In *A Simple Story*, Inchbald creates a kind of drag through a plot and structure in which the gentleman is a construct, and she asserts her authorial powers by mechanizing the gentleman for her plots. What makes Rushbrook a drag version of Miss Milner is not his body or genitalia, metaphorical or otherwise, but his character's plot, the ways both characters are situated in scenes infused with desire, and how both construct plots to counter patriarchal tyranny. With the gentleman as a construct, a structure vulnerable to occupation, Inchbald uses one structure—her plot—to reveal the constructedness of the gentleman. In so doing, she undoes the purportedly innate aspects of gender for both masculinity and femininity. For a vehicle, she uses the patriarchal homosocial triangle coupled with the circular reading invited by her two-part structure.

The leap across seventeen years in a page turn feels like the drop of an authorial guillotine. I agree with Jo Alyson Parker that "each of the two parts of *A Simple Story* is fairly unified in itself. Put together, however, they violate our notions of textual closure."[28] Although Inchbald's individual parts seem to move toward closure, the overall structure resists it and any linear, straightforward interpretation. Craft-Fairchild argues that the structure represents the novel's commitment to parting and separation. By contrast, my reading slightly shifts Craft-Fairchild's focus on "necessary separation" to the novel's investment in a narrative that invites a different structure for reading.[29] Rather than seeing the parts as resisting each other, I argue that they play off of each other, back and forth, for a kind of circular reading. Instead of reading through from part 1 to part 2, part 1 invites a reading of part 2 that reflects back on the plot of part 1, and then a reading of it that reflects back to part 2, and so on. The drag of Miss Milner/Rushbrook is what creates this cycle. Their mirrored scenes create layers of reflection that circulate through charged exchanges with Dorriforth/Elmwood. If Rushbrook is Miss Milner, then his homosocially charged scenes with Dorriforth ask us to rethink both masculine power structures and the heterosexual plot in part 1. Inchbald plays on and foils a desire for traditional courtship and sentimental plots, thereby spoiling the very structures that they expected and that women writers traditionally used to establish their authorship, and she does it with deliberate, visible control.

Before moving into my analysis of these structures, I first want to present what I see as the blatant repetition of scenes from part 1 in part 2. The mirrored scenes between Miss Milner/Dorriforth and Rushbrook/Elmwood revolve around the guardian's desire for one of his charges to marry a partner of his choosing and their refusal to do so based on romantic desires that they must keep secret from him. The scenes of reconciliation also bear a striking resemblance to one another, with Sandford intervening in a heated crisis to reconcile the parties. Both Miss Millner and Rushbrook are restrained by Dorriforth/Elmwood's own proclamations from revealing their true desires to him: Miss Milner is prohibited from expressing her desire for him because of his priesthood, Rushbrook by Elmwood's iron mandate against mentioning Matilda's name in his presence, and both are restrained by their dependent positions as Elmwood's wards. In all of these repeated scenes, Miss Milner and Rushbrook tread the careful line of respectful but unmistakable defiance. Miss Milner responds to her guardian by stating, "No . . . my heart is not given away," and asks not to be compelled to answer his questions more clearly, claiming a preference for living single and refusing to say more (*SS* 25). In part 2, Rushbrook replies to such probing in a strikingly similar manner: "Lord Elmwood proposed a wife to him; and in a way so assured of his acquiescence," in response to which Elmwood asks him, "You have no engagements, I suppose?" (*SS* 251–252). Rushbrook prevaricates: "I have only to say, my lord . . . that although my heart may be totally disengaged, I may yet be disinclined to the prospect of marriage" (*SS* 253). In both cases, Dorriforth/Elmwood tries heatedly to compel a younger person to yield to his commands by invoking his patriarchal authority over them.

The Rushbrook-versus-Elmwood scenes are the entry point into Inchbald's play with homosociality. On one level, Elmwood's interrogations of Rushbrook depict classic Sedgwickian male homosociality. Critics such as Craft-Fairchild and Caroline Breashears have read Rushbrook and Elmwood's relationship as one of several homosocial bonds in *A Simple Story* that reserve power for men through their exchange of women. According to this structure, Rushbrook's courtship and defense of Matilda establishes his homosocial power struggle with Elmwood. In this light, Rushbrook's desire for Matilda is an "affective or social force, the glue that maintains male privilege."[30] By marrying her, he maintains his status as heir, even after the father and daughter reconcile, and thus maintains the patriarchal system of power in which women become vehicles for property exchange. Any erotic charge of these exchanges—and there are plenty—seem merely to fuel and reinforce this power structure.

A closer inspection of the role of desire in the twin plots and their erotic charge reveals how it is not binary gender that creates desire but power and narrative structure. The structures of male homosociality reverberate with homoerotics, and, as John Morillo notes, the dialogue between Rushbrook and Elmwood is "archly sexualized."[31] This charge comes from the above-described mirroring. The way in which Inchbald mirrors this desire with the desire of the courtship plot is too deliberate to ignore. The two reconciliation scenes emphasize that instead of distinguishing homosocial power struggle from heterosexual courtship, Inchbald aligns them. As a result, both Miss Milner and Rushbrook are threatened with banishment. In Miss Milner's case, it is Elmwood's intended, self-imposed banishment from her, a decision that he reaches after she defies him by attending the masquerade and allowing Lord Frederick into her company again. In Rushbrook's case, Elmwood banishes his nephew for breaking his law and mentioning Matilda's name to him. In the first, Sandford commands Elmwood, "My Lord, take this woman's marriage vows; you can ask no fairer promises of her reform" (*SS* 191). In the second, Sandford commands, "Take this young man from the depth of despair in which I see he is sunk, and say you pardon him" (*SS* 292). The similarity of the language and of Sandford's commands casts the homosocial scene in the same light and tone as the heterosexual union of the first. Inchbald thus reveals that plot, not genitalia, constructs desire. The patriarchal machines of courtship and homosocial rivalry create the same spark; however, that spark is not natural but constructed. Apart from revealing that she can control the machine and manipulate it as well as anyone else, Inchbald reveals the machine for what it is: a plot to maintain male-authored control.

At the same time, such control is also an illusion, one that relies on readers' yielding to its linear agenda. Miss Milner/Rushbrook's drag may seem to be a conservative gesture, for the coquette's feminine transgressions are made acceptable when performed by a man. However, Rushbrook himself reminds us that, "If I feel gratitude towards you [Lord Elmwood] . . . I must also feel it towards her [Miss Milner], who first introduced me to your protection" (*SS* 290). Rushbrook only enters the narrative as Miss Milner's plot device; she unites the nephew with his uncle and thus overcomes the established example of male tyranny and banishment. Rushbrook is her creation, her gentleman, her plot, and he follows through and then back again.

Reading back, the structural drag allows us to rethink the courtship plot and ending of part 1 of *A Simple Story*. In one light, Miss Milner appears to be a literary descendent of Mary Davys's Amoranda from *The Reform'd Coquet* (1724). Wealthy and willful, Miss Milner's flirtatious ways are checked and called into question by the theoretical regulation of her guardian-lover Dorriforth. As in the earlier novel, the coquette and her gentleman counterpart also battle for narrative control. Resembling a hybrid of Amoranda and Arabella, Miss Milner declares to Miss Woodly that she will test her lover: "As my guardian, I certainly did obey him; and I could obey him as a husband; but as a lover, I will not . . . for if he will not submit to be my lover, I will not submit to be his wife" (SS 154). Throughout, Miss Milner plots. She seeks to exert her version of their courtship, and Dorriforth resists. Taken as an ending, part 1 seems to contain this female authorial impulse. Part 2 seems to resign the will to narrate to the grave, with Miss Milner forever encased in the cold form of Lady Elmwood and the (f)rigid Matilda. However, if Miss Milner's character, her plot, and her power struggle with Dorriforth have been repackaged instead of dismissed, that is revelatory. The foreclosure at the end of part 1 is revealed to be a patriarchal illusion, one authored by the gentleman mentor-lover. The woman writer has not been silenced by the male author figure; instead, she has recoded her rebellious energy to live on. She resists the linearity of the courtship plot itself and, in the process, reveals it to be an unfulfilling device.

The Gentleman in Drag: Tricky Triangles and Disruptive Courtship Narratives in Mary Robinson's *Walsingham*

Robinson's *Walsingham* is a more blatant takedown of patriarchal narratives than Inchbald's *A Simple Story*. After hundreds of pages of Walsingham's frantically running hither and yon, screaming loudly enough about his rivalry with his cousin Sidney for all of England to hear (so why are you making it weird!?), with the flip of a few pages—once again—all is transformed. After Sidney's reveal, the homosocial rivalry is immediately transfigured into heterosexual love in an inverse of Inchbald's structure. After falling into gambling, being in and out of prison and funds, and flirting with several women, all of whom Sidney steals except the one woman Walsingham rapes, Walsingham, without pausing for breath, transfers his affections from Isabella Hanbury—the woman he has been raving about being in love with for the entire novel—to Sidney. The novel thus proposes that after the requisite time for Sidney to learn to be a woman, everyone who has survived will pair off and live happily ever after in proper binary bliss.

This is all entirely too strange, too suspicious, and too constructed; it is as if we can see the mechanisms of narrative, gender, and patriarchy all grinding together. Although my reading of *Walsingham* continues the tradition that views Robinson as challenging binary gender categories,[32] I add that Robinson is particularly interested in the construction of the gentleman and in using his masculinity to critique patriarchal power structures. Sidney is *the* ideal gentleman of the text, and their ability to perform this version of masculinity without detection—that is, to pass—threatens binary gender categories. It also affords them, as well as Robinson, access to the privileges and power struggles of male homosociality. Within this structure, Sidney's performativity reveals that gendered society runs on performance, that the performance makes the man, and that through genteel, masculine performance a woman can co-opt the machinations of patriarchal authority in ways that subordinate masculinity and men such as Walsingham.

The Authorial Threat of Passing for the Gentleman

Sidney's performance of the gentleman is threatening because it directly defies 1790s assumptions about gender. Robinson's critics expressed disbelief at her plot, and we need only read the anxiety of Robinson's reviewers to see why. As a critic in *The Analytical Review* (1798) wrote, "The circumstances upon which the distress turns is . . . little probable, and frequently ludicrous."[33] Most pointedly, a review in *The Monthly Mirror* (1798) stated "that a proud and unprincipled woman should resolve to educate her daughter as a youth, to prevent the family title and estates from devolving to the next male heir, may be credited without much difficulty:—but that this daughter should arrive to maturity, and mingle in the dissipations of high-life, indiscriminately associating with men, and conducting herself in all respects like those of the present age, without detection, or even incurring the slightest degree of suspicion, is an event that shocks probability and staggers belief."[34] It isn't the act of cross-dressing that surprised and upset Robinson's critics. Figures such as Charlotte Charke, Henry Fielding's 1746 *The Female Husband*, tales of female soldiers, and even Robinson herself, who performed in breeches roles, would have been familiar reference points for *Walsingham*'s readers.[35] The anxiety trigger is that nobody, not even the men Sidney associates with, ever find her out. As Wahrman and Julie Shaffer argue, it was believed that "late-eighteenth-century heroines . . .

simply could not pull it off."³⁶ Therefore, "If *Walsingham* followed the [expected] model... the real sex of the male-masquerading Sidney would be apparent to Walsingham and, indeed, to everyone else."³⁷ (For the record, readers did not share the critics' outrage. The novel itself was a success; it was published by Longman on December 7, 1797, and went into a second edition by New Year's Day.) Such critics viewed Sidney's performance as an impossibility because other men would have surely recognized Sidney as a woman. They thus attempted to reassert control over Robinson's text by emphasizing the financial motive, which has long been a way of making female-male cross-dressing *"normalized."*³⁸ It was a historical strategy to reinscribe Sidney's performance within understood structures, to recast it as something that achieved an end instead of a force for creating gender.

Even so, the text itself clearly resists such normalization because Sidney is without question the best gentleman in the novel. Even Walsingham affirms repeatedly that Sidney is not merely manly but the ideal man. When they reunite as adults, Walsingham begrudgingly admits: "Sir Sidney was exactly the being whom Isabella had described—handsome, polite, accomplished, engaging, and unaffected. He sung, he danced, he played on the mandolin, and spoke the Italian and French languages with the fluency of a native. Yet these were not his only acquirements; he fenced like a professor of the science; painted with the correctness of an artist; was expert at all manly exercises; a delightful poet; and a fascinating companion" (*Walsingham* 129). Sidney has been classically and culturally educated; has traveled; and has gained the vaunted experience of the world. Sidney excels in the gentlemanly art of fencing yet simultaneously uses the gentleman's restraint to avoid dueling; when Walsingham challenges Sidney to a duel, Sidney, despite his superior skill, fires into the air. There are no signs of the "effeminate nor... socially deviant male in the way that those writing on fops and homosexuals suggest."³⁹ Nobody notices; nobody suspects. Walsingham is a deeply unreliable narrator, and, as this chapter bears out, a bad author and reader. However, there are plenty of presumably clear-sighted characters, even among the men—Colonel Aubrey, Mr. Hanbury, the pointedly named Mr. Optic—who never question Sidney's performance. On the contrary, Sidney is hailed as "the epitome of the perfect man."⁴⁰

Robinson exposes how permeable the boarders of narrative passing are. A close look reveals how the features that mark Sidney as a gentleman resemble the accomplishments of an upper-class woman: dancing, charm, painting, music, poetry, etc. However, instead of outing Sidney, these features go unnoticed. Robinson illustrates how the supposedly contrasting features of gender are made to look distinct by social reaction, not innate difference. Sidney also emphatically out-gentlemans Walsingham at every turn, which comes to serve as the foundation of their homosocial rivalry. Between ravings, Walsingham *intends* to do good. He *intends* to help the noble but impoverished Colonel but instead ends up reneging on his commitment, rapes his fiancée, Amelia Woodford, and then murders her in an act of sentimental violence. Sidney, by contrast, defies his mother by providing funds for the Colonel and supports and protects Isabella and numerous other women throughout the novel. Walsingham loses track of his own debts, and his attempts to help others navigate their social and financial woes fall apart; he is forever moving and never achieving. Meanwhile, Sidney outmaneuvers, outmanners, and outmans Walsingham in every possible way.

By comparing Sidney and Walsingham, Robinson emphasizes that what makes a gentleman desirable is not his innate gender but his treatment of women. Sidney repeatedly seduces women away from Walsingham, and although Sidney ultimately reveals her gender to them, the initial play at heterosexual seduction is clearly superior to Walsingham's. For example, as Sidney wins over Lady Emily, one of the women whom Walsingham flirts with, the text gloats, "[Lady Emily] has never had such a lover as Sidney Aubrey" (*Walsingham* 163). This appeal is the core of the gentleman, and the ability to invoke desire in women is what defines his heterosexual masculinity. Robinson makes a point to connect Sidney's desirability to the influence of women. As Sidney explains, "Wherever I go, I make woman my companion; whatever I meditate, I consult a woman: in short, when I abandon the sex I cease to live" (*Walsingham* 131). Whereas Sidney has been raised by women and sees "woman [as] a charming creature . . . a gentle associate where she has power to command," Walsingham is routinely misogynistic (*Walsingham* 193).[41] He both refers to and treats Isabella as his property throughout the novel and proclaims that "the lovely Lady Arabella, who had hitherto *appeared* to be the most affected of high-bred triflers, was, in reality, a reasonable being" (*Walsingham* 423). How generous, how insightful. Robinson thus reveals that the power of the gentleman is in pleasing women, not in private character or body. Audaciously, what pleases women turns out to be treating them as subjects and not as objects.

The fact that Sidney's version of the gentleman has been authored by women is what makes Sidney the better man. In Butlerian terms, Sidney is a gentleman because *her* mother "names" *him* a boy: "The naming is at once the setting of a boundary, and also the repeated inculcation of a norm."[42] The moment is one of authorship, for Lady Aubrey creates and authorizes Sidney's masculinity. She is also the one, as my epigraph illustrates, who insists that Sidney seek the society of women. In the aforementioned debate with Mr. Hanbury, Lady Aubrey insists, "by woman alone can man be rendered amiable," and she repeats the phrase three times during their dialogue. When she insists on a female influence for her child, Mr. Hanbury accuses her of supporting the education system of Lord Chesterfield, but Lady Aubrey surprises him and possibly Robinson's readers by declaring, "The precepts of Chesterfield are generally either useless or criminal" (*Walsingham* 92). Chesterfield's influence involves a homosocial system that uses women, and Lady Aubrey rejects it, just as she rejects the homosocial, classical education of the ancients, because she views both systems as excluding the influence of women. In this way, Lady Aubrey's status as a coquette connects to metaphors of female authorship. The coquette has again returned to insist that she be allowed to create narrative, specifically the narrative of the gentleman.

Lady Aubrey is one of many women who "author" Sidney's status as the ideal man. Every time that a woman chooses Sidney over Walsingham, they authorize Sidney's masculinity as more ideal, more desirable, and more gentlemanly. Pointedly, Isabella also pens Sidney in a letter to Walsingham and becomes the first character to define adult Sidney. Already "half in love" with Sidney, she writes: "Sir Sidney is an angel! Never did nature form so wonderful a creature! How shall I describe him? What pen can do justice to the model which mocks the powers of description? . . . –Oh Walsingham! I will not attempt to delineate them; they would mock the powers of a more experienced artist. Then, his manners are so fascinating, so polished, so animated!" (*Walsingham* 127–128). A defining feature of the ideal gentleman continues to be the attraction of a woman and the interest that he creates in women. I argue that the way in which Isabella directs attention to her authorship and her role as the artist aligns her with the woman writer. Even her modesty and her claim to have limited experience and prowess echo the litany of women writers' prefaces. Her description is also reaffirmed by Walsingham: "Sir Sidney was exactly the being whom Isabella had described" (*Walsingham* 129). It is Isabella's authority and the wider array of women characters that continue to authorize Sidney's position as the gentleman.

But the connections between ideal masculinity and authorship go even further, because Walsingham is a failed gentleman author. The epistolary form of the text self-consciously positions Walsingham as an author, one who writes to Rosanna to instruct her and give her the benefit of his masculine experience of the wider world. He repeatedly draws attention to his authorial role: "Rosanna, my pen trembles as I proceed; but you have commanded, and I will obey your wishes" (*Walsingham* 119). The words not only repeat the convention of the gentleman's seeming to instruct and seek sympathy from female readers but also reiterate the false language of gallantry and masculine subservience, for Walsingham never delivers on being a gentleman. Robinson frequently reveals that Walsingham is a poor excuse for a literary gentleman. As a reader, Walsingham pathologically misinterprets everything and everyone around him. He misreads Isabella, Emily, and Arabella's defections to Sidney; he misreads Sidney's love for him as hatred and rivalry; and he mistakes Amelia for Isabella at a ball. In fact, he mistakes several women for Isabella at balls. Despite his claims to sentiment and prophetic insight, he does not qualify as a sympathetic reader.[43]

As a male author and male-authored gentleman, Walsingham is revealed to be misogynistic and self-serving, and his supposedly innate masculinity is guided by all of the traditional modes of hegemonic masculinity. He is taught by other men to embrace reason, to sympathize with nature, and to seek truth and virtue, but the product of this education is violent misogyny and ineffective authorship. He repeatedly rewrites women as blamable for their loss of virtue, which is sometimes the figment of his own imagination. When he believes that Isabella loves Sidney, he describes her "as the dupe of her own vanity." He even walks back his accusation that Sidney is a libertine, because "Sir Sidney's youth and inexperience were ill suited to the machinations of seduction; and I concluded that Isabella was more than half to blame, in yielding to his passion" (*Walsingham* 163).

After Walsingham rapes Amelia, he revises her rape in his narrative to assuage his guilt. He initially claims, "I could have loved her, had I not known Isabella." After raping her, he laments, "I knew not how to meliorate her fate," even despite acknowledging "I ought to have married her" only a semicolon later. In the next breath, he argues, "There was mercy in refusing" because their marriage would be followed "with all the hideous train of reproach, indifference, repentance, and disgust." In the next paragraph, he distances himself further from his guilt by claiming, "She was, in fact, the victim of her own fatal curiosity" (*Walsingham* 296). Even more despicably, when Mr. Optic urges Walsingham to marry Amelia by arguing that it is his duty to restore her good name, Walsingham blames "the frailty which had rendered her my victim, made me suspect that she would scarcely fulfill, with honour, the duties of a wife" (*Walsingham* 300). He thus repeats the same argument that he used with Sidney and Isabella. Robinson, perhaps drawing on her own experience as a publicly ridiculed "fallen" woman, uses Walsingham to dramatize the conventions of male authorship. Walsingham literally writes his way out of his own guilt by displacing his masculine violence onto women. He demonstrates how male authors, whether symbolically or literally, rewrite situations of women's sexual vulnerability to their own advantage by making women responsible for protecting their virtue and clearing all male participants in the narrative of blame.

Poetry within the novel becomes the ultimate symbol of masculine authorship and at once the product of the female author. Walsingham, who can't arrive anywhere on time or be useful to anyone, always manages to find a scrap of paper on which to scrawl some verses. However, Sidney also surpasses him in the art of poetry, for Sir Sidney is both a better author and a better reader than Walsingham. In fact, Sidney writes a sonnet so well that Walsingham assumes the lines are "merely a translation; they are not my cousin's composition . . . they bear evident traits of that romantic tenderness which distinguished the Italian poets" (*Walsingham* 146). As Ellen Arnold argues, the genre of Sidney's sonnets speaks to a gentlemanly education, and his "poem convincingly acts the part of a poem written by a well-educated man."[44] Sidney can write like the gentlemen, which helps to make him a gentleman. Although Walsingham writes more poems within the novel, they all have their own kind of drag effect, and many were reprinted or had already been printed in Robinson's own collections of poetry. Some contemporary critics of Robinson's may have found the plot "perplexed"[45] or even "disgusting,"[46] but many praised the inset poetry as having "great delicacy and beauty"[47] and for being "very superior to those with which novel-writers usually treat us."[48] The value of Walsingham's poetry is the product of Robinson's own literary reputation. Known as an "English Sappho," Robinson had gained a high reputation for her poetry before beginning to write novels. Similar to Charlotte Smith, she was admired by and influenced the Romantics; Samuel Coleridge was a particular correspondent and admirer. Walsingham's literal authorship is celebrated but relies on the reputation and awareness of the woman writer behind it. The threat of Sidney's passing reveals the pulse of how women authors power the gentleman.

Infiltrating the Homosocial Triangle

Sidney's passing is threatening because, as Halberstam writes, "at various moments, the successful pass may cohere into something akin to identity. At such a moment, the passer has *become*."[49] By successfully performing masculinity, Sidney is indeed a gentleman. He demonstrates that the gentleman's masculinity is a performance, one that women can execute as successfully as men, if not better. Such possibility has unique ramifications for homosocial relationships within the text, because for most of the novel Walsingham treats Sidney as his homosocial rival to almost hyperbolic proportions. Meanwhile, as Katherine Binhammer and Emily Allen point out, there is a simultaneous structure in which, "as the true object of Sidney's affection, [Walsingham] is essentially traded from female hand to female hand."[50] The dynamic creates provocative potential for the text. Sidney's performance of masculinity is so authentic that it allows her and consequently Robinson to infiltrate the structures of male homosocial desire and gain access to patriarchal power. This works on two levels: the traditional homosocial triangle (i.e., male-female-male) and the inverted homosocial triangle (i.e., female-male-female). In the traditional configuration, Sidney's drag allows Robinson to reveal the charged undercurrent of homosocial desire, its homoerotic anxieties, and how it is used to reinforce patriarchal courtship narratives. Through the inverted configuration, the novel's triangulation allows Robinson to place Walsingham in the objectified position. By positioning the biological man as an object of exchange, Robinson reveals the objectification of women to be a superficial construct based on power, not the state of their being.

Robinson makes the structure of male homosociality viscerally transparent, including its layer of homoerotic desire. According to Walsingham, the motivation for all of his actions and his misfortunes is his rivalry with Sidney, which is played out hyperbolically and mechanically through the bodies of women. Isabella is the first; she is Walsingham's childhood companion, and although he claims to have loved her always, his "feelings" for Isabella are set in motion by his rivalry with Sidney. Walsingham's desire for Isabella is always mediated by distance and obstacle. Looking back, he recalls, "It was not till I was separated from Isabella [at University] that I knew how tenderly I loved her... fatally conscious, that she was the object of my enthusiastic idolatry" (*Walsingham* 126). When Sidney seems to abandon Isabella for Lady Emily or Arabella, rather than seeking out the woman whom he claims to love beyond all reason, Walsingham never acts. However, when Sidney seems to renew his relationship with Isabella, Walsingham kidnaps her and brings her to Lord Kencarth's house. She shouts for help: "Oh, my lord [Kencarth]... rescue me from this monster!" To that, Walsingham replies, "My Lord, I command your absence... this lady is my property" (*Walsingham* 395). This is textbook male homosocial desire: Isabella only becomes truly desirable when Walsingham can use her as an object of exchange with another man.

Walsingham's relationship with Amelia is even more emphatically Sedgwickian. Most critics take Walsingham's word for it that Amelia "fatally, strikingly resembled Isabella." As with Inchbald, this seeming truth is superficial and ultimately suspicious—a narrative trap. A closer look at Amelia's physical and intellectual description instead aligns her more closely with Sidney than with Isabella. Amelia and Sidney also share the rather distinct feature of auburn hair, whereas Isabella's is golden. Immediately before claiming that Amelia fatally resembles Isabella, Walsingham notes, "To these attractions [of mind] Nature had given a person beautifully commanding! Tall, fair, finely formed, with light *auburn hair*, and eyes beaming with sensibility that bespoke the purest and most genteel affections" (*Walsingham* 261). When meeting Sidney as a child, Walsingham remembers, "He was indeed beautiful! His countenance was fresh and animated; his person well formed, and his eyes expressive of sense and benevolence... while the deep glow which mantled over his cheek was contrasted with a *profusion of dark auburn hair*, falling in natural ringlets" (*Walsingham* 89, emphasis mine). Amelia shares other features with Sidney as well. She is tall, her manners too are "unaffected," and she has been "polished by a foreign education" and "a correct judgment, joined to extreme delicacy of sentiment" (*Walsingham* 261). In the carnivalesque confusion of the second masquerade scene that precedes the rape, Walsingham has a heated exchange with Sidney before absconding with Amelia. Although he claims to be searching for Isabella, what lights the fuse of his sexual aggression is his dialogue with Sidney. Robinson thus captures the homoerotics within the homosocial rivalry and the ways that they are masked through supposedly heterosexual vessels. If Amelia equals Isabella then this is a heterosexual rivalry. If Amelia equals Sidney, however, then the homoerotics of the narrative equation come to the fore.

If we connect the overtly homosocial structure with Walsingham's status as a would-be gentleman author, then we can trace how Robinson reveals male homosociality as a violent plot of patriarchy. Male homosocial structures are plots authored by men, and Walsingham's perceived entitlement to Isabella is thus a false, tyrannical narrative of patriarchal lineage. Walsingham does not spontaneously fall in love with Isabella; on the contrary, their union is proposed to him and crafted by Mr. Randolph, Isabella's uncle, and Mr. Hanbury, her brother. When Mr. Hanbury and Walsingham arrive to collect Isabella from her uncle, Mr. Randolph teasingly calls Walsingham "Isabella's intended husband" (*Walsingham* 118). Mr. Hanbury even promises Mr. Randolph "to render them worthy of each other" (*Walsingham* 119). Isabella and Walsingham are set up to be complementary. He is dark; she is fair. Supposedly he is masculine (i.e., rational and passionate), whereas she is feminine (i.e., sympathetic and nurturing). When Mr. Randolph leaves his fortune to Walsingham and Isabella, he promises Walsingham a larger portion if he marries Isabella. Their marriage is thus the machination of a patriarchal courtship plot designed to reinforce the ideals of complementary gender, all of which is tied to financial gain and power. Walsingham's rhapsodizing about nature and his love for Isabella acts out this patriarchal script. His frantic commitment to it is the righteous fury of patriarchy attempting to actualize its own systems of power.

Walsingham's violent outbursts become metaphors of male narrative violence. Because they are manipulative narratives, Isabella becomes the primary narrator of the counterplot and reveals that the courtship plot is entirely of Walsingham's making and one of patriarchal construction. Kept silent throughout much of the novel, Isabella finally confronts Walsingham with his own delusion. Facing one of his many fits of rage about her unfaithfulness, she exclaims, "Are you frantic . . . Will you never hear reason . . . I declare, that you, who ought to be the first to credit my assertion, are the only being upon earth that suspects me of dishonor." She denies his claim to her and her affections: "In what instance have I merited resentment from you . . . I have ever loved you as a brother." Seeking to regain narrative control, Walsingham responds, "Would to God my affection had been of that cold and tranquil nature which might suit a brother's bosom." In reply, Isabella explains, "Then you deceived yourself . . . your virtues, your attachment charmed my mind, but never touched my heart. I have not deceived you, Walsingham.—I have never entertained a thought beyond the intercourse of friendship . . . I frankly own that my heart is devoted to—" here Walsingham inserts his claims to a homosocial plot by interrupting Isabella midsentence with "Sir Sidney Aubrey" (*Walsingham* 415). The words undercut Walsingham's entire narrative and reveal the tyrannical bias of his first-person narration. All along, we have heard of Isabella's betrayal and theoretically been asked to trust in Walsingham's declarations of love for Isabella, which most critics have done. However, Isabella reveals that it has all been a fantasy—a fabrication imagined by Walsingham and, in turn, by Mr. Hanbury and Mr. Randolph—and thus the male homosocial plot is outed by a woman author figure.

If Walsingham is the reflection of the patriarchal male-authored text, then Robinson's women characters present a counternarrative. Sidney's reveal at the end of the novel creates a kind of rapid rereading of the text.[51] As Binhammer points out, in the first reading, which assumes Sidney is a biological man, the classic homosocial rivalry seems to inscribe natural gender binaries. However, upon rereading, a female homosocial plot structure is revealed, one in which Walsingham becomes the object of exchange within a network of women authors, which becomes a structure of resistance. By extension, instead of being a victim of vanity, Isabella is revealed to be a loyal friend who has protected and supported Sidney. She has absorbed her genteel education too well to be an object of male homosocial exchange; instead of learning the socially constructed lessons of the "trivial claims of sexual rivalry," she has learned that "she is capable of prouder, nobler acquirements! That she is born with reason, which should break through the trammels of custom, and assert its equal rights with those tyrants who would enervate her mind, and bend her lofty spirit to the yoke of ignorance and slavery" (*Walsingham* 117). The irony is that the education that was supposed to make Isabella the ideal companion for Walsingham has made her alert to his deficiencies and unwilling to play the flattened role that he has selected for her.

Within the network of women, Sidney is the greatest author of them all. They perform the gentleman to perfection, create his and her multivalent homosocial plots, and wield ultimate control over the larger narrative. Sidney plays the rival with Walsingham while at once constructing female homosocial relationships that cast him as the object. Woman after woman gives up Walsingham in favor of supporting Sidney. In this light, Walsingham's rage and constant outcries against tyranny are not a genuine call for human liberty but the tantrum of a man affronted at being denied the privilege that he regards as his right. As a result of Sidney's superior performance of masculinity, Walsingham occupies a subordinate, objectified position. Even as a child, he had been instructed "never to contradict Sir Sidney; never to interrupt him when speaking; never to call him cousin, or to refuse obeying whatever he should think proper to command, Sir Sidney was amiable and would have been the delight of my bosom, had nature been permitted to take place of compulsion; but the stern authority which enforced obedience, chilled the young buds of friendship and esteem" (*Walsingham* 111). Put differently, Walsingham has been expected to perform the role of the woman in a binary system of gender: to yield, listen, be submissive, and even love her gentleman rulers. The role is what nearly every heroine and most eighteenth-century women were expected to play, and the language of binary gender required their grateful obedience and bound them to it as if it were natural.

There are, as the double-plot structure reveals, two layers of Robinson's critique. On one level, Walsingham's outrage is revealed to be a gender double standard. Time and again, the Isabellas and the Amelias are expected to yield, accept, and obey, and when they refuse, they are subjected to verbal and physical gendered violence. On another, Walsingham's defiance and his chaffing despite Sidney's benevolence and generosity speak to the oppression of women under even the enlightened rule of the gentleman. As Woodworth articulates, such is the soft tyranny of the gentleman that makes women complicit in their own oppression while continuing to consolidate male power and privilege.[52] Therefore, Walsingham's outcries against tyranny reveal the injustice of the very gender system that his courtship narrative attempts to enact.

Robinson uses this dual-plot structure to interrogate the naturalness of gender ideals and the plots that seek to enforce them. Walsingham is not denied power because he is insufficiently masculine. On the contrary, he is outmanned by Sidney within his own system of gender privilege. Robinson reveals that this system functions on performance, not naturalness, and that the best performer of masculinity can run the machine. If Walsingham is feminized, then it is owing to his position as an object, not his failure of innate masculinity. Nature does not create the system; the system creates nature.

Conclusion: Unfinished, Resistant Endings and Authorial Power

To conclude, I would like to address the strange, ambivalent endings of the two novels, which I hope will yield an un-ambivalent ending to this chapter. In their construction of the gentleman as a form of drag, both Robinson and Inchbald disrupt patriarchal power structures. From this position, they confidently critique the power and behavior of the more traditional plots within their texts. However, the endings of both novels have been read as capitulations. Such is the perpetual paradox of many eighteenth-century women writers: the feminist or protofeminist potential of their texts seems forever trapped, foreclosed, or reduced by ending along the traditional trajectory of the courtship plot. Walsingham, after nearly killing Sidney accidentally, is happily reunited with his "transcendent Sidney" who has now "completely...changed" (*Walsingham* 495). Meanwhile, Rushbrook has declared his love for Matilda to Lord Elmwood, and the novel closes with his proclaiming his love to Matilda herself. Rushbrook tells his cousin, "I boldly told 'Elmwood' of my presumptuous love, and he has yielded to you alone, the power over my happiness or misery.—Oh! do not doom me to the latter" (*SS* 337). Both texts, after struggling against the strictures of convention for so long, seem to slip back into it at the last minute.

However, because Robinson and Inchbald used their novels to interrogate plot structure, gender, and authorship, we are able to recontextualize their endings as maintaining instead of abjuring resistance. Because Robinson has exposed Walsingham's perspective and authorship as unreliable, we should not inherently trust that Sidney has radically transformed. After all, as mentioned, Sidney as a man already resembled both Isabella and

Amelia in manner and education. Therefore, instead of reinscribing binary gender roles, as so many critics fear, the novel's ending maintains the constructed nature of gender. Walsingham, the pathologically mistaken, codes Sidney now as wonderfully feminine but intelligent, nevertheless. However, these features are the same that already marked Isabella and Amelia. Robinson is not equating these features with womanliness or marking them as innately feminine; instead, she is demonstrating how gender is constructed by perception. Walsingham now perceives Sidney to be a woman, so he regards her features as being feminine. His narrative and his perspective transform her from rival to wife, neither of which is a role innate to her. We should know better than to trust his narrative.

By closing the novel with an epistolary frame, Robinson clearly directs attention to the relationship between gender and authorship. We are abruptly reminded that Walsingham has been writing retrospectively to a female reader in a bid to present himself as an object of sympathy and desire. At the same time, Robinson redeems the moral position of female ambition. Lady Aubrey's great sin is supposedly ambition and what led her to author Sidney's masculinity in the first place, which is a metaphor for female authorship in general. Women writers were ambitious. Lady Aubrey may be castigated for her vanity, but her authorship wins the competition because she produces the best gentleman. Despite her flaws, her authorship is superior to that of her gentleman peers. To further validate this connection, Isabella, so often dismissed as Walsingham's object, has created her own secret subplot by marrying Lord "dash his wig" Kencarth. Although seemingly abrupt, it also seems to be a moment of female-desired authorship. Isabella has been silenced for most of the novel, not because she has no plans or subjectivity but because Walsingham has forcefully cast her within the patriarchal plot of homosocial exchange and courtship. However, in defiance of that triangulation, she has sought and achieved her own desired end. Leaving a letter—a literal artifact of authorship—she elopes with Kencarth and is ultimately positioned as the powerful, superior force in their relationship. The viscount is now "a repentant rover" under his "gentle amiable monitress, the happy origin of a reformation which graces her power and evinces his understanding" (*Walsingham* 496). Isabella's power, as a figure of female authorship, has reformed Kencarth, and we can only assume in Sidney's image, not Walsingham's.

Finally, even Sidney—the infiltrating gentleman—has plotted her own fate. Governed by figures of female authorship, Sidney has managed to maintain her fortune, pursue and win the man whom she desires, and cultivate strong, positive, rivalry-transcending relationships with other women, and she still remains the best gentleman in the novel. Her courtship plot—the pursuit of Walsingham—has beaten Walsingham's own plot: the pursuit of Isabella and homosocial rivalry. Sidney is not discovered, and similar to the late-eighteenth-century female author, she chooses to be revealed and claims a moral high ground and authority while doing so.

Inchbald is perhaps even more successfully resistant than Robinson. She does not guarantee Rushbrook and Matilda's marriage. Instead she writes and, in the process, inserts her opinionated narrator into the dramatic void: "Whether the heart of Matilda, including as it has been described *could* sentence him to misery, the reader is left to surmise—and if he supposes that it did not, he has every reason to suppose their wedded life was a life of happiness" (*SS* 337). Although the fact that Inchbald directs her notes to a male reader could be a gesture to the male-universal, but the clear implication is that Inchbald feels entitled to gesture to both male and female readers and to instruct men on the moral possibilities of her ending. She ultimately resists closure, just as she has done throughout, and she resists not only one courtship plot but two, one in each part, and in both cases does so with direct authorial intervention. She claims as her right the ability to govern readerly desire. As Hye-Soo Lee argues, Inchbald "exposes the fictionality of the fabricated image of a coquette as a projection of male desire and fear."[53] However, she also reveals how these kinds of courtship plots create desire for the gentleman and for the patriarchal power and regulation that he represents. Inchbald disrupts these forms, and that is the effect of the turn of the page from part 1 to part 2: "Courtship and marriage in *A Simple Story* do not involve tenderness—instead they are revealed as erotically charged power struggles that contain implications of dissolution in their very origin."[54] Inchbald does not dramatize the dutiful, patriarchally constructed Matilda doing her duty and wedding Rushbrook; instead, she calls out to her reader. In the end, she asserts her own power by stepping out of the dynamics of plot to reveal her own authority.

In both Robinson's and Inchbald's novels, we find a departure from the tactics of Mary Davys, Eliza Haywood, Charlotte Lennox, and Samuel Richardson's women correspondents explored in the first four chapters of this book. This is the fulfillment of the eighteenth-century gentleman as a tool for the woman writer. She has so revised him that he is not merely her vehicle but her subject, and the authorial power that attends him is now open to her. Both Inchbald and Robinson cast themselves in the role of didactic author and presented their texts as morally instructive. Through their plots, figures of female authorship, and narrators, they also revealed themselves to be the most insightful, sympathetic, moral readers. As proper critics, both also critiqued plot structures within their works and engaged in literary criticism. Last, they performed the roles of the gentleman author and made these roles their own. Although the gentleman is not a figure of revolution, women writers slowly but surely manipulated his position of conservative power for their own ends.[55] These positions are rightfully theirs, and from this vantage point, women writers such as Edgeworth, Austen, Mary Shelley, and others, secure in their right to voice and influence masculinity and patriarchal structures, would continue to critique and construct the gentleman and other iconic representatives of masculinity.

Coda

But They Were All Written by Women

Figure 1. Kate Beaton, "Jane Austen Comics," *Hark! A Vagrant*, 2006–2018, web comic, http://www.harkavagrant.com/index.php?id=4.

It is a truth universally acknowledged that if one is going to write about the gentleman, one must acknowledge Jane Austen. It is also a truth universally conventional that when writing about Austen, one cannot help but to play on her famous opening lines to *Pride and Prejudice*. Austen's gentlemen have been the looming exception to the thesis of my project. Critics and the populace alike have never stopped talking about them, though some would argue they have done so to cross-purposes. This difference in reading Austen is the premise of Kate Beaton's "Jane Austen Comics" from *Hark! A Vagrant*: although Austen writes serious social commentary, the modern Austen fan is more interested in her "hunky dreamboats." However, my hope is that *A Genealogy of the Gentleman* demonstrates that writing "hunky dreamboats" *is* social commentary and influence.

Austen's men are often presented as anomalies. They emerge dressed in the finery of the English gentleman and have rocked the popular imagination with resurgences throughout their history. From a cultural standpoint, there is a sense that Austen is the exception that proves the rule when it comes to women's ability to write men. The consensus seems to be that even if she did not emerge out of nowhere, what Austen was doing was nevertheless somehow innovative and unprecedented. Thus, from a critical standpoint, there is a desire to position Austen as producing a forward-looking legacy, and this perspective has become the precedent for reading

CODA

Austen's men. Michael Kramp's foundational *Disciplining Love: Austen and the Modern Man*, his edited collection *Jane Austen and Masculinity*, and Claudia Johnson's *Jane Austen's Cults and Cultures* all position Austen as an innovator and have decidedly forward-looking trajectories.[1] As these works suggest, we are frequently as interested in our current fascination with Austen as with her original context. When we look at Austen in her moment, she is often presented as extraordinary; even if the "complexity of Austen's men" is not "unique," it nevertheless reminds us that "she created novels within the context of volatile social transformation."[2] Kramp argues that Austen's men were a response to the tumultuous era of revolutions but locates them specifically in the late eighteenth and early nineteenth centuries as a distinctive, relatively new cultural response.[3] Much of this understanding comes from our very contemporary attachment to Austen, fueled by the resurgence of Austen films and paraphernalia in the 1990s in particular. Kramp opens *Disciplining Love* with a discussion of Austen's "Late-Millennial Moment,"[4] and the edited collection includes the section "Austen's Afterlives." None of these moves are unjustified or even misguided, but they have perhaps given the impression that Austen is a novelty.

In studies of eighteenth-century literature Austen is frequently our end point—our coda—and approaching the moment of her works often gives a sense of having arrived at a cultural juncture. When it comes to her men, there is also a sense of exceptionality. Austen is the focus of the last chapter of Jason Solinger's *Becoming the Gentleman: British Literature and the Invention of Modern Masculinity, 1660–1815*, and one of the only women whom his book treats at such depth.[5] Sharing the stage with Maria Edgeworth, Austen is also a major focus of the final three chapters of Megan Woodworth's *Eighteenth-Century Women Writers and the Gentleman's Liberation Movement: Independence, War, Masculinity, and the Novel, 1778–1818*.[6] While I too end my book by addressing Austen, I hope I can light a distinct path by positioning Austen as participating in a woman-authored tradition of the gentleman. For Solinger, up until the moment of Burney and Austen, the gentleman is a creature of male authors along the lines of Joseph Addison, Richard Steele, and Alexander Pope. Although Woodworth positions Austen on the larger trajectory of women's influence and investment in masculinity, she presents Samuel Richardson's *Sir Charles Grandison* (1753) as the literary progenitor of this movement. Though Austen most definitely loved Richardson's novel—as established in chapter 4, her appreciation is a primary justification for studying Richardson's least popular novel—her depictions of the gentleman draw on an array of woman-authored traditions.

In this coda, my goal is to situate Austen, the über-author of the gentleman, as part of a long-standing literary legacy that entitles women to authority over masculinity and the gentleman. Although Austen is not the end of the line, she is dramatically representative of the traditions that preceded her. Here, I argue that her first published novel, *Sense and Sensibility* (1811), most overtly presents the legacy of eighteenth-century women writers on the character of the gentleman. Given the wider appeal of some of Austen's later gentlemen—Mr. Darcy and Captain Wentworth—reading *Sense and Sensibility* as carrying this particular legacy may seem counterintuitive. With the exception of Edmund Bertram in *Mansfield Park* (1814), there are few leading Austen men who readers and critics typically find to be as disappointing as Edward Ferrars and Colonel Brandon. However, I contend that of all of Austen's novels, *Sense and Sensibility* most blatantly displays the power of women as authors of masculinity. In a visceral way, Edward and Brandon come into being only as a result of the deliberate attention of the Dashwood women. In fact, the novel is littered with acts of women's authoring, authorizing, and reshaping masculinity to suit their own agendas, all of which reflect the legacy of the eighteenth-century woman writer's genealogy of the gentleman. Although Austen is perhaps the most subdued but also most insistent owner of both the gentleman and the right of women writers to dictate the contours of masculinity, her propensity did not emerge from nowhere.

> I require so much! He must have all Edward's virtues, and his person and manners must ornament his goodness with every possible charm
> —Marianne Dashwood in Jane Austen's *Sense and Sensibility*

Marianne's declaration that she, at seventeen, has not yet seen a man who fits her ideal or whom she could love is meant to reflect her immature sensibility.[7] However, her particular statement "I require so much" is perhaps more weighty than it first appears. Here, at the beginning of the nineteenth century, the gentleman was an unattainable ideal. Kramp argues that Austen's men are inherently adaptable: "Rather than attempting to imitate a single and stable paragon of masculinity, [they] must negotiate numerous intertwined and contradictory standards for proper maleness" that are "perpetually debated and revised."[8] My argument is that the gentleman's required negotiation of these standards is a direct by-product of the eighteenth-century gentleman. To meet all of the standards of goodness, attraction, and desirability "with every possible charm" is quite a laundry list for masculinity. Even so, the women of *Sense and Sensibility* repeatedly reveal that the creation of the ideal is just that—a construction—one that they make for themselves time and again. There is a process of creation, revision, and rewriting of masculinity that repeats throughout the novel until the various women find their way to endings that satisfy their desires. As part of this process, the male figures of Edward, Brandon, and John Willoughby are all dressed with the fabric of the eighteenth-century gentleman using patterns woven by women authors. Moreover, the tools that the Dashwood women use are the ones outlined in the rest of my project—criticism, authorship, reform, and reveals—all fueled through an alternative structure of female homosociality in which the gentleman is an object of exchange.

Sense and Sensibility showcases a distinctive structural pattern in which women conjure the man that they imagine and speak his masculinity into being. Following this pattern is how Marianne exerts authorial power, initially by practically summoning Willoughby into existence. Her wishes seem to be answered with the abrupt arrival of this "young man of good abilities, quick imagination, lively spirits, and open, affectionate manners," one who "was *exactly formed* to engage Marianne's heart, for with all this, he joined not only a captivating person, but a natural ardour of mind" (*S and S* 37, italics mine). From there, Willoughby's character undergoes several reforms and revisions, all of which are dictated by the Dashwood sisters. Structurally, his initial appearance presents as a moment of female-authored creation. He emerges, seemingly from nowhere, as a product of Marianne's imagination, and, in this light, his failings may reflect the underdeveloped nature of her initial authorship. Less ambiguously, Marianne's dramatic imagination reveals the mechanisms of female authorship in the text, structures that her older sister, Elinor, uses in her more subtle but no less controlled construction of men. We see from the first that masculinity is tied to the female imagination and that its contours and structures depend on women's authorial power. Like Richardson's correspondents, the Dashwood girls create the men and determine who counts as a good one and who does not.

For their part, the leading men of *Sense and Sensibility* desperately need an author. Edward Ferrars and Colonel Brandon are especially notable for their silence and reserve in their initial scenes and lack the striking handsomeness of Willoughby. Although neither Edward nor Brandon is bad-looking—upon closer inspection, they are even physically attractive—the fact that they reveal their masculine value only upon inspection reflects the pull and power of female authorship in the novel. On one level, Brandon and Edward seem to be rejections or at least interrogations of the eighteenth-century gentleman. Speaking of Edward, Marianne remarks to her mother, "I love him tenderly. But yet—he is not the kind of young man—there is something wanting—his figure is not striking; it has none of the grace which I should expect in the man who could seriously attach my sister. His eyes want all that spirit, that fire, which at once announces virtue and intelligence. And besides this, I am afraid, mama, that he has no real taste" (*S and S* 14). Gone is the immediate impact of Alanthus, D'elmont, Grandison, Rushbrook, Glanville, and Sidney. From this baseline, what Austen reveals over the course of the novel is that the characteristics of the gentleman hero are not inherent in the man but always available for construction.

Indeed, Elinor Dashwood is the most overt, influential author of the novel precisely because she is the one who remakes Edward and Brandon. The keys of Mr. Spectator's supposed taciturnity are now turned over to the women writers, and the men, far from printing themselves out as gentlemen, graciously wait for the ladies to do it for them. A few pages after Marianne's pronouncement that Edward's gentlemanly credentials are lacking, Elinor fundamentally rewrites his character:

> I have seen a great deal of him, have studied his sentiments and heard his opinion on subjects of literature and taste; and, upon the whole, I venture to pronounce that his mind is well-informed, his enjoyment of books exceedingly great, his imagination lively, his observation just and correct, and his taste delicate and pure. His abilities in every respect improve as much upon acquaintance as his manners and person. At first sight, his address is certainly not striking; and his person can hardly be called handsome, till the expression of his eyes, which are uncommonly good and the general sweetness of his countenance, is perceived. At present, I know him so well, that I think him really handsome; or, at least, almost so. (*S and S* 16)

With her words, Elinor highlights the ways in which authorship authorizes the gentleman: she declares, after studying and conversing with Edward, that he is indeed all that he should be. She deploys the structures of heterosociality advocated by Haywood and Hume but with the confidence of Haywood and with more effect than Hume. (Hume wishes he had the Dashwoods' skills.) It is Elinor's interpretation that carries the day, for Marianne answers her, "I shall very soon think him handsome, Elinor, if I do not now" (*S and S* 16). The same pattern is repeated with Brandon. Elinor, again deploying the construct of heterosocial conversation, discovers Brandon's worthiness and writes it into being for the reader. She is also the one who ferrets out that reserve is not "natural" to him and "appeared rather the result of some oppression of spirits, than of any natural gloominess of temper" (*S and S* 38). If reserve is not natural, then this aspect of their characters can be revised through proper cultivation. The attraction of the gentleman is thus malleable; it is not ingrained but can be determined, decided, and created for the audience, and the creator of this phenomenon is the woman writer. Just as Arabella and Melliora reform their gentlemen, Elinor, Marianne, and Mrs. Dashwood all take similarly innocuous men and transform them into gentlemen. They prove Lady Aubrey's maxim that by woman only is man made agreeable.

The women's ability to construct male characters goes hand in hand with their status as critics of masculinity. As with the other novels examined in this book, *Sense and Sensibility* is a work that runs on women's critiquing men. It begins with the critique of the "old gentleman," Dashwood, who problematically entails his estate on John Dashwood, thereby leaving the Dashwood women without financial support. It immediately continues with John's failure to live up to his vow to his father. Although the influence of his wife, Fanny, over him reinforces the power that women exert over men in the novel, the merits of the gentleman characters who come onto the scene are either entirely established or deconstructed in the debates between the Dashwood sisters and their mother. Marianne and Elinor often discuss their different opinions of men and men's behavior; they initially debate Edward's appeal as a suitor and a gentleman as well as argue over the propriety of Marianne's courtship with Willoughby. Within this circle, Mrs. Dashwood frequently weighs in. She and Elinor both counter Marianne's notion that "thirty-five [i.e., Brandon's age] has nothing to do with matrimony" (*S and S* 29). Later, Elinor begins shifting the reader's approval away from Willoughby and toward Brandon even before Willoughby absconds to London. Although Elinor likes Willoughby, she pointedly criticizes his and Marianne's combined meanness toward Brandon. After all, "in Colonel Brandon alone, of all her new acquaintance, did Elinor find a person who could in any degree claim the respect of abilities, excite the interest of friendship, or give pleasure as a companion" (*S and S* 42). While Elinor's opinions hold the most sway in the Dashwoods' discussions, it is symbolic that Austen situates the character of masculinity within women's conversations with each other. As a result, Mrs. Dashwood debates and even convinces Elinor to not cast immediate judgment on Willoughby's departure. Austen repeatedly empowers women to determine the value of men and just as repeatedly stresses how having keen judgment when it comes to masculinity is vital for women because the stakes are so incredibly high. At the same time, these reiterations reinforce a sense that the opinions that determine the men's character and guide the novel's action are those of women. Criticizing masculinity is unquestionably the province of women, and it is a both a literal and literary tool that they rely on to author texts as well as their lives.

Ultimately, what makes men worthy and what qualifies them to be rewarded with statuses as gentlemen within *Sense and Sensibility* is their willingness to be narrated by the Dashwood women. In this way, Austen echoes the women correspondents who determined the character of her beloved Sir Charles Grandison. Almost from the outset, Colonel Brandon proves to be wonderfully malleable to Elinor's purposes. His character's worth is something that she discovers, and it is Willoughby's treatment of Brandon that first signals the former's failings and the latter's superiority. Elinor chastises Willoughby for (supposedly) having no real reason to dislike Brandon and even defends Brandon: "My protégé, as you call, him, is a sensible man; and sense will always have attractions for me" (*S and S* 39). Willoughby's characterization of Brandon as Elinor's "protégé" is not inaccurate, for Brandon is the character whom Elinor creates. She praises him for having seen the world, for having read widely, and for his politeness. In retrospect, the scene is the first sign of Willoughby's dishonorable connection to Brandon. Elinor thus plants the narrative seeds of the novel's later twist in the minds of readers, through her construction and criticism of various masculinities.

Brandon and Edward also both defer to Elinor to narrate their lives. After recounting his history and Willoughby's seduction of Eliza, Brandon's ward, Brandon tells Elinor, "Use your own discretion . . . in communicating to [Marianne] what I have told you" and thus authorizes Elinor to act as his author (*S and S* 157). Rewarding Edward with a living is a perfect example of this structure. Brandon offers this position to Edward because Elinor has narrated Edward's character to him, and as Edward himself notes to Elinor, "I cannot be ignorant that you, to your goodness I owe it all.—I feel it—I would express it if I could—but, as you well know, I am no orator" (*S and S* 128). Edward is properly conscious that the structure of his life, including this helpful turn, is the working of Elinor's authorship. He is not an orator, which is for the best, because Elinor can now construct and characterize him herself. Edward and Brandon both reinforce that power over masculinity, and the larger structure of the novel is the province of women, especially Elinor.

Austen's Dashwood women exert their critical and authorial powers to also construct reform and reveal narratives for the gentlemen of the text. Such revisions echo trends described in the earlier chapters of my book as tropes of eighteenth-century, women-authored gentlemen. Both Willoughby and Brandon undergo reforms that are symbolically women-authored revisions of their character. In Brandon's case, the seemingly innocuous, even boring, mentor figure is reimagined as a sentimental hero with a romantic past. Earlier in the novel, Elinor reflects, "What could a silent man of five and thirty hope, when opposed by a very lively one of five and twenty?" (*S and S* 38). The answer is rewritten by the women of the text. Through his accounts to Elinor and Mrs. Dashwood, Brandon is revealed to be a romance figure; he fights a duel with Willoughby, has a tragic backstory of a failed first love, and repeatedly proves himself to be useful to the Dashwood women in times of crisis. After rushing off to fetch Mrs. Dashwood during the height of Marianne's illness, Brandon indirectly confesses his love for Marianne to Mrs. Dashwood: "Colonel Brandon loves Marianne. He has told me so himself" and "made me acquainted with his earnest, tender, constant, affection for Marianne. He has loved her, my Elinor, ever since the first moment of seeing her" (*S and S* 255). In this moment, Brandon's presentation as a constant lover casts the previous volumes of the novel into new light such that he becomes the restrained hero in disguise who takes the highly gentlemanly position of prioritizing Marianne's feelings over his own. Austen also highlights the constructed nature of Brandon's revision: "Here, however, Elinor perceived,—not the language, not the professions of Colonel Brandon, but the natural embellishments of her mother's active fancy, which fashioned every thing delightful to her as it chose" (*S and S* 255). Kramp reads these words as Mrs. Dashwood's "recreat[ing] Brandon, describing him as a desperate sentimental man who will also be useful to her family."[9] With Mrs. Dashwood and Elinor's exchange, Austen highlights how the stories that women tell about men are decisive; their narratives are what construct heroism and desirability but not the man himself or the flannel of his waistcoat (*S and S* 30).[10]

Initially formed from Marianne's sensibility-fueled imagination, Willoughby is first revealed to be a libertine, not a gentleman. In this light, just as the coquette to the gentleman in chapter 1 of this book, he manifests as a narrative competition for the women authors and as a rival able to foil their plots. He has seduced and abandoned Eliza, and he jilts Marianne in favor of an heiress after his misdeeds have been discovered. Although Willoughby initially seems to defy the authorial controls of the Dashwood sisters, even Marianne has absolute faith in her sister's power to dictate masculinity. At the traumatic ball with Willoughby, Marianne pleads, "Go to him, Elinor . . . and force him to come to me" (*S and S* 132). He then writes Marianne a cruel letter that denies their attachment and announces his engagement. In response, as Austen writes, "[Marianne] felt the loss of Willoughby's character yet more heavily than she had felt the loss of his heart; his seduction and desertion of Miss Williams, the misery of that poor girl, and the doubt of what his designs might *once* have been on herself, preyed... on her spirits" (*S and S* 159). More important than losing Willoughby's love is the blow that Marianne was not in control of his character: that her version of Willoughby, the character formed from her imagination, does not take hold and is not the real Willoughby. The rake has seemingly triumphed over the women-authored version of the gentleman.

However, Willoughby's rake undergoes a kind of reform that, though failing to transform him into the gentleman, reasserts the woman writer's power over his masculinity. He retrospectively describes how the Dashwoods disrupted his rakish trajectory: "I endeavored, by every means in my power, to make myself pleasing to [Marianne], without any design of returning her affection" (*S and S* 242). Nevertheless, he too later falls under Marianne's sway, even to the point of declaring, "It is astonishing, when I reflect on what it was, and what *she* was, that my heart should have been so insensible!" Through her affections and her desire to make Willoughby the gentleman hero, Marianne effects literal and literary change over his character. Echoing Lord Lofty, as described in chapter 1, he even proclaims, "The happiest hours of my life were what I spent with her, when I felt my intentions were strictly honourable, and my feelings blameless" (*S and S* 243). Even after his retreat to London, Willoughby reverts to his old ways until receiving Marianne's note, which he tells Elinor "made me know myself better" (*S and S* 247). After he confesses that Marianne's authorship seems to have recreated the version of himself that he knows better, we are invited, via Elinor, to feel sympathy, if not forgiveness, for him: "Willoughby, he, whom only half an hour ago she had abhorred as the most worthless of men, Willoughby, in spite of all his faults, excited a degree of commiseration" (*S and S* 252). In this way, the combined force of Marianne and Elinor reconfigures the rake as permeable to the influence of woman writers. His initial plot is irrevocably swayed by theirs, and he cannot compete with them. Thus, though Willoughby is dismissed from being a D'elmont—that is, a reformed rake—the rake does not depart the text untouched by the authority of the women whom he encounters.

The generational line of women at the center of *Sense and Sensibility* is symbolic of women's authorship of the gentleman. Although Elinor is often separated, both in demeanor and temper, from her mother and sisters, it is significant that this family of women navigates the patriarchal landscape that frequently denies them access and recourse. As explored throughout *A Genealogy of the Gentleman*, a major incentive for women to author the gentleman was to gain access to his authority. *Sense and*

Sensibility makes us keenly aware of the ways in which women are vulnerable to the machinations of patriarchal society; however, through their authorship of the gentleman, the Dashwood women are able to deploy the inverted structure of female homosociality, as discussed in chapter 5. Through their debates about men, their plotting, and their narrating, they recast the gentlemen as an object of exchange, which facilitates their emotional and financial security.

When Marianne initially rejects the idea of Colonel Brandon as a suitor, she declares that a marriage to a man of thirty-five, even by a woman of twenty-seven, could "only [be] a commercial exchange, in which each wished to be benefitted at the expense of the other" (*S and S* 29). In this traditional system, she refuses to be the object of exchange. The dynamics of the exchange are corrected by rewriting Brandon as a romantic hero, which is the combined effect of Mrs. Dashwood and Elinor's authorship. Even Marianne is ultimately able to exert her transformative power in order to rewrite a marriage that starts with a foundation of economic comfort and security into a happy, romantic ending: "Colonel Brandon was now as happy, as all those who best loved him, believed he deserved to be;—in Marianne he was consoled for every past affliction;—her regard and her society restored his mind to animation, and his spirits to cheerfulness ... Marianne could never love by halves; and her whole heart became, in time, as much devoted to her husband, as it had once been to Willoughby" (*S and S* 288). Thus, as the gentlemanly object of exchange for the Dashwood women, Brandon transforms via their combined revision of his character as a hopeless, past-his-prime stodge into a dueling figure of true love and conjugal bliss.

Likewise, Edward's family presents obstacles to Elinor's interests that she removes by reworking Brandon, and abetted by the plotting of another woman, Lucy Steele, perhaps another compelling woman author in the novel, Edward becomes sufficiently reconciled with his family to merit financial support for himself and Elinor, with the added convenience of now having a living on the Brandons' estate. Thus, the Dashwood women, now comfortably and conveniently situated, have their initial distress, dismissal, and displacement replaced with financial security, happy marriages, and familial affection, all of which have come to pass by way of their authorship. They have written the men at hand into the gentlemen whom they needed—or, in Willoughby's case, written them out. They have escaped the patriarchal plots that disadvantaged them—patrilineal inheritance, mercenary suitors, and seduction—and instead of serving men's interests, the men serve theirs.

"The Pen Has Been in Their Hands"

To close, I would like to briefly consider another iconic scene in Austen's oeuvre. In her final novel, *Persuasion* (1817),[11] Austen's Anne Elliot has a quiet debate with Captain Harville on the gendered nature of love. Harville insists that men love longer than women, and Anne famously declares that it is women who love the longest, at least when all hope is lost. To support his case, Harville presents the literary canon: "But let me observe that all histories are against you, all stories, prose and verse." Harville then anticipates, "But perhaps you will say, these were all written by men," to which Anne responds, "Perhaps I shall . . . Men have had every advantage of us in telling their own story . . . the pen has been in their hands."[12] This line has reflected much of what drives feminist scholarship, the need for gender studies, and examinations such as this book. When the stories we consult for histories of authorship and gender come only from men, or only from one side or one source, we overlook the broader picture. Historically, we have always envisioned the pen of masculinity as being in men's hands and, in so doing, have disregarded the long history of how and why women have shaped normative masculinity, along with the clear influence and power that they have had over its structures. We have done so due to the challenges of thinking about normative masculinity in performative terms and perhaps also because we do not always like the gentlemen whom women's pens have produced. There is only so much that Colin Firth in a wet shirt can do before the gentleman's patriarchal features start to sour.

In response, it is high time for us to recognize the role women have played in masculinity's evolution. By doing so, we can trace an important new chain of influence for women writers, one that places them more equally with their male contemporaries. It also allows us to examine masculinity more honestly and more directly, in ways that unite the panels from the comic at the opening of this coda. The gentleman plays upon desires because he is designed to do so. However, this model is deeply rooted in the structure of power, social dynamics, and cultural history. Even though we may sometimes prefer it, the pen of masculinity has not always been in men's hands. Women have also held and deployed it for their own ends, often quite effectively even if not always progressively. It is time to recognize this reality and to view it not as the work of a singular exceptional woman such as Austen but as the collective literary inheritance of a century of women writers.

To return to Virginia Woolf's statement that opened this entire endeavor: women have been writing books about men for a long time. The pen has been in their hands; we simply haven't looked for it there.

Notes

Introduction

Epigraphs: Virginia Woolf, *A Room of One's Own* (New York: Mariner Books, 2005), 27.

Mary Hays, *The Memoirs of Emma Courtney*, ed. Miriam L. Wallace (Glen Allen, VA: College Publishing, 2004), 48.

1. Woolf, *A Room of One's Own*, 27.
2. Hays, *Emma Courtney*, 270.
3. Miriam Wallace, introduction to *Emma Courtney*, 15.
4. Hays, *Emma Courtney*, 634.
5. Eleanor Wikborg, *The Lover as Father Figure in Eighteenth-Century Women's Fiction* (Gainesville: University Press of Florida, 2002); and Megan A. Woodworth, *Eighteenth-Century Women Writers and the Gentleman's Liberation Movement: Independence, War, Masculinity, and the Novel, 1778–1818* (Burlington, VT: Ashgate, 2011). See also Sarah S. G. Frantz and Katharina Rennhak, eds., *Women Constructing Men: Female Novelists and Their Male Characters, 1750–2000* (Lanham, MD: Lexington Books, 2010). A forthcoming special issue of *Women's Writing* titled "Women Writing Men" will also address the topic.
6. Janet Todd and Jane Miller express skepticism and disappointment about the literary value and quality of such male characters when compared with their female counterparts. See Janet Todd, introduction to *Men by Women* (Boulder, CO: Holmes & Meier, 1981); and Jane Miller, *Women Writing about Men* (New York: Pantheon, 1986).
7. Shawn Lisa Maurer's *Proposing Men: Dialectics of Gender and Class in the Eighteenth-Century English Periodical* (Stanford, CA: Stanford University Press, 1998) considers how the gentleman, or the "bourgeois family man," emerged "as the prototype of desirable masculinity" in a way that usurped the dominance of the rake (3). This evolution is the arc of Thomas King's *The Gendering of Men, 1600–1750: The English Phallus* (Madison: University of Wisconsin Press, 2004). Erin Mackie, in *Rakes, Highwaymen, and Pirates: The Making of the Modern Gentleman in the Eighteenth Century* (Baltimore, MD: Johns Hopkins University Press, 2009), positions the emergence of the gentleman to frame her analysis of criminal forms of masculinity. Michèle Cohen's *Fashioning Masculinity: National Identity and Language in the Eighteenth Century* (New York: Routledge, 1996) examines how the shift from relatively violent models of the rake toward the gentleman was shaped by English responses to French culture. G. J. Barker-Benfield's *The Culture of Sensibility: Sex and Society in Eighteenth-Century Britain* (Chicago: University of Chicago Press, 1992) ties economic and cultural evolution to changes in ideals of masculinity, particularly from the rake to the gentleman.
8. For the rake as consumer, see Mackie, *Rakes, Highwaymen, and Pirates*, 35; and Barker-Benfield, *Culture of Sensibility*, 45, xxvii. For more on the rake's bi- or

pansexual modes in contrast to the heterosexuality required of the gentleman, see King, *The Gendering of Men*, 5–6; Mackie, *Rakes, Highwaymen, and Pirates*, 8–9; and Randolph Trumbach, *Sex and the Gender Revolution*, vol. 1, *Heterosexuality and the Third Gender in Enlightenment London* (Chicago: University of Chicago Press, 1998), 14.

9. King, *Gendering of Men*, 3; and Mackie, *Rakes, Highwaymen, and Pirates*, 35. King and Mackie both explore how the rake was defined by his personal sovereignty—that is, his ability to exert his will over others.

10. Elizabeth Kraft, "Wit and the Spectator's Ethics of Desire," *Studies in English Literature, 1500–1900* 45, no. 3 (2005): 636–637.

11. See Maurer's second and third chapters in *Proposing Men* for a thorough explanation of the gentleman's chastity.

12. King, *Gendering of Men*, 8.

13. R. W. Connell, *Masculinities*, 2nd ed. (Berkeley: University of California Press, 2005), 76–77.

14. Connell, *Masculinities*, 68.

15. Erin Mackie, *Market à la Mode: Fashion, Commodity, and Gender in* The Tatler *and* The Spectator (Baltimore, MD: Johns Hopkins University Press, 1997), 146.

16. Whereas "the rake's prestige resides in the culturally confirmed success of his social performance" (Mackie, *Rakes, Highwaymen, and Pirates*, 35), the gentleman's masculinity was presented as an internal part of his private self. In *Rakes, Highwaymen, and Pirates*, Mackie writes that "the paradigm of sexual difference locates gender within an individual's innate character, his or her subjectivity; it makes gender a personal, private matter fixed inwardly" (7). Such "political and personal privacy" is often considered to be a major shift in gender and especially in eighteenth-century masculinity (King, *Gendering of Men*, 5). See Dror Wahrman, *Making of the Modern Self: Identity and Culture in Eighteenth-Century England* (New Haven, CT: Yale University Press, 2004); and Thomas Laqueur, *Making Sex: Body and Gender from the Greeks to Freud* (Cambridge, MA: Harvard University Press, 1990).

17. Jason D. Solinger, *Becoming the Gentleman: British Literature and the Invention of Modern Masculinity, 1660–1815* (New York: Palgrave Macmillan, 2012), 3.

18. Manushag Powell, *Performing Authorship in Eighteenth-Century English Periodicals* (Lewisburg, PA: Bucknell University Press, 2012), 4. See Solinger, *Becoming the Gentleman*, 3; King, *Gendering of Men*, 14–15, 125; Mackie, *Market à la Mode*, 20–21; Mackie, *Rakes, Highwaymen, and Pirates*, 7; and Maurer, *Proposing Men*, 7.

19. Rebecca Tierney-Hynes, *Novel Minds: Philosophers and Romance Readers, 1680–1740* (New York: Palgrave Macmillan, 2012), 37.

20. Solinger, *Becoming the Gentleman*, 74. See also Laura Runge, *Gender and Language in British Literary Criticism, 1660–1790* (New York: Cambridge University Press, 1997), 89; Janet Todd, *The Sign of Angellica: Women, Writing, and Fiction, 1660–1800* (New York: Columbia University Press, 1989), 46; and Margaret Anne Doody, *The True Story of the Novel* (New Brunswick, NJ: Rutgers University Press, 1996), 277.

21. Solinger, *Becoming the Gentleman*, 30.

22. Carolyn D. Williams, *Pope, Homer, and Manliness: Some Aspects of Eighteenth-Century Classical Learning* (New York: Routledge, 1993), 15.

23. Karen Harvey, *The Little Republic: Masculinity, Domesticity, and Authority in Eighteenth-Century Britain* (New York: Oxford University Press, 2014); King, *Gendering of Men*; and Maurer, *Proposing Men*.

24. Barker-Benfield, *Culture of Sensibility*, 139–140; Cohen, *Fashioning Masculinity*, 9; King, *Gendering of Men*, 67. As a hegemonic structure, the gentleman is defined "in terms of what he was not": woman, rake, fop, molly, and so on (Solinger, *Becoming the Gentleman*, 17–18). The structure of the binary gender system increasingly defined the gentleman's masculinity through its relationships with women. As Barker-Benfield and Cohen have argued, along with Philip Carter, *Men and the Emergence of Polite Society, Britain, 1660–1800* (New York: Pearson Education, 2001), manners, politeness, and the increased social mixing with women played decisive roles in defining genteel masculinity in the eighteenth century. See also Harriet Guest's *Small Change: Women, Learning, Patriotism, 1750–1810* (Chicago: University of Chicago Press, 2000), 2. The gentleman demonstrates his domesticity, virtue, heterosexuality, and economy through his dealings with women. Thus, while the gentleman patriarch, no matter how benevolently, was supposed to rule women, he also depended on them. See Cohen, *Fashioning Masculinity*, 4, and Timothy Hitchcock and Michèle Cohen, eds., *English Masculinities 1660–1800* (New York: Longman, 1999), 19.

25. Barker-Benfield, *Culture of Sensibility*, xxvi; Guest, *Small Change*, 4; and E. J. Clery, *The Feminization Debate in Eighteenth-Century England: Literature, Commerce and Luxury* (New York: Palgrave MacMillan, 2004), 10. See also Carter, *Men and the Emergence of Polite Society*, 2.

26. Todd W. Reeser, *Masculinities in Theory: An Introduction* (New York: Wiley-Blackwell, 2010), 1.

27. Powell, *Performing Authorship*, 33; and Connell, *Masculinities*, 76.

28. Some of the most vibrant studies on eighteenth-century masculinity have focused on the period's more flamboyant structures of masculinity—the salacious Restoration libertine or rake, the criminal, the queer, and effeminate masculinity—or how they were deployed. See Declan Kavanagh, *Effeminate Years: Literature, Politics, and Aesthetics in Mid-Eighteenth-Century Britain* (Lewisburg, PA: Bucknell University Press, 2017). See also George Haggerty's *Men in Love: Masculinity and Sexuality in the Eighteenth Century* (New York: Columbia University Press, 1999), and Mackie's *Rakes, Highwaymen, and Pirates*. Both Clery and Kavanagh have investigated how the terminology of feminization and effeminacy has been deployed to maintain normative masculinity's contrast-based contours. Meanwhile, other critics have approached normative masculinity through other lenses; see Carter, *Men and the Emergence of Polite Society*; Lawrence Klein, *Shaftesbury and the Culture of Politeness: Moral Discourse and Cultural Politics in Early Eighteenth-Century England* (New York: Cambridge University Press, 1994); and Cohen, *Fashioning Masculinity*. Carter, Klein, and Cohen have approached masculinity as manifest in social practices such as politeness. By comparison, Williams and Solinger have used the lens of education to define genteel masculinity. Carolyn D. Williams's *Pope, Homer, and Manliness* is a foundational work on eighteenth-century masculinity, one that traces the links between classic ideas and education to manliness in the eighteenth century, while Solinger's *Becoming the Gentleman* is a more recent study on the gentleman. King, in *Gendering of Men*,

rethinks privacy and embodiment to construct a history of English masculinity; the work is a foundational bridge in studies on eighteenth-century masculinity to the idea that masculinity and gender have evolved and been performed.

29. Solinger includes two chapters on women—Frances Burney and Jane Austen—although neither woman is positioned as responding to an established male tradition created by figures such as Joseph Addison, Richard Steele, and Alexander Pope.

30. Judith Halberstam, *Female Masculinity* (Durham, NC: Duke University Press, 1998), 1. See also Marjorie Garber, *Vested Interests: Cross-Dressing and Cultural Anxiety* (New York: Harper Perennial, 1992).

31. Todd, *Men by Women*, 3.

32. See Betty A. Schellenberg, *The Conversational Circle: Rereading the English Novel, 1740–1775* (Lexington: University Press of Kentucky, 1996), 26; and Janet Todd, *Sensibility: An Introduction* (New York: Methuen, 1986), 165, where Todd articulates the assumption that characters such as David Simple are somehow "quintessentially female." Linda Bree, in the introduction to *The Adventures of David Simple and The Adventures of David Simple, Volume the Last*, by Sarah Fielding (New York: Penguin Books, 2002), says, "In place of the traditional masculine qualities . . . David demonstrates qualities more often associated, then and even now, with femininity" (xxiv).

33. Both Clery and Kavanagh explore the important but overlooked relationships between masculinity, the feminine, and the effeminate. Clery, in *Feminization Debate*, distinguishes "effeminate," an overreliance on women, and being properly feminized, all of which were vital components of proper masculinity in the eighteenth century (10). Meanwhile, Kavanagh, in *Effeminate Years*, explores how terms such as "effeminacy," instead of exclusively marking a homosexual identity, were used to structure the contours of heterosexual masculinity during the period (xxii).

34. Frantz and Rennhak, *Women Constructing Men*, 2.

35. Jan Fergus, *Provincial Readers in Eighteenth-Century England* (New York: Oxford University Press, 2006), 43. Fergus demonstrates that men, especially schoolboys, were the primary consumers of fiction, and that "the tastes of male and female readers of all classes were not as different as many scholars have supposed." Meanwhile, Doody and Runge have both argued that the figure of the female reader was more ideological than factual; see Doody, *True Story of the Novel*, 278; and Runge, *Gender and Language*, 89.

36. Katherine Sobba Green, introduction to *The Courtship Novel, 1740–1820: A Feminized Genre* (Lexington: University Press of Kentucky, 1991). See also Susan Lanser, "Of Closed Doors and Open Hatches: Heteronormative Plots in Eighteenth-Century (Women's) Studies," *Eighteenth Century* 53, no. 3 (2012): 273–290.

37. Jane Spencer, *The Rise of the Woman Novelist: From Aphra Behn to Jane Austen* (New York: Basil Blackwell, 1986), 32.

38. Patricia Meyer Spacks, *Desire and Truth: Functions of Plot in Eighteenth-Century English Novels* (Chicago: University of Chicago Press, 1990), 3. See also Patricia Meyer Spacks, *Novel Beginnings: Experiments in Eighteenth-Century English Fiction* (New Haven, CT: Yale University Press, 2006).

39. Woodworth, *Eighteenth-Century Women Writers*, 3.

40. Green, introduction to *The Courtship Novel*.

41. This is the thesis of Spacks's *Desire and Truth*.

42. Paul Kelleher, *Making Love: Sentiment and Sexuality in Eighteenth-Century British Literature* (Lewisburg, PA: Bucknell University Press, 2015), 6.

43. King, *Gendering of Men*, 11.

44. Catherine Gallagher, *Nobody's Story: The Vanishing Act of Women Writers in the Marketplace, 1670–1820* (Berkeley: University of California Press, 1995), 167–168.

45. Of course, exceptions abound, including in periodical studies, a field that takes the performative nature and structures of these works as its foundation; see Manushag Powell, *Performing Authorship in Eighteenth-Century English Periodicals* (Lewisburg, PA: Bucknell University Press, 2012).

46. Powell, *Performing Authorship*, 7.

47. Solinger, *Becoming the Gentleman*, 3.

48. Catherine A. Craft, "Reworking Male Models: Aphra Behn's *Fair Vow-Breaker*, Eliza Haywood's *Fantomina*, and Charlotte Lennox's *Female Quixote*," *Modern Language Review* 86, no. 4 (1991): 822. See also Catherine Craft-Fairchild, *Masquerade and Gender: Disguise and Female Identity in Eighteenth-Century Fictions by Women* (Philadelphia: University of Pennsylvania Press, 1993), 832; and Mary Anne Schofield, *Eliza Haywood* (Boston: Twayne Publishers, 1985), 5.

49. George Haggerty, "Male Privilege in Frances Burney's *The Wanderer*," in *Women Constructing Men: Female Novelists and Their Male Characters, 1750–2000*, ed. Sarah S. G. Frantz and Katharina Rennhak (Lanham, MD: Lexington Books, 2010), 42.

50. Elizabeth Kowaleski-Wallace, *Their Fathers' Daughters: Hannah Moore, Maria Edgeworth, and Patriarchal Complicity* (New York: Oxford University Press, 1991), 9. See also Wikborg, *Lover as Father Figure*, 8.

51. Margaret Case Croskery, "Masquing Desire: The Politics of Passion in Eliza Haywood's *Fantomina*," in *The Passionate Fictions of Eliza Haywood: Essays on Her Life and Work*, ed. Kirsten T. Saxton and Rebecca P. Bocchicchio (Lexington: University Press of Kentucky, 2000), 70.

52. Wikborg, *Lover as Father Figure*, 2.

53. Connell, *Masculinities*, 76–77.

54. Lanser, "Of Closed Doors," 284.

55. Kowaleski-Wallace, *Their Fathers' Daughters*, ix.

56. An oft-cited example is that nearly 40 percent of women voted for candidate Donald J. Trump in the 2016 presidential election when he ran against Hillary Clinton; many women articulated that they prefer voting for men over women. Pew Research Center, "An Examination of the 2016 Electorate, Based on Validated Voters," Pew Research, August 9, 2018, https://www.pewresearch.org/politics/2018/08/09/an-examination-of-the-2016-electorate-based-on-validated-voters/.

57. Tania Modleski, introduction to *Loving with a Vengeance: Mass-Produced Fantasies for Women* (New York: Routledge, 2007).

Chapter 1. Gentleman Spectator as Desiring Author

Epigraphs: Mary Davys, *The Reformed Coquet; or, the Memoirs of Amoranda* in *Popular Fiction by Women 1660–1730 an Anthology*, ed. Paula R. Backscheider and

John J. Richetti (New York: Oxford University Press, 1996), 289, emphasis mine. Hereafter, *The Reform'd Coquet* will be cited in text with the abbreviation *RC*.

Joseph Addison and Richard Steele, *The Spectator*, ed. Donald Bond (New York: Oxford University Press, 1965), 1:5.1711, emphasis mine. Hereafter, *The Spectator* will be cited in text by volume, page, and year, with the abbreviation *Spectator*.

1. Jason D. Solinger, *Becoming the Gentleman: British Literature and the Invention of Modern Masculinity, 1660–1815* (New York: Palgrave Macmillan, 2012), 30.

2. Solinger, *Becoming the Gentleman*, 15; Thomas King, *The Gendering of Men, 1600–1750*, vol. 1, *The English Phallus* (Madison: University of Wisconsin Press, 2004).

3. Shawn Lisa Maurer, *Proposing Men: Dialectics of Gender and Class in the Eighteenth-Century English Periodical* (Stanford, CA: Stanford University Press, 1998), 7; Manushag Powell, *Performing Authorship in Eighteenth-Century English Periodicals* (Lewisburg, PA: Bucknell University Press, 2012), 4; Erin Mackie, *Market à la Mode: Fashion, Commodity, and Gender in The Tatler and The Spectator* (Baltimore, MD: Johns Hopkins University Press, 1997), 152.

4. Kristina Straub, *Sexual Suspects: Eighteenth-Century Players and Sexual Ideology* (Princeton, NJ: Princeton University Press, 1992), 6; King, *Gendering Men*, 125.

5. R. W. Connell, *Masculinities*, 2nd ed. (Berkeley: University of California Press, 2005), 67–68.

6. Connell, *Masculinities*, 45.

7. This is the primary subject of Powell's essay "See No Evil, Hear No Evil, Speak No Evil: Spectation and the Eighteenth-Century Public Sphere" in *Eighteenth-Century Studies* 45, no. 2 (2012): 255–276.

8. King, *Gendering Men*, 7–8.

9. Powell, "See No Evil," 262.

10. Addison and Steele, *The Spectator*, no. 261.

11. Anthony Ashley Cooper Shaftesbury, Third Earl of Shaftesbury, *Characteristics of Men, Manners, Opinions, Times*, ed. Lawrence E. Klein (New York: Cambridge University Press, 1999), 409.

12. Powell, *Performing Authorship*, 50.

13. Powell, *Performing Authorship*, 4.

14. Mackie, *Market à la Mode*, 152.

15. Powell, *Performing Authorship*, 7.

16. Christina Lupton, "Sincere Performances: Franklin, Tillotson, and Steele on the Plain Style," *Eighteenth-Century Studies* 40, no. 2 (2007): 187.

17. Bonnie Latimer, "Courting Dominion: Sir Charles Grandison, Sir George Ellison, and the Organizing Principle of Masculinity," *The Eighteenth-Century Novel* 9 (2012): 113.

18. Powell, *Performing Authorship*, 3–4, emphasis mine.

19. Mackie, *Market à la Mode*, 21.

20. Maurer, *Proposing Men*, 2.

21. Maurer, *Proposing Men*, 97. Maurer discusses the power and erotics of the male gaze in periodicals.

22. Powell, *Performing Authorship*, 9.

23. Powell, *Performing Authorship*, 3.

24. Powell, *Performing Authorship*, 15.

25. Addison and Steele, *The Spectator*, nos. 4, 37, 79, 92, 205, 572; all the issues touch on women's reading and libraries in some way, with Mr. Spectator refusing to actually list readings outside of his own publication. Steele did publish *The Ladies Library* in three volumes in 1714, but in it he adopts the persona of a lady. This is further evidence of Steele performing his gentlemanly prerogative.

26. Addison and Steele, *The Spectator*; there are numerous entries that reference or touch on the features of female vanity in ways that implicate the coquette. Some of the most clear and striking are: no. 45, which criticizes an excess of "gaiety" in women; no 79, which presents a letter from a supposed coquette, which is contrasted by a letter from another, less superficially frivolous woman reader; and no. 73, which claims that women love praise more than men and how this leads them into folly when they seek the vain applause like a coquette; it castigates women who seek "to Seduce Men to their Worship" (*Spectator* 1:313.1711).

27. Juliette Merritt, "Reforming the Coquette? Eliza Haywood's Vision of a Female Epistemology," in *Fair Philosopher: Eliza Haywood and* The Female Spectator, ed. Lynn Marie Wright and Donald J. Newman (Lewisburg, NJ: Bucknell University Press, 2006), 177, 180.

28. Merrit, "Reforming the Coquette?," 180.

29. Powell, "See No Evil," 259.

30. Martha Bowden, "Mary Davys: Self-Presentation and the Woman Writer's Reputation in the Early Eighteenth Century," *Women's Writing* 3, no. 1 (1996): 26.

31. Victoria Joule, "Mary Davys's Novel Contribution to Women and Realism," *Women's Writing* 17, no. 1 (2010): 31. William H. McBurney, "Mrs. Mary Davys: Forerunner of Fielding," *PMLA* 74, no 4 (1959): 348–355.

32. McBurney, "Mrs. Mary Davys," 350.

33. Some critics, like B. G. MacCarthy, biographer Martha Bowden, and Jane Spencer, place Davys within the "female school of moral didacticism" made up of authors like Elizabeth Singer Rowe, Jane Barker, and Penelope Aubin (see MacCarthy, B.G. *The Female Pen: Women Writers Their Contribution to the English Novel 1621-1744*. New York: William Salloch, 1948). MacCarthy calls Davys and Jane Barker "priggish" writers who create heroines who "are all righteous, matter-of-fact prigs" (252). Bowden is more sympathetic to Davys, seeing her conservatism as the product of cultural constraints. MacCarthy and Eleanor Wikborg identify Davys's *The Reform'd Coquet* as a forerunner of the mentor-lover, but neither treats Davys with any real, sustained critical attention. Jean B. Kern sees Davys as uneasily negotiating a sort of middle ground between conservative and protofeminist. Meanwhile, critics like Natasha Sajé, Virginia Duff, and Tiffany Potter read Davys as a subtle but definitely subversive protofeminist writer. Potter and Sajé authored, perhaps, the two most current and compelling pieces on *The Reform'd Coquet*.

34. Eleanor Wikborg, *The Lover as Father Figure in Eighteenth-Century Women's Fiction* (Gainesville: University Press of Florida, 2002), 2. Wikborg's *The Lover as Father Figure in Eighteenth-Century Women's Fiction* categorizes different versions of the father figure in her exploration of what she terms "the patriarchal lover." Wikborg categorizes Formator as Mentor in her fourth chapter.

35. Wikborg, *The Lover as Father Figure*, 2, 6.

36. Davys, *Reform'd Coquet*, 287. Speaking to Lord Lofty: "Pugh! said *Amoranda*, is that all? you know, my Lord, there are Misfortunes in all Families, as Sir *Roger de Coverley* says, come come, drink a Dish of Tea and wash away Sorrow" (287). This line is from *The Spectator* no. 109 (July 5, 1711). The specific line from *The Spectator* is "there are Misfortunes in all families" (1:451.1711). It is intriguing that Amoranda quotes this line to Lofty. This scene is part of one Mr. Spectator's visits to Sir Roger's family estate, and the specific scene in no. 109 is one where Roger boasts about his family history to Mr. Spectator. He explains how the portraits mark the powers, foibles, and progressions of his family, for "[Sir Roger] is a Gentleman who does not a little value himself upon his ancient Descent." Sir Roger describes how the "the Persons of one Age differ from those of another, merely by . . . the Force of Dress," "only" Amoranda is speaking to Lord Lofty here, laying the foundation that will trick him into marrying Altemira. One minute calling out and laughing at his gallant declarations of love, the next he goes pale after receiving news of "a considerable loss" from his steward (actually news that Altemira has regained her contract). There is something challenging about the coquettish heroine parroting the stuffy country gentleman's pompous pride in his heritage to the class- and status-conscious rake. There is also something to be said about Amoranda, the narratively threatening coquette, referencing a scene depicting homosociality amid the evidence of patriarchal heritage. Sir Roger is telling his gentleman friend, Mr. Spectator, of his family, where men are strong or soft, and women become valued through their marriages. The coquette is demonstrating an authority of her own: the right to co-opt the gentleman author's language for her own plotting—in this case, the plot to get Lofty to fulfill his contract with Altemira. Sir Roger describes one ancestor, an heiress, who was whisked away for her fortune. Lofty thinks this will be his role, but instead he is the one trapped into marriage by the clever coquette.

37. Powell, " Spectation and the Eighteenth-Century Public Sphere," 58, 275.

38. Catherine Gallagher, *Nobody's Story: The Vanishing Act of Women Writers in the Marketplace, 1670–1820* (Berkeley: University of California Press, 1995), xxiv.

Chapter 2. The Gentleman of Letters as Passionate Reader

Epigraphs: David Hume, *A Treatise of Human Nature*, ed. P. H. Nidditch, 2nd ed. (New York: Oxford University Press, 1978), 365. Hereafter, *A Treatise on Human Nature* will be cited in text with the abbreviation *Treatise*.

Eliza Haywood, *The Female Spectator, Volumes 1 and 2: Selected Works of Eliza Haywood 2*, ed. Kathryn R. King and Alexander Pettit (London: Pickering and Chatto, 2001), 10:363.

1. See Brian Michael Norton, *Fiction and the Philosophy of Happiness: Ethical Inquiries in the Age of Enlightenment* (Lewisburg, PA: Bucknell University Press, 2012); Karen O'Brien, *Women and Enlightenment in Eighteenth-Century Britain* (New York: Cambridge University Press, 2009); and Eve Tavor Bannet, *The Domestic Revolution: Enlightenment Feminism and the Novel* (Baltimore, MD: Johns Hopkins University Press, 2000).

2. Rebecca Tierney-Hynes, *Novel Minds: Philosophers and Romance Readers, 1680-1740* (New York: Palgrave Macmillan, 2012). Tierney-Hynes is a good model of a critic who investigates similar themes in a way that considers how male and female authors were in mutually influential dialogue, even if the male authors consistently positioned themselves in opposition to what they considered to be feminine forms.

3. G. J. Barker-Benfield, *The Culture of Sensibility: Sex and Society in Eighteenth-Century Britain* (Chicago: University of Chicago Press, 1992), 132.

4. John Bender, *Imagining the Penitentiary: Fiction and the Architecture of the Mind in Eighteenth-Century England* (Chicago: University of Chicago Press, 1987); John Mullan, *Sentiment and Sociability: The Language of Feeling in the Eighteenth Century* (Oxford: Clarendon Press, 1988); Jerome Christensen, *Practicing Enlightenment: Hume and the Formation of a Literary Career* (Madison: University of Wisconsin Press, 1987); and Betty A. Schellenberg, *The Conversational Circle: Rereading the English Novel, 1740-1775* (Lexington: University Press of Kentucky, 1996). Bender explores Hume's philosophy as a means of formulating the self as a narrative construction; Mullan explores the intersections between Hume's form and his philosophy of sympathy; and Christensen uses Hume's career as a case study for intersections between authorship, the rise of capitalism, and power. See also the introduction in Schellenberg, *Conversational Circle*. More recently, in *Novel Minds*, Tierney-Hynes argues that the philosophy of Hume's fictional self draws on novelistic conventions and passionate conceptions of the imagination.

5. Catherine Gallagher, *Nobody's Story: The Vanishing Act of Women Writers in the Marketplace, 1670-1820* (Berkeley: University of California Press, 1995), 167-168.

6. See Kathleen Lubey, *Excitable Imaginations: Eroticism and Reading in Britain, 1660-1760* (Lanham, MD: Bucknell University Press, 2012); Rebecca Tierney-Hynes, "Fictional Mechanics: Haywood, Reading, and the Passions," *The Eighteenth Century: Theory and Interpretation* 51, nos. 1-2 (2010): 153-172; and Tierney-Hynes, *Novel Minds*. Lubey and Tierney-Hynes have begun bringing Haywood into discussions about the philosophical and moral implications of the passions on eighteenth-century culture, particularly in the realm of epistemologies of the self and the imagination. See Lubey's chapter on Haywood, "'Too Great Warmth': Joseph Addison, Eliza Haywood, and the Pleasures of Reading," in *Excitable Imaginations*. Tierney-Hynes explores the relationship between Haywood's amatory passion and philosophies of the passions in her article "Fictional Mechanics," and although she does not focus extensively on Haywood, her book *Novel Minds* discusses similar relationships between Enlightenment philosophers such as Hume and women writers and feminine genres. Also representative of the trend are Bannet, *The Domestic Revolution*; O'Brien, *Women and Enlightenment*; and Norton, *Fiction and the Philosophy of Happiness*.

7. Paul Kelleher, *Making Love: Sentiment and Sexuality in Eighteenth-Century British Literature* (Lewisburg, PA: Bucknell University Press, 2015); Stephen Ahern, *Affected Sensibilities: Romantic Excess and the Genealogy of the Novel, 1680-1810* (New York: AMS Press, 2007); April Alliston, "Aloisa and Melliora (*Love in Excess*, Eliza Haywood, 1719-1720)," in *The Novel, Volume 2: Forms and Themes*, ed. Franco Moretti (Princeton, NJ: Princeton University Press, 2006), 515-533. At the Aphra Behn Society conference, Kathryn King presented a paper postulating that Haywood sought to be remembered

as a poet of sensibility and sympathy. In *Making Love*, Kelleher writes that "Haywood is both a great arbitress *and* a canny theorist of passionate love" (99). Alliston argues that Haywood's novel seeks "to convert curiosity into sympathy, a passion that, like love in Haywood's book, refuses to objectify and commodify the other" (523).

8. An emerging exception is King's most recent work, still in the form of a conference paper, who has begun postulating that Haywood sought to be remembered as a poet whose work in many ways anticipates sentiment. My work approaches Haywood from a different angle and connects her work to masculinity instead of poetry and traditions of homosocial female praise.

9. Barker-Benfield, *Culture of Sensibility*; Mullan, *Sentiment and Sociability*; Schellenberg, *Conversational Circle*; and Harriet Guest, *Small Change: Women, Learning, Patriotism, 1750–1810* (Chicago: University of Chicago Press, 2000). Barker-Benfield links this to the reform of male manners, whereas Mullan argues that it emerges from the need to represent newly important social bonds. Somewhat similarly, Schellenberg ties it to the growing desire for social and moral consensus via polite society. Guest links it to shifting ideas—"small changes"—in gender definitions and the relationship between public and private.

10. Barker-Benfield, *Culture of Sensibility*, xxvi.

11. Barker-Benfield, *Culture of Sensibility*, 247, 145.

12. The shift from the rake to the gentleman was a revision of class status, not an erasure. Whereas the rake's power came from lineage and birth and from his aristocratic position, the gentleman's class status came from his manners, education, and birth. The expansive category of the rake remained deeply based in class but created a slightly wider access point for privilege for men of means and education born into less illustrious circumstances. For more on the class connections of the gentleman and the rake, see Thomas King, *The Gendering of Men, 1600–1750: The English Phallus* (Madison: University of Wisconsin Press, 2004); Michele Cohen, *Fashioning Masculinity: National Identity and Language in the Eighteenth Century* (New York: Routledge, 1996); and Jason D. Solinger, *Becoming the Gentleman: British Literature and the Invention of Modern Masculinity, 1660–1815* (New York: Palgrave Macmillan, 2012).

13. Ahern, *Affected Sensibilities*, 82.

14. David Oakleaf, introduction to *Love in Excess; or, the Fatal Enquiry* by Eliza Haywood, 2nd ed. (Peterborough, ON: Broadview Literary Texts, 2000), 12.

15. Lubey, *Excitable Imaginations*, 6; and Gallagher, *Nobody's Story*, 168.

16. Tierney-Hynes, *Novel Minds*, 30. See also Bender, *Imagining the Penitentiary*.

17. Gallagher, *Nobody's Story*, 168.

18. David Hume, *Essays: Moral, Political, and Literary; The Philosophical Works*, vol. 3, ed. Thomas Hill Green and Thomas Hodge Grose (Darmstadt, Germany: Scientia Verlag Aalen, 1992). In *An Enquiry Concerning the Principles of Morals* (1751), Hume explicitly connects literature with moral instruction: "The great charm of poetry consists in lively pictures ... which warm the heart, and diffuse over it similar sentiments and emotions" (238 Hume, David. *Essays: Moral, Political, and Literary*. Vol 1. *The Philosophical Works*. Vol 3. Ed Thomas Hill Green and Thomas Hodge Grose. Germany: Scienta Verlag Aalen, 1992. In his *Treatise*, Hume writes, "Poets themselves, tho' liars by profession," can create pleasure in their readers, which is significant

because pleasure—feeling pleasure or pain—becomes the key indicator of sensibility for Hume (121). Hereafter, *Essays: Moral, Political, and Literary; The Philosophical Works* will be cited in text with the abbreviation *Essays*.

19. Solinger, *Becoming the Gentleman*, 7.

20. Solinger, *Becoming the Gentleman*, 15. See also Barker-Benfield, *The Culture of Sensibility*, 115.

21. Barker-Benfield, *The Culture of Sensibility*, 118.

22. Barker-Benfield, *Culture of Sensibility*, 115.

23. Kelleher, *Making Love*, 101.

24. Robert W. Jones, *Gender and the Formation of Taste in Eighteenth-Century Britain* (New York: Cambridge University Press, 1998), 84–85; Cohen, *Fashioning Masculinity*, 4; Barker-Benfield, *Culture of Sensibility*, xxvi; Schellenberg, *Conversational Circle*, 9; and Guest, *Small Change*, 2.

25. Barker-Benfield, *Culture of Sensibility*, xxvi.

26. Cohen, *Fashioning Masculinity*, 4.

27. Cohen's sentiments are echoed by Barker-Benfield, *Culture of Sensibility*, 249, and by Guest, *Small Change*, 2.

28. Shawn Lisa Maurer, *Proposing Men: Dialectics of Gender and Class in the Eighteenth-Century English Periodical* (Stanford, CA: Stanford University Press, 1998), 65; and Erin Mackie, *Rakes, Highwaymen, and Pirates: The Making of the Modern Gentleman in the Eighteenth Century* (Baltimore, MD: Johns Hopkins University Press, 2009), 9–10.

29. See T. King, *Gendering of Men*, 3; Cohen, *Fashioning Masculinity*, 4–7; and Mackie, *Rakes, Highwaymen, and Pirates*, 1.

30. Toni Bowers, *Force or Fraud: British Seduction Stories and the Problem of Resistance, 1660–1760* (New York: Oxford University Press, 2011), 229.

31. Kelleher, *Making Love*, 99. Although Kelleher acknowledges D'elmont's centrality and even connects Haywood to sensibility, he does not directly examine how Haywood anticipates dominant models of masculinity. Instead, Kelleher frames D'elmont's reform within the broader context of heterosexual love as a vehicle for moral instruction. See also Oakleaf, introduction to *Love in Excess*: "Partly centered on a hero, it is a Bildungsroman representing its narrowly ambitious hero's education in the ways of the heart" (23).

32. See Jennifer Airey, "'He Stood Like One Transfixed with Thunder': Male Rape and the Punishment of Libertinism in Eliza Haywood's *Love in Excess*," *Women's Writing* 26, no. 3 (2019): 328–341. In her essay, Airey brings much-needed critical attention to the ways in which Haywood's text repeatedly places D'elmont in traditionally feminine positions of sexual vulnerability, including during his rape by Melantha and the inverted seduction scenes of Ciamara and Melliora in volume 3, a pattern that she reads as the punishment of male libertinism.

33. Kelleher, *Making Love*, 123.

34. Ahern, *Affected Sensibilities*, 76; and Kelleher, *Making Love*, 99.

35. Bowers, *Force or Fraud*, 230.

36. Lubey, "Eliza Haywood's Amatory Aesthetic," 314. Lubey, Kathleen. "Eliza Haywood's Amatory Aesthetic." *Eighteenth-Century Studies* 39, no. 3 (2006) 309–321.

37. Aside from Lubey and Bowers, see Margaret Case Croskery, "Masquing Desire: The Politics of Passion in Eliza Haywood's *Fantomina*," in *The Passionate Fictions of Eliza Haywood: Essays on Her Life and Work*, ed. Kirsten T. Saxton and Rebecca P. Bocchicchio (Lexington: University Press of Kentucky, 2000), 70.

38. Jennifer Thom, "'A Race of Angels': Castration and Exoticism in Three Exotic Tales by Eliza Haywood," in *The Passionate Fictions of Eliza Haywood*, 184. Thorn notes "Philidore's astonishingly un-Haywoodian refusal of amorous dalliance."

39. For more on the influence and importance of character types during the eighteenth century, see Deidre Shauna Lynch's *The Economy of Character: Novels, Market Culture, and the Business of Inner Meaning* (Chicago: University of Chicago Press, 1998), especially her introduction.

40. Haywood, *Love in Excess*, 266. This is not to say that the female characters are not dynamic or complex but only that their central motives and characters do not change over the course of the novel. Alovisa is always jealous; Ciamara is always selfish and lustful; Melantha is thoroughly a coquette; Melliora is passionate yet virtuous; Violetta is self-sacrificing; and so on. By contrast, D'elmont evolves from being an ambitious rake to a sympathetic gentleman. Hereafter, *Love in Excess* will be cited in the text with the abbreviation *LE*.

41. Christine Blouch, "'What Ann Lang Read': Eliza Haywood and Her Readers," in *The Passionate Fictions of Eliza Haywood*, 307.

42. John Richetti, *Popular Fiction before Richardson: Narrative Patterns, 1700–1739* (New York: Oxford University Press, 1969); Janet Todd, *The Sign of Angellica: Women, Writing, and Fiction, 1660–1800* (New York: Columbia University Press, 1989), 46; Ros Ballaster, *Seductive Forms: Women's Amatory Fiction from 1684 to 1740* (New York: Oxford University Press, 1992), 30–31; Bowers, *Force or Fraud*, 4, 229; and Lubey, *Excitable Imaginations*, 92.

43. Laura Runge, *Gender and Language in British Literary Criticism, 1660–1790* (New York: Cambridge University Press, 1997), 89; and William B. Warner, *Licensing Entertainment: The Elevation of Novel Reading in Britain, 1684–1750* (Berkeley: University of California Press, 1998), 89–90.

44. Jan Fergus, *Provincial Readers in Eighteenth-Century England* (New York: Oxford University Press, 2006), 10–12; and Manushag Powell, *Performing Authorship in Eighteenth-Century English Periodicals* (Lanham, MD: Bucknell University Press, 2012), 151.

45. Eliza Haywood, *Lasselia: or, the Self-Abandon'd. A novel, Written by Mrs. Eliza Haywood*, 2nd ed. (London: 1724), Eighteenth Century Collections Online, https://www.gale.com/primary-sources/eighteenth-century-collections-online, vi–vii; emphasis mine.

46. Runge, *Gender and Language*, 92.

47. Bowers, *Force or Fraud*, 229.

48. Mackie, *Rakes, Highwaymen, and Pirates*, 50. See also Barker-Benfield, *Culture of Sensibility*, 45.

49. Haywood, *LE*, 37. As T. King argues in *Gendering of Men*, according to Restoration standards, "Manliness was not a set of privileges accruing to the membership of a 'natural group' of biological men, but the performative effect of preferment and

autonomy within a patriarchal society" (4–5). From the opening passages of the text, Haywood signals that D'elmont's masculinity is founded on aristocratic masculine privilege. D'elmont is rewarded for his military service according to aristocratic rules with a reception by the king and court. Barker-Benfield, in *Culture of Sensibility*, argues that rakish masculinity was "traditionally bound up with classical and warrior ideals" (104). In *Rakes, Highwaymen, and Pirates*, Mackie states that "closer proximity to the monarch" equated to manliness and status (50), whereas T. King explains that "the sovereign body [was] the primary place and the center around which power relations were exercised" (3). Furthermore, Cohen argues in *Fashioning Masculinity* that with the rise of the gentleman, Frenchness came to signify refinement but also a dangerous seductiveness.

50. D'elmont's aristocratic status meant that he was beholden only to his ambition for wealth. Amena's father is not wealthy enough to pressure D'elmont to marry her, and Alovisa is desirable because of her fortune and high status.

51. In *Affected Sensibilities*, Ahern describes the trajectory as "the arena of action mov[ing] from the battlefield to the bedroom" (41–42).

52. Airey, "'He Stood Like One Transfixed,'" 5.

53. Here I refer to both the Baron and the Marquess. However, to a lesser extent, young Frankville also begins as a would-be rake who is uninterested in marriage and who never follows through on any rakish impulses because he meets Camilla.

54. Kelleher, in *Making Love*, also makes this characterization and is one of the few critics to engage with the Chevalier's sympathetic potential in any way, namely by labeling the Chevalier's function as an "explicit invocation of 'sympathy'" (107).

55. Unlike the rakish D'elmont, the Chevalier has been susceptible to Cupid's bow and fallen in love with Ansellina, who in classic romance fashion "is not indifferent" to the Chevalier and whose beauty and virtue fill his noble breast with sighs and "something of an awe which none but those who truly love can guess at." Haywood, *Love in Excess*, 68, 70. Romance heroes were typically defined by their radical, subservient devotion to their ladies and the extreme feats they performed as marks of service for them.

56. Patricia Meyer Spacks, *Desire and Truth: Functions of Plot in Eighteenth-Century English Novels* (Chicago: University of Chicago Press, 1990), 2.

57. Ballaster, *Seductive Forms*, 170.

58. In fact, most of the inset tales in *Love in Excess* are between men, including one between D'elmont and the younger Frankville, in which D'elmont is again the sympathetic listener. Melliora's tale of abduction by the Marquess that she relates to D'elmont is the exception to the male homosocial rule.

59. Ballaster, *Seductive Forms*, 46. Ballaster also writes that a key feature of romance as a genre is that "love is perceived as the sole motivating force of history and our only means of understanding its processes" (47).

60. Bowers, *Force or Fraud*, 233.

61. Schellenberg, *Conversational Circle*, 4.

62. Maurer, *Proposing Men*, 97.

63. Airey, "'He Stood Like One Transfixed,'" 9–10. Airey also notes that the third part of the novel continually places D'elmont in the traditionally female position of vulnerable sexual prey. She reads the positioning as punishment for his earlier libertine

behavior: "In his relations with Melantha, Ciamara and eventually even Melliora, D'elmont finds himself on the receiving end of libertine sexual objectification, and these experiences soften him into a loving companion for . . . Melliora" (2).

64. Airey, "'He Stood Like One Transfixed,'" 10.

65. Ciamara's comment surfaces in a scene in which she uses the ruse, easily penetrated, of dropping her jewels to start a private conversation with D'elmont. Ciamara, a sexually predatory woman, attempts to play on D'elmont's former reputation and the seeming innocence of the encounter and conversation to make an attempt on his virtue.

66. Bowers, *Force or Fraud*, 234.

67. Unlike in passionate scenes in the first two volumes, the scene emphasizes reciprocal passion and pleasure, and instead of male taking and female yielding, there is mutuality: "Breathless with bliss . . . would *they* pause and gaze, then joyn [sic] again, with ardour [sic] still encreasing [sic], and looks, and sights, and straining grasps" (Haywood, *LE*, 258; italics mine).

68. Glanville is the romantic lead in Charlotte Lennox's *The Female Quixote* (1752); Orville is the same in Frances Burney's *Evelina*; Sir Charles Grandison is the titular hero of Samuel Richardson's *Sir Charles Grandison* (1753); Lovelace is the rakish villain of Richardson's *Clarissa* (1748); and Tom Jones is the lovable scamp of Henry Fielding's *Tom Jones* (1749).

69. Ballaster, *Seductive Forms*, 24.

70. Richetti, *Popular Fiction*, 201.

71. Lubey, *Excitable Imaginations*, 100.

72. Ahern, *Affected Sensibilities*, 86.

73. Barker-Benfield, *Culture of Sensibility*, xxvi.

74. Bowers, *Force or Fraud*, 229–231. Bowers argues that nearly all aggressive female desire is punished except Melliora's careful balance of passive obedience.

75. Lubey, *Excitable Imaginations*, 6.

76. See Oakleaf, introduction to Haywood, *Love in Excess*.

77. Christensen uses Hume as a case study to explore the roles of capitalism, market culture, and gender in defining the author's role as a vehicle of Enlightenment ideology. Christensen, one of the few critics to extensively analyze the trajectory of Hume's career, presents Hume as a representative case of how masculinity became tied to Enlightenment principles via authorship and examines how Hume represents his own actual social practice and self. Barker-Benfield positions Hume as a piece of a larger cultural apparatus that is concerned with masculinity.

78. Critics draw on both Hume's early *Treatise* and his later essays, as do I, because although Hume's philosophical outlook remained consistent in many ways throughout his works, he writes that many of his essays in his *Treatise* are "cast anew" ("My Own Life," 3). Hume, David. "My Own Life". *Essays: Moral, Political, and Literary*. Vol 1. *The Philosophical Works*. Vol 3. Ed Thomas Hill Green and Thomas Hodge Grose. Germany: Scienta Verlag Aalen, 1992. p. 1–7.

79. Spacks, *Desire and Truth*, 6.

80. Hume, *An Enquiry Concerning the Principles of Morals*, 238.

81. Tierney-Hynes, *Novel Minds*, 5.

82. Hume also wrote *History of the Rebellion and Civil Wars in England (1646–1669)*.

83. The removal provides titillating possibilities about Hume's attempt to cultivate his image at the end of his career, but other than interesting speculation there is no definite answer about why the essay was removed from subsequent editions of his work. However, perhaps Hume and his later publishers found an essay about his attempt to seduce a young woman into desiring him a bit ungentlemanly, as he would later write.

84. Solinger, *Becoming the Gentleman*, 26.

85. Joseph Addison and Richard Steele, *The Spectator*, ed. Donald Bond (New York: Oxford University Press, 1965), 10, 1:44.1711.

86. Within this masculine cultural context, "Any man who wishes to be distinguished from boys and beasts should begin by differentiating himself from women; he must avoid female influences, and eliminate or control all those elements in his own nature, including irrationality, that he perceives as feminine"; Carolyn D. Williams, *Pope, Homer, and Manliness: Some Aspects of Eighteenth-Century Classical Learning* (New York: Routledge, 1993), 11. The distinction derives from Shaftesbury's versions of the man of letters and polite masculinity, which were far more stoic and removed from society than Hume's. The duty of men—exclusively aristocratic men, in Shaftesbury's version—was to work and study for the good of society. For Shaftesbury, two forces could corrupt a man unequivocally: "the quest for commodities, or the consumption of particular goods and services; and the desire for (and ultimately the desires of) women" (Jones, *Gender and the Formation of Taste*, 21). Although Shaftesbury writes to foster the reform of male manners and critiques of the rake as an unrestrained consumer, the harsh assessment of women as frivolous and distracting to men is in direct opposition to the heterosociality of the gentleman and the cult of sensibility.

87. Schellenberg, *Conversational Circle*, 1.

88. Hume writes, "By that Means, every Thing of what we call *Belles Lettres* became totally barbarous, being cultivated by Men without any Taste of Life or Manners, and without that Liberty and Facility of Thought and Expression, which can only be acquir'd by Conversation. Even Philosophy went to Wrack.... And Indeed, what cou'd be expected from Men who never consulted Experience in any of their reasonings, or who never search'd for that Experience, where alone it is to be found, in common Life and Conversation?" (*Essays* 3).

89. Hume's works were not completely unnoticed; over the course of his life, as Hume writes, "notwithstanding this variety of winds and seasons, to which my writings had been exposed, they had still been making such advances," which were enough to keep him comfortably independent ("My Own Life," 6). But the winds and seasons of readership did not ultimately favor Hume in his lifetime.

90. See Mullan, *Sentiment and Sociability*, 11; and Gallagher, *Nobody's Story*, 167–168, for a discussion of Hume's popularity or lack thereof.

91. Tierney-Hynes, *Novel Minds*, 30.

92. Bender, *Imagining the Penitentiary*, 37; and Lubey, *Excitable Imaginations*, 8.

93. Haywood, *The Female Spectator*, 10:363.

94. Haywood, *The Female Spectator*, 10:363.

Chapter 3. Romancing the Gentleman Critic

Epigraphs: Samuel Johnson, *A dictionary of the English language: in which the words are deduced from their originals, and illustrated in their different significations by examples from the best writers. To which are prefixed A history of the language, and An English grammar. By Samuel Johnson, A.M. In two volumes*, 2nd ed. (London: 1756), Eighteenth Century Collections Online, https://www.gale.com/primary-sources/eighteenth-century-collections-online, 1:203.

Norbert Schürer, ed., *Charlotte Lennox: Correspondence and Miscellaneous Documents* (Lewisburg, PA: Bucknell University Press, 2012), 16–17. The quotation comes from a letter that Lennox wrote to Richardson dated November 22, 1751.

1. Susan Carlile, *Charlotte Lennox: An Independent Mind* (Toronto: University of Toronto Press, 2018).

2. Kathleen Nulton Kemmerer, *"A Neutral Being between the Sexes": Samuel Johnson's Sexual Politics* (Lewisburg, PA: Bucknell University Press, 1998); Sarah R. Morrison, "Samuel Johnson, Mr. Rambler, and Women," *The Age of Johnson* 14, no. 3 (2003): 23–50; Manushag N. Powell, "Johnson and His 'Readers' in the Epistolary *Rambler* Essays," *Studies in English Literature, 1500–1900* 44, no. 3 (2004): 571–594; and Jacqueline Pearson, *Women's Reading in Britain, 1750–1835* (New York: Cambridge University Press, 1999). Kemmerer's book explores how Johnson in his own writing, and contrary to Boswell's depiction, resists key aspects of misogyny, advocates for women's education, and interrogates gender categories. Meanwhile, Morrison investigates Johnson's uses of pronouns and gendered language. Regarding Johnson in his gender relations, Powell reads him as "not a feminist, but a moralist" (582), while Pearson reads him as not quite a misogynist but definitely "ambivalent" (31).

3. Carlile, *Charlotte Lennox*, 4.

4. Carlile, *Charlotte Lennox*, 3.

5. James Boswell, *Life of Johnson*, ed. R. W. Chapman (New York: Oxford University Press, 1980), 1278.

6. Susan Carlile, introduction to *Masters of the Marketplace: British Women Novelists of the 1750s*, ed. Susan Carlile (Bethlehem, PA: Lehigh University Press, 2011), 11.

7. Jane Spencer, *The Rise of the Woman Novelist: From Aphra Behn to Jane Austen* (New York: Basil Blackwell, 1986), 92.

8. Carlile, *Charlotte Lennox*, 4.

9. Schürer, *Charlotte Lennox*, 15.

10. Schürer, *Charlotte Lennox*, 92.

11. Schürer, *Charlotte Lennox*, 26.

12. Debra Malina, "Rereading the Patriarchal Text: *The Female Quixote, Northanger Abbey*, and the Trace of the Absent Mother," *Eighteenth-Century Fiction* 8, no. 2 (1996): 277.

13. Schürer, *Charlotte Lennox*, 29.

14. The proposed cure, according to Schürer, most likely involved Arabella's reading Richardson's *Clarissa*. Richardson advised against this very ending in a letter dated January 13, 1752 (Schürer, *Charlotte Lennox*, 21). Prioritizing Lennox's desire for expediency, he instead recommended that she continue with two volumes instead of the three that the new ending would seem to entail.

15. Patricia Meyer Spacks, *Desire and Truth: Functions of Plot in Eighteenth-Century English Novels* (Chicago: University of Chicago Press, 1990), 15.

16. Paul J. Korshin, "Johnson, the Essay, and *The Rambler*," in *The Cambridge Companion to Samuel Johnson*, ed. Greg Clingham (New York: Cambridge University Press, 1997), 52.

17. Patricia Meyer Spacks, *Novel Beginnings: Experiments in Eighteenth-Century English Fiction* (New Haven, CT: Yale University Press, 2006), 8.

18. Powell, "Johnson and His 'Readers,'" 572. See also Eithne Henson, *"The Fictions of Romantick Chivalry": Samuel Johnson and Romance* (Madison, WI: Fairleigh Dickinson University Press, 1992), 54; and Freya Johnson and Lynda Mugglestone, *Samuel Johnson: The Arc of the Pendulum* (New York: Oxford University Press, 2012). Other critics who make much of Johnson's inconsistency or incongruity, especially in *The Rambler*, include Morrison and Kemmerer.

19. Manushag Powell, *Performing Authorship in Eighteenth-Century English Periodicals* (Lanham, MD: Bucknell University Press, 2012), 32.

20. Laura Runge, *Gender and Language in British Literary Criticism, 1660–1790* (New York: Cambridge University Press, 1997). Runge's book has been formative for my chapter. See also Kathleen Lubey, *Excitable Imaginations: Eroticism and Reading in Britain, 1660–1760* (Lanham, MD: Bucknell University Press, 2012), which connects erotic images in amatory fiction with empirical and epistemological philosophies; Marta Kvande, "Reading Female Readers: *The Female Quixote* and *Female Quixotism*," in *Masters of the Marketplace*, 220; and Pearson, *Women's Reading*.

21. Runge, *Gender and Language*, 17.

22. Alexander Pope, "An Essay on Criticism," in *The Norton Anthology of English Literature*, vol. 100, ed. James Noggle and Lawrence Lipking, 9th ed. (New York: W. W. Norton, 2012): 2669–2684, ll. 315–317.

23. Samuel Johnson, *The Rambler: The Yale Edition of the Works of Samuel Johnson*, ed. W. J. Bate and Albrecht B. Strauss (New Haven, CT: Yale University Press, 1969), 3:99.1750. Hereafter, *The Rambler* will be cited in text, with the abbreviation *Rambler*, by volume, page, and year.

24. Henson, *"Fictions of Romantick Chivalry*," 69.

25. Morrison, "Samuel Johnson, Mr. Rambler, and Women," 36–37.

26. Powell, "Johnson and His 'Readers,'" 572, 575; Powell, *Performing Authorship*, 55; and Kemmerer, "Neutral Being," 60.

27. Powell, *Performing Authorship*, 26–27.

28. Powell, *Performing Authorship*, 26.

29. Kemmerer, "Neutral Being," 64.

30. Boswell, *Life of Johnson*, 302.

31. Powell, *Performing Authorship*, 32.

32. Helen Deutsch, *Loving Dr. Johnson* (Chicago: University of Chicago Press, 2005), 4. Deutsch writes that one Johnson—the masculine, überman of letters—is "the picture of a gentleman," with "pure manners," clever anecdotes, and confident prose, or the literary giant that he came to be and was beloved for being; whereas another Johnson was "awkward, ungainly, and plainly dressed," a figure who "could only imitate well-bred behavior."

33. Powell, *Performing Authorship*, 32.

34. Korshin, "Johnson, the Essay, and *The Rambler*," 61.

35. Morrison, "Samuel Johnson, Mr. Rambler, and Women," 24; and Kemmerer, "Neutral Being," 23.

36. Powell, "Johnson and His Readers," 582; Kemmerer, "Neutral Being," 20; Morrison, "Samuel Johnson, Mr. Rambler, and Women," 24; and Korshin, "Johnson, the Essay, and *The Rambler*," 62.

37. Kemmerer, "Neutral Being," 76.

38. Morrison calls the essays the "marriage group" (Morrison, "Samuel Johnson, Mr. Rambler, and Women," 39); they include nos. 34 and 35 (by a male letter writer); 39 and 45 (by a correspondent of unclear gender); 113, 115, and 116 (by Hymenaeus); 119 (by Tranquilla); and 167 (by Hymenaeus and Tranquilla).

39. Runge, *Gender and Language*, 28.

40. Boswell, *Life of Johnson*, 36.

41. Ellen Gardiner, "Writing Men Reading in Charlotte Lennox's *The Female Quixote*," *Studies in the Novel* 28, no. 1 (1996): 7.

42. Laurie Langbauer, *Women and Romance: The Consolations of Gender in the English Novel* (Ithaca, NY: Cornell University Press, 1990), 64.

43. Henson, "Fictions of Romantick Chivalry," 70.

44. Although the first reference of the "heroes of literature" is in no. 21 (May 29, 1750), Johnson repeats the language throughout *The Rambler* and uses the same phrase in no. 137 (July 9, 1751). Aside from this phrase, Johnson's imagery frequently refers to a knight or challenger on a quest for glory.

45. Runge, *Gender and Language*, 18–19.

46. Joseph Addison and Richard Steele, *The Spectator*, ed. Donald Bond (New York: Oxford University Press, 1965), 1:21.1711.

47. For recent work on the importance of Quixote and quixotes to eighteenth-century ideologies and literature, see Aaron R. Hanlon, *A World of Disorderly Notions: Quixote and the Logic of Exceptionalism* (Charlottesville: University of Virginia Press, 2019).

48. For explanations on the variety and categories of quixotes, see Hanlon's introduction; see also Eve Tavor Bannet, "Quixotes, Imitations, and Transatlantic Genres," *Eighteenth-Century Studies* 40, no. 4 (2007): 554.

49. *Rambler* 93 and 145 are both defenses of these writers.

50. See also *Rambler* 37 and 158.

51. John Mullan, *Sentiment and Sociability: The Language of Feeling in the Eighteenth Century* (Oxford: Clarendon Press, 1988), 77.

52. See *Rambler* 88, 92, and 168.

53. See also *Rambler* 137.

54. Carlile, *Charlotte Lennox*, 92. For example, Carlile makes a compelling argument that *Rambler* 148 on parental tyranny "could have been inspired by Harriot's short-sighted parents" (92).

55. Spacks, *Desire and Truth*, 14.

56. Janet Todd, *The Sign of Angellica: Women, Writing, and Fiction, 1660–1800* (New York: Columbia University Press, 1989), 157; Langbauer, *Women and Romance*, 2;

Margaret Ann Doody, introduction to *The Female Quixote* by Charlotte Lennox (New York: Oxford University Press, 1998), xi–xxxii; and Ros Ballaster, *Seductive Forms: Women's Amatory Fiction from 1684 to 1740* (New York: Oxford University Press, 1992), 46. Initially, critics such as Todd and Langbauer argued that Lennox's novel is a relatively open-and-shut case about the dangers of reading romances for young women. Gradually, other critics such as Doody and Ballaster began seeing a subversive, feminist potential in Arabella's romance code. The debate largely continues today.

57. Nicole Horejsi, *Novel Cleopatras: Romance Historiography and the Dido Tradition in English Fiction, 1688–1785* (Buffalo, NY: University of Toronto Press, 2019). For another approach to rethinking genre in *The Female Quixote*, see chapter 3 in Horejsi, which presents romance as an alternative kind of feminist history. In a sense, Horejsi does for history what I am attempting to do for literary criticism.

58. Gardiner, "Writing Men Reading," 1. Although Gardiner reads *The Female Quixote* as a "form of literary criticism," she frames her reading as part of the romance debate, hence the criticism reflective of "the need to control and contain women's desire for romance."

59. Gardiner, "Writing Men Reading," 2; and David Marshall, "Writing Masters and 'Masculine Exercises' in *The Female Quixote*," *Eighteenth-Century Fiction* 5, no. 2 (1993): 121. Although Gardiner aptly identifies that the true problem is that "reading the romance produces the desire to write," she does not read Arabella as an authorial figure but instead positions her as an example of problematic female reading and focuses on the male figures, especially Sir George, as authorial figures. More drastically, Marshall argues that Arabella "can be a heroine but never an author" because she is too bound by imitation.

60. Patricia Meyer Spacks, "The Subtle Sophistry of Desire: Dr. Johnson and *The Female Quixote*," *Modern Philology* 85, no. 4 (1988): 534.

61. Catherine A. Craft, "Reworking Male Models: Aphra Behn's *Fair Vow-Breaker*, Eliza Haywood's *Fantomina*, and Charlotte Lennox's *Female Quixote*," *Modern Language Review* 86, no. 4 (1991): 833.

62. Todd, *Signs of Angellica*, 152.

63. Catherine Gallagher, *Nobody's Story: The Vanishing Act of Women Writers in the Marketplace, 1670–1820* (Berkeley: University of California Press, 1995), xix. This is what Gallagher famously argues to be women writers' "author-selves," which were "not pretenses or mystifications, but as the partly disembodied entities required by the specific exchanges that constituted their careers."

64. Gallagher, *Nobody's Story*, 148.

65. I steal the phrase "Mr. Blandville"—similar to "Boreville" instead of "Orville" in *Evelina*—from Powell, who is fairly convinced that she acquired it elsewhere. However, because this is as far as the trail leads at the present juncture, I attribute the witticism to her.

66. Deidre Shauna Lynch, *The Economy of Character: Novels, Market Culture, and the Business of Inner Meaning* (Chicago: University of Chicago Press, 1998), 55.

67. Spacks, "Subtle Sophistry," 535.

68. Charlotte Lennox, *The Female Quixote: or the Adventures of Arabella*, ed. Margaret Dalziel (New York: Oxford University Press, 1989), 153. Hereafter, *The Female Quixote* will be cited in text, with the abbreviation *FQ*.

69. Runge, *Gender and Language*, 22.

70. Lennox, *Female Quixote*, 153, 149–150, 267–269.

71. Glanville tells his father, "'Her fine Sense, and the native Elegance of her Manners give an inimitable Grace to her Behavior; and as much exceed the studied Politeness of other Ladies I have conversed with, as the Beauties of her Person do all I have ever seen.'" Lennox, *Female Quixote*, 64.

72. Gardiner, "Writing Men Reading in Charlotte Lennox's *The Female Quixote*," 2. See Marshall "Writing Masters," 113; and Christine Roulston, "Histories of Nothing: Romance and Femininity in Charlotte Lennox's *The Female Quixote*," *Women's Writing* 2, no. 1 (1995): 36.

73. See also nos. 121 and 154.

74. For an analysis of Mr. Selvin as a patriarchal historian, see Horejsi, *Novel Cleopatras*, 111–112.

75. See Runge, *Gender and Language*, 32; and Carolyn D Williams, *Pope, Homer, and Manliness: Some Aspects of Eighteenth-Century Classical Learning* (New York: Routledge, 1993), 27.

76. Bannet, "Quixotes," 562.

77. Langbauer, *Women and Romance*, 67.

78. Wendy Motooka, "Coming to a Bad End: Sentimentalism, Hermeneutics, and *The Female Quixote*," *Eighteenth-Century Fiction* 8, no. 2 (1996): 263.

79. Lennox also criticizes people who crow too loudly for fame and glory for making a "Kind of Traffick between Virtue and Glory, barter just so much of the one for the other, and expect like other Merchants, to make Advantage by the Exchange" (*FQ* 304). She even criticizes women who take too much care with their dress: "How mean and contemptible a Figure must a Life spent in such idle Amusements make in History?" (*FQ* 279). Turning the tables, however, she is even harsher with the men of society whose "Figures so feminine, Voices so soft, such tripping Steps, and unmeaning Gestures, have ever signalized either their Courage or Constancy" (*FQ* 279).

80. Katherine M. Rogers, "Dreams and Nightmares: Male Characters in the Feminine Novel of the Eighteenth Century," *Men by Women: Women and Literature* 2 (1982): 13.

81. Craft, "Reworking Male Models," 836.

82. Spacks, *Desire and Truth*, 14.

83. David Marshall, "Writing Masters and 'Masculine Exercises' in The Female Quixote." *Eighteenth-Century Fiction* 5, no. 2 (1993): 105–136.

84. Gallagher, *Nobody's Story*, xxiv.

85. Margaret Ann Doody, "Shakespeare's Novels: Charlotte Lennox Illustrated," in "Women and Early Fiction," special issue, *Studies in the Novel* 19, no. 3 (1987): 296.

86. Runge, *Gender and Language*, 128.

87. Runge, *Gender and Language*, 13; Doody, "Shakespeare's Novels," 297; and Jonathan Brody Kramnick, "Reading Shakespeare's Novels: Literary History and Cultural Politics in the Lennox-Johnson Debate," *Modern Language Quarterly* 55, no. 4 (1994): 429–453. Kramnick's essay positions Lennox's critical work as contributing to literary history's idea of the novel but ultimately declares Johnson's to have been the dominant voice.

88. Runge, *Gender and Language*, 138.

89. Carlile, *Charlotte Lennox*, 117.

90. In fact, the scandal was even mentioned in the proposal, perhaps as an incentive for the folio edition: "She was thought by some to have treated SHAKSPEARE with less reverence than might have been wished. Nevertheless the Public was pleased to see so much merit in the performance" (1). "Proposal," *Johnson on Shakespeare: The Yale Edition of the Works of Samuel Johnson*. Vols. 7–8, edited by Arthur Sherbo. New Haven, Yale University Press, 1968, pp. 1–3.

91. Carlile, *Charlotte Lennox*, 128.

92. *Monthly Review* 9 (August 1753): 145, as cited in Carlile, *Charlotte Lennox*,129.

93. As cited in Carlile, *Charlotte Lennox*, 131.

94. Kramnick, "Reading Shakespeare's Novels," 431.

95. Carlile, *Charlotte Lennox*, 122.

96. Charlotte Lennox, *Shakespear illustrated: or the novels and histories, on which the plays of Shakespear are founded, collected and translated from the original authors. With critical remarks. In two volumes By the author of The female Quixote* (London: 1753), Eighteenth Century Collections Online, https://www.gale.com/primary-sources/eighteenth-century-collections-online, 1:x. Hereafter, *Shakespear Illustrated* will be cited in text, with the abbreviation *SI*, by volume and page.

97. Schürer, *Correspondence*, 45, emphasis mine.

98. Runge, *Gender and Language*, 165.

99. Carlile, *Charlotte Lennox*, 135. Carlile points out how much more Lennox is cited than other women: twenty times "is significantly more than the four other women who are included once each, and the one, Jane Collier, who appears three times" (136).

100. Samuel Johnson, *Samuel Johnson*, ed. Donald Green (New York: Oxford University Press, 1984), 69.

101. Johnson, *Samuel Johnson*, 710.

102. Johnson, *Samuel Johnson*, 716.

103. Henry Fielding, "*The Covent Garden Journal*, No. 24," in *The Criticism of Henry Fielding*, ed. Ioan Williams (New York: Barnes & Noble, 1970), 193, 194.

104. Carlile, *Charlotte Lennox*, 113.

105. Carlile, *Charlotte Lennox*, 118.

106. Samuel Johnson, *Johnson on Shakespeare*, 7:59.

107. Johnson, *Johnson on Shakespeare*, 7:71.

108. Johnson, *Johnson on Shakespeare*, 7:104.

109. Carlile, *Charlotte Lennox*, 122.

110. Carlile, *Charlotte Lennox*, 121.

111. Carlile, *Charlotte Lennox*, 278.

112. Carlile, *Charlotte Lennox*, 123. In the proposal he declares that many of Shakespeare's plots "are generally borrowed from novels" and that he most likely read the source text for *Romeo and Juliet* in an English translation, not in the original Italian (82, 86). These details, facts, and arguments come directly from Lennox; she goes unmentioned.

113. Carlile, *Charlotte Lennox*, 121.

114. Johnson, *Johnson on Shakespeare*, 7:91.

Chapter 4. "Smartly Dealt With; Especially by the Ladies"

Epigraph: Samuel Richardson, *The Cambridge Edition of the Correspondence of Samuel Richardson: Richardson's Correspondence with Lady Bradshaigh & Lady Echlin (1748–1753)*, ed. Peter Sabor, vols. 5–7 (New York: Cambridge University Press, 2016), 5:186.

1. Jocelyn Harris, *Samuel Richardson* (New York: Cambridge University Press, 1987), 132.

2. Sylvia Kasey Marks, *Sir Charles Grandison: The Compleat Conduct Book* (Lewisburg, PA: Bucknell University Press, 1986), 13.

3. Richardson, *The Cambridge Edition*, 6: 469. This chapter cites both the new *Cambridge Edition* of Richardson's correspondence and the Anna Laetitia Barbauld edition. From here on the *Cambridge Edition of the Correspondence* will be cited in text by volume and page with the abbreviation *CC*, and the Barbauld with the abbreviation *Letters*. At the time of writing this, the new Cambridge edition of Hester Mulso and Susanna Highmore's correspondence is still forthcoming. Therefore, I am relying on the Barbauld edition of Richardson's correspondence for my Mulso and Highmore citations.

4. Elaine McGirr, "Manly Lessons: *Sir Charles Grandison*, the Rake, and the Man of Sentiment," *Studies in the Novel* 39, no. 3 (2007): 269.

5. Megan A. Woodworth, *Eighteenth-Century Women Writers and the Gentleman's Liberation Movement: Independence, War, Masculinity, and the Novel, 1778–1818* (Burlington, VT: Ashgate, 2011), 11.

6. McGirr, "Manly Lessons," 281.

7. Emily Friedman, "The End(s) of Richardson's *Sir Charles Grandison*," *SEL* 52, no. 3 (2012): 653.

8. Harris, *Samuel Richardson*, 134. See also Juliet McMaster, "*Sir Charles Grandison*: Richardson on Body and Character," in *Passion and Virtue: Essays on the Novels of Samuel Richardson*, ed. David Blewet (Toronto: University of Toronto Press, 2001), 252.

9. McGirr registers, "Masculinity was in crisis: traditional and defining masculine characteristics like strength, power, and roughness were at odds with the social ideals of polite society—the virtues of delicacy, conversation, and grace traditionally coded as feminine (see Mangan, Carter, Mackie, and Shoemaker)" ("Manly Lessons," 267). Meanwhile, Kathleen Oliver, in *Samuel Richardson, Dress, and Discourse* (New York: Palgrave Macmillan, 2008), 144, declares that Sir Charles is both a "domestic woman in drag" and "the literary manifestation and articulation of the bourgeois masculine ideal." This combination of newness and femininity often then lead to declarations of Grandison's male type as fantasies and fairy tales. McGirr doesn't debate the fantasy nature of Grandison, just "the degree of wish-fulfillment that Richardson achieves in *Grandison*" (277). Sir Charles has been both a "Jesus Christ in breeches" (Terry Eagleton, *The Rape of Clarissa* [Minneapolis: University of Minnesota Press, 1982], 96) and an "Anglican Knight Errant" (McGirr, "Manly Lessons," 279). Gerard Barker, *Grandison's Heirs: The Paragon's Progress in the Late Eighteenth-Century English Novel* (Newark: University of Delaware Press, 1985), 71; again, Orville is positioned as an echo of Sir Charles for this very reason: "—'a young girl's dream,' to quote Walter Allen, 'of a nobleman based on Richardson's Grandison.'"

10. E. J. Clery, *The Feminization Debate in Eighteenth-Century England: Literature, Commerce and Luxury* (New York: Palgrave MacMillan, 2004), 1–13. Declan Kavanagh,

Effeminate Years: Literature, Politics, and Aesthetics in Mid-Eighteenth-Century Britain (Lewisberg, PA: Bucknell University Press, 2017), xi–xvi. See Clery's and Kavanagh's introductions.

11. McGirr, "Manly Lessons"; McMaster, "Richardson on Body and Character," 246–267; Barbara Zonitch, *Familiar Violence: Gender and Social Upheaval in the Novels of Frances Burney* (Newark: University of Delaware Press, 1997), 53; Bonnie Latimer, *Making Gender, Culture, and the Self in the Fiction of Samuel Richardson: The Novel Individual* (Burlington, VT: Ashgate, 2013), 145; and Martha Koehler, *Models of Reading: Paragons and Parasites in Richardson, Burney, and Laclos* (Lewisburg, PA: Bucknell University Press, 2005), 149. McGirr and McMaster bring an awareness to the complexity of reading Sir Charles as a reward figure. However, Zonitch, as one example, sees Orville as conservative foreclosure, a reward for Evelina learning to play by the patriarchy's rules; similarly, Latimer and Koehler see Sir Charles as a much more conservative, misogynistic vision of male superiority.

12. This is the core premise of Barker's *Grandison's Heirs*.

13. Bonnie Latimer, "Courting Dominion: *Sir Charles Grandison, Sir George Ellison*, and the Organizing Principle of Masculinity," *Eighteenth-Century Novel* 9 (2012), 118; Barker, *Grandison's Heirs*, 19; Mary V. Yates, "The Christian Rake in *Sir Charles Grandison*," *Studies in English Literature, 1500–1900* 24, no. 3 (1984): 557.

14. William McCarthy, "What Did Anna Barbauld Do to Samuel Richardson's Correspondence? A Study of Her Editing," *Studies in Bibliography* 54 (2001): 191–223.

15. T. C. Duncan Eaves and Ben D. Kimpel, *Samuel Richardson: A Biography* (Oxford, UK: Clarendon Press, 1971), 199.

16. Harris, *Samuel Richardson*, 130.

17. John A Dussinger, introduction to *Correspondence with Sarah Wescomb, Frances Grainger, and Laetitia Pilkington*, by Samuel Richardson (New York: Cambridge University Press, 2015), xxxiv.

18. Harris, *Samuel Richardson*, 130.

19. Harris, *Samuel Richardson*, 131.

20. Peter Sabor, "Rewriting *Clarissa*: Alternative Endings by Lady Echlin, Lady Bradshaigh, and Samuel Richardson," *Eighteenth-Century Fiction* 29, no. 2 (2016–2017): 148.

21. Shirley Van Marter, "Richardson's Debt to Hester Mulso Concerning the Curse in *Clarissa*," *Papers on Language and Literature* 14, no. 1 (1978): 22–31.

22. Peter Sabor, introduction to *The Correspondence of Samuel Richardson: Richardson's Correspondence with Lady Bradshaigh & Lady Echlin 1748–1753*, by Samuel Richardson, vols. 5–7 (New York: Cambridge University Press, 2016), xlvi.

23. Samuel Richardson, *The Correspondence of Samuel Richardson; selected from the original manuscripts bequeathed by him to his family; to which are prefixed a biographical account of that author and observations on his writings by Anne Laetitia Barbauld*, 6 vols. (London: Lewis & Rodem, 1804), 3:177. Hereafter, *The Correspondence of Samuel Richardson* will be cited in the text by volume and page, with the abbreviation *Letters*.

24. Sabor, introduction to *Correspondence of Samuel Richardson*, xliv.

25. Betty A. Schellenberg, *The Conversational Circle: Rereading the English Novel, 1740–1775* (Lexington: University Press of Kentucky, 1996), 51.

26. Betty A. Schellenberg, *Literary Coteries and the Making of Modern Print Culture* (New York: Cambridge University Press, 2016), 49.

27. Schellenberg, *Literary Coteries*, 49.

28. Schellenberg, *Literary Coteries*, 85–86.

29. Schellenberg, *Literary Coteries*, 45.

30. Sabor, "Rewriting *Clarissa*," 148.

31. Betty A. Schellenberg, "Using 'Femalities' to 'Make Fine Men': Richardson's *Sir Charles Grandison* and the Feminization of Narrative," *Studies in English Literature, 1500–1900* 34, no. 3 (1994): 600.

32. Harris, *Samuel Richardson*, 134.

33. Samuel Richardson, *The History of Sir Charles Grandison*, ed. Jocelyn Harris, 3 vols. (New York: Oxford University Press, 1972), 1:22. Hereafter, *The History of Sir Charles Grandison* will be cited in the text by volume and page, with the abbreviation *SCG*.

34. Tita Chico, "Details and Frankness: Affective Relations in *Sir Charles Grandison*," *Studies in Eighteenth-Century Culture* 38 (2009): 53.

35. McGirr, "Manly Lessons," 269.

36. Dussinger, introduction to *Correspondence with Sarah Wescomb*, xlix.

37. Barker, *Grandison's Heirs*, 15.

38. Notably, Orme is one of Harriet Byron's initial suitors, a kind of ghost of Hickman's past, who is set up to be set aside. This indicates that this exchange happens right before the reveal of Sir Charles himself.

39. McMaster, "Richardson on Body and Character," 249.

40. Bradshaigh wrote in June 1754, "My Sister [Echlin] has now taken it into her head, to be very *sure*, that I wrote some of her letters. I am pleas'd with *that*, and shall not undeceive her *yet*. give me leave to turn pirate for a *time*, the prize too tempting to resist" (*CC* 6:461).

41. Jean Baptiste de Fravel wrote to Richardson on April 17, 1751 (*CC* 10.49) for a description of how the good man would navigate Paris with a virtuous balance. In a letter written on May 10, 1751, Philip Skelton asks Richardson to make Sir Charles "rather a Christian hero than a saint" (*CC* 10.51).

42. Schellenberg, *Conversational Circle*, 59; Chico, "Details and Frankness," 46.

43. Richardson, *Letters*, 6:348.

44. Elizabeth Carter, *A series of letters between Mrs. Elizabeth Carter and Miss Catherine Talbot, from 1741 to 1770. To which are added, letters from Mrs. Elizabeth Carter to Mrs. Vesey, between 1763 and 1787, published from the original manuscripts in the possession of the rev. Montagu Pennington, m.a.*, 4 vols. (London: Rivington, 1809), 2:141–142.

45. George Haggerty, "*Sir Charles Grandison* and the 'Language of Nature,'" in *Passion and Virtue*, 319.

46. Richardson, *CC*, 6:501.

47. Schellenberg, *Literary Coteries*, 45.

48. Jocelyn Harris, introduction to *The History of Sir Charles Grandison*, xii.

49. Harris, *Samuel Richardson*, 134.

50. Chico, "Details and Frankness," 54.

51. Koehler, *Models of Reading*, 147.

52. Latimer, *Making Gender*, 168.

53. Schellenberg, *Conversational Circle*, 56.

54. Cameron Esposito, *Rape Jokes*, 2018, https://www.cameronesposito.com/. My framing of this relief was actually inspired by Cameron Esposito's comedy special *Rape Jokes* (2018). During the special, Esposito recounts her personal experience of sexual assault while in college. She also describes how, after her assaulter discovered her sexuality, he came screaming across the quad. She recalls how a male co-worker just stepped in front of her, got in the way, calmed the attacker, and got him to leave. Then he made sure she got safely back to her room. This structure, this sense of relief in the face of patriarchal-fueled danger, is, in part, where I started thinking about the appeal and the desire of the gentleman for this chapter.

55. Latimer, "Courting Dominion," 112. Latimer's use of the word "protean" is a direct link to Harris's analysis of Lovelace's protean nature.

56. McMaster, "Richardson on Body and Character," 253.

57. McMaster, "Richardson on Body and Character," 265.

58. Woodworth, *Eighteenth-Century Women Writers*, 10–11; Yates, "The Christian Rake," 554; and Harris, *Samuel Richardson*, 134.

59. Harris, *Samuel Richardson*, 134.

60. Philip Carter, *Men and the Emergence of Polite Society, Britain 1660–1800* (New York: Pearson Education Limited, 2001), 20; Latimer, "Courting Dominion," 113.

61. Latimer, "Courting Dominion," 113.

62. Latimer, "Courting Dominion," 112.

63. Helen Thompson, "Secondary Qualities and Masculine Form in *Clarissa* and *Sir Charles Grandison*," *Eighteenth-Century Fiction* 24, no. 2 (2011–2012): 222; McGirr, "Manly Lessons," 277, Harris, *Samuel Richardson*, 133.

64. Wendy Jones, "The Dialectic of Love in *Sir Charles Grandison*," in *Passion and Virtue*, 309.

65. McMaster, "Richardson on Body and Character," 255.

66. Burney, Frances, *The Early Journals and Letters of Fanny Burney*, ed. Lars E. Troide, vol. 1 (Montreal: McGill-Queen's University Press, 1988), 47.

67. Barker, *Grandison's Heirs*, 20. Barker reads Alanthus as a male paragon, which I interrogate in chapter 1. However, I think Barker's instinct that women-authored works influenced *Grandison* is both vital and sound.

68. McGirr, "Manly Lessons," 281.

69. Barker, *Grandison's Heirs*, 36.

70. Eleanor Wikborg, *The Lover as Father Figure in Eighteenth-Century Women's Fiction* (Gainesville: University Press of Florida, 2002), 2.

71. Koehler, *Models of Reading*, 149.

72. Latimer, *Making Gender*, 145.

Chapter 5. The Gentleman as Authorial Drag

Epigraph: Mary Robinson, *Walsingham; or, The Pupil of Nature*, ed. Julie Shaffer (Peterborough, ON: Broadview Press, 2003), 92. Hereafter, this edition of the work will be cited in text with the abbreviation *Walsingham*.

1. Judith Halberstam, *Female Masculinity* (Durham, NC: Duke University Press, 1998), 1.

2. Ben Robertson, *Elizabeth Inchbald's Reputation: A Publishing and Reception History* (New York: Routledge, 2015), 3.

3. Emily Hodgeson Anderson, "Revising the Theatrical Conventions in *A Simple Story*: Elizabeth Inchbald's Ambiguous Performance," *Journal for Early Modern Cultural Studies* 6, no. 1 (2006): 5–6.

4. Dror Wahrman, *Making of the Modern Self: Identity and Culture in Eighteenth-Century England* (New Haven, CT: Yale University Press, 2004), 47. See also Thomas W. Laqueur, *Making Sex: Body and Gender from the Greeks to Freud* (Cambridge, MA: Harvard University Press, 1990). Gender historians Wahrman and Laqueur argue that a more fluid perception of gender as a spectrum in the early eighteenth century was gradually replaced by an attitude that the genders were innate, separate, and complementary later in the century. Most critics on the period agree with the general thesis that gender shifted into a biological binary model by the latter half of the century.

5. Megan A. Woodworth, *Eighteenth-Century Women Writers and the Gentleman's Liberation Movement: Independence, War, Masculinity, and the Novel, 1778–1818* (Burlington, VT: Ashgate, 2011), 22; George Haggerty, *Men in Love: Masculinity and Sexuality in the Eighteenth Century* (New York: Columbia University Press, 1999), 82, 109; Candace Ward, "Inordinate Desire: Schooling the Senses in Elizabeth Inchbald's *A Simple Story*," *Studies in the Novel* 31, no. 1 (1999): 1.

6. Eve Tavor Bannet, *The Domestic Revolution: Enlightenment Feminism and the Novel* (Baltimore, MD: Johns Hopkins University Press, 2000), 1–2; Karen O'Brien, *Women and Enlightenment in Eighteenth-Century Britain* (New York: Cambridge University Press, 2009), 12; Harriet Guest, *Small Change: Women, Learning, Patriotism, 1750–1810* (Chicago: University of Chicago Press, 2000), 16.

7. Woodworth, *Eighteenth-Century Women Writers*, 21.

8. Woodworth, *Eighteenth-Century Women Writers*, 14; Guest, *Small Change*, 13–25; and Nancy Armstrong, *Desire and Domestic Fiction: A Political History of the Novel* (New York: Oxford University Press, 1987), 4–8. See also Bannet's introduction to *Domestic Revolution* and Karen O'Brien's introduction to *Women and Enlightenment in Eighteenth-Century Britain*. The critical focus has been on the heroines, whether they are viewed as conservative models of domesticity and virtue (e.g., Evelina or Belinda), as warnings of the dangers of radical philosophy (e.g., Amelia Opie's Adeline Mowbray), or as progressive victims of patriarchal oppression (e.g., Wollstonecraft's Maria or Mary Hays's Emma Courtney). However, this focus has not meant that masculinity is never displayed or of interest to such critics—for instance, Bannet, *Domestic Revolution*, 52, and Eleanor Wikborg's *The Lover as Father Figure in Eighteenth-Century Women's Fiction* (Gainesville: University Press of Florida, 2002), which explores the figure but not as an influence on men—the emphasis of and vehicle for the critique is usually determined to be the heroine, who is presented as a model for female readers and a proper object for masculine sympathy or protection (Bannet, *Domestic Revolution*, 61).

9. Mary Hays, *The Memoirs of Emma Courtney*, ed. Miriam L. Wallace (Glen Allen, VA: College Publishing, 2004), 48.

10. One of the best manifestations of Glenthorn's being a gentleman puppet animated by the plot is when he finds himself at Geraldine's "feet . . . making very serious love, before [he] knew where [he] was" (Maria Edgeworth, *Castle Rackrent and Ennui* (New York: Penguin Classics, 2007), 236.

11. Katharine Kittredge, "Proto-Butch or Temporally-Challenged Trans? Considering Female Masculinities in Eighteenth-Century Britain," *Developments in the Histories of Sexualities: In Search of the Normal, 1600–1800*, ed. Chris Mounsey (Lewisburg, PA: Bucknell University Press, 2013), 175.

12. Judith Butler, *Bodies That Matter: On the Discursive Limits of Sex*, 2nd ed. (New York: Routledge, 2011), 85.

13. R. W. Connell, *Masculinities*, 2nd ed. (Berkeley: University of California Press, 2005), 79. As Connell argues, "Not many men actually meet the normative standards" of hegemonic masculinity.

14. Madeleine Kahn, *Narrative Transvestism: Rhetoric and Gender in the Eighteenth-Century English Novel* (Ithaca, NY: Cornell University Press, 1991), 14, 17.

15. I use both masculine and feminine pronouns to refer to Sidney throughout this chapter. At other times, by performing the gentleman, Sidney *is* the gentleman. At these moments I refer to Sidney as "he/him." Meanwhile, at other times, I use "she/her" to emphasize not only that a woman can play the part of the gentleman but also what I see as the drag structure of the character and the plot. I will also occasionally use "they/them" to indicate the duality of the character's identity. I do not think that any or all of these strategies are the sole or even unquestionably correct way to approach the character or text. However, at this point, my hope is that such variety makes my analysis and larger argument clearer to the reader—that is, that the gentleman's masculinity was actualized through performance, and that women, both characters and writers, were able to don this masculinity at will.

16. I am drawing on Kittredge's explanation of "theatrical drag," which "depend[s] less on the development of actual distinct character personalities than on the audience's familiarity with certain stylized character types" (Kittredge, "Proto-Butch or Temporally-Challenged Trans?," 179).

17. Eve Kosofsky Sedgwick, *Between Men: English Literature and Male Homosocial Desire* (New York: Columbia University Press, 1985), 22.

18. Todd W. Reeser, *Masculinities in Theory: An Introduction* (New York: Wiley-Blackwell, 2010), 62, 64.

19. Reeser, *Masculinities*, 65.

20. Elizabeth Inchbald, *A Simple Story*, ed. J.M.S. Tompkins (New York: Oxford University Press, 1988), 94. Hereafter, *A Simple Story* will be cited in text with the abbreviation *SS*.

21. Terry Castle, *Masquerade and Civilization: The Carnivalesque in Eighteenth-Century English Culture and Fiction* (Stanford, CA: Stanford University Press, 1986), 294.

22. Jane Spencer, introduction to *A Simple Story*, by Elizabeth Inchbald (New York: Oxford University Press, 1988), xx. Nearly all critics read Matilda as the parallel or reincarnation of her mother, and, as Patricia Meyer Spacks notes, "Most readers have found Miss Milner a more compelling figure than her daughter"; Patricia Meyer Spacks, *Desire and*

Truth: Functions of Plot in Eighteenth-Century English Novels (Chicago: University of Chicago Press, 1990), 196. Spencer, J.M.S. Tompkins, Spacks, and others—nearly everyone except Castle—find the more submissive Matilda thoroughly dissatisfying. For readings that align Matilda and Miss Milner but with a more Castle-like reading, see George Haggerty, "Female Abjection in Inchbald's *A Simple Story*," *Studies in English Literature, 1500–1900* 36, no. 3 (1996): 670; Caroline Breashears, "Defining Masculinity in *A Simple Story*," *Eighteenth-Century Fiction* 16, no. 3 (2004): 467; and Ward, "Inordinate Desire," 16.

23. Spacks, *Desire and Truth*, 196. See also Castle, *Masquerade and Civilization*, 323.

24. Catherine Craft-Fairchild, *Masquerade and Gender: Disguise and Female Identity in Eighteenth-Century Fictions by Women* (Philadelphia: University of Pennsylvania Press, 1993), 7.

25. Craft-Fairchild, *Masquerade and Gender*, 7.

26. Haggerty, "Female Abjection," 669.

27. John Morillo, "Editing Eve: Rewriting the Fall in Austen's *Persuasion* and Inchbald's *A Simple Story*," *Eighteenth-Century Fiction* 23, no. 1 (2010): 219. See also Breashears, "Defining Masculinity," 469; Spacks, *Desire and Truth*, 336; Craft-Fairchild, *Masquerade and Gender*, 15; and Haggerty, "Female Abjection," 667–668.

28. Jo Alyson Parker, "*A Simple Story*: Inchbald's Two Versions of Female Power," *Eighteenth-Century Studies* 30, no. 3 (1997): 256.

29. Craft-Fairchild, *Masquerade and Gender*, 102–103.

30. Sedgwick, *Between Men*, 2.

31. Morillo, "Editing Eve," 219.

32. Most critics follow in the footsteps of Chris Cullens's formative article "Mrs. Robinson and the Masquerade of Womanliness," which reads Sidney's gender performance through the lens of Judith Butler's gender theory. Whether critics interpret Sidney as a transvestite figure or one of androgyny, they agree that Robinson plays with and challenges binary gender. Cullens, Eleanor Ty, Amy Garnai, Sharon Setzer, Julie Shaffer, and Katherine Binhammer all read Sidney's cross-dressing as a kind of transvestism. Ellen Arnold, Stephanie Russo, and A. D. Cousins, by contrast, see Sidney as figure of androgyny, whereas Whitney Arnold and Leigh Bonds read *Walsingham* through the lens of Robinson's own drive for celebrity and performance, especially her connection to breeches roles.

33. "*The Analytical Review* 27 (1798)," review, in Robinson, *Walsingham*, 501.

34. "*The Monthly Mirror* 5 (March 1798)," review, in Robinson, *Walsingham*, 506.

35. I am not arguing that all these forms of cross-dressing are the same. For an outstanding analysis of the different forms of masculine performance by women, see Kittredge, "Proto-Butch or Temporally-Challenged Trans?"

36. Wahrman, *Making of the Modern Self*, 27.

37. Julie Shaffer, "Cross-Dressing and the Nature of Gender in Mary Robinson's *Walsingham*," in *Presenting Gender: Changing Sex in Early-Modern Culture*, ed. Chris Mounsey (Lewisburg, PA: Bucknell University Press, 2001), 149.

38. Garber, *Vested Interest*, 69.

39. Shaffer, "Cross-Dressing," 158.

40. Stephanie Russo and A. D. Cousins, "'Educated in Masculine Habits': Mary Robinson, Androgyny, and the Ideal Woman," *Journal of the Australasian Universities*

Language and Literature Association 115 (2011): 40. See also Shaffer, "Cross-Dressing," 156; Katherine Binhammer, "Female Homosociality and the Exchange of Men: Mary Robinson's *Walsingham*," *Women's Studies* 35, no. 3 (2006): 229; and Ellen Arnold, "Genre, Gender, and Cross-Dressing in Mary Robinson's *Walsingham*," *Postscript* 16 (1999): 61.

41. Lady Emily further illustrates Walsingham's misogyny when Sidney hears that Lady Emily is attracted to Walsingham and asks, "'Pray, my gallant cousin, what is this Lady Emily Delvin?' . . . 'A woman,' answered I . . . 'Pshaw!' cried he peevishly; 'I mean what sort of woman?' . . . 'Handsome, lively, and rich,' replied I. 'Young enough to make hearts ache, and too old to be the dupe of her own'" (Robinson, *Walsingham*, 193). To Walsingham, she is merely a woman, whereas Sidney can see women as individuals with nuance and variety.

42. Butler, *Bodies That Matter*, xvii. My mid-sentence shift in pronouns is an attempt to illustrate how the naming—that is, the labeling—shifts Sidney's gender in a tangible way.

43. At one point, Walsingham claims to be prophetic: "A painful sensation, which has never failed to inform me with prophetic horror, when any event nearly interested my feelings, at the moment chilled my breast" (Robinson, *Walsingham*, 329).

44. Arnold, "Genre, Gender, and Cross-Dressing," 61.

45. "*The Anti-Jacobin* I (1798)," review, in Robinson, *Walsingham*, 503.

46. "*The Monthly Mirror* 5 (March 1798)," review, in Robinson, *Walsingham*, 506.

47. "*The Analytical Review* 27 (1798)," review, in Robinson, *Walsingham*, 500.

48. "*British Critic* 12," review, in Robinson, *Walsingham*, 509.

49. Halberstam, *Female Masculinity*, 21.

50. Emily Allen, "Loss Incommensurable: Economies of Imbalance in Mary Robinson's *Walsingham*," *Eighteenth-Century Novel* 5 (2006): 88. Throughout Binhammer's entire article, an exploration of female homosociality and its potential erotics in *Walsingham*, she points out the simultaneity of the homosocial structures by writing that, until the very end of the novel, "Female homosociality appears to be precisely the opposite: male homosocial desire played out over the exchange of Isabella" (Binhammer, "Female Homosociality," 225).

51. Allen, "Loss Incommensurable," 68; and Binhammer, "Female Homosociality," 230.

52. She aptly asks, "Does the enlightened despot or benevolent dictator lose any power by being enlightened or benevolent, or is his power increased because obedience is cheerfully given in exchange for mild treatment and the appearance of free will?" Woodworth, *Eighteenth-Century Women Writers*, 17.

53. Hye-Soo Lee, "Women, Comedy, and *A Simple Story*," *Eighteenth-Century Fiction* 20, no. 2 (2007–2008): 213.

54. Craft-Fairchild, *Masquerade and Gender*, 102.

55. More specifically, I mean that the gentleman is designed to perform a rather conservative, steady type of masculinity. As Michael Kramp in *Disciplining Love: Austen and the Modern Man* and Woodworth both argue, the late century was the era of Revolutions, and this shaped the late- and turn-of-the-century gentleman.

Coda

1. Michael Kramp, *Disciplining Love: Austen and the Modern Man* (Columbus: Ohio State University Press, 2007); Michael Kramp, *Jane Austen and Masculinity* (Lewisburg, PA: Bucknell University Press, 2018); and Claudia L. Johnson, *Jane Austen's Cults and Cultures* (Chicago: University of Chicago Press, 2014).

2. Kramp, *Disciplining Love*, 13.

3. Kramp emphasizes this perspective in *Disciplining Love* and his introduction to *Jane Austen and Masculinity*; in the former, he argues that Austen's men are the "modernization of English men," which, though not entirely discounting the eighteenth century, continuously positions them as a new form of man rather than the recurrence of the gentleman (Kramp, *Disciplining Love*, 1).

4. Kramp, *Disciplining Love*, ix.

5. Jason D. Solinger, *Becoming the Gentleman: British Literature and the Invention of Modern Masculinity, 1660–1815* (New York: Palgrave Macmillan, 2012).

6. Megan A. Woodworth, *Eighteenth-Century Women Writers and the Gentleman's Liberation Movement: Independence, War, Masculinity, and the Novel, 1778–1818* (Burlington, VT: Ashgate, 2011).

7. Jane Austen, *Sense and Sensibility*, ed. James Kinsley (New York: Oxford University Press, 2008), 14. Hereafter this work will be cited in text as *Sense and Sensibility*.

8. Kramp, *Disciplining Love*, 5.

9. Kramp, *Disciplining Love*, 70.

10. Marianne initially uses Brandon's discussion of wearing "flannel waistcoats" as evidence that he is too old and infirm to think of love.

11. Jane Austen, *Persuasion*, ed. Patricia Meyer Spacks (New York: W. W. Norton, 1995), 156.

12. Austen, *Persuasion*, 156.

Bibliography

Addison, Joseph, and Richard Steele. *The Spectator*. Edited by Donald Bond. 5 vols. New York: Oxford University Press, 1965.

Ahern, Stephen. *Affected Sensibilities: Romantic Excess and the Genealogy of the Novel, 1680–1810*. New York: AMS Press, 2007.

Airey, Jennifer L. "'He Stood Like One Transfixed with Thunder': Male Rape and the Punishment of Libertinism in Eliza Haywood's *Love in Excess*." *Women's Writing* 26, no. 3 (2019): 328–341.

Allen, Emily. "Loss Incommensurable: Economies of Imbalance in Mary Robinson's *Walsingham*." *Eighteenth-Century Novel* 5 (2006): 67–92.

Alliston, April. "Alovisa and Melliora (*Love in Excess*, Eliza Haywood, 1719–1720)." In *The Novel, Volume 2: Forms and Themes*, edited by Franco Moretti, 515–533. Princeton, NJ: Princeton University Press, 2006.

"*The Analytical Review* 27 (1798)." Review, in *Walsingham; or the Pupil of Nature*, by Mary Robinson, edited by Julie Shaffer, 500–502. Peterborough, ON: Broadview Press, 2003.

Anderson, Emily Hodgson. "Revising the Theatrical Conventions in *A Simple Story*: Elizabeth Inchbald's Ambiguous Performance." *Journal for Early Modern Cultural Studies* 6, no. 1 (2006): 5–30.

"*The Anti-Jacobin* I (1798)." Review, in *Walsingham; or the Pupil of Nature*. By Mary Robinson, edited by Julie Shaffer, 502–504. Peterborough, ON: Broadview Press, 2003.

Armstrong, Nancy. *Desire and Domestic Fiction: A Political History of the Novel*. New York: Oxford University Press, 1987.

Arnold, Ellen. "Genre, Gender, and Cross-Dressing in Mary Robinson's *Walsingham*." *Postscript* 16 (1999): 57–68.

Arnold, Whitney. "Mary Robinson's *Memoirs* and the Terrors of Literary Obscurity." *Women's Studies* 43, no. 6 (2014): 733–749.

Austen, Jane. *Persuasion*. Edited by Patricia Meyer Spacks. New York: W. W. Norton, 1995.

———. *Sense and Sensibility*. Edited by James Kinsley. New York: Oxford University Press, 2008.

Austin, Andrea. "Shooting Blanks: Potency, Parody, and Eliza Haywood's *The History of Miss Betsy Thoughtless*." In *The Passionate Fictions of Eliza Haywood: Essays on Her Life and Work*, edited by Kirsten T. Saxton and Rebecca P. Bocchicchio, 259–282. Lexington: University Press of Kentucky, 2000.

Ballaster, Ros. *Seductive Forms: Women's Amatory Fiction from 1684 to 1740*. New York: Oxford University Press, 1992.

BIBLIOGRAPHY

Bannet, Eve Tavor. *The Domestic Revolution: Enlightenment Feminism and the Novel.* Baltimore, MD: Johns Hopkins University Press, 2000.

———. "Quixotes, Imitations, and Transatlantic Genres." *Eighteenth-Century Studies* 40, no. 4 (2007): 553–569.

Barchas, Janine. "*Grandison*'s Grandeur as Printed Book: A Look at the Eighteenth-Century Novel's Quest for Status." *Eighteenth-Century Fiction* 14, nos. 3–4 (2002): 673–714.

Barker, Gerard. *Grandison's Heirs: The Paragon's Progress in the Late Eighteenth-Century English Novel.* Newark: University of Delaware Press, 1985.

Barker-Benfield, G. J. *The Culture of Sensibility: Sex and Society in Eighteenth-Century Britain.* Chicago: University of Chicago Press, 1992.

Beaton, Kate. "Jane Austen Comics." In *Hark! A Vagrant* (2006–2018). http://www.harkavagrant.com/index.php?id=4.

Bender, John. *Imagining the Penitentiary: Fiction and the Architecture of the Mind in Eighteenth-Century England.* Chicago: University of Chicago Press, 1987.

Binhammer, Katherine. "Female Homosociality and the Exchange of Men: Mary Robinson's *Walsingham*." *Women's Studies* 35, no. 3 (2006): 221–240.

Blouch, Christine. "'What Ann Lang Read': Eliza Haywood and Her Readers." In *The Passionate Fictions of Eliza Haywood: Essays on Her Life and Work*, edited by Kirsten T. Saxton and Rebecca P. Bocchicchio, 300–325. Lexington: University Press of Kentucky, 2000.

Boardman, Michael. "Inchbald's *A Simple Story*: An Anti-Ideological Reading." In *Ideology and Form in Eighteenth-Century Literature*, edited by David H. Richter, 207–222. Lubbock: Texas Tech University Press, 1999.

Bonds, Leigh. "The Power of the Puff: Mary Robinson's Celebrity and the Success of *Walsingham*." *CEA Critic* 75, no. 1 (2013): 44–50.

Boswell, James. *Life of Johnson.* Edited by R. W. Chapman. New York: Oxford University Press, 1980.

Bowden, Martha F. "Mary Davys: Self-Presentation and the Woman Writer's Reputation in the Early Eighteenth Century." *Women's Writing* 3, no. 1 (1996): 17–33.

Bowers, Toni. *Force or Fraud: British Seduction Stories and the Problem of Resistance, 1660–1760.* New York: Oxford University Press, 2011.

Breashears, Caroline. "Defining Masculinity in *A Simple Story*." *Eighteenth-Century Fiction* 16, no. 3 (2004): 451–470.

Bree, Linda. Introduction to *The Adventures of David Simple and the Adventures of David Simple, Volume the Last*, by Sarah Fielding, xi–xxxvi. New York: Penguin Books, 2002.

Burney, Frances. *The Early Journals and Letters of Fanny Burney.* Vol. 1, edited by Lars E. Troide. Montreal: McGill–Queen's University Press, 1988.

Butler, Judith. *Bodies That Matter: On the Discursive Limits of Sex.* 2nd ed. New York: Routledge, 2011.

Carlile, Susan. *Charlotte Lennox: An Independent Mind.* Toronto: University of Toronto Press, 2018.

———. Introduction to *Masters of the Marketplace: British Women Novelists of the 1750s*, 11–28. Edited by Susan Carlile. Bethlehem, PA: Lehigh University Press, 2011.

Carter, Elizabeth. *A series of letters between Mrs. Elizabeth Carter and Miss Catherine Talbot, from 1741 to 1770. To which are added, letters from Mrs. Elizabeth*

Carter to Mrs. Vesey, between 1763 and 1787, published from the original manuscripts in the possession of the rev. Montagu Pennington, m.a. 4 vols. London: Rivington, 1809.

Carter, Philip. *Men and the Emergence of Polite Society, Britain, 1660–1800.* New York: Pearson Education, 2001.

Castle, Terry. *Masquerade and Civilization: The Carnivalesque in Eighteenth-Century English Culture and Fiction.* Stanford, CA: Stanford University Press, 1986.

Chaber, Lois A. "'Sufficient to the Day': Anxiety in *Sir Charles Grandison.*" In *Passion and Virtue: Essays on the Novels of Samuel Richardson,* edited by David Blewet, 268–294. Toronto: University of Toronto Press, 2001.

Chico, Tita. "Details and Frankness: Affective Relations in *Sir Charles Grandison.*" *Studies in Eighteenth-Century Culture* 38 (2009): 45–68.

Christensen, Jerome. *Practicing Enlightenment: Hume and the Formation of a Literary Career.* Madison: University of Wisconsin Press, 1987.

Clarke, Norma. *Dr. Johnson's Women.* New York: Hambledon and London, 2000.

Clery, E. J. *The Feminization Debate in Eighteenth-Century England: Literature, Commerce and Luxury.* New York: Palgrave MacMillan, 2004.

Cohen, Michèle. *Fashioning Masculinity: National Identity and Language in the Eighteenth Century.* New York: Routledge, 1996.

Connell, R. W. *Masculinities.* 2nd ed. Berkeley: University of California Press, 2005.

Craft, Catherine A. "Reworking Male Models: Aphra Behn's *Fair Vow-Breaker,* Eliza Haywood's *Fantomina,* and Charlotte Lennox's *Female Quixote.*" *Modern Language Review* 86, no. 4 (1991): 821–838.

Craft-Fairchild, Catherine. *Masquerade and Gender: Disguise and Female Identity in Eighteenth-Century Fictions by Women.* Philadelphia: University of Pennsylvania Press, 1993.

Croskery, Margaret Case. "Masquing Desire: The Politics of Passion in Eliza Haywood's *Fantomina.*" In *The Passionate Fictions of Eliza Haywood: Essays on Her Life and Work,* edited by Kirsten T. Saxton and Rebecca P. Bocchicchio, 69–94. Lexington: University Press of Kentucky, 2000.

Cullens, Chris. "Mrs. Robinson and the Masquerade of Womanliness." In *Body and Text in the Eighteenth-Century,* edited by Veronica Kelly and Dorothea E. von Mücke, 266–289. Stanford, CA: Stanford University Press, 1994.

Davys, Mary. *The Reformed Coquet; or, the Memoirs of Amoranda.* In *Popular Fiction by Women, 1660–1730: An Anthology,* edited by Paula R. Backscheider and John J. Richetti, 251–320. New York: Oxford University Press, 1996.

Deutsch, Helen. *Loving Dr. Johnson.* Chicago: University of Chicago Press, 2005.

"Divinity, Morality." *The Gentleman's Magazine: and Historical Chronicle, Jan. 1736–Dec. 1833* 22 (1752): 145–147. ProQuest.

Doody, Margaret Ann. Introduction to *The Female Quixote,* by Charlotte Lennox, xi–xxxii. New York: Oxford University Press, 1998.

———. "Shakespeare's Novels: Charlotte Lennox Illustrated." In "Women and Early Fiction." Special issue, *Studies in the Novel* 19, no. 3 (1987): 296–310.

———. *The True Story of the Novel.* New Brunswick, NJ: Rutgers University Press, 1996.

Duff, Virginia. "'I Should Not Care to Mix My Breed': Gender, Race, Class, and Genre in Mary Davys's *The Accomplished Rake, or Modern Fine Gentleman*." *Eighteenth-Century Novel* 1 (2001): 311–325.

Dussinger, John A. Introduction to *Correspondence with Sarah Wescomb, Frances Grainger, and Laetitia Pilkington*, by Samuel Richardson, xxxiv–lxx. Edited by John A. Dussinger. New York: Cambridge University Press, 2015.

Eaves, T.C.D., and Ben D. Kimpel. *Samuel Richardson: A Biography*. Oxford: Clarendon Press, 1971.

Edgeworth, Maria. *Castle Rackrent and Ennui*. New York: Penguin Classics, 2007.

Esposito, Cameron. *Rape Jokes*. 2018. https://www.cameronesposito.com/rape-jokes/.

Fergus, Jan. *Provincial Readers in Eighteenth-Century England*. New York: Oxford University Press, 2006.

Fielding, Henry. "*The Covent Garden Journal*, No. 24." In *The Criticism of Henry Fielding*, edited by Ioan Williams, 191–193. New York: Barnes & Noble, 1970.

Frantz, Sarah S. G., and Katharina Rennhak, eds. *Women Constructing Men: Female Novelists and Their Male Characters, 1750–2000*. Lanham, MD: Lexington Books, 2010.

Freeman, Lisa A. *Character's Theater: Genre and Identity on the Eighteenth-Century English Stage*. Philadelphia: University of Pennsylvania Press, 2002.

Friedman, Emily. "The End(s) of Richardson's *Sir Charles Grandison*." *Studies in English Literature* 52, no. 3 (2012): 651–667.

Gallagher, Catherine. *Nobody's Story: The Vanishing Act of Women Writers in the Marketplace, 1670–1820*. Berkeley: University of California Press, 1995.

Garber, Marjorie. *Vested Interests: Cross-Dressing and Cultural Anxiety*. New York: Harper Perennial. 1992.

Gardiner, Ellen. "Writing Men Reading in Charlotte Lennox's *The Female Quixote*." *Studies in the Novel* 28, no. 1 (1996): 1–11.

Garnai, Amy. *Revolutionary Imaginings in the 1790s: Charlotte Smith, Mary Robinson, Elizabeth Inchbald*. New York: Palgrave MacMillan, 2009.

Green, Katherine Sobba. *The Courtship Novel, 1740–1820: A Feminized Genre*. Lexington: University Press of Kentucky, 1991. Kindle.

Guest, Harriet. *Small Change: Women, Learning, Patriotism, 1750–1810*. Chicago: University of Chicago Press, 2000.

Haggerty, George. "Female Abjection in Inchbald's *A Simple Story*." *Studies in English Literature, 1500–1900* 36, no. 3 (1996): 655–671.

———. "Male Privilege in Frances Burney's *The Wanderer*." In *Women Constructing Men: Female Novelists and Their Male Characters, 1750–2000*, edited by Sarah S. G. Frantz and Katharina Rennhak, 31–43. Lanham, MD: Lexington Books, 2010.

———. *Men in Love: Masculinity and Sexuality in the Eighteenth Century*. New York: Columbia University Press, 1999.

———. "*Sir Charles Grandison* and the 'Language of Nature.'" In *Passion and Virtue: Essays on the Novels of Samuel Richardson*, edited by David Blewet, 317–331. Toronto: University of Toronto Press, 2001.

Halberstam, Judith. *Female Masculinity*. Durham, NC: Duke University Press, 1998.

Hanlon, Aaron R. *A World of Disorderly Notions: Quixote and the Logic of Exceptionalism*. Charlottesville: University of Virginia Press, 2019.

Harris, Jocelyn. Introduction to *The History of Sir Charles Grandison*, by Samuel Richardson, vii–xxiv. New York: Oxford University Press, 1972.

———. "Protean Lovelace." In *Passion and Virtue: Essays on the Novels of Samuel Richardson*, edited by David Blewet, 92–113. Toronto: University of Toronto Press, 2001.

———. *Samuel Richardson*. New York: Cambridge University Press, 1987.

Harvey, Karen. *The Little Republic: Masculinity, Domesticity, and Authority in Eighteenth-Century Britain*. New York: Oxford University Press, 2014.

Hays, Mary. *The Memoirs of Emma Courtney*. Edited by Miriam L. Wallace. Glen Allen, VA: College Publishing, 2004.

Haywood, Eliza. *The Female Spectator, Volumes 1 and 2: Selected Works of Eliza Haywood 2*. Edited by Kathryn R. King and Alexander Pettit. London: Pickering & Chatto, 2001.

———. *Lasselia: or, the Self-Abandon'd. A novel*. Written by Mrs. Eliza Haywood. 2nd ed. (London: 1724). Eighteenth Century Collections Online. https://www.gale.com/primary-sources/eighteenth-century-collections-online.

———. *Love in Excess; or, the Fatal Enquiry*. Edited by David Oakleaf. 2nd ed. Peterborough, ON: Broadview Literary Texts, 2000.

Henson, Eithne. *"The Fictions of Romantick Chivalry": Samuel Johnson and Romance*. Madison, NJ: Fairleigh Dickinson University Press, 1992.

Hitchcock, Timothy, and Michele Cohen, eds. *English Masculinities, 1660–1800*. New York: Longman, 1999.

Horejsi, Nicole. *Novel Cleopatras: Romance Historiography and the Dido Tradition in English Fiction, 1688–1785*. Buffalo, NY: University of Toronto Press, 2019.

Hume, David. *Essays: Moral, Political, and Literary; The Philosophical Works*. Vol. 3, edited by Thomas Hill Green and Thomas Hodge Grose. Darmstadt, Germany: Scienta Verlag Aalen, 1992.

———. *A Treatise of Human Nature*. Edited by P. H. Nidditch. 2nd ed. New York: Oxford University Press, 1978.

Inchbald, Elizabeth. *A Simple Story*. Edited by J.M.S. Tompkins. New York: Oxford University Press, 1988.

Johnson, Claudia L. *Jane Austen's Cults and Cultures*. Chicago: University of Chicago Press, 2014.

Johnson, Freya, and Lynda Mugglestone. *Samuel Johnson: The Arc of the Pendulum*. New York: Oxford University Press, 2012.

Johnson, Samuel. *A dictionary of the English language: in which the words are deduced from their originals, and illustrated in their different significations by examples from the best writers. To which are prefixed A history of the language, and An English grammar. By Samuel Johnson, A.M. In two volumes*. 2nd ed. (London: 1756). Eighteenth Century Collections Online. https://www.gale.com/primary-sources/eighteenth-century-collections-online.

———. *Johnson on Shakespeare: The Yale Edition of the Works of Samuel Johnson*. Vols. 7–8, edited by Arthur Sherbo. New Haven, CT: Yale University Press, 1968.

———. *The Rambler*. In *The Yale Edition of the Works of Samuel Johnson*. Vols. 3–5, edited by W. J. Bate and Albrecht B. Strauss. New Haven, CT: Yale University Press, 1969.

———. *Samuel Johnson*. Edited by Donald Green. New York: Oxford University Press, 1984.

Jones, Robert W. *Gender and the Formation of Taste in Eighteenth-Century Britain*. New York: Cambridge University Press, 1998.

Jones, Wendy. "The Dialectic of Love in *Sir Charles Grandison*." In *Passion and Virtue: Essays on the Novels of Samuel Richardson*, edited by David Blewet, 295–316. Toronto: University of Toronto Press, 2001.

Joule, Victoria. "Mary Davys's Novel Contribution to Women and Realism." *Women's Writing* 17, no. 1 (2010): 30–48.

Kahn, Madeleine. *Narrative Transvestism: Rhetoric and Gender in the Eighteenth-Century English Novel*. Ithaca, NY: Cornell University Press, 1991.

Kavanagh, Declan. *Effeminate Years: Literature, Politics, and Aesthetics in Mid-Eighteenth-Century Britain*. Lewisburg, PA: Bucknell University Press, 2017.

Kelleher, Paul. *Making Love: Sentiment and Sexuality in Eighteenth-Century British Literature*. Lewisburg, PA: Bucknell University Press, 2015.

Kemmerer, Kathleen Nulton. *"A Neutral Being between the Sexes": Samuel Johnson's Sexual Politics*. Lewisburg, PA: Bucknell University Press, 1998.

Kern, Jean B. "Mrs. Mary Davys as Novelist of Manners." *Essays in Literature* 10, no. 1 (1983): 29–38.

King, Kathryn R. *A Political Biography of Eliza Haywood*. New York: Routledge, 2012.

King, Thomas. *The Gendering of Men, 1600–1750*. Vol. 1, *The English Phallus*. Madison: University of Wisconsin Press, 2004.

Kittredge, Katharine. "Proto-Butch or Temporally-Challenged Trans? Considering Female Masculinities in Eighteenth-Century Britain." In *Developments in the Histories of Sexualities: In Search of the Normal, 1600–1800*, edited by Chris Mounsey, 173–208. Lewisburg, PA: Bucknell University Press, 2013.

Klein, Lawrence E. *Shaftesbury and the Culture of Politeness: Moral Discourse and Cultural Politics in Early Eighteenth-Century England*. New York: Cambridge University Press, 1994.

Koehler, Marta. "'Faultless Monsters' and Monstrous Egos: The Disruption Model Selves in Frances Burney's *Evelina*." *Eighteenth Century* 43, no. 1 (2002): 19–41.

———. *Models of Reading: Paragons and Parasites in Richardson, Burney, and Laclos*. Lewisburg, PA: Bucknell University Press, 2005.

Korshin, Paul J. "Johnson, the Essay, and *The Rambler*." In *The Cambridge Companion to Samuel Johnson*, edited by Greg Clingham, 51–66. New York: Cambridge University Press, 1997.

Kowaleski-Wallace, Elizabeth. *Their Fathers' Daughters: Hannah Moore, Maria Edgeworth, and Patriarchal Complicity*. New York: Oxford University Press, 1991.

Kraft, Elizabeth. "Wit and the Spectator's Ethics of Desire." *Studies in English Literature, 1500–1900* 45, no. 3 (2005): 625–646.

Kramnick, Jonathan Brody. "Reading Shakespeare's Novels: Literary History and Cultural Politics in the Lennox-Johnson Debate." *Modern Language Quarterly* 55, no. 4 (1994): 429–453.

Kramp, Michael. *Disciplining Love: Austen and the Modern Man*. Columbus: Ohio State University Press, 2007.

———. *Jane Austen and Masculinity*. Lewisburg, PA: Bucknell University Press, 2018.

Kvande, Marta. "Reading Female Readers: *The Female Quixote* and *Female Quixotism*." In *Masters of the Marketplace: British Women Novelists of the 1750s*, edited by Susan Carlile, 219–241. Bethlehem, PA: Lehigh University Press.

Langbauer, Laurie. *Women and Romance: The Consolations of Gender in the English Novel*. Ithaca, NY: Cornell University Press, 1990.

Lanser, Susan. "Of Closed Doors and Open Hatches: Heteronormative Plots in Eighteenth-Century (Women's) Studies." *Eighteenth Century* 53, no. 3 (2012): 273–290.

———. *The Sexuality of History*. Chicago: University of Chicago Press, 2014.

Laqueur, Thomas W. *Making Sex: Body and Gender from the Greeks to Freud*. Cambridge, MA: Harvard University Press, 1990.

Latimer, Bonnie. "Courting Dominion: *Sir Charles Grandison*, *Sir George Ellison*, and the Organizing Principle of Masculinity." *Eighteenth-Century Novel* 9 (2012): 109–131.

———. *Making Gender, Culture, and the Self in the Fiction of Samuel Richardson: The Novel Individual*. Burlington, VT: Ashgate, 2013.

Lee, Hye-Soo. "Women, Comedy, and *A Simple Story*." *Eighteenth Century Fiction* 20, no. 2 (2007–2008): 197–217.

Lennox, Charlotte. *The Female Quixote: or the Adventures of Arabella*. Edited by Margaret Dalziel. New York: Oxford University Press, 1989.

———. *Shakespear illustrated: or the novels and histories, on which the plays of Shakespear are founded, collected and translated from the original authors. With critical remarks. In two volumes. By the author of The female Quixote*. Vol. 1. London: 1753. Eighteenth Century Collections Online. https://www.gale.com/primary-sources/eighteenth-century-collections-online.

Looser, Devoney. "Jane Austen 'Responds' to the Men's Movement." *Persuasions* 18 (1996): 159–170.

Lubey, Kathleen. "Eliza Haywood's Amatory Aesthetic." *Eighteenth-Century Studies* 39, no. 3 (2006): 309–321.

———. *Excitable Imaginations: Eroticism and Reading in Britain, 1660–1760*. Lewisburg, PA: Bucknell University Press, 2012.

Lupton, Christina. "Sincere Performances: Franklin, Tillotson, and Steele on the Plain Style." *Eighteenth-Century Studies* 40, no. 2 (2007): 177–192.

Lynch, Deidre Shauna. *The Economy of Character: Novels, Market Culture, and the Business of Inner Meaning*. Chicago: University of Chicago Press, 1998.

MacCarthy, B. G. *The Female Pen: Women Writers: Their Contribution to the English Novel, 1621–1744*. New York: William Salloch, 1948.

Mackie, Erin. *Market à la Mode: Fashion, Commodity, and Gender in* The Tatler *and* The Spectator. Baltimore, MD: Johns Hopkins University Press, 1997.

———. *Rakes, Highwaymen, and Pirates: The Making of the Modern Gentleman in the Eighteenth Century*. Baltimore, MD: Johns Hopkins University Press, 2009.

Malina, Debra. "Rereading the Patriarchal Text: *The Female Quixote*, *Northanger Abbey*, and the Trace of the Absent Mother." *Eighteenth-Century Fiction* 8, no. 2 (1996): 271–292.

Marks, Sylvia Kasey. *Sir Charles Grandison: The Compleat Conduct Book*. Lewisburg, PA: Bucknell University Press, 1986.

Marshall, David. "Writing Masters and 'Masculine Exercises' in *The Female Quixote*." *Eighteenth-Century Fiction* 5, no. 2 (1993): 105–136.

Maurer, Shawn Lisa. *Proposing Men: Dialectics of Gender and Class in the Eighteenth-Century English Periodical*. Stanford, CA: Stanford University Press, 1998.

McBurney, William H. "Mrs. Mary Davys: Forerunner of Fielding." *PMLA* 74, no. 4 (1959): 348–355.

McCarthy, William. "What Did Anna Barbauld Do to Samuel Richardson's Correspondence? A Study of Her Editing." *Studies in Bibliography* 54 (2001): 191–223.

McGirr, Elaine. "Manly Lessons: *Sir Charles Grandison*, the Rake, and the Man of Sentiment." *Studies in the Novel* 39, no. 3 (2007): 267–283.

McMaster, Juliet. "*Sir Charles Grandison*: Richardson on Body and Character." In *Passion and Virtue: Essays on the Novels of Samuel Richardson*, edited by David Blewet, 246–267. Toronto: University of Toronto Press, 2001.

Merritt, Juliette. "Reforming the Coquette? Eliza Haywood's Vision of a Female Epistemology." In *Fair Philosopher: Eliza Haywood and* The Female Spectator, edited by Lynn Marie Wright and Donald J. Newman, 176–192. Lewisburg, PA: Bucknell University Press, 2006.

Miller, Jane. *Women Writing About Men*. New York: Pantheon, 1986.

Modleski, Tania. *Loving with a Vengeance: Mass-Produced Fantasies for Women*. New York: Routledge, 2007.

"*The Monthly Mirror* 5 (March 1798)." *Walsingham; or the Pupil of Nature*. By Mary Robinson, edited by Julie Shaffer, 506–507. Peterborough, ON: Broadview Press, 2003.

"*The Monthly Review* n.s. 26 (August 1798)." *Walsingham; or the Pupil of Nature*. By Mary Robinson, edited by Julie Shaffer, 497–499. Peterborough, ON: Broadview Press, 2003.

Morillo, John. "Editing Eve: Rewriting the Fall in Austen's *Persuasion* and Inchbald's *A Simple Story*." *Eighteenth-Century Fiction* 23, no. 1 (2010): 195–223.

Morrison, Sarah R. "Samuel Johnson, Mr. Rambler, and Women." *Age of Johnson* 14, no. 3 (2003): 23–50.

Motooka, Wendy. "Coming to a Bad End: Sentimentalism, Hermeneutics, and *The Female Quixote*." *Eighteenth-Century Fiction* 8, no. 2 (1996): 251–270.

Mullan, John. *Sentiment and Sociability: The Language of Feeling in the Eighteenth Century*. Oxford: Clarendon Press, 1988.

Norton, Brian Michael. *Fiction and the Philosophy of Happiness: Ethical Inquiries in the Age of Enlightenment*. Lewisburg, PA: Bucknell University Press, 2012.

Oakleaf, David. Introduction to *Love in Excess; or, the Fatal Enquiry*, by Eliza Haywood, 7–24. 2nd ed. Peterborough, ON: Broadview Literary Texts, 2000.

O'Brien, Karen. *Women and Enlightenment in Eighteenth-Century Britain*. New York: Cambridge University Press, 2009.

Oliver, Kathleen M. *Samuel Richardson, Dress, and Discourse*. New York: Palgrave Macmillan, 2008.

Parker, Jo Alyson. "*A Simple Story*: Inchbald's Two Versions of Female Power." *Eighteenth-Century Studies* 30, no. 3 (1997): 255–270.

Pearson, Jacqueline. *Women's Reading in Britain, 1750–1835*. New York: Cambridge University Press, 1999.

Pew Research Center. "An Examination of the 2016 Electorate, Based on Validated Voters." Pew Research, August 9, 2018. https://www.pewresearch.org/politics/2018/08/09/an-examination-of-the-2016-electorate-based-on-validated-voters/.

Pollock, Anthony. *Gender and the Fictions of the Public Sphere, 1690–1755*. New York: Routledge, 2009.

Pope, Alexander. "An Essay on Criticism." In *The Norton Anthology of English Literature*, Vol. C, edited by James Noggle and Lawrence Lipking, 2669–2684. 9th ed. New York: W. W. Norton, 2012.

Potter, Tiffany. "Decorous Disruption: The Cultural Voice of Mary Davys." *Eighteenth-Century Women* 1 (2001): 63–93.

Powell, Manushag N. "Johnson and His 'Readers' in the Epistolary *Rambler* Essays." *Studies in English Literature* 44, no. 3 (2004): 571–594.

———. *Performing Authorship in Eighteenth-Century English Periodicals*. Lewisburg, PA: Bucknell University Press, 2012.

———. "See No Evil, Hear No Evil, Speak No Evil: Spectation and the Eighteenth-Century Public Sphere." *Eighteenth-Century Studies* 45, no. 2 (2012): 255–276.

Reeser, Todd W. *Masculinities in Theory: An Introduction*. New York: Wiley-Blackwell, 2010.

Richardson, Samuel. *The Cambridge Edition of the Correspondence of Samuel Richardson: Correspondence Primarily on Sir Charles Grandison (1750–1754)*. Vol. 10, edited by Betty A. Schellenberg. New York: Cambridge University Press, 2014.

———. *The Cambridge Edition of the Correspondence of Samuel Richardson: Richardson's Correspondence with Lady Bradshaigh and Lady Echlin (1748–1753)*. Vols. 5–7, edited by Peter Sabor. New York: Cambridge University Press, 2016.

———. *The Cambridge Edition of the Correspondence with Sarah Wescomb, Frances Grainger, and Laetitia Pilkington*. Vol 3, edited by John A. Dussinger. New York: Cambridge University Press, 2015.

———. *The Correspondence of Samuel Richardson; selected from the original manuscripts bequeathed by him to his family; to which are prefixed a biographical account of that author and observations on his writings by Anne Laetitia Barbauld*. 6 vols. London: Lewis & Rodem, 1804.

———. *The History of Sir Charles Grandison*. Edited by Jocelyn Harris. 3 vols. New York: Oxford University Press, 1972.

Richetti, John. *Popular Fiction before Richardson: Narrative Patterns, 1700–1739*. New York: Oxford University Press, 1969.

Robertson, Ben. *Elizabeth Inchbald's Reputation: A Publishing and Reception History*. New York: Routledge, 2015.

Robinson, Mary. *Walsingham; or, The Pupil of Nature*. Edited by Julie Shaffer. Peterborough, ON: Broadview Press, 2003.

Rogers, Katherine M. "Dreams and Nightmares: Male Characters in the Feminine Novel of the Eighteenth Century." *Men by Women: Women and Literature* 2 (1982): 9–24.

Roulston, Christine. "Histories of Nothing: Romance and Femininity in Charlotte Lennox's *The Female Quixote*." *Women's Writing* 2, no. 1 (1995): 25–42.

Runge, Laura. *Gender and Language in British Literary Criticism, 1660–1790*. New York: Cambridge University Press, 1997.

Russo, Stephanie, and A. D. Cousins. "'Educated in Masculine Habits': Mary Robinson, Androgyny, and the Ideal Woman." *Journal of the Australasian Universities Language and Literature Association* 115 (2011): 37–50.

Sabor, Peter. Introduction to *The Correspondence of Samuel Richardson: Richardson's Correspondence with Lady Bradshaigh and Lady Echlin, 1748–1753*, by Samuel Richardson, xxxvi–lvii. Vols. 5–7. New York: Cambridge University Press, 2016.

———. "Rewriting *Clarissa*: Alternative Endings by Lady Echlin, Lady Bradshaigh, and Samuel Richardson." *Eighteenth-Century Fiction* 29, no. 2 (2016–2017): 131–150.

Saje, Natasha. "'The Assurance to Write, the Vanity of Expecting to be Read': Deception and Reform in Mary Davys's *The Reform'd Coquet*." *Essays in Literature* 23, no. 2 (1996): 165–177.

Saxton, Kirsten T. Introduction to *The Passionate Fictions of Eliza Haywood: Essays on Her Life and Work*, edited by Kirsten T. Saxton and Rebecca P. Bocchicchio, 1–18. Lexington: University Press of Kentucky, 2000.

———. "Telling Tales: Eliza Haywood and the Crimes of Seduction in *The City Jilt* or, *The Alderman turn'd Beau*." In *The Passionate Fictions of Eliza Haywood: Essays on Her Life and Work*, edited by Kirsten T. Saxton and Rebecca P. Bocchicchio, 115–142. Lexington: University Press of Kentucky, 2000.

Schellenberg, Betty A. *The Conversational Circle: Rereading the English Novel, 1740–1775*. Lexington: University Press of Kentucky, 1996.

———. *Literary Coteries and the Making of Modern Print Culture*. New York: Cambridge University Press, 2016.

———. "Using 'Femalities' to 'Make Fine Men': Richardson's *Sir Charles Grandison* and the Feminization of Narrative." *Studies in English Literature, 1500–1900* 34, no. 3 (1994): 599–616.

Schofield, Mary Anne. *Eliza Haywood*. Boston: Twayne Publishers, 1985.

Schürer, Norbert, ed. *Charlotte Lennox: Correspondence and Miscellaneous Documents*. Lewisburg, PA: Bucknell University Press, 2012.

Sedgwick, Eve Kosofsky. *Between Men: English Literature and Male Homosocial Desire*. New York: Columbia University Press, 1985.

Setzer, Sharon. "The Dying Game: Crossdressing in Mary Robinson's *Walsingham*." *Nineteenth-Century Contexts* 22, no. 3 (2000): 305–328.

Shaffer, Julie. "Cross-Dressing and the Nature of Gender in Mary Robinson's *Walsingham*." In *Presenting Gender: Changing Sex in Early-Modern Culture*, edited by Chris Mounsey, 136–167. Lewisburg, PA: Bucknell University Press, 2001.

Shaftesbury, Anthony Ashley Cooper, Third Earl of Shaftesbury. *Characteristics of Men, Manners, Opinions, Times*. Edited by Lawrence E. Klein. New York: Cambridge University Press, 1999.

Solinger, Jason D. *Becoming the Gentleman: British Literature and the Invention of Modern Masculinity, 1660–1815*. New York: Palgrave Macmillan, 2012.

Spacks, Patricia Meyer. *Desire and Truth: Functions of Plot in Eighteenth-Century English Novels*. Chicago: University of Chicago Press, 1990.

———. *Novel Beginnings: Experiments in Eighteenth-Century English Fiction*. New Haven, CT: Yale University Press, 2006.

———. "The Subtle Sophistry of Desire: Dr. Johnson and 'The Female Quixote.'" *Modern Philology* 85, no. 4 (1988): 532–542.

Spedding, Patrick. *A Bibliography of Eliza Haywood*. New York: Routledge, 2004.

Spencer, Jane. Introduction to *A Simple Story*, by Elizabeth Inchbald, vii–xx. New York: Oxford University Press, 1988.

———. *The Rise of the Woman Novelist: From Aphra Behn to Jane Austen*. New York: Basil Blackwell, 1986.

Straub, Kristina. *Sexual Suspects: Eighteenth-Century Players and Sexual Ideology*. Princeton, NJ: Princeton University Press, 1992.

Thompson, Helen. "Secondary Qualities and Masculine Form in *Clarissa* and *Sir Charles Grandison*." *Eighteenth-Century Fiction* 24, no. 2 (2011–2012): 195–226.

Thorn, Jennifer. "'A Race of Angels': Castration and Exoticism in Three Exotic Tales by Eliza Haywood." In *The Passionate Fictions of Eliza Haywood: Essays on Her Life and Work*, edited by Kirsten T. Saxton and Rebecca P. Bocchicchio, 168–193. Lexington: University Press of Kentucky, 2000.

Tierney-Hynes, Rebecca. "Fictional Mechanics: Haywood, Reading, and the Passions." *Eighteenth Century: Theory and Interpretation* 51, nos. 1–2 (2010): 153–172.

———. *Novel Minds: Philosophers and Romance Readers, 1680–1740*. New York: Palgrave Macmillan, 2012.

Todd, Janet. *Men by Women*. Boulder, CO: Holmes & Meier, 1981.

———. *Sensibility: An Introduction*. New York: Methuen, 1986.

———. *The Sign of Angellica: Women, Writing, and Fiction, 1660–1800*. New York: Columbia University Press, 1989.

Ty, Eleanor. *Empowering the Feminine: The Narratives of Mary Robinson, Jane West, and Amelia Opie, 1796–1812*. Toronto: University of Toronto Press, 1998.

Van Marter, Shirley. "Richardson's Debt to Hester Mulso Concerning the Curse in *Clarissa*." *Papers on Language and Literature* 14, no. 1 (1978): 22–31.

Wahrman, Dror. *Making of the Modern Self: Identity and Culture in Eighteenth-Century England*. New Haven, CT: Yale University Press, 2004.

Wallace, Miriam L. Introduction to *The Memoirs of Emma Courtney* by Mary Hays and *Adeline Mowbray; or the Mother and the Daughter* by Amelia Opie, 1–38. Glen Allen, VA: College Publishing, 2004.

Ward, Candace. "Inordinate Desire: Schooling the Senses in Elizabeth Inchbald's *A Simple Story*." *Studies in the Novel* 31, no. 1 (1999): 1–18.

Warner, William B. *Licensing Entertainment: The Elevation of Novel Reading in Britain, 1684–1750*. Berkeley: University of California Press, 1998.

Wikborg, Eleanor. *The Lover as Father Figure in Eighteenth-Century Women's Fiction*. Gainesville: University Press of Florida, 2002.

Williams, Carolyn D. *Pope, Homer, and Manliness: Some Aspects of Eighteenth-Century Classical Learning*. New York: Routledge, 1993.

Woodworth, Megan A. *Eighteenth-Century Women Writers and the Gentleman's Liberation Movement: Independence, War, Masculinity, and the Novel, 1778–1818*. Burlington, VT: Ashgate, 2011.

Woolf, Virginia. *A Room of One's Own*. New York: Mariner Books, 2005.
Yates, Mary V. "The Christian Rake in *Sir Charles Grandison*." *Studies in English Literature, 1500–1900* 24, no. 3 (1984): 545–561.
Zonitch, Barbara. *Familiar Violence: Gender and Social Upheaval in the Novels of Frances Burney*. Newark: University of Delaware Press, 1997.

Index

Addison, Joseph: criticism of the coquette, 34, 94; and Davys, 48–49; essays of, 10; and the gentleman's masculinity, 29; and Haywood, 55; and Hume, 76, 82; and S. Johnson, 93; and Lennox, 116; and Mr. Spectator, 23, 26, 27, 28, 37; as periodicalist, 29–30, 78. See also *Spectator*; Steele, Richard
Ahern, Stephen, 56, 60, 203n51
Airey, Jennifer, 60, 64, 70, 201n32, 203n63
Allen, Emily, 172
Alliston, April, 56
amatory fiction, 61, 83–84
Arnold, Ellen, 171
Arnold, Whitney, 218n32
Austen, Jane: appreciation of *Sir Charles Grandison*, 151, 181, 186; continuation of eighteenth-century women writers, 17, 157, 179, 182; exceptionality of, 2, 180–181; legacy of, 180–182; male characters of, 17, 220n3. See also *Persuasion*; *Pride and Prejudice*; *Sense and Sensibility*
authenticity of the gentleman, 4, 12, 21, 28–29, 33
authorial network, 127, 128, 138, 174
authorial prerogative, 102

Ballaster, Ros, 73, 203n59, 209n56
Bannet, Eve Tavor, 112, 156, 216n8
Barbauld, Anna Laetitia, 126
Barker, Gerard, 134, 150, 151, 215n67
Barker, Jane, 197n33
Barker-Benfield, G. J.: on Hume, 75, 204n77; on rakish masculinity, 203n49; on the reform of male manners, 75, 193n24, 200n9; on the reform of masculinity, 6, 56, 193n24; on the reform of the rake, 3, 191n7
Beaton, Kate, 180
Belfour. *See* Bradshaigh, Lady Dorothy
Bender, John, 199n4

binary gender, 17, 155–156, 157, 193n24, 216n4
Binhammer, Katherine, 172, 174, 218n32, 219n50
Bonds, Leigh, 218n32
Bowden, Martha, 197n33
Bowers, Toni, 60, 68, 204n74
Bradshaigh, Lady Dorothy: and *Clarissa*, 127, 133, 135; construction of *Sir Charles Grandison*, 122, 123, 127, 131–137, 140–144, 146, 152; correspondence with Richardson, 122, 123, 126–138, 140–145, 152, 214n40; similarity to Harriet Byron, 137–138, 144; similarity to Lady Grandison, 130
Breashears, Caroline, 163
Burney, Frances, 88, 125, 150–151, 156, 204n68
Butler, Judith, 157, 168, 218n32

Carlile, Susan, 88–89, 101, 117–118, 120–121, 208n54, 211n99
Carter, Elizabeth: construction of *Sir Charles Grandison*, 122, 123, 127, 142–143; correspondence with Richardson, 126, 128, 130, 138, 142–143; similarity to Harriet Byron, 130
Carter, Philip, 147, 193n24, 193n28
Castle Rackrent (Edgeworth), 156
Castle, Terry, 159, 217n22
Charke, Charlotte, 166
Chico, Tita, 138
Christensen, Jerome, 75, 81, 199n4, 204n77
Cibber, Colley, 137
Clarissa Harlowe (character), 8, 9, 85, 129–130, 133, 138, 145–146
Clarissa (Richardson), 122–123, 124, 127, 133–135, 204n68, 206n14
class status: of eidolons versus authors, 28; of the gentleman, 5, 57; of periodical readership, 28; of the rake versus gentleman, 59, 200n12

INDEX

Clery, E. J., 6, 8, 193n28, 194n33
Cohen, Michèle, 3, 191n7, 193n24, 193n28, 203n49
Connell, R. W., 4, 19, 25, 217n13
Cooper, Anthony Ashley. *See* Shaftesbury, 3rd Earl of
coquette, figure of the: authority of, 169, 198n36; cleverness of, 198n36; criticism of, 33–34; reform of, 42–43; threat of, 11, 33–34, 42
Correspondence of Samuel Richardson, The (Barbauld), 126
coterie, 128
courtship plot, 10–12, 13, 19, 23, 35, 98, 115–116, 176
Cousins, A. D., 218n32
Craft, Catherine. *See* Craft-Fairchild, Catherine
Craft-Fairchild, Catherine, 102, 114, 160, 162, 163
critic, role of the, 86, 100, 106
cross-dressing, 166. *See also* drag; transvestism
Cullens, Chris, 218n32
cultivation of taste. *See* taste, cultivation of
cult of sensibility, 55, 56–57, 58, 59, 64, 68–69, 205n86

David Simple (S. Fielding), 8, 194n32
Davys, Mary: as admirer of *The Spectator*, 24, 34, 36; authorial persona of, 47–51; authorial power of, 24, 47, 50; construction of the gentleman, 36, 37; correspondence with Jonathan Swift, 34; criticism on, 34, 35, 197n33; cultivation of masculinity, 24; disinterestedness of, 103; and Haywood, 55, 103; male readership of, 50; and moral didacticism, 197n33; and periodical conventions, 24, 35, 36, 41, 48; professional performance of, 14–15, 35, 50. See also *Reform'd Coquet, The*
Desmond (Smith), 156
Deutsch, Helen, 93, 207n32
Dictionary (S. Johnson), 86, 88, 92, 119, 211n99
didactic authorship, 14, 32, 58, 178
domesticity of the gentleman, 6, 57, 95, 124, 132
Doody, Margaret Ann, 194n35, 209n56

drag, 153, 157. *See also* cross-dressing; transvestism
Duff, Virginia, 197n33
Dussinger, John, 126, 134

Eaves, T. C. Duncan, 126
Echlin, Lady Elizabeth, 122, 123, 126–127, 128, 130, 214n40
Edgeworth, Maria, 156–157, 179. See also *Castle Rackrent*; *Ennui*; *Harrington*
eidolon, 27, 93, 27–28, 48
Enlightenment ideology, 53, 204n77
Ennui (Edgeworth), 156–157
Enquiry Concerning the Principles of Morals, An (Hume), 82, 200n18
Esposito, Cameron, 215n54
Essay on the Learning of Shakespeare, An (Farmer), 117
Evelina (Burney), 125, 156, 204n68, 209n65, 213n11, 216n8

fantasy of the gentleman, 125, 150–151
Farmer, Richard, 117
female audience. *See* female readership
female desire, 19, 44, 45, 60, 62, 101, 115, 148
female homosociality, 174, 183, 189, 219n50
Female Husband, The (H. Fielding), 166
female masculinities, 154
Female Quixote, The (Lennox), 15–16, 89–90, 101–115: amatory fiction in, 102; Arabella as author figure in, 103, 109, 110–111, 115; construction of the gentleman (critic) in, 102, 104, 105, 108, 109, 112; courtship plot of, 87, 102, 104–106, 107–108; on critics and criticism, 102, 106; as dialogue, 90, 107, 114; and *Don Quixote*, 120; final chapter of, 89–90; influence on Sir Charles Grandison, 122; publication of, 86–87, 89–90, 101; relationship with *The Rambler*, 101, 102; romance in, 101–102, 112–113, 114–115
female readership, 2, 27, 44, 51, 62, 157, 194n35
Female Spectator (Haywood), 84
female vanity, 37–38, 48–49
Fergus, Jan, 61, 194n35

234

Fielding, Henry, 35, 48, 96, 119, 125, 166, 204n68
Fielding, Sarah, 8
Frantz, Sarah S. G., 9
Freval, Jean Baptiste de, 128, 214n41
Friedman, Emily, 124

Gallagher, Catherine, 12, 13, 55, 58, 103, 116, 209n63
gallantry. *See* romance (genre)
Garber, Marjorie, 7, 154
Gardiner, Ellen, 209n58, 209n59
Garnai, Amy, 218n32
Garrick, David, 117, 137
gender binary. *See* binary gender
genre. *See* amatory fiction; courtship plot; romance; sentimental fiction
gentleman author, figure of the: benevolence of, 106; female readership of, 6, 30, 33, 36, 76, 141, 150; need for readership, 30, 32, 45, 141; need to regulate female readership, 76; performativity of, 36, 47; performed authenticity of, 28, 29; performed neutrality of, 14, 28, 37, 39, 51
gossip, 110
Guest, Harriet, 6, 56, 156, 200n9

Haggerty, George, 18, 139, 156
Halberstam, Jack, 7, 154, 171
Hark! A Vagrant (Beaton), 80
Harrington (Edgeworth), 156
Harris, Jocelyn, 124, 126–127, 142, 144, 148, 215n55
Harvey, Karen, 6
Hays, Mary, 1–2, 156, 216n8
Haywood, Eliza: amatory fiction of, 61, 73–74, 75, 150; criticism on, 56, 60, 61–62, 75, 85, 199n6; cult of sensibility, 55, 57; disinterestedness of, 103; as instructive woman writer, 75; literary authority of, 75; male characters of, 60–61; and male class privilege, 59; male readership of, 61–62; and moral sympathy, 56, 57, 81; and philosophy, 55, 56, 84; popularity of, 54, 75, 82, 85; and reform of the rake, 54, 55, 57, 59; and sympathetic reading, 58, 74. See also *Female Spectator*; *Lasselia; or the Self-Abandon'd*; *Love in Excess*

hegemonic masculinity: and authorship, 24–25; character of, 19, 170; and eidolon–author relationship, 28; of the gentleman, 3, 4, 157; idealism of, 217n13; mechanisms of, 28, 34, 121. *See also* patriarchy
Henson, Eithne, 97
"heroes of literature" (S. Johnson), 97, 102, 103, 208n44
heroism, paradigm of, 16, 17, 70, 98–99, 101–103, 203n55, 216n8. *See also* romance (genre)
heterosociality of the gentleman, 6, 24, 26, 58, 64, 68–69, 76, 80–83, 125, 184, 205n86
Highmore, Susanna, 122, 123, 126, 127, 128, 133, 141, 143
homosocial rivalry, 164, 165, 174
homosocial triangulation, 17, 158, 172. *See also* female homosociality; male homosociality
Horejsi, Nicole, 209n57
Hume, David: authorial anxiety of, 54 76, 78, 81–82; criticism on, 56, 75–76; and the cult of sensibility, 55, 76, 80, 200–201n18; and cultivation of taste, 79; and desirability, 54–55, 76, 77, 78, 81; and Enlightenment ideology, 53, 204n77; essays of, 10, 78; failed seduction in, 77–79; and heterosociality, 80–82; and Lennox, 116; love of reading, 78, 79; on the "minds of men," 53; and moral instruction, 78, 200n18; on poetry, 78, 200n18; performed disinterest of, 79; readership of, 205n89; regulation of readers and women, 54, 55, 76–77, 79, 85; self-construction as a gentleman, 54–55, 58, 76–77, 79, 80, 82, 83, 205n83; and sympathetic reading, 57–58; unpopularity of, 82–83, 85. See also *Enquiry Concerning the Principles of Morals, An*; "My Own Life"; "Of Morals"; "Of the Delicacy of Taste and Passion"; "Of the Study of History"; *Treatise of Human Nature, A*

Inchbald, Elizabeth: authorial drag of, 154; authorial power of, 178; and courtship plots, 154; as didactic

Inchbald, Elizabeth (cont.)
  author, 178; public image of, 155; self-fashioning of, 155. See also *Simple Story, A*
inset poetry. See under *Walsingham* (Robinson): poetry in
inset tale. See under *Love in Excess* (Haywood)

Johnson, Claudia, 181
Johnson, Samuel: anxiety of, 91–92, 108; correspondence with Lennox, 86–87, 88–89, 90, 119; as (gentleman) critic, 86, 91–94, 96, 99–101, 105, 116, 118, 120, 207n32; on critics and criticism, 87, 93, 97–100, 105; essays of, 10, 91–100; Lennox's influence on, 87, 101, 119–120; and Mr. Rambler, 93; and Mr. Spectator, 92; performance as gentleman, 91, 94, 105; performed neutrality of, 92, 93, 94, 96, 105; relationship with Lennox, 87, 88, 89, 96, 100, 111–112, 114, 118, 120, 121; and romance (genre), 96–99, 100, 103; suspicions of literary hierarchies, 99, 108, 110; and women readers, 94–96; and women writers, 88, 96. See also *Dictionary*; *Rambler*; *Shakespeare*
Jones, Robert, 81

Kahn, Madeleine, 157
Kavanagh, Declan, 8, 193n28, 194n33
Kelleher, Paul, 10, 56, 60, 200n7, 201n31
Kemmerer, Kathleen Nulton, 93, 94, 206n2, 207n18
Kern, Jean B., 197n33
Kimpel, Ben D., 126
King, Kathryn, 56, 61, 199n7, 200n8
King, Thomas, 3, 6, 24, 26, 191n7, 192n9, 193n28, 202n49
Klein, Lawrence, 193n28
Koehler, Martha, 213n11
Kowaleski-Wallace, Elizabeth, 20
Kramnick, Jonathan Brody, 118, 210n87
Kramp, Michael, 181, 182, 187, 219n55, 220n3
Kvande, Marta, 91

Ladies Library, The (Steele), 197n25
Laqueur, Thomas W., 4, 216n4

Langbauer, Laurie, 112, 209n56
Lanser, Susan, 19
Lasselia; or the Self-Abandon'd (Haywood), 61
Latimer, Bonnie, 145, 147, 148, 213n11, 215n55
Lee, Hyo-Soo, 178
Lennox, Charlotte: authorial ambition of, 87, 89, 101, 103, 108; authorial control of, 89, 90; correspondence with S. Johnson, 86–87, 88–89, 90, 119; correspondence with Richardson, 86–87, 89, 206n14; as (gentleman) critic, 116–118, 119, 120, 210n79; relationship with S. Johnson, 87, 88, 89, 96, 100, 111–112, 114, 118, 120, 121; relationship with Richardson, 86–87, 89; and romance (genre), 99, 101; S. Johnson's (lack of) reference to, 88, 119, 121, 211n99, 211n112. See also *Female Quixote, The*; *Shakespear Illustrated*
literary circle. See authorial network; coterie
literary coterie. See coterie
literary market, 29–30, 45
Love in Excess (Haywood), 15, 55–74: amatory style in, 74, 75; authorial control in, 72; construction of the gentleman in, 62–63, 68, 73, 75, 77, 79; criticism on, 60; failed seduction in, 64, 70; female desire in, 60; heterosociality in, 64–65, 67–69; inset tales in, 65–66, 72, 203n58; misreading in, 65; rakish masculinity in, 63; reform of the rake in, 55, 60, 62–64, 67, 69, 70–71, 73, 74; sympathetic reading in, 65–69, 72, 74, 203n54
Lubey, Kathleen, 73, 91, 199n6
Lupton, Christina, 29

MacCarthy, B. G., 197n33
Mackie, Erin, 3, 24, 29, 192n9, 192n16, 203n49
male gaze, 32, 196n21
male homosociality, 154, 158. See also homosocial rivalry
male manners, reform of, 54–59, 75, 80, 130, 200n9, 205n86

man of letters, figure of the, 16, 75, 79–81, 82, 88, 100, 127, 205n86
Man of Sense, figure of the, 40, 44, 45
Marshall, David, 115, 209n59
masculine hegemony. *See* hegemonic masculinity
masculine privilege, 17, 34, 59, 158, 200n203
masculinity, models of: as authentic self, 4; against binary gender, 160; conservative versions of, 92, 125; coquette as, 154; entrenchment of, 190; fantasy of, 151; under French influence, 190; and the gentleman's persona, 84; Haywood's, 59, 84; without heterosociality, 80; reform of, 56; and sympathetic reading, 74
Maurer, Shawn Lisa, 3, 6, 24, 30, 191n7, 196n21
McBurney, William, 35
McGirr, Elaine, 124, 138, 212n9, 213n11
McMaster, Juliet, 135, 147, 148, 213n11
Memoirs of Emma Courtney, The (Hays), 1–2, 156
Men of Sense. *See* Man of Sense, literary figure of
Merritt, Juliette, 34
Millar, Andrew, 89
Miller, Jane, 191n6
Milton, John, 99, 119
moral instruction, 47, 75, 78, 200n18, 201n31
moral sympathy, 56, 59, 63, 76, 79, 81, 84
Morillo, John, 164
Morrison, Sarah, 92, 94, 206n2, 207n18, 208n38
Mullan, John, 56, 199n4, 200n9
Mulso, Hester: and *Clarissa*, 127; construction of *Sir Charles Grandison*, 122, 123, 127, 128, 132, 140, 152; correspondence with Richardson, 126, 128, 130, 132, 133, 134, 138, 140, 141, 152
"My Own Life" (Hume), 79, 80, 82

narrative self, 28
normative masculinity, 157, 190

O'Brien, Karen, 156
Oakleaf, David, 60, 201n31

"Of the Delicacy of Taste and Passion" (Hume), 79
"Of Morals" (Hume), 82
"Of the Study of History" (Hume), 76–78, 80, 81, 205n83
Oliver, Kathleen, 212n9

Pamela (Richardson), 123, 124, 129
Parker, Jo Alyson, 162
patriarchy: authorial negotiation of, 52, 179; dependence on women, 75; gendered violence of, 149; the gentleman's perpetuation of, 5, 18, 19, 33; and male homosocial desire, 158, 173; malleability/permeability of, 21, 151, 158, 166; as masked by hegemonic masculinity, 28; women's attraction to, 20; women's complacency in, 151; women's unattainability of, 8; women's writing within, 1, 14, 18, 179. *See also* hegemonic masculinity
Pearson, Jacqueline, 206n2
Perdita (Robinson), 155
performed disinterest. *See* performed neutrality
performed neutrality, 26, 81, 96
periodical: and construction and circulation of the gentleman, 23, 26; and construction and circulation of (hegemonic) masculinity, 26, 28; eidolon–author relationship in, 28; eidolons in, 27; emergence of, 24; market culture of, 29–30; mobility of, 29; and the narrative self, 28
Persuasion (Austen), 190
politeness of the gentleman, 4, 28, 98, 106, 125, 146, 149, 193n24
Pope, Alexander, 78, 80, 91–92, 131
Potter, Tiffany, 197n33
Powell, Manushag: on eidolon–author relationship, 27; on Haywood's readership, 61; on the literary market, 29; on Mr. Spectator, 26; on the narrative self in periodicals, 12, 24, 28; on S. Johnson's gender relations, 206n2; on women in periodicals, 43
Pride and Prejudice (Austen), 19

quixotism, 98, 101. *See also* heroism, paradigm of; romance (genre)

INDEX

rake, figure of the: behavior of, 22, 63, 64, 67; class status of, 200n12; versus the gentleman, 4, 18, 26, 27, 29, 30, 39, 40, 42, 57, 59, 69, 70, 136, 146; the gentleman's replacement/revision of, 4, 5–6, 33, 56–57, 59, 63, 66, 69, 74, 124, 134, 191n7, 200n12; poor reading skills of, 63, 65; rakish masculinity, 203n49; reform of, 23, 57, 73, 187–188; similarity to the gentleman, 147

Rambler (S. Johnson), 15–16, 90–100; critical legacy of, 90–91; eidolon of, 92–93; "marriage group," 208n38; mixed-gender readership of, 95; no. 1, 92, 100; no. 2, 97, 108; no. 3, 97; no. 4, 92, 96, 109; no. 14, 93; no. 18, 93; no. 21, 208n44; no. 23, 105; no. 34, 208n38; no. 35, 208n38; no. 39, 208n38; no. 45, 208n38; no. 92, 97; no. 93, 93, 109; no. 94, 99; no. 113, 208n38; no. 115, 208n38; no. 116, 208n38; no. 137, 208n44; no. 148, 208n54, no. 167, 208n38; no. 168, 109; no. 176, 98; periodical conventions in, 92; publication of, 90; and romance (genre), 87, 92

Rape Jokes (Esposito), 215n54

Reeser, Todd, 158

Reform'd Coquet, The (Davys), 14–15, 22–24, 34–51: authorial power in, 47; construction of the gentleman in, 36–37, 42, 44–47, 49–50; courtship plot in, 24, 35, 36, 41, 47; criticism on, 35; cross-dressing in, 39–40; disguise in, 22, 37, 38, 39–40, 41, 46; eidolon-author in, 36–37, 40, 41; gentlemanly restraint in, 41; gentleman's performativity in 23, 36–37, 39, 40, 41, 45–46; legacy of, 35; performed neutrality in, 41; periodical's influence on, 36, 197n33, 198n36; readership of, 50, 51; reform of the rake in, 22–23; women's moral instruction in, 38, 44

regulation of women. *See* women's regulation by the gentleman

Rennhak, Katharina, 9

Restoration (cultural era), 26, 56

Richardson, Samuel: and appreciation of women's input, 128, 135–136, 137–138, 140–142; authorial anxiety of, 123, 132, 133; and correspondence of, 126, 127, 137, 152 (*see also under* Bradshaigh, Lady Dorothy; Carter, Elizabeth; Lennox, Charlotte; Mulso, Hester; see also *Correspondence of Samuel Richardson, The;* Echlin, Lady Elizabeth; Freval, Jean Baptiste de; Highmore, Susanna; Talbot, Catherine; Wescomb, Sarah); critical perception of, 126; criticism on, 127; and *The Female Quixote*, 122; on the figure of the rake, 133–137; as gentleman author, 128–129; middle-class status of, 126, 129; relationship with Lennox, 86–87, 89. See also *Clarissa*; *Pamela*; *Sir Charles Grandison*

Richetti, John, 73

Robertson, Ben, 155

Robinson, Mary: authorial drag of, 154; and courtship plots, 154; patriarchal power of, 172; poetry of, 171; public image of, 155, 170, 171; self-fashioning of, 155. See also *Walsingham*

Rogers, Katherine, 114

romance (genre), 61, 66, 84, 98, 99, 103, 203n55

Runge, Laura, 61, 91, 111, 119, 194n35, 207n20

Russo, Stephanie, 218n32

Sabor, Peter, 127–128

Sajé, Natasha, 43, 197n33

Schellenberg, Betty, 56, 68–69, 81, 128, 129, 138, 200n9

Schürer, Norbert, 88, 206n14

Sedgwick, Eve Kosofsky, 158, 163, 172. *See also* homosocial triangulation; male homosociality

Sense and Sensibility (Austen), 182–189: construction of the gentleman and masculinity in, 17, 182–186, 188, 189; critiques of men in, 185; female authorship in, 183–184, 186–187, 188–189; female heterosociality in, 184–185; female homosociality in, 183, 189; reform of the rake in, 187–188

sensibility. *See* cult of sensibility

sentiment, 8, 53, 84

sentimental fiction, 56, 57, 75, 155, 163

Setzer, Sharon, 218n32

INDEX

Shaffer, Julie, 166, 218n32
Shaftesbury, 3rd Earl of, 27, 55, 80, 205n86
Shakespeare (S. Johnson), 119–121, 211n112
Shakespear Illustrated (Lennox), 16, 87, 116–119, 211n90
Simple Story, A (Inchbald), 17, 153–154, 158–164: ambivalent ending of, 176, 178; authorial power in, 162; and binary gender, 157, 160, 162, 164, 165; construction of the gentleman in, 154, 160–161, 176; and the coquette, 154; courtship plot in, 154, 155, 160, 163, 164–165, 178; criticism on, 160; drag in, 157–158, 159, 162, 176; male homosociality in, 159, 162, 163–164; misreading in, 160; mixed-gender readership of, 178; passing in, 158; reform of the coquette in, 155, 159; two-part structure of, 158–159, 162–163
Sir Charles Grandison (Richardson), 16, 122–152: authorial network within, 139; collective construction of, 16, 122–123, 126–127, 128, 129, 134, 138, 140; construction of the gentleman in, 123, 124, 125, 132–133, 136–137, 143–144, 146, 150, 152; coterie interested in, 122, 123, 124, 125–126, 138, 140; courtship plot in, 13; criticism on, 124–125; epistolary structure of, 129; fantasy of the gentleman in, 125, 150; Harriet Byron as composite author of, 129–130, 131, 133, 139; legacy of, 150–151; performativity of the gentleman in, 148; gentlemanly politeness in, 143, 146, 149; publication of, 123, 142; rakishness in, 57, 133–137, 146–147; women's perceived ownership of, 142–143; women's appreciation of, 143, 144, 151
Skelton, Philip, 214n41
Smith, Charlotte, 156, 171
social class. *See* class status
Solinger, Jason, 7, 12, 24, 181, 193n28, 194n29
Spacks, Patricia Meyer, 10, 66, 77, 217n22
Spectator (Addison and Steele), 14, 23–34: author-eidolon relationship in, 23; authorial satisfaction in, 23, 32; construction of eidolon in, 26–29; construction of masculinity in, 25–27, 28–29; on the coquette, 33–34, 94, 197n26; courtship in, 30; and (dis)embodiment of masculinity, 25–26, 33; on female readership and libraries, 27, 33, 43, 93, 197n25; female readership of, 30, 31–32; the gentleman's performativity in, 23, 28–29; no. 4, 26–27, 197n25; no. 37, 33, 197n25; no. 45, 33, 197n26; no. 57, 27; no. 79, 197n25, 197n26; no. 73, 197n26; no. 92, 30, 197n25; no. 95, 32; no. 109, 198n36; no. 205, 197n25; no. 572, 197n25; performance of masculinity in, 24–27, 52; performed neutrality in, 14, 26, 28–29, 87; women's moral instruction and regulation in, 30–31, 32–33
Spedding, Patrick, 61
Spencer, Jane, 89, 197n33, 218n22
Steele, Richard: and criticism of the coquette, 34, 94; and Davys, 48–49; essays of, 10; gentlemanly prerogative of, 197n25; and the gentleman's masculinity, 29; and Haywood, 55; and Hume, 76, 82; and Lennox, 116; and Mr. Spectator, 23, 26, 27, 28, 37; as periodicalist, 29–30, 78; plain style of, 29. *See also* Addison, Joseph; *Spectator*
Straub, Kristina, 24
sympathetic reading, 14, 54, 57–58, 64–68, 80

Talbot, Catherine, 122, 123, 126, 127, 128, 130, 138, 141
taste, cultivation of, 24, 58, 78, 79, 82, 84
Thompson, Helen, 136, 148
Thorn, Jennifer, 202n38
Tierney-Hynes, Rebecca, 56, 199n2, 199n4, 199n6
Todd, Janet, 8, 103, 191n6, 194n32
Tom Jones (character), 16, 73, 103, 123, 204n68, 209n56
Tom Jones (H. Fielding), 125, 204n68
Tompkins, J. M. S., 218n22
transvestism, 157. *See also* cross-dressing; drag
Treatise of Human Nature, A (Hume), 12, 58, 82, 200n18
Ty, Eleanor, 218n32

INDEX

Wahrman, Dror, 4, 155, 166, 216n4
Walsingham (Robinson), 17, 153, 164–176: ambivalent ending of, 176–177; and binary gender, 157, 166, 175; construction of the gentleman in, 154, 166, 168, 176; and the coquette, 169; courtship plot in, 154, 172, 178; drag in, 154, 157–158, 167, 176; dual-plot structure of, 175–176; epistolary structure of, 169, 177; female ambition in, 177; homoerotics in, 164, 172, 173; homosociality in, 166, 168, 171–175, 177; (moral) instruction in, 155, 169, 178; misogyny in, 219n41; misreading in, 170; passing in, 158, 166, 167, 171; poetry in, 171; reception of, 166–167; Sidney as ideal gentleman in, 153, 167, 169, 175; unreliable narrator of, 167

Ward, Candace, 156

Warner, William, 61

Wescomb, Sarah, 122, 123, 126, 127, 128, 133–134

Wikborg, Eleanor, 2, 35, 151, 197n33, 197n34, 216n8

women readers. *See* female readership

women's regulation by the gentleman, 5, 14, 23, 31–32, 44, 55, 75, 76, 85

Woodworth, Megan, 2, 10, 156, 175, 181, 219n55

Woolf, Virginia, 1, 190

Zonitch, Barbara, 213n11

About the Author

Mary Beth Harris is an associate professor at Bethany College in Lindsborg, Kansas, where she teaches everything and anything English and also serves as the director of Core Education and the Bethany College Ascension Program. Her work explores the intersection of eighteenth-century genre and gender, especially with regards to performance and masculinity. Her most recent work can be found in *TSWL, The Eighteenth-Century*, as well as two edited collections, *Castration, Impotence, and Emasculation in the Long Eighteenth-Century* and *A Spy on Eliza Haywood: Addresses to a Multifarious Writer*. Prior to arriving at Bethany College, Harris received her PhD from Purdue University, her MA from Villanova University, and her BA from Saint Mary's College of Notre Dame.